Systems Analysis and Design for Advanced Modeling Methods:
Best Practices

Akhilesh Bajaj
University of Tulsa, USA

Stanisław Wrycza
University of Gdansk, Poland

INFORMATION SCIENCE REFERENCE

Hershey · New York

Director of Editorial Content:	Kristin Klinger
Senior Managing Editor:	Jamie Snavely
Managing Editor:	Jeff Ash
Assistant Managing Editor:	Carole Coulson
Typesetter:	Chris Hrobak
Cover Design:	Lisa Tosheff
Printed at:	Yurchak Printing Inc.

Published in the United States of America by
Information Science Reference (an imprint of IGI Global)
701 E. Chocolate Avenue
Hershey PA 17033
Tel: 717-533-8845
Fax: 717-533-8661
E-mail: cust@igi-global.com
Web site: http://www.igi-global.com/reference

and in the United Kingdom by
Information Science Reference (an imprint of IGI Global)
3 Henrietta Street
Covent Garden
London WC2E 8LU
Tel: 44 20 7240 0856
Fax: 44 20 7379 0609
Web site: http://www.eurospanbookstore.com

Library of Congress Cataloging-in-Publication Data

Systems analysis and design for advanced modeling methods : best practices / Akhilesh Bajaj and Stanislaw Wrycza, editors.
  p. cm.

Includes bibliographical references and index.
Summary: "This book is a collection of work representing leading research in the area of systems analysis and design practices and methodologies"--Provided by publisher.

ISBN 978-1-60566-344-9 (hardcover) -- ISBN 978-1-60566-345-6 (ebook) 1. System design. 2. System analysis. I. Bajaj, Akhilesh, 1966- II. Wrycza, Stanislaw.

QA76.9.S88S936 2009
  004.2'1--dc22

                                2009009164

British Cataloguing in Publication Data
A Cataloguing in Publication record for this book is available from the British Library.

All work contributed to this book is new, previously-unpublished material. The views expressed in this book are those of the authors, but not necessarily of the publisher.

Table of Contents

Detailed Table of Contents

Chapter I

    Andreea Sabău, Babeş-Bolyai University, Romania

In order to represent spatio-temporal data, many conceptual models have been designed and a part of them have been implemented. This chapter describes an approach of the conceptual modeling of spatio-temporal data, called 3SST. Also, the spatio-temporal conceptual and relational data models obtained by following the proposed phases are presented. The 3SST data model is obtained by following three steps: the construction of an entity-relationship spatio-temporal model, the specification of the domain model and the design of a class diagram which includes the objects characteristic to a spatio-temporal application and other needed elements. The relational model of the 3SST conceptual model is the implementation of the conceptual 3SST data model on a relational database platform. Both models are characterized by generality in representing spatial, temporal and spatio-temporal data. The spatial objects can be represented as points or objects with shape and the evolution of the spatio-temporal objects can be implemented as discrete or continuous in time, on time instants or time intervals. More than that, different types of spatial, temporal, spatio-temporal and event-based queries can be performed on represented data. Therefore, the proposed 3SST relational model can be considered the core of a spatio-temporal data model.

Chapter II

    Jeff Crawford, University of Tulsa, USA

This theoretical work draws on group development literature to propose a model for increasing the likelihood of achieving temporal success within a software development (SD) environment. The study addresses a group's temporal performance through a punctuated equilibrium (PE) lens. As a means of extending the PE model of group development for a SD project context, this research will consider social and temporal aspects of identity within each group in order to address the varying nature of temporal success. First, anthropological research on rituals in society will be applied to present a project-as-ritual perspective, where social and temporal identity are suggested to flow from the rites of passage that exist during the initial meeting and temporal midpoint of a group. Second, social identity theory will be applied to posit that both types of identity are positively associated with a group's ability to meet temporal deadlines. This theoretical piece is expected to make two primary contributions to literature. First, group development literature is enhanced by providing an extension of the PE model to address environments where social and temporal identities are variable. This contribution is significant since it will allow researchers to apply a PE perspective in real world project team environments. Second, the research contributes to SD literature by offering a clear perspective regarding key factors that can serve to impact a SD project team's ability to meet temporal deadlines.

Chapter III

Faiz Currim, University of Iowa, USA
Sudha Ram University of Arizona, USA

Cardinality captures necessary semantics in conceptual data modeling and determines how constructs are translated into relations. Business policies in a variety of domains like healthcare, education, supply chain management and geographic systems are often expressible in terms of cardinality. The knowledge about cardinality constraints is also useful during schema integration, in query transformation for more efficient search strategies, and in database testing. Practically every conceptual modeling grammar provides support for this kind of constraint, and in an effort to resolve the variations in semantics past research has studied the different types of cardinality constraints. None have been so far comprehensive, and further there has been very little coverage of the concept in temporal domain even though it provides some interesting extensions to the concept. This study considers existing work in snapshot and temporal cardinality and suggests some areas for future work.

Chapter IV

Leszek Kotulski, AGH University of Science and Technology, Poland
Dariusz Dymek, Cracow University of Economics, Poland

The UML model consists of several types of diagrams representing different aspects of the modeled system. To assure the universality and flexibility, the UML involves only a few general rules about dependence among different types of diagrams. In consequence people can have the different methodologies based on the UML, but in the same time we haven't the formal tool for assure the vertical cohesion of created model. To test and reach the vertical cohesion of the model some auxiliary information about the relations among the elements belonging to different types of diagrams should be remembered. In this chapter the authors present the method of formal representation of such information in a form of the relation, called Accomplish Relation. This method is based only on the UML properties and is independent from any methodology. Additionally, they show how to use the UML timing diagrams for representing the users' requirements in association with use cases. To illustrate the usefulness of this approach we present how it can be used for load balancing of distributed system in case of a Reporting Systems based on Data Warehouse concept.

Chapter V

Angela Mattia, Virginia Commonwealth University, USA
Heinz Roland Weistroffer, Virginia Commonwealth University, USA

Conventional wisdom has it that user participation in information systems development (ISD) is essential for systems success. Though the significance of user participation to system success has been much discussed in the literature, results from empirical studies are inconsistent and suggest that perhaps new avenues need to be explored. One approach may be viewing user participation as a social network that is, looking at the emergence of social structures and their technological expressions during the user participation process. In this chapter, a framework is presented that organizes user participation approaches that emerge from the different worldviews existing within organizations. This user participation approach (UPA) framework is used as the structure for the systematic arrangement of user participation approaches into a fourfold taxonomy based on extrinsic information attributed to them in the literature. In addition, a categorical analysis and social network analysis (SNA) are used to map and visualize the relationships between analyst and users, thus providing a conceptual and visual representation of the relational structures.

Chapter VI

Özlem Albayrak, Bilkent University, Turkey

This study is an enhancement of previous research presented at the 2nd AIS SIGSAND European Symposium on Systems Analysis and Design and its improved version presented at the 3rd National Software Engineering Symposium (UYMS) 2007. The AIS-SIGSAND 2007 study, the first phase, was part of on-going research by which systems analysis and design-teaching experiences related to course evaluation items were enlightened. This study summarizes previous studies and introduces new findings suggested by those studies that relate to teaching challenges on systems analysis and design in software engineering. The first challenge studied is to decide a suitable evaluation item set in undergraduate level system analysis and design courses for software engineers. The second challenge relates to implicit assumptions made by software engineers during the analysis phase. Based on pre-interview, test, and post-interview data, the study presents a snapshot of an analysis in software engineering regarding implicit assumptions made by analysts. Related to these challenges, the study concludes with proposals on systems analysis and design education.

Chapter VII

Przemyslaw Polak, Warsaw School of Economics, Poland

Nowadays, there are two main information systems modeling methods: structured and object-oriented. The structured methods have been widely used since the 1970s, whereas recently the object-oriented methods have attracted more attention. This chapter analyses the methods that are taught on the courses of information systems analysis and design. The curricula of information systems and computer science studies in Polish higher education institutions are compared to the Association for Computing Machinery curricula recommendations. In both cases none of the methods is prevailing. Also, the program of introducing, at the Warsaw School of Economics, Poland, all management and business administration students to the basics of systems analysis and design is presented. Thus, students majoring in information systems learn both modeling methods, whereas only structured methods are introduced to all management students.

Chapter VIII

System theories, analysis and design have been deployed within every corporate function and within a broad section of businesses and markets. Systems thinking involve changing paradigms about the way the world works, the way corporations function, and the human role in each. In systems thinking, analysis and design we look for interrelationships among the elements of a system. The chapter reflects the core insights of system modeling. This chapter addresses the core issues of system engineering, analysis, design, Simulation and modeling of real-world objects. It tells everything one needs to know to be a successful system thinker, modeler, technical manager and forecaster. The chapter focuses on: the real-world goals for, services provided by, and constraints on systems; the precise specification of system structure and behavior, and the implementation of specifications; the activities required in order to develop an assurance that the specifications and real-world goals have been met; the evolution of systems over time and across system families. It is also concerned with the processes, methods and tools for the development of systems in an economic and timely manner.

Chapter IX

This chapter includes an analysis and design of a system with a task of improving the efficiency of the information forwarding process by the institutions under obligation so that the criteria laid down by law are met. The description of the system has been created in accordance with the specifications of UML 2.0 and - based on many diagram types and the architecture - the business processes that it extends to and the database structure required to collect information about transactions are set forth. Thanks to the application of use cases the main functionality of the system is defined: searching for and bringing together particular transactions followed by transformation and the dispatching of reports. Complex business processes are presented by corresponding activity and interaction diagrams. The architecture and the placement of the system within the structure of the organization, however, are depicted with the help of structure diagrams such as class, component and deployment diagrams. The use made of the extensibility mechanisms of UML merits attention here. The database stereotype presented in the work made it possible for the database to be designed at the level of implementation, and the functionality of the CASE tool enabled the complete software script to be compiled on this basis.

Chapter X

Stanisław Wrycza, University of Gdańsk, Poland

UML 2.x version has become even more complicated and diverse set of graphical techniques than its predecessors. Therefore, system developers propose preparation of its reduced, limited or minimal version called Light UML. This problem has become also the serious challenge for the UML academic teachers. The goal of this chapter is the study of specifying the UML 2.x Light version content on the basis of the questionnaire survey registering opinions of 180 university students of the University of Gdansk, Poland. After the introduction, the methodological prerequisites of the survey are clarified. Then, the research results are presented and discussed according to seven essential UML diagrams assessment criteria, included in a questionnaire. The final UML 2.x version, resulting from the accomplished survey is exposed in the last section of the chapter.

Chapter XI

Akhilesh Bajaj, University of Tulsa, USA
Jason Knight, University of Tulsa, USA

Traditionally, the data model and the process model have been considered separately when modeling an application for construction purposes. The system analysis and design area has largely ignored the issue of the relationship between the user interface (UI) and the underlying data schema, leaving UI creation within the purview of the human computer interaction (HCI) literature. Traditional HCI methods however, underutilize the information in the data schema when designing user screens. Much of the work on automatic user interface (UI) generation has met with limited success because of the added load on the human designer to use specialized scripts for UI specification. In this research in progress, the authors propose a methodology applicable to database driven systems that (a) automatically infers a draft interface directly from an extended entity relationship (EER) model schema and (b) lists the interactions that need to take place between the designer and the tool in order to generate the final user schema.

Chapter XII

Roy Gelbard, Bar-Ilan University, Israel

Reusable code helps to decrease code errors, code units and therefore development time. It serves to improve quality and productivity frameworks in software development. The question is not HOW to make the code reusable, but WHICH amount of software components would be most beneficial (i.e. cost-effective in terms of reuse), and WHAT method should be used to decide whether to make a component reusable or not. If we had unlimited time and resources, we could write any code unit in a reusable way. In other words, its reusability would be 100%. However, in real life, resources and time are limited. Given these constraints, decisions regarding reusability are not always straightforward. The current chapter focuses on decision-making rules for investing in reusable code. It attempts to determine the parameters, which should be taken into account in decisions relating to degrees of reusability. Two new models are presented for decisions-making relating to reusability: (1) a restricted model, and (2) a non-restricted model. Decisions made by using these models are then analyzed and discussed.

Chapter XIII

This chapter encapsulates the main findings of an in-depth study of Web development practices in Ireland. The essential research objective was to build a richer understanding of the modern context of Web development and of how that context influences design practices. At the outset, a conceptual framework was derived through a synthesis of issues in the literature and an analysis of existing models of IS development. Data was then gathered through a dual-mode (Web and postal) quantitative survey which yielded 165 usable responses, and later through a series of 14 semi-structured qualitative interviews in a follow-up field study. Following an interpretive approach, elementary statistics and grounded theory were used to iteratively analyze the data until a reasonably comprehensive and stable explanation emerged. This is presented in the form of an elaborated conceptual framework of Web-based systems development as "situated action."

Chapter XIV

This chapter discusses reference modeling languages for business systems analysis and design. In particular, it reports on reference models in the context of the design-for/by-reuse paradigm, explains how traditional modeling techniques fail to provide adequate conceptual expressiveness to allow for easy model reuse by configuration or adaptation and elaborates on the need for reference modeling languages to be configurable. We discuss requirements for and the development of reference modeling languages that reflect the need for configurability. Exemplarily, we report on the development, definition and configuration of configurable event-driven process chains. We further outline how configurable reference modeling languages and the corresponding design principles can be used in future scenarios such as process mining and data modeling.

Chapter XV

This article analyzes the handling of customer complaints after shipping ordered goods by applying automated reputation and trust accounts as decision support. Customer complaints are cost intensive and difficult to standardize. A game theory based analysis of the process yields insights into unfavorable interactions between both business partners. Trust and reputation mechanisms have been found useful in addressing these types of interactions. A reputation and trust management system (RTMS) is proposed based on design theory guidelines as an IS artifact to prevent customers from issuing false complaints. A generic simulation setting for analysis of the mechanism is presented to evaluate the applicability of the RTMS. The findings suggest that the RTMS performs best in market environments where transaction frequency is high, individual complaint-handling costs are high compared to product revenues, and the market has a high fraction of potentially cheating customers.

Chapter XVI

The extent methods largely ignore the importance of integrating security requirements with business requirements and providing built-in steps for dealing with these requirements seamlessly. To address this problem, a new approach to secure network analysis and design is presented. The proposed method, called the SEACON method, provides an integrated approach to use existing principles of information systems analysis and design with the unique requirements of distributed secure network systems. We introduce several concepts including security adequacy level, process-location-security matrix, data-location-security matrix, and secure location model to provide built-in mechanisms to capture security needs and use them seamlessly throughout the steps of analyzing and designing secure networks. This method is illustrated and compared to other secure network design methods. The SEACON method is found to be a useful and effective method.

Chapter XVII

Software has been a major enabling technology for advancing modern society, and is now an indispensable part of daily life. Because of the increased complexity of these software systems, and their critical societal role, more effective software development and analysis technologies are needed. How to develop and ensure the dependability of these complex software systems is a grand challenge. It is well known that a highly dependable complex software system cannot be developed without a rigorous development process and a precise specification and design documentation. Formal methods are one of the most promising technologies for precisely specifying, modeling, and analyzing complex software systems. Although past research experience and practice in computer science have convincingly shown that it is not possible to formally verify program behavior and properties at the program source code level due to its extreme huge size and complexity, recently advances in applying formal methods during software specification and design, especially at software architecture level, have demonstrated significant benefits of using formal methods. In this chapter, we will review several well-known formal methods for software system specification and analysis. We will present recent advances of using these formal methods for specifying, modeling, and analyzing software architectural design.

Preface

Systems analysis and design (SAND) is an evolving field that still represents the point where business and technology intersects. As discussed in (Bajaj, Batra, Hevner, Parsons, & Siau, 2005), SAND represents the core of management information systems (MIS) curricula but is underrepresented in the area of MIS research. The chapters in this book represent the state of the art in several streams that are ongoing in SAND research is Europe and North America. The chapters in this book are largely taken from presentations at the 2007 AIS SIG SAND (Association of Information Systems Special Interest Group on SAND) symposia that are an annual occurrence in both North America and Europe since around 2004. While not exhaustive, these symposia represent on-going work in several different areas of SAND. As such, the papers here discuss work ranging from spatio-temporal data modeling to software project management to user interface generation to empirical evaluation of web based system development methods.

Chapter I, entitled "3SST Model: A Three Step Spatio-Temporal Conceptual and Relational Data Model" by Andreea Sabău, follows three steps: the construction of an entity-relationship spatio-temporal model, the specification of the domain model and the design of a class diagram which includes the objects characteristic to a spatio-temporal application and other needed elements. It describes the implementation of the 3SST spatio-temporal data model on a relational platform.

Chapter II is entitled "An Identity Perspective for Predicting Software Development Project Temporal Success" by Jeff Crawford investigates a project group's temporal performance through a punctuated equilibrium (PE) lens. It describes a model that considers social and temporal aspects of identity within each group in order to address the varying nature of temporal success.

Chapter III is entitled "Survey of Cardinality Constraints in Snapshot and Temporal Semantic Data Models" by Faiz Currim and Sudha Ram. It highlights the usefulness of cardinality constraints during schema integration, in query transformation for more efficient search strategies, and proposed avenues of future research in this area.

Chapter IV entitled "On the Load Balancing of Business Intelligence Reporting Systems" is co-authored by Leszek Kotulski and Dariusz Dymek. This chapter proposes a formal representation of the information that intersects across different UML diagrams in order to form a cohesive view of the domain.

Chapter V by Angela Mattia and Heinz Roland Weistroffer is entitled "Information Systems Development: Understanding User Participation as a Social Network" attempts to formally study user participation in systems development as a social network, *that is,* looking at the emergence of social structures and their technological expressions during the user participation process.

Chapter VI is entitled "Solutions to Challenges of Teaching "Systems Analysis and Design" for Undergraduate Software Engineers" and is authored by Özlem Albayrak. It presents implicit assumptions made by software engineers during analysis and also describes suitable item sets in undergraduate SAND courses.

Continuing in the teaching of SAND vein, **Chapter VII** is entitled "Systems Analysis and Design in Polish Universities Curricula: Structured or Object-Oriented" and is written by Przemyslaw Polak. It compares the curricula of information systems and computer science studies in Polish higher education institutions to the Association for Computing Machinery curricula recommendations and analyzes the prevalence of structured versus object-oriented approaches.

Chapter VIII by Kumar Saurabh, is entitled "Systems Engineering Modeling and Design" highlights the insights afforded by "systems" thinking and offers steps on how to achieve such a mindset in real world contexts.

Chapter IX, entitled "Uml 2.0 in the Modelling of the Complex Business Processes of Reporting and Control of Financial Information System" is by Sebastian Kwapisz. The chapter explores the usage of UML specifications for interagency systems development, using a specific case study.

Chapter X by Stanisław Wrycza is entitled "The Uml 2 Academic Teaching Challenge: An Integrated Approach". The author explores the essential components of UML that need to be taught in a University curriculum, based on student surveys.

Chapter XI, entitled by "User Interface Generation from the Data Schema" is co-authored by Akhilesh Bajaj and Jason Knight. It proposes a method to automatically infer a draft interface directly from an extended entity relationship (EER) model schema and lists the interactions that need to take place between the designer and the tool in order to generate the final user interface.

Chapter XII is by Roy Gelbard and is entitled "Decision Rule for Investment in Reusable Code". The author attempts to determine the parameters, which should be taken into account in decisions relating to degrees of reusability that should be injected into code.

Chapter XIII, entitled "Web-Based Systems Development: An Empirically-Grounded Conceptual Framework" is by Michael Lang. This chapter encapsulates the main findings of an in-depth study of Web development practices in Ireland. Using the results of an extended survey, it presents a conceptual framework of Web-based systems development as "situated action".

The last four chapters are not from SIGSAND symposia; but were included because they represent topics that fit well with the theme of this book. **Chapter XIV** is entitled "Configurable Reference Modeling Languages" and is authored by Jan Recker, Michael Rosemann, Wil van der Aalst, Monique Jansen-Vullers, and Alexander Dreiling. It motivates the need for conceptual expressiveness for enhancing the configurability of modeling languages.

Chapter XV, by Roman Beck and Jochen Franke is entitled "Designing Reputation and Trust Management Systems". It utilizes game theory to design a trust based system so as to reduce false complaints filed by customers in high transaction environments.

Chapter XVI, entitled "Seacon: An Integrated Approach to the Analysis and Design of Secure Enterprise Architecture–Based Computer Networks" and is authored by Surya Yadav. It illustrated how SAND principles can be used in the design of secure networks.

The final chapter is entitled "Formal Methods for Specifying and Analyzing Complex Software Systems" and is co-authored by Xudong He, uiqun Yu, and Yi Deng. It summarizes formal methods of system specification and illustrates how these can be used at the architecture stage to test complex software.

Akhilesh Bajaj, University of Tulsa, USA

Stanisław Wrycza, University of Gdansk, Poland

REFERENCES

Bajaj, A., Batra, D., Hevner, A., Parsons, J., & Siau, K. (2005). Systems Analysis and Design: Should We Be Researching What We Teach? *Communications of the AIS, 15*(April), 478-493.

Chapter I
3SST Model:
A Three Step Spatio-Temporal Conceptual and Relational Data Model

Andreea Sabău
Babeş-Bolyai University, Romania

ABSTRACT

In order to represent spatio-temporal data, many conceptual models have been designed and a part of them have been implemented. This chapter describes an approach of the conceptual modeling of spatio-temporal data, called 3SST. Also, the spatio-temporal conceptual and relational data models obtained by following the proposed phases are presented. The 3SST data model is obtained by following three steps: the construction of an entity-relationship spatio-temporal model, the specification of the domain model and the design of a class diagram which includes the objects characteristic to a spatio-temporal application and other needed elements. The relational model of the 3SST conceptual model is the implementation of the conceptual 3SST data model on a relational database platform. Both models are characterized by generality in representing spatial, temporal and spatio-temporal data. The spatial objects can be represented as points or objects with shape and the evolution of the spatio-temporal objects can be implemented as discrete or continuous in time, on time instants or time intervals. More than that, different types of spatial, temporal, spatio-temporal and event-based queries can be performed on represented data. Therefore, the proposed 3SST relational model can be considered the core of a spatio-temporal data model.

1. INTRODUCTION

Spatio-temporal databases (STDB) deal with spatial objects that are changing over time and space. In other words, these objects are characterized by spatial and temporal attributes, yet these are not static objects. There are many domains where the spatio-temporal (ST) data is used: cadastral applications, military operations, weather systems, multimedia presentations, moving objects etc.

Spatial databases and temporal databases have been studied for many years (modeling, implementing, optimizing), but the surrounding reality showed us different applications which needed to combine the spatial and temporal domains. Thus, the two dimensions were both included into spatio-temporal databases. The first attempts consisted in adding one dimension to the other: including temporal data into a spatial database or adding spatial attributes to the temporal objects. Later, other models joined space and time into one unified spatio-temporal view (Worboys, 1994).

Following these different approaches in perceiving ST data, modeling techniques and database models, many conceptual models have been designed and concrete applications have been implemented. Some of the models represent space and evolving spatial objects organized in time-stamped layers (see the Snapshot Model – Langran & Chrisman, 1988). One layer contains the state of a geographic distribution at a moment of time, but there are no explicit temporal connections between layers. Another class of spatio-temporal data models is represented by the Event-Oriented Models which record information about the events that led to spatio-temporal changes (see the Event-Oriented Spatio-Temporal Data Model (ESTDM) - Peuquet & Duan, 1995). Thus, event-oriented queries are supported and the evolution of an object has to be traced through the stored events.

Other spatio-temporal data models have been designed using and / or adapting conceptual data modeling techniques in order to satisfy some spatio-temporal requirements. Such a model is the STER model (the Spatio-Temporal Entity-Relationship Model - Tryfona & Jensen, 1999; Tryfona & Jensen, 2000) which extends the standard Entity-Relationship Model to include spatial and temporal characteristics. The entities may have spatial attributes of type point, line or region, while entities, attributes and relationships can be time-stamped using valid time, transaction time or bi-temporal data. The object-oriented data

modeling technique is used in another paper (Price, Tryfona, & Jensen, 2000), where the Unified Modeling Language (UML) is extended to include attributes and methods of spatial and temporal nature (Spatio-Temporal UML - STUML).

An original approach is the Three-Domain Model (Yuan, 1999) which separates semantic domain from spatial and temporal domains. The advantage of this model arises from the independence of the three domains at semantic and behavioral level. There are links from semantic and temporal objects to spatial objects and from spatial and temporal objects to semantic objects. Assuming that a spatial object is located in time, there are no direct links from semantic to spatial domain. The particular case of objects without temporal measures is marked with a null time value. The ST data is organized within four relations: three relations that correspond to the three domains and a relation that links the semantic objects, the time elements and the spatial entities.

A parametric ST model is the Parametric k-Spaghetti (Chomicki & Revesz, 1997). The evolving spatial data can be of type point, line segment or region. One geometry element is represented by one or more triangles (degenerate in the case of points and line segments). Therefore the ST information is stored within tuples which contain the object's id, the parametric coordinates of one triangle and a valid time interval as timestamp. Though the structure of the relation is relatively simple, the represented information can capture the continuous evolution of spatial objects in time.

Moving Object Data Models have been developed to deal explicitly with continuously moving objects. The Moving Objects Spatio-Temporal data model (MOST) (Sistla, Wolfson, Chamberlain, & Dao, 1997; Wolfson, Xu, Chamberlain, & Jiang, 1998) introduces the notion of dynamic attribute represented as functions of time in order to denote an attribute that changes continuously. Another approach consists in modeling the continuous evolution of objects using the so-called sliced representation (Erwig, Güting, Schneider, & Vazirgiannis, 1998; Güting, Böhlen, Erwig, Jensen, Lorentzos, Schneider, & Vazirgiannis, 2000).

A part of these data models were proposed as general models. Other ST data models were designed especially for a specific ST application. The paper (Wang, Fang, & Xie, 2005) considers the particular application domain of cadastral information system and proposes a new ST data model. This model is based on the parcel as primary object and is designed in order to overcome some problems like data redundancy, low query efficiency and the relationship problem between the father parcel and the son parcel. Another data model concerned with tracking land use is proposed in (Huang, & Claramunt, 2005). The proposed model extends the ODMG object model with a parameterized type, *TimeSeries<T>*, which allows the shifting of spatial types into ST types in order to represent the history of an object. Also, a spatio-temporal extension of the object query language is proposed, which helps the formulation of various spatio-temporal queries. The Volumetric Spatiotemporal Data Model (Rahim, Shariff, Mansor, Mahmud, & Alias, 2006) has been developed to manage surface movement in the Virtual Geographical Information Systems (VGIS). The authors have integrated the temporal element with the 3D object (the volumetric object), which is one of the spatial objects in VGIS. Therefore, temporal version of volumetric surface data can be stored and visualized by using this model.

In (Sabau, 2007a), a new ST conceptual data model was presented. Using the 3SST model for a spatio-temporal application domain modeling, the designer may include spatio-temporal objects, but also thematic objects, without any spatial or temporal attributes. Depending on the application, events may be modeled using particular event-type objects. Discrete and continuous evolutions are allowed for the thematic and spatial objects. One spatial object can be a point, a line or a simple polygon (therefore, spatial object with or without shape).

Three steps are proposed to be followed during the conceptual modeling process: the identification of the general entities and the relationships between them, the design of the four-domain model and the development of the detailed model which includes classes (the description and behavior of objects) and relations. The importance of each of the proposed modeling phases is mentioned regarding the identification of the characteristics or behavioral aspects of objects to be modeled.

Next, the 3SST conceptual data model is transformed into a concrete model (Sabau, 2007b) in order to be implemented on a relational database system. Despite the diversity and complexity of objects and their evolutions, the proposed objective is to represent the data using a reduced number of relations and attributes. Thus, the final goal is to obtain a spatio-temporal relational structure characterized by simplicity, generality, minimum redundancy and offering the possibility of an easy implementation of spatial and temporal operations and queries on the represented data.

The chapter is organized as follows: the next section presents the steps by which the 3SST model is obtained; the represented space and time elements and the concrete relational 3SST model are described in Section 3. The final section contains conclusions and proposed future work.

2. THE 3SST CONCEPTUAL DATA MODEL

A weakness of many existing models is that each of them deals with some common characteristics found within specific applications. The modeling process described in this chapter tries to identify and use the objects and elements needed within an application dealing, among others, with spatio-temporal data. The modeling phases do not take into account a certain ST application. This means that the model is capable to represent thematic, spatio-temporal and events alike objects.

The conceptual 3SST model is obtained by following three steps: the construction of a general entity-relationship spatio-temporal model, the specification of the domain model and the design of a class diagram which includes the objects characteristic to a spatio-temporal application and other needed elements. These steps are presented next in this section.

2.1. The Entity-Relationship Spatio-Temporal Model

The first step of the spatio-temporal modeling approached in this chapter makes use of one of the most encountered conceptual data modeling techniques, regardless of the nature of data or application - the Entity-Relationship model. Thus, the result of the first modeling step of spatio-temporal data will be simply called the Entity-Relationship Spatio-Temporal model (E-R ST model).

In order to discuss the construction of the diagrams corresponding to the three modeling steps, the concrete example of a meteorological application is considered.

The main entity such an application has to deal with is the meteorological phenomenon. These are one of the most complex spatio-temporal objects: a meteorological phenomenon is a spatial object with both position and extend, and both characteristics evolve in time. Yet, besides these attributes, the object may have non-spatial characteristics which are called thematic in this chapter. For example, to a meteorological phenomenon it can be associated: a type (rain, drizzle, fog, snow, hail, glazed frost, storm), which is a non-temporal

attribute; various parameters (atmospheric pressure, air temperature, soil dampness / moisture, nebulousness, visibility, wind speed), which can be temporal attributes if their evolution in time is recorded.

The attributes that record the evolution (the temporal attributes) are considered to be composite attributes with repetitive values (multi-value attributes), because there are zero, one or more values associated with an object's instance. The thematic temporal attributes and the spatio-temporal attributes consist of a time attribute and a thematic attribute, and a spatial attribute, respectively. The structure of the multi-value attributes within the 3SST data model is shown in Figure 1. For example, for the previously considered entity "Meteorological_phenomenon", the attribute "wind_speed" is represented as a thematic temporal attribute (see Figure 1(a)): one value of this attribute is given by the wind's speed (corresponding to the thematic attribute) at a certain moment (corresponding to the time attribute).

In order to generalize the domain of a problem and to achieve a fairly comprehensive model, the set of object types to be included within the E-R ST diagram is enlarged. For example, the domain of a meteorological application may contain spatial objects with no temporal characteristics (like table-land, town), temporal objects without spatial attributes (the usage of equipments or the measurement of the values corresponding to different parameters) or objects with no spatial or temporal attributes.

Figure 1. The structure of the multi-value attributes within the 3SST data model: (a) The thematic temporal attributes, (b) The spatio-temporal attributes

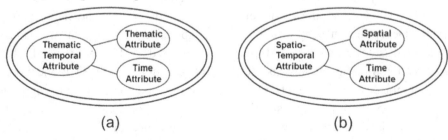

If a database contains spatio-temporal objects and their attributes along with the evolution of their values in time (the objects states are stored), the types of queries that may be efficiently answered are object-oriented, spatial-oriented, time-oriented and combinations of these. Yet, it cannot be known what caused the change of the state, the creation or destruction of an object. Therefore, information about the occurred event is also stored, to overcome this shortcoming (Peuquet & Duan, 1995).

In common usage, an event has the connotation of an occurrence, something that takes places at a particular place and time. Depending on the number of objects affected by an event, the events are classified as endogen (implies a single object; for example the creation or alteration of an object) or hexogen (at least two objects are affected, for example the split and merge processes). As an example of event that may occur in the considered application, let's consider the impact of two meteorological phenomena.

In this chapter it is considered that an event do not has associated a lifespan. In order to explain this decision, an object O is considered and two consecutive states of O, S_1 and S_2, which are valid during the time intervals $[t_s^1, t_f^1)$, and $[t_s^2, t_f^2)$ respectively. The event E is considered to be the event that triggered the change of the object's state, from S_1 to S_2. If the event E has a lifespan, then $t_f^1 < t_s^2$, and the corresponding lifespan is given by $[t_f^1, t_s^2)$. The question that arises in this case is „Which is the state of O during the time interval $[t_f^1, t_s^2)$?". In each case, if the object has a discrete or a linear continuous evolution in time, its state should be known in any moment within a contiguous time interval (except the cases when the communication with that object is broken). Therefore, it is considered that an event only happens at a certain moment in time, updates the states of the affected objects, and $t_f^1 = t_s^2$ is the timestamp of that event.

Therefore, an event object has associated as attributes a temporal-type one (a timestamp) and the location, representing the instant and the position where the event occurred. The event can be considered an individual class of objects that are connected to objects within the application domain. It is important to notice that the event objects have no evolution in time and that an event is not a spatio-temporal object even if it has spatial and temporal characteristics.

Considering that an object may have more attributes which evolve in time, the type of time-stamping at attribute level is applied in this model. The time-stamping of a tuple would lead to many data redundancies.

Despite the complexity of a ST data domain, the E-R ST diagram (see Figure 2) is very simple, identifying only two related entity types. This E-R ST diagram is not intended to be used directly for a particular application domain. It only proves that all kind of objects characteristics (thematic, spatial, temporal, ST) can be modeled by using simple and multi-valued attributes, but in order to obtain a more closed conceptual model to a concrete one, further refining steps are necessary (see subsection 2.3).

An observation has to be made in order to clarify the difference made by this chapter between time and temporal elements. It is called temporal an element (object or attribute) whose state (value) is changing over time. The timestamps associated with evolving elements are simply called time elements.

2.2. The 4-Domain Model

The data model presented by Yuan (1996) implies the spreading of data over thee domains in accordance with its nature: thematic, spatial and temporal. There are relationships set from the semantic and temporal domain to the spatial domain and from the spatial and temporal domain to the semantic domain.

The second step of the 3SST modeling process applies the same idea to the components depicted in Figure 2. The events and thematic objects are

Figure 2. The general Entity-Relationship Spatio-Temporal diagram

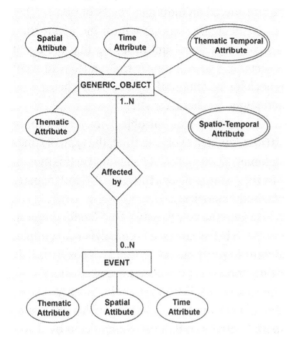

treated as two separate domains because there is a special relation among objects through events. The space and time aspects are removed from thematic objects and events, in order to be seen as individual classes, with their own attributes and behavior, and to answer efficiently spatial-based and time-based queries. Thus the domain model depicted in Figure 3 is composed by four domains, representing:

- *Thematic objects*: The objects that are included in the domain of application;
- *Event objects*: The objects that represent the cause of changes among application domain objects;
- *Space objects*: The objects that describe the spatial characteristics of a thematic or event-type object; these objects are strictly spatial and each of these objects represents shape and / or location. An observation has to be made: in this paper these objects are not called spatial objects not to be con-

founded with the spatial objects of a spatial database;

- *Time objects*: objects which represents the temporal domain that may be associated with thematic objects, event objects or space objects.

Unlike the data model proposed by Yuan (1999), the 3SST modeling allows for the establishment of direct links between any two of the four domains, without restrictions. Therefore, the representation of static spatial objects or dynamic non-spatial objects is possible.

2.3. The Object Model

Using either the E-R or the 4-Domain diagram, four types of objects may be represented in the current model:

- Non-spatial non-temporal objects (noted here as thematic objects): The objects that do not have any spatial or temporal attribute;
- (strict) Spatial objects: They have at least one spatial attribute, but its evolution in time is not recorded, and do not have any temporal attribute;
- (strict) Temporal objects: These objects do not have any spatial attribute, but they have associated at least one valid time or transaction time attribute;
- Spatio-temporal objects: They have at least one spatial attribute whose evolution in time is recorded.

Figure 3. The 4-Domain diagram

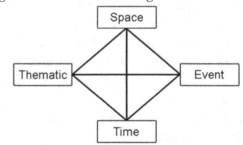

The efficient temporal data handling and the uniform treatment of spatial and temporal data are two of the main advantages of using object-oriented techniques in a ST environment. The design of the class diagram corresponding to the 3SST data model starts with the transformation of the E-R ST diagram, using the 4-Domain diagram, into the initial model represented in Figure 4.

Futher, the normalization process at object class level (Ambler, 2006) is used during the refining operations because it has the main advantage the fact that it makes possible to identify independent objects not only at characteristics level, but at behavioral level as well over the classic relation normalization. In this way, the obtained model is closer to a concrete one. For example, the space and time objects might be treated in a similar fashion regarding the resemblance between the spatial and temporal dimensions characteristics; nevertheless, the two domains present major differences at the behavioral level.

The final class diagram in 3ONF (the 3rd Object Normal Form) corresponding to the 3SST data model is depicted in Figure 5.

Some observations related to Figure 5 have to be made:

- A geometric object (space object) is represented by one or more n-dimensional points; thus, such an object can represent a point, a line segment (if there are two associated points) or any region implemented as a polygon having at least three vertices; the points are stored in counterclockwise order, in order to facilitate different computations, like area, direction, intersection, or triangulation of that region; the attribute *Next_point* is a link to the next point within the current list of points (if it is not the last point of the list). The points of a polygon are stored in counterclockwise order, in order to facilitate the implementation of different computations, like area, direction, intersection, or triangulation of regions.

- This spatio-temporal model allows both types of time objects to be used: the *valid time* (the time when the fact is true in the modeled reality) and the *transaction time* (the time when a fact is stored in database).

- The temporal domain of the 3SST data model is linear and continuous.

- The time elements can be instants or intervals.

The presented spatio-temporal model allows both types of time objects to be used: the *valid time* (the time when the fact is true in the modeled reality) and the *transaction time* (the time when a fact is stored in database).

The time elements are enriched with an attribute that represents the corresponding time zone, if needed. For example, the timetable of

Figure 4. The class diagram in 0ONF of the 3SST data model

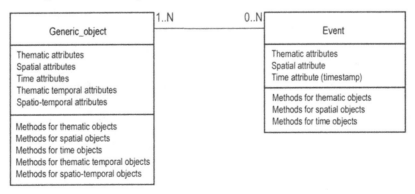

Figure 5. The class diagram in 3ONF of the 3SST data model

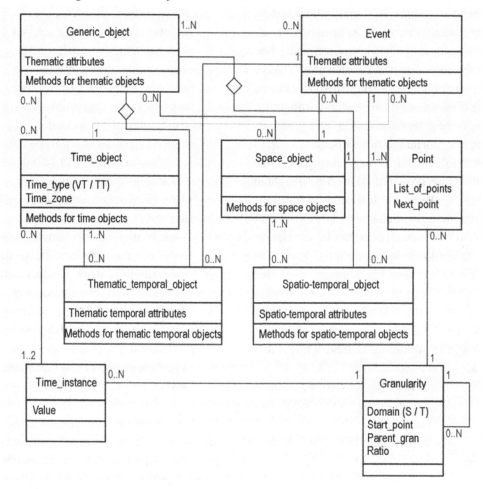

airplanes uses the local time for arrivals, but, in order to be able to compute the duration of a flight, the difference between the time zones is needed to be known.

The Figure 5 depicts relations of aggregation between the *Generic_object* class and the *Thematic_temporal_object* and *Spatio-temporal_object* classes in order to represent the dynamic attributes (non-spatial and spatial) whose evolution time intervals correspond to the lifespan of the corresponding object. Further, there are also represented relations of association between the *Generic_object* and *Space_object*, and *Time_object* respectively in the case when the thematic object has associated a spatial attribute without temporal evolution or a time attribute.

The entity *Granularity* is included in order to express spatial, time and numerical data in association with different measurement units.

The methods that define the behavior of thematic objects, space objects and time objects are not presented in detail: the methods of thematic objects may be implemented according to the nature of managed data, and the methods for spatial and temporal data correspond to different spatial and temporal operators.

The values of a spatio-temporal attribute may evolve discretely or continuously. On the other hand, regarding the spatial attributes of objects, the changes that may occur are on shape and / or position. These kinds of changes may be represented depending on data members and methods of the *Point* class: if a point object is represented by a scalar value or a constant function of time, the evolution of that point is discrete on a corresponding time interval (discrete evolution); the continuous evolution of a point object during a time interval might be represented by a non-constant function of time. Like the Parametric k-Spaghetti data model, the 3SST data model uses linear functions of time.

3. THE 3SST RELATIONAL DATA MODEL

This section presents the result of the implementation (Sabau, 2007b) of the proposed 3SST conceptual data model on top on a relational database system. During this implementation, the following decisions have been made:

- The generality regarding the number of objects' dimensions is reduced to two, because of some limitations of the used Transact SQL language and the implementation of some spatial operators. Therefore, the implemented model can represent two-dimensional spatial objects.

- The objects of class *Time_instance*, which is renamed as *Temporal* in the relational model, received the *time_zone* property. This is useful, for example, in recording the timetable of airplanes, for which the departure and the arrivals are given using the local time. In this case, the knowledge if the time zone is necessary in order to compute the duration of one flight.

- The implementation of the 3SST model uses the vector data model and represents spatial entities by their approximations: a line is represented by as set of connected line segments and a region is modeled as polygon. The set of polygons that are represented by a set of points (the vertices) are convex or

non-convex and have to be simple, non-self-intersecting polygons. The next sub-section contains the definitions of the basic spatial data types (point, line segment, line, and polygon) and the description of the time elements used within the 3SST model.

3.1. The Represented Spatial Data

The *space Sp* that includes the spatial objects is considered theoretically to be the Euclidian 2-dimensional space. Because of limitations of the *real* type of the system, the domain of values corresponding to the coordinates of points is discrete. According to this, theoretically, $Sp = R^2 = \{(x_1, x_2) \mid x_1, x_2 \in R \}$. A pair $P = (x_1, x_2)$, $x_i \in R$, i:=1..2, is a *point* of the considered space.

A *line segment* S is given by two points, P_1, $P_2 \in Sp$, $P_1 \neq P_2$, such as $S = \{P_s \mid P_s = \alpha * P1 + (1-\alpha) * P2, \alpha \in [0, 1]\}$.

In order to define the line and polygon entities, the *oriented line segment* is considered to be the vector determined by two points P_1 si P_2. Therefore, if $P_1, P_2 \in Sp$, $P_1 \neq P_2$, and $SO_1 = (P_1, P_2)$ and $SO_2 = (P_2, P_1)$ are two oriented segments, then $SO_1 \neq SO_2$.

A set of oriented segments, $L = (SO_1, SO_2, ..., SO_l)$, defines a *line* if:

PL1: $\forall$ i:=1..(l-1), $SO_i.P_2 = SO_{i+1}.P_1$ (the segments are connected at their end points);

PL2: $\forall$ i, j:=1..l, i≠j, $SO_i \cap SO_j = \varnothing \vee SO_i \cap SO_j = \{P\}$ (the segments are not overlapping, partially or totally).

Let $Pg = (SO_1, SO_2, ..., SO_p)$, p≥1, be a set of oriented segments. Pg is a *simple polygon* if the following conditions are fulfilled:

PP1: $\forall$ i:=1..p, $SO_i.P_2 = SO_{(i+1) \bmod p}.P_1$ (the segments are connected at their end points);

PP2: $\forall$ i:=1..(p-2), j:=(i+2)..p, i ≠ j, $SO_i \cap SO_j = \varnothing$ (any two non-consecutive segments are not intersecting);

PP3: $\sum_{i:=2}^{p-1} A(\Delta P_1 P_i P_{i+1}) > 0$

The notation $A(\Delta P_1 P_i P_{i+1})$ used in PP3 represents the signed area of the triangle $\Delta P_1 P_i P_{i+1}$, $i:= 2..(p-1)$. The sum of the triangles' signed areas represents the signed area of the polygon; the positive sign assures the counterclockwise orientation of the vertices of the polygon.

3.2. The Time Elements

The time objects that are used for time stamping the thematic or spatial objects can be of type instant or interval. It is considered that the time domain is the time of reality, and not simply a surrogate temporal axis, as the real numbers.

The evolution of an object O is considered to be given by a sequence of states $(S^1, S^2, ..., S^n)$. If the evolution of O is discrete and is recorded only at certain moments in time, each of its states is time stamped with a time instant. On the other side, each state is defined over a certain time interval, if the object O's evolution (discrete or continuous) is recorded during time intervals. Let I_k with the end points t^k_1 and t^k_2, $t^k_1 < t^k_2$, be the time interval corresponding to S^k state, where $k:=1..n$. If the lifespan of O is continuous and there cannot exists two different states of O at the same time, then any two time intervals I^k and I^j, k, j:=1..n, k $\neq$ j, must be disjoint. The implementation of the 3SST data model considers that they are closed at their "left" end point and open at the "right" end point. Figure 6 depicts a discrete evolution of O, which consists of four states (S^1, S^2, S^3, S^4), during time interval $[t^1, t^5]$.

3.3. The Relational Implementation of the 3SST Model

In this section the structure of the 3SST relational model (Sabau, 2007b) that corresponds to the presented conceptual 3SST model is shortly described.

Figure 6. The discrete evolution of an object over the time interval [t1, t5)

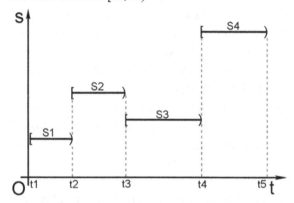

The relations depicted in Figure 7 are currently implemented on a Microsoft SQL-Server database system and the operation routines and queries are written using the Microsoft SQL-Server's Transact-SQL language. The set of implemented routines includes operations and queries with numerical result (for spatial or temporal objects), predicates (topologic, metric and directional, also for spatial or temporal objects), operations with result of type *Direction* (Sabau, 2007b) (only for spatial data of type point), operations and queries with result of type spatial or time.

A few comments about the diagram structure depicted in Figure 7 are given next:

- The property of generality is inherited by the relational model from the conceptual data model. Therefore, the 3SST relational model can be considered the core of a ST data model. For example, even if the current structure contains one relation *Object* which includes the static data of the application domains entities, more *Object*-like relations can be included in the database, depending on a particular application.

- A measurement unit is included into a single family of granularities, each of these having a parent granularity.

- Each spatial element has associated a unique ID (SOID) and each point identified by a

Figure 7. The diagram of the 3SST relational model

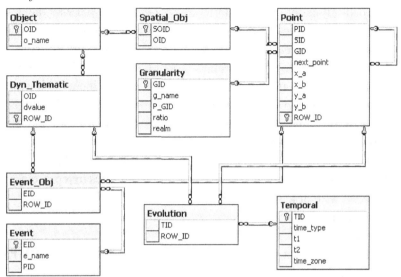

PID corresponds to a certain spatial element (see the foreign key *Point* (SID) referencing *Spatial_Obj* (SOID)).

- The type of the ROW_ID columns is *Timestamp*. This decision was made because this data type assures that the automatically generated values are unique within the entire database, not only within a relation.
- A static object or a static point does not have associated any tuple within the relation *Evolution*.
- Any point is identified by the value PID, and a state of a point is identified by ROW_ID. Therefore, the evolution of a point is given by the set of tuples of the *Point* relation that contain the given PID value.
- In the previous sub-sections were described the spatial and time objects that can be represented using the 3SST relational model. The non-spatial temporal objects and the spatio-temporal objects are not described explicitly because they are implemented using the *Evolution* relation. This relation actually contains the complete history of an object (*Dyn_Thematic* or *Point*).

- The events that trigger the objects' changes are recorded in the *Event* relation. The associations within an event and the new states of the affected objects are contained within the *Event_obj* relation, where the ROW_ID can represent the new state of a thematic object or the new state of a point object.

3.4. The Characteristics of the 3SST Relational Data Model

The characteristics that recommend the 3SST data model as a core in modeling data within a ST application are presented next:

- *Generality* at the level of:
  - *ST application*: the modeling process does not take into account a specific type of application, and can be used within different applications, like the management of terrains, transportation systems, ecology, and many others;
  - *Types of objects (as being included into one of the four mentioned domains)*: it is possible the representation of:

> *thematic static objects* (without thematic dynamic, spatial static or spatial dynamic attributes),

> *spatial static objects* (with at least one spatial static attribute and without dynamic attributes),

> *thematic dynamic objects* (with at least one thematic dynamic attribute and without spatial attributes),

> *spatial dynamic objects* or *ST objects* (with at least one spatial dynamic attribute);

○ *Types of spatial objects*: the 3SST data model allows the geometric representation of objects without shape, with linear or region shape; the approximation of the regions is made using convex or concave simple polygons;

○ *Types of evolutions*: the model can represent the discrete and the continuous evolutions of spatial objects using linear functions of time as their approximations. As another aspect of the generality within the context of spatial objects' evolutions, it is emphasized the fact that the representation of the evolution of spatial objects of type line segment or polygon allows the *independent evolution of their extremities*, without storing redundant data.

• *Extensibility*:

○ The main idea of the 3SST data model development is obtaining a core in modeling ST data. The presented model can be extended by new structures and new fields can be added to the existing structures, without influence on what was mentioned before. For example: there is a single table *Object* and a single table *Dyn_Thematic*; but, according to the number or the diversity of ST objects within the data domain of a ST application, there can be added new tables

within the relational database, as long as the way the objects and their states are identified is the same.

• *Independence* against the domain of the problem: the spatial and spatio-temporal data is included into structures that are not affected by the expansion of the database.

• *Simplicity*: not the last, the simplicity of the 3SST structures can be noticed, as the number of tables and fields vis-à-vis the possibilities in representing data and operating on it.

CONCLUSION AND FUTURE WORK

Any application needs first a conceptual model of data. The 3SST data modeling process proves the benefit of using two or more modeling techniques in order to identify various types of objects, the relationships among them, how they communicate or what behavior they have. The entity-relationship diagram was first used because is simple and provides a clear point of view on data. The domain model resulted from different observations and it was rather an intermediate step, than a separate modeling phase. The class diagram finished the process by identifying the objects and some of their attributes and methods.

Next, it is shown the capability of a relational database system to store ST data with discrete or continuous evolution in time. The spatial attributes of considered objects may be of type point, line or simple polygon. The implementation of spatial evolution allows the defining points of the geometric objects to change independently, with a different frequency, on different time intervals. Also, the implemented model is able to perform different spatial, temporal and ST operations and queries on the stored data, with the help of a set or routines written in the standard query language.

The current work will be continued by the implementation of a visual interface. In order to implement in a more elegant and efficient fashion the data structures and the corresponding routines, the proposed future work also includes their implementation on top of an object-relational database system and the study of queries performance on large sets of data.

REFERENCES

Ambler, S. W. (last updated 2006). *Introduction to class normalization.* Retrieved 2008, from http://www.agiledata.org

Chomicki, J., & Revesz, P. (1997). Constraint-based interoperability of spatiotemporal databases. *Proc. of the 5th Intl. Symposium on Large Spatial Databases, LNCS 1262,* 142-162. Springer-Verlag.

Erwig, M., Güting, R. H., Schneider, M., & Vazirgiannis, M. (1998). Abstract and discrete modeling of spatio-temporal data types. *In Proceedings of ACM International Symposium on Geographic Information Systems,* (pp. 131-136).

Güting, R. H., Böhlen, M. H., Erwig, M., Jensen, C. S., Lorentzos, N. A., Schneider, M., & Vazirgiannis, M. (2000). A foundation for representing and querying moving objects. *ACM Transactions on Database Systems, 25*(1), 1-42.

Huang, B., & Claramunt, C. (2005). Spatiotemporal Data Model and Query Language for Tracking Land Use Change. *Transportation Research Record: Journal of the Transportation Research Board, 1902,* 107-113.

Langran, G., & Chrisman, N. R. (1988). A framework for temporal geographic information systems. *Cartographica, 25*(3), 1-14.

Peuquet, D., & Duan, N. (1995). An Event-Based Spatio-temporal Data Model (ESTDM) for Temporal Analysis of Geographical Data. *Int. Journal of Geographical Information Systems, 9*(1), 7-24.

Price, R. J., Tryfona, N., & Jensen, C. S. (2000). Extended SpatioTemporal UML: Motivations, Requirements and Constructs. *Journal of Database Management, 11*(4), 14-27.

Rahim, M. S. M., Shariff, A. R. M., Mansor, S., Mahmud, A. R., & Alias, M. A. (2006). Volumetric spatiotemporal data model. *In Innovations in 3D Geo Information Systems, Lecture Notes in Geoinformation and Cartography,* (pp. 547-556).

Renolen, A. (1996). History graphs: Conceptual modeling of spatio-temporal data. *In Proceedings of GIS Frontiers in Business and Science,* International Cartographic Association, 2, Brno.

Sabau, A. (2007a). The 3SST Model: A three step spatio-temporal conceptual model. *In Proceedings of the 2nd AIS SIGSAND European Symposium on System Analysis and Design,* Gdansk.

Sabau, A. (2007b). The 3SST Relational Model. *Studia Universitatis "Babeş-Bolyai", Informatica, LII*(1), 77-88.

Sistla, A. P., Wolfson, O., Chamberlain, S., & Dao, S. (1997). Modeling and querying moving objects. *Proceedings of the 13th IEEE International Conference on Data Engineering,* Birmingham, (pp. 422-432).

Tryfona, N., & Jensen, C. S. (1999). Conceptual data modeling for spatiotemporal applications. *GeoInformatica, 3*(3), 245-268.

Tryfona, N., & Jensen, C. S. (2000). Using abstractions for spatio-temporal conceptual modeling. *Proceedings of the 2000 ACM Symposium on Applied Computing,* Italy, (pp. 313-322).

Wang, Z., Fang, Y., & Xie, X. (2005). A spatio-temporal data model based on the parcel in cadastral. *In Proceedings of Geoscience and Remote Sensing Symposium, 2.*

Wolfson, O., Xu, B., Chamberlain, S., & Jiang, L. (1998). Moving objects databases: Issues and solutions. *Proceedings of the 10th International*

Conference on Scientific and Statistical Database Management (SSDBM98), (pp. 111-122).

Worboys, M. F. (1994). A Unified Model for Spatial and Temporal Information. *The Computer Journal, 37*(1), 27-34.

Yuan, M. (1996). Modeling semantical, temporal, and spatial information in geographic information systems. In M. Craglia & H. Couclelis (Eds.),

Geographic Information Research: Bridging the Atlantic (pp. 334-347). London: Taylor & Francis.

Yuan, M. (1999). Use of a three-domain representation to enhance GIS support for complex spatiotemporal queries. *Transactions in GIS, 3*(2), 137-159.

Chapter II
An Identity Perspective for Predicting Software Development Project Temporal Success

Jeff Crawford
The University of Tulsa, USA

ABSTRACT

This theoretical work draws on group development literature to propose a model for increasing the likelihood of achieving temporal success within a software development (SD) environment. The study addresses a group's temporal performance through a punctuated equilibrium (PE) lens. As a means of extending the PE model of group development for a SD project context, this research will consider social and temporal aspects of identity within each group in order to address the varying nature of temporal success. First, anthropological research on rituals in society will be applied to present a project-as-ritual perspective, where social and temporal identity are suggested to flow from the rites of passage that exist during the initial meeting and temporal midpoint of a group. Second, social identity theory will be applied to posit that both types of identity are positively associated with a group's ability to meet temporal deadlines. This theoretical piece is expected to make two primary contributions to literature. First, group development literature is enhanced by providing an extension of the PE model to address environments where social and temporal identities are variable. This contribution is significant since it will allow researchers to apply a PE perspective in real world project team environments. Second, the research contributes to SD literature by offering a clear perspective regarding key factors that can serve to impact a SD project team's ability to meet temporal deadline.

INTRODUCTION

Software development (SD) projects have been the subject of a tremendous amount of attention in the academic world. Within this research stream, the most frequent goal has been to evaluate, elucidate and ultimately predict factors which enhance the likelihood of achieving SD project success. Issues such as project structure and SD methodology usage have been suggested as important factors that influence project success (Hardgrave, Davis, & Riemenschneider, 2003; Khalifa & Verner, 2000; Kirsch, Sambamurthy, Ko, & Purvis, 2002). However, little research has considered the role of group dynamics in shaping SD project success. Since SD projects are often the result of team efforts, a key source of SD project success must lie in how the group develops and approaches their tasks over time.

As a first step in addressing the role of group dynamics in a SD context, this paper will present a theoretical model which attempts to explain the role of group development in promoting SD project success. Because project success is a broad and complex construct, the theory detailed here will focus only on one aspect of success, that of meeting temporal deadlines. A punctuated equilibrium (PE) model of group development (Gersick, 1988) will serve as the theoretical foundation for addressing the temporal pacing of work activities within a SD project. While a PE model provides a general framework to evaluate SD project temporal success, its interpretive power is limited with regards to several of the idiosyncrasies inherent in SD project work. For example, SD environments are often characterized by fluid project specifications, shifting task and project deadlines, workplace demands which compete with project expectations, and a need to interweave independent development activities within interdependent project goals. To accommodate these issues, this research will extend the PE model by considering both the social and temporal identity possessed by each SD project team. The resulting view of SD group development is expected to explain the variance that often exists in project team temporal success.

This paper will proceed as follows. First, the PE model of group development will be discussed in terms of its strengths and limitations for predicting SD project success. Next, the PE model will be extended by considering the role of social and temporal identity in a SD context, specifically focusing on the impact of identity on the group's ability to navigate its temporal midpoint. Following this, the theoretical model will be presented and propositions discussed. Finally, the paper will conclude with an overview of expected contributions and future directions of this research stream.

THEORETICAL PERSPECTIVES ON GROUP DEVELOPMENT

Group development literature has a long, rich and somewhat divided history[1]. Early researchers of group development suggested that productive groups progress sequentially through a series of well defined stages during their life (Tuckman & Jensen, 1977). While a sequential view of group development doesn't preclude the existence of behaviors in any given stage (i.e., work activities in the forming stage), it does suggest that each phase is characterized by a dominant set of behaviors specific to that phase (Wheelan, 1994). A sequential perspective suggests that groups *must* navigate in a linear fashion through each developmental stage before they can have a chance of attaining task success. In the late 1980s, the idea of gradual sequential development was challenged by the research of Connie Gersick (1988, 1989), who used a widely accepted theory of biological evolution (PE) to frame the task-related behavior of small groups. The PE perspective illustrated that groups are likely to complete tasks on-time provided they share a consistent sensitivity to temporal deadlines and demonstrate that sensitivity through increased activity at the group's temporal midpoint. While often positioned as competing and tangential explanations of group development (Wheelan, Davidson, & Tilin, 2003), recent work has suggested that both perspectives offer valid explanations of group behavior, but from different points of reference. Specifically, sequential models of group development focus on the socio-emotional development of groups throughout their life while a PE model illustrates group development in light of work activity over time (Chang, Bordia, & Duck, 2003). Since this research focuses on the temporal nature of SD projects, a PE model of group development is the most appropriate framework for understanding the role of group development in temporal SD project success.

A PE Model of Group Development

The PE perspective of group development grew out of evolutionary research which sought to understand how biological systems change over time (Wollin, 1999). Rather than proposing that species evolve only through smooth and gradual change, scientists began to theorize that new forms often result from revolutionary events (Eldredge & Gould, 1972). Over time, researchers began to apply this perspective in understanding phenomena within different domains. In particular, group development researchers such as Gersick (1988) observed that groups did not follow a smooth and gradual development pattern as suggested in previous research (Tuckman & Jensen, 1977) but rather exhibited characteristics that were analogous with the development of biological systems. Specifically, she found that groups tended to experience two stable phases of their life, punctuated by a radical shift at their temporal midpoint (Gersick, 1988, 1989). During the first half of a group's life, a group's modus operandi appeared to result from the first meeting and stayed fairly consistent until the temporal midpoint. At the midpoint, groups typically experienced a sharp point of crisis (i.e.,

uncertainty regarding completion of the task) which resulted in a radical re-evaluation and reformation of group behavior and task work. This new group structure then stabilized for the second phase of a group's life, where members intently focused on behaviors which would help them complete the assigned work task before the temporal deadline.

A key finding of this perspective is that windows of opportunity for influencing a group's trajectory exist and are somewhat predictable. Specifically, Gersick found that both inertial phases of a group's life are preceded by a window of opportunity (1988, 1989). The first is evident during a group's initial meeting, where members are brought together to consider the assigned task and member roles for the first time. Decisions made during this first period strongly influence group structure and work during the first period of the group's life. The second window of opportunity occurs at the midpoint transition, where group members are forced to reconsider their task progress in light of a rapidly approaching deadline. Rather than incrementally changing direction, the midpoint results in a radical shift of group direction which serves to define task work during the second period of inertia.

This perspective holds several promises for SD research addressing temporal project success. First, the PE model suggests two key points in a group's life, the initial meeting and the temporal midpoint, that can serve as windows of opportunity for management to help direct SD project teams towards a successful end. At the initial meeting, efforts made to promote a unified view of project expectations and goals can help to ensure that the first period of inertia isn't wasted time but rather a period when a healthy team structure is implemented. At the temporal midpoint, the model suggests that drawing attention to project deadlines can serve as an important means of moving the SD team into a highly productive period where attaining project deadlines are more likely. Second, a PE model of group development *implicitly* illustrates the importance of identity in achieving positive group outcomes. PE research has most often investigated groups convened to complete a *specific task* within a *clearly understood time frame* (Chang et al., 2003; Gersick, 1988, 1989), resulting in project teams with strong social and temporal identities.

THEORETICAL PERSPECTIVES ON IDENTITY

A PE model of group development has been examined and validated within groups that possess two distinct types of identity. First, groups examined in PE research seemed to enjoy a strong *social identity*, defined as the summation of group member "self-concept which derives from his knowledge of his membership of a social group (or groups) together with the value and emotional significance attached to that membership" (Tajfel, 1981, p. 255). This social identity is most clearly expressed in the group's consensus regarding project goals and objectives. Second, groups examined in PE research also evidenced a strong *temporal identity,* defined as group member understanding for and allegiance to the final project deadline. Temporal identity is most clearly illustrated in groups where project deadlines are clear and unambiguous.

Unfortunately, SD project environments are subject to variations in social and temporal identities within the project and an assumption of strong social and temporal identity will not suffice. As such, it is important to address how identity is achieved within a SD project as a means of inducing positive project outcomes. A PE perspective suggests two points in a group's life where a group is most agreeable for shaping identity, the initial group meeting and the group's temporal midpoint. These periods can be understood in terms of *rites of passage* that serve to transition individuals into a new project-related identity.

Rites of Passage in a SD Context

Rites can be defined as "relatively elaborate, dramatic, planned sets of activities that consolidate various forms of cultural expressions into one event, which is carried through social interactions, usually for the benefit of an audience" (Trice & Beyer, 1984, p. 655). The existence of rites provides a means of achieving stability within an organization in the face of unpredictable change (Robey & Markus, 1984; Trice & Beyer, 1984). Within the context of project work, rites of passage become paramount since they provide a door through which member identity can be shaped into one that is project-focused. Anthropological research on rites of passage in society, originating in the early 1900s with French anthropologist Arnold van Gennep (1960) and coming to prominence in the latter half of the 20th century with the ethnographic work of Victor Turner (Turner, 1974), provides a procedural view which provides an important insight into the formation of developer identity within a SD project. Drawing on the work of van Gennep, Turner formalized a ritual-as-process perspective where individuals are suggested to traverse three separate stages of behavior during an identity transition: (a) separation, (b) liminality, and (c) aggregation (Deflem, 1991)[2]. In the initial stage of separation, the individual divorces from existing social structures in preparation to receive their new identity. This initial stage is followed by a liminal period where the individual is "betwixt and between", having abandoned their previous identity but yet to take hold of the new one (Turner, 1995). Finally, a period of aggregation occurs where the individual absorbs their new identity and finalizes the shift between social roles. Turner's intense interest in this process focused on the liminal period since he was convinced that "liminality is not only *transition* but also *potentiality*, not only 'going to be' but also 'what may be'" (Turner & Turner, 1978, p. 3). As such, Turner suggests that the liminal period can be dangerous to the existing institutional environment since communitas (anti-structure) develop which can produce social structures incompatible with existing norms (Turner, 1995).

Organizational worker identities shift over time within an organization, as can be evidenced within the day to day roles required of a SD project worker. For example, a software developer will often wear different hats based on specific organizational needs, playing the part of coder, mentor, standards bearer, technical support, project worker, manager, etc. With so many potential outlets for identity, how does a project worker acquire a social and temporal identity within the context of a SD project? Within organizations, worker identity is often altered through the use of rites of passage, such as that of a worker being promoted to management whose existing workspace (cubicle) is abandoned for an office with a door (a transitory rite of passage). Rites are prevalent within the software development process (Robey & Markus, 1984) and often serve as mechanisms through which developer identity is aligned with the project.

The first rite of passage in a SD project exists during the group's initial meeting, where individuals are faced with creating a social identity relating to the project itself. At this early stage of the project, individuals must unfreeze their current social identity in order to incorporate new roles and responsibilities required within the project. The second rite of passage is evident at the group's midpoint transition, where group members must solidify a temporal identity, locking into the project's completion date in order to encourage and support productive behaviors. As such, rites of passage play an important role in shaping project identity, and consequently enabling or constraining temporal success.

The strength of SD project social and temporal identities can vary greatly between projects. With social identity, team members are often saddled with divergent organizational demands that preclude them from deeply identifying with the project. In addition, temporal identity might be discouraged because of competing and/or ambiguous project deadlines. Using a rites of passage perspective, SD environments would exhibit weak social or temporal identities in light of two conditions. First, project-related rites of passage might not encourage sufficient separation for members, hampering the formation of a strong social identity. For example, replacing the initial project meeting with an e-mail message could be interpreted by team members as an indication of low project importance. Second, project-related rites of passage might not be sufficient to move an individual from the liminal stage into aggregation with the new identity. For example, a SD group might not develop a concrete and cohesive understanding of the project deadline at the midpoint but rather continue living in a state of project-related temporal ambiguity.

RESEARCH PROPOSITIONS

Drawing on the theoretical framework presented earlier, several propositions can be asserted. The first considers how a project team can achieve temporal success. PE research demonstrates that task productivity primarily occurs during the period of a group's life following their midpoint transition **provided that the team exhibited a proper awareness of time and deadlines**. Groups unable to refocus at their temporal midpoint were found to be prone to failure (Gersick, 1989). As such, a PE perspective suggests the following within a SD project context:

P1: *SD project temporal success is positively related to a project team's ability to successfully navigate their temporal midpoint.*

However, there are several idiosyncrasies within a SD project environment that prevent one from blindly applying a PE perspective to understand SD project temporal success. First, groups studied in PE research have a very clear project-related social identity. While some SD projects are characterized by developers working solely on one project, many developers are saddled daily with competing organizational demands. For example, it is not uncommon for a developer to provide support and maintenance for past SD projects while also working on new development initiatives. In addition, developers are often assigned to projects based on their expertise (i.e., security expert, database expert, etc.) which can force them to span multiple projects at one time. In situations where developers are asked to identify with multiple initiatives, it is likely that they will experience problems in identifying with any one particular project. Second, the PE perspective has typically been applied to groups where members were required to "make interdependent decisions about what to create and how to proceed" (Gersick, 1988, p. 13). While SD projects do require interdependent activity, developers often function independently of the project team while completing tasks within the project. As such, developers are frequently insulated from the overall project through their attention to the completion of specific project-related tasks. Third, the idea of a temporal midpoint transition requires that group members have an unambiguous knowledge of the project deadline. Gersick acknowledged this in her work when she stated that "synchrony in group members' expectations about deadlines may be critical to groups' abilities to accomplish successful transitions in their work" (1989, pp. 305-306). SD projects often require SD methodologies which embrace need for user requirements to be progressively elaborated over time (DeGrace & Stahl, 1990; McConnell, 2004), limiting the degree to which team members can clearly understand the project deadline. Even when a project deadline can be crystallized, developers are often required to focus on the completion of individual tasks rather than the project as a whole, and as such are not tuned into the overall project deadline.

While there is value in drawing on a PE model for understanding SD project temporal success, it is clear that the model alone won't address the complexities of SD environments. The next paragraphs will illustrate how the concept of identity can be used to extend the PE model to a SD project context.

The Role of Identity in SD Project Temporal Success

Project identity is expressed in the PE model of group development through both social and temporal identities. While social identity is established in the initial meeting of a group, temporal identity grows from the group's inception and is only solidified at the group's temporal midpoint. The impact of identity on temporal success will first be addressed through social identity since it occurs early in the group's life, followed by a discussion of the influence of temporal identity on success.

The role of social identity on group outcomes can be understood through a social identity theory lens. Social identity theory was developed to explain the means by which individuals ascribe identification with a given group, and the resulting dynamics of relationships with other groups (Tajfel, 1981). Social identity is important since it provides the individual with cognitive structuring regarding the social environment while also enabling a means of positioning themselves within that environment (Ashforth & Mael, 1989). While social identity theory has most frequently been used to explain the drivers of group identification (Bhattacharya, Rao, & Glynn, 1995; Dwyer, Richard, & Shepherd, 1998; Laverie & Arnett, 2000; Underwood, Bond, & Baer, 2001), the theory has also been applied to understanding outcomes such as adherence to organizational norms (Hogg & Terry, 2000) and stakeholder mobilization (Rowley & Moldoveanu, 2003).

Social identity theory offers several important lessons with regards to a SD group's ability to meet temporal deadlines. First, individuals possess multiple social identities which might impose competing and conflicting demands upon them (Ashforth & Mael, 1989). Research has consequently suggested that individuals in organizations are more likely to participate in activities that are viewed as consistent with their identities (Ashforth & Mael, 1989), or conversely that individuals might eschew activities that aren't consistent. Further, research has posited that social group attraction encourages compliance with in-group norms (Hogg & Terry, 2000), consequently discouraging compliance with out-group norms. These two assertions suggest that a project team's social identity, defined as "the intersection of the social identities of the individuals in that group" (Rowley & Moldoveanu, 2003, p. 211), should positively influence that team's attention to project tasks, which has a direct bearing on their ability to navigate the temporal midpoint transition described in a PE perspective. As such, the PE model of group development is extended for a SD project environment through the following proposition:

P2: *The project-related social identity within a group is positively related to a project team's ability to successfully navigate their temporal midpoint.*

Another important application of social identity theory within this context is its implications for a project team's ability to develop a temporal identity. Temporal identity is more than just knowing the date a project should be complete. Rather, temporal identity requires that a group ingest the due date in a way that is reflected through their collective behavior. While SD project team members are understood to have multiple social identities within the organization, there are likely to be inconsistencies between these different identities. Rather than integrating the various social identities, research has suggested that individuals will

identify more strongly with one than the others and as such exert more efforts on activities that support that foremost identity (Ashforth & Mael, 1989). In the case of SD projects, this suggests that the strength of a SD project team's social identity will impact the formation of their temporal identity by providing a justification and motivation for project work over other competing demands.

P3: *The project-related social identity within a group is positively related to a project team's project-related temporal identity.*

Finally, the temporal identity of a SD project team is also expected to have direct implications on their ability to manage the temporal midpoint transition suggested in a PE perspective. Research on polychronic orientations within a workgroup suggests that as worker preferences regarding polychronicity (i.e., a desire to work on multiple tasks simultaneously) align with the reality of how activities are actually accomplished in the group, members have a greater willingness to exert effort and in fact increase their desire to remain in that group (Slocombe & Bluedorn, 1999). This finding underlies the idea that temporal synchrony within a group provides an intra-group paradigm that allows them to more closely focus on project activities regardless of other temporal pressures. As such, it is expected that the strength of a SD project team's temporal identity will provide a means for effectively handling the shock of the temporal midpoint transition.

P4: *The project-related temporal identity within a group is positively related to a project team's ability to successfully navigate their temporal midpoint.*

Figure 1 provides a graphical depiction of the process theory outlined in propositions one through four.

Figure 1. Theoretical model[3]

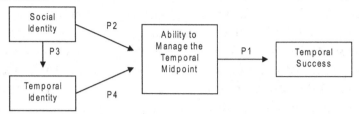

CONTRIBUTIONS, LIMITATIONS AND FUTURE DIRECTIONS

The preceding research propositions suggest that a PE model of group development can be used to predict temporal success within a SD project team provided that social and temporal identities are sufficient to provide a team the ability to survive and thrive in light of the shock at the group's temporal midpoint. The resulting model is expected to make three primary contributions to literature. First, group development literature is furthered by extending the PE model to address "real-world" project environments where project identity can substantially vary. Second, the research contributes to SD literature by offering a theoretical view regarding conditions that can encourage SD project team's ability to meet temporal deadlines. Finally, this research contributes to project management literature by stepping outside the procedural aspects of project management and addressing social considerations in enabling project success.

In addition, the propositions in this research offer a platform from which managerial interventions can be derived to induce temporal project success. For example, the proposed model stresses the importance of two points in a group's life (the initial meeting and the temporal midpoint) that are most conducive to altering the trajectory of a group. This research contributes to practitioners by providing a project-as-ritual view where individual identity is shaped through rites of passage at each key point in the project's life. As such,

the model suggests that interventions aimed at increasing project team identity (for example, providing a greater emphasis on the initial project meeting) can improve the project team's ability to meet temporal deadlines.

REFERENCES

Ashforth, B. E., & Mael, F. (1989). Social identity Theory and the Organization. *Academy of Management Review, 14*(1), 20-39.

Bhattacharya, C. B., Rao, H., & Glynn, M. A. (1995). Understanding the Bond of Identification: An Investigation of its Correlates Among Art Museum Members. *Journal of Marketing, 59*(4), 46-57.

Chang, A., Bordia, P., & Duck, J. (2003). Punctuated equilibrium and Linear Progression: Toward a New Understanding of Group development. *Academy of Management Journal, 46*(1), 106-117.

Deflem, M. (1991). Ritual, Anti-Structure, and Religion: A Discussion of Victor Turner's Processual Symbolic Analysis. *Journal for the Scientific Study of Religion, 30*(1), 1-25.

DeGrace, P., & Stahl, L. H. (1990). *Wicked Problems, Righteous Solutions: A Catalogue of Modern Software Engineering Paradigms.* Englewood Cliffs, NJ: Prentice Hall, Inc.

Dwyer, S., Richard, O., & Shepherd, C. D. (1998). An Exploratory Study of Gender and Age Matching in the Salesperson-Prospective Customer

Dyad: Testing Similarity-Performance Predictions. *The Journal of Personal Selling & Sales Management, 18*(4), 55.

Eldredge, N., & Gould, S. J. (1972). Punctuated Equilibria: An Alternative to Phyletic Gradualism. In T. J. M. Schopf (Ed.), *Models in Paleobiology* (pp. 82-115). San Francisco, CA: Freeman.

Gersick, C. J. G. (1988). Time and Transition in Work Teams: Toward a New Model of Group development. *Academy of Management Journal, 31*(1), 9-41.

Gersick, C. J. G. (1989). Marking Time: Predictable Transitions in Task Groups. *Academy of Management Journal, 32*(2), 274-309.

Hardgrave, B. C., Davis, F. D., & Riemenschneider, C. K. (2003). Investigating Determinants of Software Developers' Intentions to Follow Methodologies. *Journal of Management Information Systems, 20*(1), 123-151.

Hogg, M. A., & Terry, D. J. (2000). Social identity and Self-Categorization Processes in Organizational Contexts. *Academy of Management Review, 25*(1), 121-140.

Khalifa, M., & Verner, J. M. (2000). Drivers for Software development Method Usage. *IEEE Transactions on Engineering Management, 47*(3), 360-369.

Kirsch, L. J., Sambamurthy, V., Ko, D.-G., & Purvis, R. L. (2002). Controlling Information Systems Development Projects: The View from the Client. *Management Science, 48*(4), 484-498.

Laverie, D. A., & Arnett, D. B. (2000). Factors Affecting Fan Attendance: The Influence of Identity Salience and Satisfaction. *Journal of Leisure Research, 32*(2), 225.

Markus, M. L., & Robey, D. (1988). Information Technology and Organizational Change: Causal Structure in Theory and Research. *Management Science, 34*(5), 583-598.

McConnell, S. (2004). *Code Complete* (2nd ed.). Redmond, WA: Microsoft Press.

Robey, D., & Markus, M. L. (1984). Rituals in Information Systems Design. *MIS Quarterly, 8*(1), 5-15.

Rowley, T. J., & Moldoveanu, M. (2003). When Will Stakeholder Groups Act? An Interest- and Identity-based Model of Stakeholder Group Mobilization. *Academy of Management Review, 28*(2), 204-219.

Slocombe, T. E., & Bluedorn, A. C. (1999). Organizational Behavior Implications of the Congruence Between Preferred Polychronicity and Experienced Work-unit Polychronicity. *Journal of Organizational Behavior, 20*, 75-99.

Tajfel, H. (1981). *Human Groups and Social Categories: Studies in Social Psychology.* Cambridge, England: Cambridge University Press.

Trice, H. M., & Beyer, J. M. (1984). Studying Organizational Cultures Through Rites and Ceremonials. *Academy of Management Review, 9*(4), 653-669.

Tuckman, B. W., & Jensen, M. A. C. (1977). Stages in Small Group development Revisited. *Group & Organization Studies, 2*(4), 419-427.

Turner, V. W. (1974). *Dramas, Fields, and Metaphors: Symbolic Action in Human Society.* London, England: Cornell University Press.

Turner, V. W. (1995). *The Ritual Process: Structure and Anti-Structure* (Reprint ed.). Chicago: Aldine Transaction.

Turner, V. W., & Turner, E. (1978). *Image and Pilgrimage in Christian Culture.* New York: Columbia University Press.

Underwood, R., Bond, E., & Baer, R. (2001). Building Service Brands via Social identity: Lessons from the Sports Marketplace. *Journal of Marketing Theory and Practice, 9*(1), 1.

Van Gennep, A. (1960). *The Rites of Passage* (M. B. Vizedom & G. L. Caffe, Trans.). London, England: University of Chicago Press

Wheelan, S. A. (1994). *Group Processes: A Developmental Perspective.* Needham Heights, MA: Allyn and Bacon.

Wheelan, S. A., Davidson, B., & Tilin, F. (2003). Group development Across Time: Reality or Illusion? *Small Group Research, 34*(2), 223-245.

Wollin, A. (1999). Punctuated equilibrium: Reconciling Theory of Revolutionary and Incremental Change. *Systems Research and Behavioral Science, 16*(4), 359-367.

ENDNOTES

[1] For a comprehensive review of group development literature, see: Chidambaram, L., and Bostrom, R.P. "Group Development (I): A Review and Synthesis of Development Models," *Group Decision and Negotiation* (6:2), March 1997, pp 159-187.

[2] It is interesting to note the parallel between Turner's three stages and those proposed by Kurt Lewin to explain behavioral change: unfreeze, change and freeze. More information on Lewin's model of change can be found at: Lewin, K. "Group Decision and Social Change," in: *Readings in Social Psychology,* T.M. Newcomb and E.L. Hartley (eds.), Henry Holt & Co., New York, NY, 1947, p. 344.

[3] Antecedent variables in Figure 1 are considered necessary, but not sufficient, conditions required in attaining temporal success. The model in Figure 1 is an example of a process theory, as discussed in (Markus & Robey, 1988)

Chapter III
Survey of Cardinality Constraints in Snapshot and Temporal Semantic Data Models

Faiz Currim
University of Iowa, USA

Sudha Ram
University of Arizona, USA

ABSTRACT

Cardinality captures necessary semantics in conceptual data modeling and determines how constructs are translated into relations. Business policies in a variety of domains like healthcare, education, supply chain management and geographic systems are often expressible in terms of cardinality. The knowledge about cardinality constraints is also useful during schema integration, in query transformation for more efficient search strategies, and in database testing. Practically every conceptual modeling grammar provides support for this kind of constraint, and in an effort to resolve the variations in semantics past research has studied the different types of cardinality constraints. None have been so far comprehensive, and further there has been very little coverage of the concept in temporal domain even though it provides some interesting extensions to the concept. This study considers existing work in snapshot and temporal cardinality and suggests some areas for future work.

INTRODUCTION

The last three decades have seen active research in the area of database design and modeling. A number of modeling grammars and implementation techniques have been proposed, including popular standards like the Entity Relationship (ER) model and the Unified Modeling Language (UML). Both ER and UML were designed as general-purpose models, and we have seen the development of model extensions to capture the semantics in specialized domains (e.g., for scientific, healthcare, and temporal applications). In various forms, these models all address important design needs of documenting and communicating the database schema, and are consequently popular in industry and academia. One would be hard-pressed to find a database textbook that did not include some conceptual model variant, and likewise most database CASE tools incorporate them in as well.

A number of grammars have been developed for snapshot and temporal data. Their popularity and importance can also be measured via a surrogate of the number of surveys and research commentaries developed for conceptual modeling (Gregersen & Jensen, 1999; Hull & King, 1987; Parent *et al.*, 1999; Peckham & Maryanski, 1988; Tryfona & Jensen, 1999; Wand & Weber, 2002). An important aspect of such models is the expression of data constraints (Ram & Khatri, 2005). The visible representation of rules helps organizations in a number of ways including better capturing of semantics, as an aid to translation of the schema, in search and query strategies.

Most conceptual models capture business policies that determine cardinality. However, there is a wide variation in how grammars treat the semantics of cardinality and how many different types of cardinality constraints they represent. Some consider cardinality as applied to relationships, while others also take into account attributes and classes. Cardinality for attributes is often integrated into the semantic model constructs by use of special symbols such as shading mandatory attributes (i.e., minimum cardinality of 1) or using some symbolic construct like a double-lined oval for a multi-valued attributes (maximum cardinality $\geq$ 2). Other useful and related structural constraints like identification (where the cardinality of the attribute domain exactly matches the cardinality of its associated entity set) and composition (attributes with degree > 1 or component attributes) are also represented. In Figure 1, which uses the

notation syntax adopted by a popular database text book[1] (Elmasri & Navathe, 2006), we see EmpID is an identifier, Name is a composite attribute, and Phone is a multi-valued attribute for the EMPLOYEES class.

There are a number of other data constraints besides cardinality. For instance, when discussing attributes, one could include constraints on the range of values an attribute can take, including restrictions determined by membership in relationships or subclasses. Often, a simple annotation to the schema or data dictionary is made. For example, the Semantic Database Model (SDM) (Hammer & McLeod, 1981) uses value classes and derivations which are specified in the schema data-dictionary. Aiming to survey and classify all possible rules is a huge task, and would go well beyond the scope of a single chapter.

In this work, we focus on cardinality rules. This is a subset of the possible data integrity rule types, and we refer the reader to work by Thalheim (Thalheim, 1996) that discusses the various constraint categories. Cardinality is an interesting type of rule for a number of reasons, including the variety of constraint sub-types, the ability to formalize rule semantics via first-order-logic and consequently reason about the rules and potential conflicts. Further, a lack of understanding of the distinction among cardinality types can lead to miscommunication (for those following a different scheme) about the data semantics and consequent translation, or a persistent misconception that cardinality is a difficult concept in conceptual modeling.

Figure 1. An example of employees working on projects

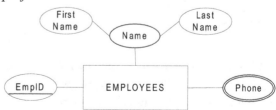

The purpose of this survey is to provide a comparative reference of cardinality semantics. For traditional snapshot models, we provide a meta-survey by making reference to previous papers in the field that have examined a number of conceptual modeling grammars. Since a survey has not been done yet for temporal models, we proceed to provide one for the well-known temporal conceptual models, explaining and classifying their support for different kinds of cardinality. Our goal is to assist current and future efforts by cataloging available features and providing recommendations for future modeling research efforts and implementation development. Thus, it is aimed at both academicians and practitioners engaged in database design and development, including those in the temporal data management area.

In the rest of this chapter, we examine some of the constraint types currently modeled. We begin with traditional snapshot (i.e., non-temporal) models and their handling of attribute and relationship cardinalities and subsequently move on to the treatment of cardinality in temporal, temporal models. Finally we also consider general-purpose rule-based frameworks and constraint modeling languages and how they deal with cardinality.

1.1 Cardinality in Traditional Conceptual Models

Relationship cardinality is a business rule type normally captured in semantic models like the ER approach or UML, and the term *cardinality* in most models is synonymous with cardinalities associated with interaction relationships (Elmasri & Navathe, 2006; Rob & Coronel, 2001). Relation-ship cardinality is used to represent the semantics of "how many", in connection with members of entity classes being associated with other entity classes in relationship instances. For example in a relationship involving employees working on projects (Figure 2), a cardinality constraint could specify that an employee may not work in any projects (i.e., minimum of 0) and could work in up to 5 projects at a maximum. Each project should have at least 10 employees (with no constrained maximum). This information is then used in translating the diagram into the relational model. The minimum and maximum components of the cardinalities are sometimes referred to as existence dependencies and mapping constraints (Silberschatz *et al.*, 1997).

The conventional (snapshot) semantic models do not explicitly capture semantics of time. Implicitly however, the cardinality constraints do have a time frame of evaluation associated with them. For example, when stating that an employee may work in a minimum of 0 and a maximum of 5 projects, the implicit evaluation frame is at a point in time.

In most grammars, attribute cardinality is used to denote either *single-valued* or *multi-valued* attributes, with implications for logical design (Elmasri & Navathe, 1994; McFadden *et al.*, 2002). Additional semantics that capture the cardinality for attributes in terms of specific minimum and maximum values (i.e., natural numbers specifying the minimum and maximum number of values an attribute can have) and entity classes (minimum and maximum number of members in the entity class) has also been suggested (Lenzerini & Santucci, 1983; Liddle *et al.*, 1993).

Figure 2. An example of employees working on projects

1.1.1. A Summary of Relationship Cardinality

Different types of cardinality constraints have been identified for relationships beginning with Lenzerini and Santucci's detailed study of cardinality in the early eighties (Lenzerini & Santucci, 1983). Since then a number of framework papers have been written on cardinality, and we present the basic classifications (using the example in Figure 2) to help explain the concepts presented in previous work (and the differences among them). The subsequent section (1.1.2) contains the discussion of existing literature on cardinality in a snapshot context.

Participation constraints look at a relationship (e.g., *employees* **work on** *projects*), and ask the question, "How many times can an entity (e.g., an employee) participate in the relationship?" The generalized version of this rule type considers not just a single entity class, but also entity combinations, for example "How many times can a given combination of employee and project participate in the Works_On relationship?" The syntax we use to denote relationship participation constraints is: PARTICIPATION(R, C_1,...,C_i), $i \in [1, ..., n]$, where the relationship is denoted by R, each entity class within the relationship by C_i, and n is the degree of the relationship

Projection constraints look at the relationship and restrict how many distinct entity instances can occur across the set of relationship instances. Thus, "How many different employees can exist across all instances of the Works_On relationship?" is an example of the projection constraint. The generalized version of this constraint examines entity combinations from multiple entity classes. The syntax we use to denote this constraint is: PROJECTION(R, C_1,...,C_i), $i \in [1, ..., n]$, where R, C_i, and n have the same semantics as for participation constraints.

Co-occurrence constraints consider an entity already known to be participating in a relationship, and ask how many members of another entity class can co-occur with it. Thus, for example, one could ask, "Given an employee that exists in the Works_On relationship, how many distinct projects can co-occur with it?" The syntax we use to denote this constraint is: CO_OCCURRENCE(R, (C_1,...,C_i), (C_{i+1},...,C_k)), $i \in [1, ..., n\text{-}1]$ and $k \in [2, ..., n]$, and the other terms have the same semantics as before.

Appearance constraints are relevant in relationships where the same entity-class plays more than one role. Common examples are unary relationships, e.g., a **pre-requisite** relationship in Figure 3 where a task can serve as a pre-requisite for another task; i.e., it must be completed before the other task can start. The appearance constraint restricts the number of roles a single entity can play in a particular relationship instance (if a task can be a pre-requisite for another task, but not for itself, then it plays a single role since the same task cannot appear on both sides of the relationship). The syntax used for this constraint is: APPEARANCE (R, C, L_1,..., L_j)), where $j \in [1, ..., m]$, and L_j are roles played by entity class C in the relationship R.

Now that we have a basic vocabulary for describing the kinds of constraints, we consider the common interpretation of cardinality described in many textbooks (Elmasri & Navathe, 1994; McFadden et al., 2002; Rob & Coronel, 2001; Silberschatz et al., 1997). The semantics of these are: "For a given member of one class participating in a relationship, how many members of another

Figure 3. An example of projects and pre-requisites

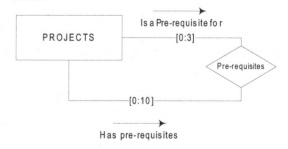

class can it be associated with?" Using the example in Figure 2, "For a given employee, how many projects can he/she be working in (minimum, maximum)?" This is also the interpretation adopted by UML (OMG, 2004) when referring to *associative multiplicity* (the UML equivalent of cardinality). Since this variant of cardinality appears often in literature we give it a moniker for easy reference, *textbook cardinality*. The interesting aspect of this cardinality is that the minimum cardinality corresponds to a specific kind of participation cardinality, while the maximum maps to a co-occurrence constraint. When generalized to ternary or higher-order relationships the semantics is of "look-across" constraints that encompass n-1 entity classes on the constraining side, while counting the association with the remaining entity class (where n is the degree of the relationship). For instance in Figure 4, the "0:M" cardinality attached to suppliers asks: "for a given project-part pair, how many suppliers can they be associated with at a minimum and maximum?" The general understanding is that an arbitrarily chosen project-part pair may never exist together (i.e., never participate in the relationship together), so the minimum would likely be 0, while the maximum is some upper bound "M" (signifying at most how many suppliers co-occur with this project-part pair). Formally, the minimum maps to: PARTICIPATION($R, C_1, ..., C_i$), where $i = n$ (i.e., no sub-combinations where $i < n$ are considered), while the maximum is CO_OCCURRENCE(R, $(C_1, ..., C_{i-1})$, (C_i)), where $i = n$ and we can interpret the constrained class as the ith class without loss

of generality in this case. Note: we could replace "i" with "n" in the formal constraint specification, but leave it in to emphasize the missing aspect of "generality" in these definitions.

Another point to note is that in most cases the meaning of the *max(Cardinality)* for the co-occurrence and participation constraints is the same for binary relationships, this is not the case for ternary or higher order relationships where we may wish to consider a constraint on a subset of the entity classes in the relationship. For example, in Figure 4 we may wish to limit how often a part α, can co-occur with a supplier β irrespective of the projects shipped to. Additionally, with a shipment history involved, co-occurrence and participation cardinalities can differ even for binary relationships (since time is an implicit third dimension in the relationship).

1.1.2. Snapshot Cardinality Discussions in Literature

Ferg (Ferg, 1991) has summarized the notation and semantics of interaction relationship cardinality in three commonly entity-relationship model variants, *Information Engineering* (Finkelstein, 1990; Martin, 1990), *Merise* (Rochfeld, 1986) and *Chen* (Chen, 1976). In comparing them, he comes up with three types of cardinality, i.e., *Lookacross, Participation* and *Visibility* constraints. Ferg's version of *Lookacross* cardinality corresponds to the traditional understanding of cardinality constraints described in the previous paragraph. His *Participation* cardinalities are a

Figure 4. An example of part shipments made by suppliers to projects

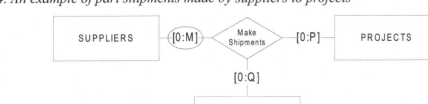

subset of the possible cardinalities, and take the form of how often an entity in a class participates in a relationship, "How often does any employee (e.g., John Doe) from the Employees entity class participate in the relationship?", and does not consider entity-combinations. There is an overlap between the *min*(*Cardinality*) of his *Lookacross* and *Participation* cardinality (i.e., they refer to the same concept). *Visibility* cardinality maps to a subset of what we classify as Projection constraints, specifically the non-generalized form that only considers a single entity class at a time. Ferg does not consider cardinality constraints on constructs other than interaction relationships.

Liddle et al. (Liddle et al., 1993) formally defined (using predicate calculus and relational algebra) and compared (in the context of interaction relationships) the semantics of cardinality in thirteen different conceptual data models. This was the first serious attempt to come up with a broad understanding of cardinality as seen in various grammars. The models he examined included a number of variants of the original ER model, and also the Semantic Binary Data Model (Abrial, 1974), Semantic Association Model (Su, 1983), Semantic Database Model (Hammer & McLeod, 1981), NIAM/ORM, IRIS (N. Derrett, 1985), Object Modeling Technique (OMT) (Rumbaugh *et al.*, 1991), and Object-oriented Systems analysis (OSA) (Embley *et al.*, 1992). OSA was used as the reference model in the paper (having been developed by Liddle's co-authors). Rumbaugh et al.'s OMT is similar to UML in its constraint semantics. One observation that is evident from the comparison is that even variants of the same ER model have ended up with different semantics for cardinality. This stresses the need for a unifying framework. A useful concept introduced by this chapter is using expressions and variables for the *min*(*Cardinality*) and *max*(*Cardinality*) specifications. This allows the user to come up with relative constraints as well, for example the size of the student population can be placed as a restricted on some multiple of the number of faculty (i.e., based

on a maximum desired student-faculty ratio). In terms of cardinality for interaction relationships, Liddle et al. come up with the classification of constraints into three types, *mapping*, *participation* and *co-occurrence*. Mapping constraints are related to the maximum *co-occurrence* cardinality for interaction relationships (or more specifically $CO\_OCCURRENCE(R, (C_1,...,C_{i-1}), (C_i))$, $i = n$. They typically are of the form "1:1", "1:M", "M:M" (or "M:M:M" in the case of ternary relationships), where [1, M] refer to the maximum cardinality of association for a member (or members) of that entity class ("M" simply meaning "Many")[2]. For example, if an employee can work in only one department at most, but a department can have many employees, this gives rise to a "1:M" type mapping. These constraints are important for translation into the relational design. Our framework does not explicitly consider mapping constraints since they can be derived from the maximum cardinality of the relevant co-occurrence constraint. Liddle et al.'s *participation* and *co-occurrence* constraints are a subset of the participation and co-occurrence constraints in our framework. Specifically, the participation constraint takes the form $PARTICIPATION(R, C_1, ..., C_i)$, $i = n$, and the co-occurrence constraint takes the form $CO\_OCCURRENCE\ (R, (C_1,..., C_{i-1}), (C_i))$, $i = n$, where n is the degree of the relationship. Thus, these are identical to the corresponding definition adopted by Ferg. Like the textbook definition, these do not consider varying combinations of entity classes. This is not surprising since ER/UML modeling variants usually represent a single constraint on the schema diagram.

Ferg and Liddle et al. distinguish the notions of *participation*, *co-occurrence* and *projection* cardinalities for interaction relationships. However, these notions of cardinality are not *generalized*. By generalization, we mean constraints that consider different possible combinations of participating entities. For example, in Figure 5, given a ternary relationship R, and participating entity classes A, B, C, the conventional constraints capture the following three forms of co-occurrence: (A, B) with C [min_1:max_1], (A, C) with B [min_2:max_2], and (B, C) with A [min_3:max_3]. A generalized version would consider in addition: A with B, A with C, B with A, B with C, C with A, C with B, A with (B, C), B with (A, C), and C with (A, B). Generalized constraints are particularly significant for relationships of degree greater than two (i.e., ternary or higher-order relationships). The conventional, or non-generalized, definitions of cardinality involve either one entity class or n-1 entity classes considered at a time (where n is the degree of the relationship).

Thalheim (Thalheim, 2000) has generalized these three types of cardinalities to cover participation, co-occurrence and projection constraints with one or more associated entity classes. His definition of the $comp(R, R_1, ..., R_n)$ constraint maps to what we define as participation constraint, while $comp^*(R, R_1, ..., R_n)$ maps to the co-occurrence constraint and $comp{+}(R, R_1, ..., R_n)$ maps to the projection constraint. The superiority over the previous two approaches is the generalized version of the constraint, as also support for a user-specified set of integers (as opposed to simply a range) to which the cardinality maps.

McAllister also provides a generalization of cardinalities (i.e., for combinations of entities rather than a single entity), and suggests a tabular notation for capturing the constraints (McAllister, 1998). His framework is unique in that it uses the semantics of co-occurrence for $max(Cardinality)$ and participation for $min(Cardinality)$. This is possibly because the author does not specify the semantics using first order logic and instead uses intuitive operations to define the semantics. The author mentions projection cardinality, but deliberately chooses not to consider it in the current paper. Thus, while a claim of completeness is made, we do not agree with it because not only are projection constraints not considered, but also, no distinction is made between co-occurrence and participation constraints. Instead of having achieved completeness, we feel the author really means to have achieved generalization of the cardinalities. The article does however present a very detailed analysis of inter-relationships between constraints.

The papers previously discussed do not cover appearance cardinalities for interaction relationships. Another limitation is that they only consider cardinalities for attributes, entity classes and interaction relationships. Thus, generalization/specialization relationships, grouping relationships and composite relationships are not considered.

Rundensteiner et al. have proposed a framework for set-based integrity constraints specifically for semantic groupings (Rundensteiner *et al.*, 1991). These constraints have been included in a taxonomy for modeling set-based business rules at the conceptual design stage proposed by Ram and Khatri (Ram & Khatri, 2005). Their framework encompasses previous classification schemes, adds the concept of appearance constraints for interaction relationships, and addresses

Figure 5. Cardinality in a ternary relationship

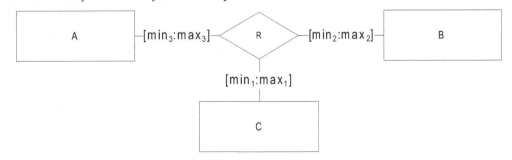

the gaps in extant cardinality frameworks that do not have much by way of a formal classification for cardinality constraints for generalization/specialization relationships, grouping relationships and composite relationships. To that extent, it is the most detailed framework for classifying cardinality in traditional conceptual models.

In terms of notation, a variety of styles have been presented, including Crow's feet (McFadden et al., 2002), specifying only the maximum, and specifying a minimum-maximum combination (Batini *et al.*, 1992). Essentially, most of these notation formats specify a range denoted by the minimum and maximum values for relationship cardinalities. Some notations are more expressive than others and specify numbers for minimum and maximum rather than simply allowing [*optional, mandatory*] for the minimum and [*one, many*] for maximum. A more flexible notion of having a specification system where the cardinality is not restricted to a [⟨min⟩, ⟨max⟩] pair has also been suggested (Zhou & Baumann, 1992), where a set of possible values may be specified for the cardinality, rather than a range. This can be useful for example to specify that a tennis match can have either two or four players, but not three, or that there must be an even number of wheels for a vehicle (or some user-defined valid range for "number of wheels"). Other extensions to the notion of cardinality include the inclusion of variables and expressions in specifying cardinality and the inclusion of averages (in addition to the [⟨min⟩, ⟨max⟩] pair) (Liddle et al., 1993).

A key aspect that past frameworks have not covered is proof for completeness of the classification. There was no formal approach to determine what possible kinds of constraints existed and whether any future extensions were needed. This is one of the reasons the author and a collaborator introduced previous work on completeness in cardinality (Currim & Ram, 2006). In doing so, they introduced a distinction between set and instance-level constraints and established comprehensiveness in the classification of cardinality constraints in semantic data modeling.

1.2 Cardinality in Temporal Models

Temporal ER models cover various aspects related to time while defining the conceptual model and the semantics of cardinality. We assume the notational style earlier in this chapter (a variation of earlier work (Ram & Khatri, 2005)) when mapping the cardinality types from each of the models to ours. We do not describe the models themselves in detail, just the cardinality aspect. Descriptions and comparisons between the semantic models is available in previous research (Gregersen & Jensen, 1999; Khatri *et al.*, 2004).

1.2.1. Cardinality in Temporal Models

Temporal conceptual models focus on adding support for time-varying information to conventional snapshot models. The models are considered in the approximate sequence they appeared in literature.

RAKE: The Relationships, Attributes, Keys and Entities (RAKE) model considers time-varying relationships and attributes (entity classes per se are not considered time varying). It focuses on the valid time dimension and includes facts that are either events or states. As for cardinality, the author only considers maximum cardinality for interaction relationships (textbook convention), which is extended to each "state" (i.e., should hold at each point in time, or in other words a "sequenced" semantics). Specifically: CO_OCCURRENCE(R, $(C_1...C_{i-1})$ (C_i)) sequenced[3]; where R is the relationship, $(C_1...C_{i-1})$ is the entity combination under consideration (e.g., a supplier-project pair) and C_i is the entity class being "counted" (e.g., "How many distinct parts" appear with each supplier-project pair).

TEER and STEER: The Temporal EER (TEER) (Elmasri & Wuu, 1990; Elmasri *et al.*, 1993) and Semantic Temporal EER (STEER) model (Elmasri *et al.*, 1990) adapt the EER model (Elmasri & Navathe, 1994) to handle the time dimension. While the models have some differences with respect to temporal constructs, there is no perceptible difference in terms of cardinality; additionally the first author on both these models is the same and they appear in literature at about the same time. Both models have no explicit discussion of cardinality. However, reference is made to the *max*(*Cardinality*) for interaction relationships. Since TEER is based on EER, and EER considers *min*(*Cardinality*), we assume the detailed model specification includes *min*(*Cardinality*). The authors also discuss the possibility of attributes being multi-valued at a point in time or over an entity's lifetime. We therefore infer that the authors wish to represent the attribute cardinality constraint using a sequenced and lifetime window of evaluation; where *A* represents any attribute possessed by entity class *C*. For relationships the cardinality inferred relates to participation of a combination of entities, in a sequenced and lifetime context.

ERT: The Entity-Relationship-Time (ERT) Model (Theodoulidis *et al.*, 1991) was developed as part of the TEMPORA modeling paradigm (Loucopoulos *et al.*, 1990). It supports state data (referred to as *history*) and event data (associated with a single time unit). The ERT model makes distinctions between three types of relationships interaction, generalization/specialization and aggregation (termed as an "*is_part_of*" relationship). Cardinality is described for all of the relationship types. However, there is no reference to non-sequenced or lifetime cardinality, and the assumption is the authors intend to convey sequenced semantics. For interaction relationships, the cardinality is a sequenced extension of the traditional textbook cardinality. Thus, *min*(*Cardinality*) it corresponds to the *min*(*Cardinality*) of participation, PARTICIPATION(R, C_1, ..., C_i), sequenced. The *max*(*Cardinality*) maps to the *max*(*Cardinality*) of CO_OCCURRENCE(R, (C_1...C_{i-1}), (C_i)), sequenced . In both cases, *n* represents the degree of the relationship, and $i = n$. For generalization/specialization (GS) relationships with a given superclass *C* and subclasses

C_j, we see GS-PARTICIPATION(C, C_1, ..., C_j), sequenced. Finally, for aggregation relationships (AG), we see two types of cardinality, one from the base class to the aggregate of the form AG-PARTICIPATION(Ag, C_1, ..., C_k), sequenced, and the next from the aggregate to the base class of the form AG-PROJECTION (Ag, C_1, ..., C_k), sequenced. *Ag* is the aggregate entity class (or complex object), and C_k is the participating base class. In both cases, *k* represents the number of participating base entity classes forming the aggregate.

TER: The Temporal Entity-Relationship (TER) extends the entity-relationship model by introducing the concepts of *snapshot* and *lifetime* cardinality for relationships (Tauzovich, 1991). TER is the first model to emphasize the distinction between snapshot and lifetime cardinality (though traces of this division have been referred to previously) and the need to represent both. On the negative side, they restrict the applicability of cardinality to binary relationships and do not recommend allowing a "many-to-many" type relationship (based on maximum cardinality). This limits the generalizability of cardinality constraints. The semantics of the cardinality types proposed by them map to: PARTICIPATION(R, C_1, ..., C_i) for *min*(*Cardinality*) and the *max*(*Cardinality*) maps to CO_OCCURRENCE(R, (C_1...C_{i-1}), (C_i)), both of which are applicable in sequenced and lifetime context.

TempEER: The Temporal Enhanced Entity-Relationship Model (TempEER)[4] discusses temporal extensions to the entity-relationship model and how it can be mapped to the relational model (Lai *et al.*, 1994). The discussion of cardinality is almost identical to TEER/STEER and the authors additionally discuss attributes being multi-valued at a point in time or over an entity's lifetime, which we could interpret as: ATTRIBUTE(C, A) over the sequenced and lifetime windows of evaluation. Once again, the authors' intent for relationship cardinality is inferred from a schema used and we consider it as translating to the same semantics as that for TEER/STEER.

TEERM: The Temporal Event-Entity Relationship Model (TEERM) (Dey *et al.*, 1995) extends the entity-relationship model by introducing events as an additional construct. They distinguish between static, quasi-static and temporal relationships and attributes. In TEERM, cardinality is defined as the minimum (or maximum) number of relationship instances in which any instance of an entity class can participate. This maps to our definition of participation cardinality, specifically PARTICIPATION $(R, C_1, ..., C_i)$ in a sequenced context. There is no indication to whether the authors wished to consider a lifetime cardinality interpretation. Thus, on this front it is less expressive than models we have recently discussed.

TERC+: As one of the more recent research efforts, the TERC+ conceptual model (Zimányi *et al.*, 1997) incorporates a number of temporal concepts. It distinguishes between valid time, transaction time as well as user-specified time dimensions (though only implements valid time). Temporal facts are classified as either events or states, and all constructs (entity classes, relationships and attributes) have associated time varying semantics. The TERC+ model expresses cardinality for attributes, interaction relationships, generalization/specialization relationships and aggregation relationships. For cardinality a distinction is made between snapshot and lifetime cardinality. While they only discuss the *max(Cardinality)* relative to lifetime cardinalities, the concept can be generalized to include the *min(Cardinality)*. When only the two extremes of snapshot and lifetime cardinalities are considered, the corresponding *min(Cardinality)* must be the same (since at the beginning—the lifetime of an item is a single unit of time). Summarizing the various kinds of cardinalities that are expressible in TERC+, we have both at the sequenced and lifetime level:

- Cardinality constraints for Attributes,
- Interaction Relationships: Participation (rather than co-occurrence),

- Generalization / Specialization Relationships: Participation (i.e., how many subclasses a superclass entity instance can be a member of),
- Aggregation Relationships: Both the participation and projection constraints.

The cardinality types in TERC+ for Generalization/Specialization and Aggregation are similar to that of ERT, but have and implicit extension of lifetime cardinalities. We say "implicit", because the authors only discuss snapshot cardinality for these. However, for the other abstractions, the authors discuss lifetime cardinality, and so we assume they also intend to consider lifetime cardinalities for Generalization/Specialization and Aggregation as well.

Chrono: The Chrono conceptual model (Bergamaschi & Sartori, 1998) is designed as a temporal extension to the IDEF1X (Publication, 1993) model (itself an extension of the entity-relationship model). It focuses on representing the valid time dimension of facts and supports both states and events. Entity classes and relationships are considered temporal (time varying attributes lead to the corresponding class being designated as temporal). The model emphasizes the need for correctly capturing integrity constraints that can then be translated into triggers. However, in terms of cardinality, only the *max(Cardinality)* for interaction relationships is mentioned. Since Chrono is based on IDEF1X, it is restricted to binary relationships. Therefore the cardinality corresponds to: CO_OCCURRENCE(R, C_i, C_j), where $i, j \in [1, 2] \wedge i \neq j$ (we assume here that each role will be conceptually have a distinct number, in the case of unary relationships). Based on the discussion in the paper, we conclude that only a sequenced semantics is intended.

TimeER: The temporal semantic model TimeER (Gregersen & Jensen, 1998) incorporates the sequenced version of the snapshot participation constraint. Interestingly, they do not follow the convention of the snapshot conceptual database models in adopting a combination of participation and co-occurrence constraints as the cardinality. Their definition of both the minimum and maximum cardinality maps to PARTICIPATION(R, C_1, ..., C_i) sequenced, where $i = n$. As we might have learned to expect, based on the conceptual models examined so far, the authors do not get into much detail about cardinality, and do not discuss generalizability of cardinality for higher-order relationships (i.e., ternary or above). They do however include "lifespan constraints", a special type of a temporal cardinality constraint where the cardinalities are defined over the lifetime of the relationship in question, and derive a useful relationship in terms of: $min(Cardinality)$ lifespan $\geq min(Cardinality)$ snapshot; $max(Cardinality)$ lifespan $\geq max(Cardinality)$ snapshot.

1.3 Other Temporal Integrity Constraints

Temporal integrity constraints have long been studied in relational database research (Gertz & Lipeck, 1995; Koubarakis, 1995). In addition to temporal keys and referential integrity (Snodgrass, 1999), a variety of constraints and implementation considerations (e.g., efficient constraint checking using temporal logic (Chomicki, 1995), constraint conflict resolution using temporal logic (Chomicki *et al.*, 2003), constraints and access control permissions (Bertino *et al.*, 1998)). Most of these efforts have been focused at the logical level, and other than the cardinality constraints present in temporal entity-relationship models (see Section 1.2.1), not much attention has been paid to a framework for classifying temporal cardinality constraints.

1.4 Constraint Definition Languages

In order to overcome the inherent lack of constraint specification ability in most semantic models, and allow for richer specification of constraints, constraint definition languages and constraint enforcement systems have been developed (Cal-

vanese *et al.*, 1998; Morgenstern, 1984; Shepard & Kerschberg, 1984; V. C. Storey *et al.*, 1996; Urban & Lim, 1993). While these papers are relevant from the standpoint of representing modeled constraints at the logical design phase, they are not suitable for the higher-level of abstraction in conceptual modeling. Most are also not designed to allow analysts to handle temporal semantics.

The other limitation of such languages (taking OCL (OMG, 2006) as an example) is that they try and allow for a high-level pseudo-code definition of a constraint. Every OCL specification of a co-occurrence constraint would include the for-loop counting associated entities rather than simply saying it was a "co-occurrence constraint". The consequence of this lack of abstraction is that each time the same constraint type is seen, the pseudo-code must be rewritten, and the productivity is lost. Complex constraints expressed in such languages are hard to understand by users and may be inadequate for communicating business rules between users and database designers. However, if the user is looking for a language to represent constraints and generate inferences based upon axiomatic representations of constraints (rather than a means to classify or understand constraint semantics), then constraint definition languages are the appropriate choice.

1.5 Business Rules Frameworks

We briefly discuss two well-known business rules frameworks that deal with conceptual modeling, the Ross Method (and classification), and BRO-COM. While they do an excellent job considering the various types of constraints applicable for businesses, their focus is not on cardinality, and instead is on providing a general purpose constraint framework. This leads to a similar limitation for both, in that they do not distinguish the different kinds of cardinality. Further, while time is considered in terms of how it affects sequencing of operations, neither model was designed for temporal data.

The Ross Method (Ross, 1997) offers a classification scheme that spans seven rule types including instance verifiers (counts instances), type verifiers (logical AND / OR connectivity between rules to derive more complex rules), and mathematical evaluators (functions to perform calculations). In terms of cardinality—the category that is applicable is instance verifiers. Ross offers two operators: **mandatory** and **limited** (upper and lower bounds) that can be used with entities or attributes. While this provides a simple and elegant approach, there is no semantic distinction between participation, co-occurrence or projection constraints. The BROCOM or Business Rule Oriented Conceptual Modeling (Herbst, 1997) approach aims to conceptually (through a simplified SQL-like syntax that is closer to natural language) represent database triggers. It adopts a general-purpose classification scheme that breaks down rules into four components: *triggering event* (e.g., order inserted into table), *check condition* (is the order worth more than $50,000?), action on meeting the condition (expedite the order processing and set its priority to `high`), and action on the failure of condition (set the priority to `normal`). A rule-repository facilitates storage and implementation (typically via triggers or procedures) of the rules. Since BROCOM is a general-purpose framework, it has the limitation of not providing a discussion of semantics for the different kinds of cardinality.

1.6 Conclusion

A summary of cardinality support in the different models is provided in Tables 1 and 2. These

Table 1. Summary of snapshot cardinality frameworks

Framework	Constraint Aspects Included in Framework						
	Constructs	Predicate Support?	PT	CO	PJ	AP	Set-Level?
Lerenzini	E A R	No	No	Yes	Non-generalized	No	No
Ferg	R	No	Non-generalized	Non-generalized	Non-generalized	No	No
Liddle	E A R	No	Non-generalized	Non-generalized	No	No	No
Thalheim	R	No	Yes	Yes	Yes	No	No
McAllister	R	No	Yes	Yes	Yes	No	No
Rundensteiner	H	No	Yes	Yes	Yes	No	No
Ram & Khatri	E A R S H	Yes	Yes	Yes	Yes	Yes	No
(work by Authors)	E A R S H	Yes	Yes	Yes	Yes	Yes	Yes

Table Legend

Constructs for which Cardinality is Defined	E: Entity Classes
	A: Attributes
	R: Interaction Relationships
	S: Subclass and superclass relationships
	H: Higher order relationships (groupings, composites)
Kinds of Interaction Cardinality supported	PT: Participation cardinality
	CO: Co-occurrence cardinality
	PJ: Projection cardinality
	AP: Appearance cardinality

highlight the differences in previous work when dealing with constraints. We demonstrate what kinds of constructs cardinality is supported on (entity classes, attributes, interaction relationships, etc.). We also present whether the constraints allow for predicates in snapshot models (for selectively restricting counts of say "red" parts instead of all parts), and whether the distinction between instance and set-level cardinality is supported. Since relationship cardinality is the most common type of constraint, we provide additional details on the kinds of relationship cardinality covered, and if the generalized form of the constraint can be modeled.

Efforts to standardize the various cardinality interpretations using some form of a classification framework have been undertaken both in snapshot (Liddle et al., 1993; Ram & Khatri, 2005) as well as temporal contexts (Currim, 2004). The standardization frameworks serve two purposes. To begin with, they provide a consistent interpretation to understand constraints. Additionally, they

allow analysts to have a structured approach to considering the different kinds of rules that may exist in an application being developed.

In the snapshot domain, the most detailed treatment of constraints appear in work by Ram and Khatri (Ram & Khatri, 2005). Temporal extensions for attribute cardinality were introduced in TEER (Elmasri & Wuu, 1990; Elmasri et al., 1993). Extending these constraint schemes to include specific consideration of evaluation windows and applicability bounds in a temporal (and spatial) context has been proposed (Currim & Ram, 2008), but we find there is much room for future work along three different directions.

First, there is room for taxonomy augmentation to new branches of related research such as extending frameworks to include rules that lie at the intersection of data and process modeling. Managing the rules in a federated environment particularly when schema evolution occurs would also be a challenging area of work that would also have to resolve the issue of since constraint con-

Table 2. Support for cardinality in common temporal data models

Model	Constraint Types Included in Framework					
	Constructs	PT	CO	PJ	Evaluation Window	Applicability Bounds
RAKE	R	No	Non-generalized	No	Seq	None
TEER and STEER	A R	Non-generalized	No	No	Seq, Lifetime	None
ERT	R S H (partial)	Textbook	Textbook	No	Seq	None
TER	R	Textbook	Textbook	No	Seq, Lifetime	None
TempEER	A R	Non-generalized	No	No	Seq, Lifetime	None
TERM	None	N/A	N/A	N/A	N/A	N/A
TEERM	R	Non-generalized	No	No	Seq	None
TERC+	A R S H (partial)	Non-generalized	No	No	Seq, Lifetime	None
Chrono	R	No	Non-generalized	No	Seq	None
TimeEER	R	Non-generalized	No	No	Seq, Lifetime	None

flicts and address how differences in granularity among schemas can be handled while merging constraints.

Second, application and evaluation, both in terms of building proof-of-concept prototypes or extending CASE tools to handle different kinds of constraints, as well as evaluation of the rule frameworks in a field study or case study to measure expressiveness and ease of use.

Finally, a tough but rewarding area of work would be in theory building. Here researchers could seek to adopt and develop theories that explain, for example, under what circumstances analysts using the additional complexity of the rules perform better (perhaps due to the taxonomy leading to automated translation algorithms for constraint code) and what the challenges to adoption of additional constraint complexity are. Currently, established ways of data modeling among practitioners focus on limited number of constraints. We recommend the inclusion of a richer variety of constraints at the conceptual design stage since rule visibility improves the quality of the conceptual schema.

REFERENCES

Abrial, J. R. (1974). Data semantics. In J. W. Klimbie & K. L. Koffemen (Eds.), *Data base management* (pp. 1–59). Amsterdam: North-Holland.

Batini, C., Ceri, S., & Navathe, S. B. (1992). *Conceptual database design: An entity-relationship approach*: The Benjamin/Cummings Publishing Company.

Bergamaschi, S., & Sartori, C. (1998). *Chrono: A conceptual design framework for temporal entities*. Paper presented at the 17th International Conference on Conceptual Modeling, Singapore.

Bertino, E., Bettini, C., Ferrari, E., & Samarati, P. (1998). An access control model supporting periodicity constraints and temporal reasoning.
ACM Transactions on Database Systems, 23(3), 231-285.

Bettini, C., Jajodia, S., & Wang, S. X. (2000). *Time granularities in databases, data mining, and temporal reasoning*: Springer-Verlag.

Calvanese, D., Lenzerini, M., & Nardi, D. (1998). Description logics for conceptual data modeling. In J. Chomicki & G. Saake (Eds.), *Logics for databases and information systems* (pp. 229-263). Kluwer.

Chen, P. P. (1976). The entity-relationship model - toward a unified view of data. *ACM Transactions on Database Systems, 1*(1), 9-36.

Chomicki, J. (1995). Efficient checking of temporal integrity constraints using bounded history encoding. *ACM Transactions on Database Systems, 20*(2), 149-186.

Chomicki, J., Lobo, J., & Naqvi, S. A. (2003). Conflict resolution using logic programming. *IEEE Transactions on Knowledge and Data Engineering, 15*(1), 244-249.

Currim, F. (2004). *Spatio-temporal set-based constraints in conceptual modeling: A theoretical framework and evaluation*. Unpublished Doctoral Dissertation, University of Arizona, Tucson.

Currim, F., & Ram, S. (2006). *Understanding the concept of "completeness" in frameworks for modeling cardinality constraints*. Paper presented at the 16th Workshop on Information Technologies and Systems, Milwaukee, WI.

Currim, F., & Ram, S. (2008). Conceptually modeling windows and bounds for space and time in database constraints. *Communications of the ACM, 51*(11), 125-129.

Dey, D., Barron, T. M., & Storey, V. C. (1995). A conceptual model for the logical design of temporal databases. *Decision Support Systems, 15*(4), 305-321.

Elmasri, R., Ihab El-Assal, & Kouramajian, V. (1990, October 8-10). *Semantics of temporal data in an extended er model*. Paper presented at the Ninth International Conference on Entity-Relationship Approach, Lausanne, Switzerland.

Elmasri, R., & Navathe, S. B. (1994). *Fundamentals of database systems* (Second ed.): Benjamin Cummings Publishing Co., Redwood City, CA.

Elmasri, R., & Navathe, S. B. (2006). *Fundamentals of database systems* (Fifth ed.): Addison Wesley.

Elmasri, R., & Wuu, G. T. J. (1990). *A temporal model and query language for er databases*. Paper presented at the Sixth International Conference on Data Engineering, Los Angeles, California, USA.

Elmasri, R., Wuu, G. T. J., & Kouramajian, V. (1993). A temporal model and query language for eer databases. In A. U. Tansel, J. Clifford, S. K. Gadia, A. Segev & R. T. Snodgrass (Eds.), *Temporal databases: Theory, design, and implementation* (pp. 212-229): Benjamin/Cummings.

Embley, D. W., Kurtz, B. D., & Woodfield, S. N. (1992). *Object-oriented systems analysis: A model-driven approach*. Englewood Cliffs, N J: Prentice-Hall.

Ferg, S. (1991, 23-25 October, 1991). *Cardinality constraints in entity-relationship modeling*. Paper presented at the 10th International Conference on Entity-Relationship Approach, San Mateo, alifornia, USA.

Finkelstein, C. (1990). *An introduction to information engineering: From strategic planning to information systems*.

Gertz, M., & Lipeck, U. W. (1995, September 17-18). *Temporal" integrity constraints in temporal databases*. Paper presented at the International Workshop on Temporal Databases, Zürich, Switzerland.

Gregersen, H., & Jensen, C. S. (1998). *Conceptual modeling of time-varying information* (No. TR-35): TimeCenter.

Gregersen, H., & Jensen, C. S. (1999). Temporal entity-relationship models - a survey. *IEEE Transactions on Knowledge and Data Engineering, 11*(3), 464-497.

Hammer, M., & McLeod, D. (1981). Database description with sdm: A semantic database model. *ACM Transactions on Database Systems, 6*(3), 351-386.

Herbst, H. (1997). *Business rule-oriented conceptual modeling*. Heidelberg: Physica-Verlag.

Hull, R., & King, R. (1987). Semantic database modeling survey, applications, and research issues. *ACM Computing Surveys*, 210-260.

Jensen, C. S., Dyreson, C. E., Böhlen, M. H., Clifford, J., Elmasri, R., Gadia, S. K., et al. (1998). The consensus glossary of temporal database concepts - february 1998 version. In C. S. Jensen, J. Clifford, R. Elmasri, S. K. Gadia, P. J. Hayes & S. Jajodia (Eds.), *Temporal databases: Research and practice* (pp. 367-405): Springer.

Khatri, V., Ram, S., & Snodgrass, R. T. (2004). Augmenting a conceptual model with geo-spatio-temporal annotations. *IEEE Transactions on Knowledge and Data Engineering, forthcoming*.

Koubarakis, M. (1995, September 17-18). *Databases and temporal constraints: Semantics and complexity*. Paper presented at the International Workshop on Temporal Databases, Zürich, Switzerland.

Lai, V. S., Kuilboer, J.-P., & Guynes, J. L. (1994). Temporal databases: Model design and commercialization prospects. *DATA BASE, 25*(3), 6-18.

Lenzerini, M., & Santucci, G. (1983). *Cardinality constraints in the entity-relationship model*. Paper presented at the 3rd International Conference on Entity-Relationship Approach, Anaheim, California.

Liddle, S. W., Embley, D. W., & Woodfield, S. N. (1993). Cardinality constraints in semantic data models. *Data and Knowledge Engineering, 11*(3), 235-270.

Loucopoulos, P., McBrien, P., Persson, U., Schmaker, F., & Vasey, P. (1990, November). *Tempora-integrating database technology rule based systems and temporal reasoning for effective software.* Paper presented at the ESPRIT Conference, Brussels, Belgium.

Martin, J. (1990). *Information engineering, Book II: Planning and analysis*: Pearson Education.

McAllister, A. (1998). Complete rules for n-ary relationship cardinality constraints. *Data and Knowledge Engineering, 27*(3), 255-288.

McFadden, F. R., Hoffer, J. A., & Prescott, M. B. (2002). *Modern database management* (Sixth ed.): Prentice Hall.

Morgenstern, M. (1984). *Constraint equations: Declarative expression of constraints with automatic enforcement.* Paper presented at the 10th Conference on Very Large Databases, Singapore.

N. Derrett, W. K. a. P. L. (1985). Some aspects of operations in an object-oriented database. *IEEE Database Engineering Bulletin, 8*(4), 66-74.

OMG. (2004). Unified modeling language (uml), v2.0.

OMG. (2006). Object constraint language specification, v 2.0.

Parent, C., Spaccapietra, S., & Zimanyi, E. (1999). *Spatio-temporal conceptual models: Data structures + space + time.* Paper presented at the 7th ACM Symposium on Advances in Geographic Information Systems, Kansas City, USA, 1999.

Peckham, J., & Maryanski, F. (1988). Semantic data models. *ACM Computing Surveys, 20*(3), 153-189.

Publication, F. I. P. S. (1993). *Integration definition for function modeling (idef1x)* (No. Technical Report 184): National Institute of Standards and Technology, Gaithersburg, MD 20899.

Ram, S., & Khatri, V. (2005). A comprehensive framework for modeling set-based business rules during conceptual database design. *Information Systems, 30*(2), 89-118.

Rob, P., & Coronel, C. (2001). *Database systems: Design, implementation, and management* (Fifth ed.): Course Technology.

Rochfeld, A. (1986, November 17-19). *Merise, an information system design and development methodology, tutorial.* Paper presented at the Fifth International Conference on Entity-Relationship Approach, Dijon, France.

Ross, R. G. (1997). *The business rule book: Classifying, defining and modeling rules, version 4.0* (Second ed.): Business Rule Solutions, Incorporated.

Rumbaugh, J., Blaha, M., Premerlani, W., Eddy, F., & Lorensen, W. (1991). *Object-oriented modeling and design.* Englewood Cliffs, NJ: Prentice-Hall.

Rundensteiner, E. A., Bic, L., Gilbert, J. P., & Yin, M.-L. (1991, April 8-12). *A semantic integrity framework: Set restrictions for semantic groupings.* Paper presented at the Seventh International Conference on Data Engineering, Kobe, Japan.

Shepard, A., & Kerschberg, L. (1984). *Prism: A knowledge-based system for semantic integrity specification and enforcement in database systems.* Paper presented at the ACM SIGMOD Conference, Boston.

Silberschatz, A., Korth, H., & Sudarshan, S. (1997). *Database system concepts* (Third Edition ed.): McGraw Hill.

Snodgrass, R. T. (1999). Developing time-oriented database applications in sql. *Morgan Kaufmann Series in Data Management Systems.*

Storey, V. C. (1993). Understanding semantic relationships. *The VLDB Journal — The International Journal on Very Large Data Bases, 2*(4), 455-488.

Storey, V. C., Yang, H., & Goldstein, R. C. (1996). Semantic integrity constraints in knowledge-based database design systems. *Data and Knowledge Engineering, 20*(1), 1-37.

Su, S. Y. W. (1983). A semantic association model for corporate and scientific statistical databases. *Journal of Information Sciences, 29*, 151-199.

Tauzovich, B. (1991). *Towards temporal extensions to the entity-relationship model.* Paper presented at the 10th International Conference on Entity-Relationship Approach, San Mateo, California.

Thalheim, B. (1996, December 1-10, 1996). *An overview on semantical constraints for database models.* Paper presented at the 6th International Conference on Intellectual Systems and Computer Science, Moscow, Russia.

Thalheim, B. (2000). *Entity-relationship modeling: Foundations of database technology*: Springer-Verlag.

Theodoulidis, C. I., Loucopoulos, P., & Wangler, B. (1991). A conceptual modelling formalism for temporal database applications. *Information Systems, 16*(4), 401-416.

Tryfona, N., & Jensen, C. S. (1999). Conceptual data modeling for spatiotemporal applications. *Geoinformatica, 3*(3), 245-268.

Urban, S. D., & Lim, B. B. (1993). An intelligent framework for active support of database semantics. *International Journal of Expert Systems, 6*(1), 1-37.

Wand, Y., & Weber, R. (2002). Research commentary: Information systems and conceptual modeling - a research agenda. *Information Systems Research, 13*(4), 363-376.

Zhou, J., & Baumann, P. (1992, October 7-9, 1992). *Evaluation of complex cardinality constraints.* Paper presented at the 11th International Conference on the Entity-Relationship Approach, Karlsruhe, Germany.

Zimányi, E., Parent, C., Spaccapietra, S., & Pirotte, A. (1997, November 26-28). *Terc+: A temporal conceptual model.* Paper presented at the International Symposium on Digital Media Information Base (DMIB '97), Nara, Japan.

ENDNOTES

[1]   In this particular syntax, there is no symbolic representation of whether an attribute is optional or mandatory.

[2]   Some authors use the symbol * in place of M, for example in (Veda C. Storey, 1993).

[3]   We assume the reader is familiar with basic temporal database terminology, and refer to previous work in the temporal domain (Bettini *et al.*, 2000; Jensen *et al.*, 1998) for more information.

[4]   Note: While the authors refer to their model with the acronym TEER, we use TempEER to avoid confusion with (Elmasri & Wuu, 1990).

Chapter IV
On the Load Balancing of Business Intelligence Reporting Systems

Leszek Kotulski
AGH University of Science and Technology, Poland

Dariusz Dymek
Cracow University of Economics, Poland

ABSTRACT

The UML model consists of several types of diagrams representing different aspects of the modeled system. To assure the universality and flexibility, the UML involves only a few general rules about dependence among different types of diagrams. In consequence people can have the different methodologies based on the UML, but in the same time we haven't the formal tool for assure the vertical cohesion of created model. To test and reach the vertical cohesion of the model some auxiliary information about the relations among the elements belonging to different types of diagrams should be remembered. In this chapter the authors present the method of formal representation of such information in a form of the relation, called Accomplish Relation. This method is based only on the UML properties and is independent from any methodology. Additionally, they show how to use the UML timing diagrams for representing the users' requirements in association with use cases. To illustrate the usefulness of this approach we present how it can be used for load balancing of distributed system in case of a Reporting Systems based on Data Warehouse concept.

INTRODUCTION

In modern concepts of using IT in business organizations, one of the crucial elements are systems supporting business decision processes generally called Business Intelligence systems. This class of information systems includes data warehouses, OLAP systems, report generating systems etc.

Their complex structures reflect the multifaceted of modern business decision processes and the large scale of necessary information. The common feature of all mentioned kinds of systems is a large amount of data and a high computational complexity. Additionally, there are time limits[1] set on response time of these systems which result in high hardware requirements. On the second hand, some parts of these systems are not used all the time with full efficiency. Generally, BI applications generate several periodical cycles of a hardware nodes workload. The basic time cycles are relevant to periodical reports and adequate processes: we can distinguish daily, weekly, decadal and monthly cycles and a few longer cycles: quarterly, half-yearly and annual ones. Beside periodical processes we have also processes linked with everyday analytical tasks, which generate system workload, and must be taken into account.

Analyzing of the workload schedule for the whole system, based on aggregated time cycles, we must take into consideration the structure of the system. Usually, it consists of many single components: subsystems, software applications and hardware nodes. Considering the workload schedule for each hardware nodes we can indicate the situations in which one node is overloaded whereas other nodes are on low level of their efficiency. To assure optimal resource utilization, throughput, or response time we can increase the computing system power (by redundantion of some hardware components) or reschedule some processes. Such techniques, called load balancing, strongly depend on the software structure. So it seems to be useful to start considering the timing characteristic of the developed software from the software modeling phase. This situation forces formalization of this phase.

Unified Modeling Language (UML), being an uncontested modeling standard, in version 2.x offers 13 types of diagrams (Object Management Group, 2007a). In the load balancing context we are especially interested in *timing* diagrams

introduced for describing timing properties of the modeled system. However, we suggest using them to describe timing characteristic of user requirements (represented at *use case* diagrams) and to trace their influence to other stages of the software modeling processes, represented by *class*, *object* and *deployment* diagrams.

Let's note that UML as a tool became a base for some software development methodologies like RUP (IBM Rational Unified Process) or ICONIC (Rozenberg & Scott, 2001). It bases on such a fundamental concepts like an object-oriented paradigm or a distributed and parallel programming but is independent from those methodologies. This fact gives UML some advantages; especially it can be treated as a universal tool for many purposes. On the other hand, UML needs to be supplemented when we consider the vertical consistency of the model (Kuźniarz, Reggio, Sourrooille, & Huzar, 2002; Dymek & Kotulski, 2007a; Kotulski & Dymek, 2008), i.e. when we are interested in the formal description how one type of the UML diagrams influences on the model described by the other types of the UML diagrams. In the section below, the relational model, based on the graph theory, is proposed for describing the vertical consistency of the model.

Timing diagrams are one of many new artifacts introduced by second version of UML. They are the tool for describing the dynamical aspect of the modeled system and expressing the time characteristic of system components. The brief description of *timing* diagrams concept is presented in the following section. We also present the way of using the timing diagrams in cooperation with previously presented the relational model for obtaining the time characteristic for elements from different kinds of UML diagrams.

Successive section presents an example of using previously described models and methods, in case of the Reporting Data Mart based on the Data Warehouse concept. We describe how to use timing diagrams to obtain the time characteristic of system components, and how these characteristics can be used for checking the system properties (e.g. workload). We also present how the achieved results can be used to workout some decision about the system structure.

The last section is a summary of presented solution. It describes the main features of this approach and points out the possibility of using it in different situations.

Described solution is the summary of a few years investigation presented in a few publications (Dymek & Kotulski, 2006; Dymek & Kotulski, 2007a; Dymek & Kotulski, 2007b; Dymek & Kotulski, 2008; Kotulski & Dymek, 2007; Kotulski & Dymek, 2008). We still continue our research; especially concentrate on practical aspect of its application.

ASSURANCE OF VERTICAL CONSISTENCY

UML itself defines the relation between elements from the given kind of diagrams or among diagrams from the same class. Generally, UML does not formally define the relation between various kinds of diagrams. Version 2.0 introduces <<trace>> and <<refine>> stereotypes for specifying model elements that represent the same concept in different models (Object Management Group, 2007a). but does not extend their use at the metamodel level. The limitation itself to the specification connections inside only a given type of UML diagrams allows using different kinds of reasoning methods for development methodologies and is one of advantages of the UML. But lack of the formal linkage among elements from different kinds of diagrams can cause loosing some information during the software system designing, e.g. it's hard to find the connections between users' requirements and servicing them software components.

The problem of considering both the horizontal and the vertical consistency of UML model has been already pointed out a few years ago (Kuźniarz, Reggio, Sourrooille, & Huzar, 2002), but in practice those investigations has been concentrated on the horizontal consistency.

The consideration of the vertical consistency of the model i.e. relations among the information maintained by different kinds of diagrams needs remembering, inside this model, the "associations" introduced by the system modeler during the system development phase. Let's note that this information is not only strongly dependent on the methodology of the system creation, but dynamically changes in time. As there are many examples of the usefulness of the graph transformations mechanism for specification and controlling dynamically changing systems (Rozenberg, 1997; Ehrig, Engels, Kreowski & Rozenberg, 1999a; Ehrig, Kreowski, Montanari, & Rozenberg, 1999b), so it seams to be natural use this formalism for our purpose.

Fortunately, the UML diagrams can be expressed as graphs using XMI standard (Object Management Group, 2006). During the process of software system designing we can translate each UML diagrams into a form of a graph and create it representation in the Graph Repository, which will gather the information from each phase of the designing process. It gives us a possibility to take advantages of graph grammar to trace the software system designing process, treating this process as a sequence of graphs transformations. We are able to participate in the designing process and simultaneously modify the Graph Repository. In (Kotulski, 2006) it was proved that, with the help of the aedNLC graph transformation system (Kotulski, 2000), we can control the generation of such a Graph Repository with $O(n^2)$ computational complexity. This solution enables us to establish the formal linkage between elements from different kinds of UML diagrams as the Vertical Relation. To illustrate the capability of the Vertical Relation we present below one of its exemplifications called the Accomplish Relation (AR) (Dymek & Kotulski, 2006; Dymek & Kotulski, 2007b).

In the Graph Repository we can distinguish various layers (relevant to UML diagrams): the use case layer (UL), the sequence layer (SL), the class layer (CL) (divided onto the class body layer (CBL) and the class method layer (CML)), the object layer[2] (OL) (divided onto the object body layer (OBL) and the object method layer (OML)), the timing layer (TML) and the hardware layer (HL).

In the presented solution (Dymek & Kotulski, 2006) we can:

- Represent deployment of the final objects to the proper computing nodes,
- Show nested software structure (introduced by packages),
- Trace, inside which class (in the case of class inheritance) the given objects method has been defined.

Finally in the same way we can extend this representation by:

- The association of the object's method with the proper edges in the interaction diagrams,
- The association a graph representing the interaction diagram with the given use case activity.

For any G, representing a subgraph of the graph repository R, the notation G|XL means the graph, with the nodes belonging to the XL layer (where XL stands for any UML type of diagram) and the edges induced from the connections inside R. For example, $R|UL \cup OL$ means the graph with all the nodes ($n\_set\ (R|UL \cup OL)$) representing user requirements and all the objects, servicing these requirements, with the edges ($e\_set(R|UL \cup OL)$) representing both horizontal and vertical relation inside the graph repository. Now we can present a definition of Accomplish Relation function:

$AR:(Node,Layer) \rightarrow AR(Node,Layer) \subset n\_set(R|Layer)$ is the function where:

$Node \in n\_set\ (R|XL) : XL \in \{UL, CBL, CML, OBL, OML, HL\}$

$Layer \in \{UL, CBL, CML, OBL, SL, OML, TML, HL\}, Layer \neq XL$

In the chapter we will be interested in following exemplification of the AR function: AR(Node,Layer) is a subset of nodes from $n\_set(R|Layer)$, which stay in the relationship of the following type: "support service" or "is used to" with given Node, based on the role performed in the system structure. For better explanation, let's see some examples:

- For any user requirement $r \in n\_set\ (R|UL)$, AR(r,OBL) returns a set of objects which supports this requirement service,
- For any object $o \in n\_set\ (R|OBL)$, AR(o,UL) returns a set of requirements that are supported by any of its methods,
- For any object $o \in n\_set\ (R|OBL)$, AR(o,HL) returns a set consists of the computing (hardware) node, in which given object is allocated,
- For any object $x \in n\_set (R|UL \cup CBL \cup OBL \cup SL \cup HL)$, AR(x,TML) returns a set consists of the timing diagram describing the timing properties of its behavior,
- For any class $c \in n\_set\ (R|CBL)$, AR(c,UL) returns a set of requirements that are supported by any of its method

The above relations are embedded into the graph repository structure, so there are no complexity problems with their evaluation. Moreover, the graph repository is able to trace any software or requirement modification, so these relations are dynamically changing during the system life time. In (Kotulski & Dymek, 2008) we suggest to specify timing behavior of the actors appearing in the *use case* diagrams by using the *timing* diagrams associated (by some vertical relation) with them, and to trace how this specification influences on the software creation process (especially preparation of some software component for distribution). We also consider this problem later, in successive section.

TIMING DIAGRAMS AND THEIR APPLICATION

Timing diagrams are one of the new artifacts added to UML 2.x. They enrich the UML by adding the possibility of expressing and analyzing some dynamical properties of modeled system based on its (and its elements) behavior in time. Below, we present some basic concept of *timing* diagram and show how, in cooperation with Accomplish Relation, we can use them to calculate the time characteristic of system or its components.

Timing Diagram Concept

In the OMG documentation (Object Management Group, 2007b) the *timing* diagram is defined as an "interaction diagram that shows the change in state or condition of a lifetime (representing a Classifier Instance or Classifier Role) over linear time. A classifier itself is characterized as "a collection of instances that have something in common. A classifier can have features, that characterize its instances. Classifiers include interfaces, classes, data types, and components" (Object Management Group, 2007b). While timing diagrams has been primary used by electrical engineers for designing electronic state machines, the most common usage is to show how software object interact with each other. They have a simple representation as a diagram with the time along the horizontal axis and object states or attribute value along the vertical axis. Its usefulness for modeling of the real time systems is presented by Valiente, Genova and Cerretero (2005).

It should be outlined, that the mentioned in OMG UML Superstructure examples of Classifiers are not only those mentioned above. Below we will consider *timing* diagrams associated with Actors in *use case* diagrams in order to characterize the behavior of the modeled system environment. We will also consider a different interpretation of the Lifeline state, designated both as the possible subsystem states and as the values of eventual attributes of the Lifeline.

A Figure 3.1 represents the robust notation of the timing diagrams for one Lifeline (:report), two states (on, off) and linear time representation. A few Lifelines can appear in the same package, and all the events are synchronized with respect of

Figure 3.1. A lifetime for a discrete object

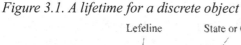
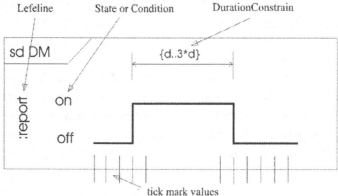

the tick values of the common clock. The Lifeline has not to be necessarily expressed in metric time, so some events, duration and time constrains or synchronization edges can appears in the *timing* diagrams notation, but they are not necessary for the presentation of the introduced in the paper methodology of *timing* diagram application, so they are not considered here.

Characterizing the behavior of the systems environment, it is easy to note that its influence on the system depends not only on the type of Actors cooperated with the system, but also on the number of particular Actor instances and frequency of the request generation made by them. This creates the problem of the Lifeline states representation by enumerate number of states. The solution can be the introduction of some continuous space of states and marking the Lifeline value as pointed by some its attribute. For example if we are interested in how many times a given actor A interacts with the pointed out *uses case* U representing the part of the modeled the system; then the state space can be designated as number of interactions per day. Actors may represent human users, external hardware, or other subjects, what means that each of them represents a number of the physical instances in the real world. So, the final value represented by the Lifeline should be evaluated by multiplying the number of single actor interactions by the number of its instances.

Analyzing the *use case* diagram we can evaluate the whole use cases overhead by summing up the interactions of actors and the other *use cases*. If we are able to estimate the time complexity of the algorithms implementing *use case* then we are able to estimate the final system workload, otherwise we can treat this values as a desired timing constrains of the designated system. Two problems appear when we try to use this idea in practice:we can estimate the time complexity of the particular algorithms of the system, but it is difficult to trace how this estimation influences the final workload of the particular function of the system represented by the use case,

the mentioned estimation is usually made after implementation of the system (at the testing and the integration stage), so it can be too late to improve the system effectiveness.

Using AR for Generation of Timing Diagrams for Elements from Different kinds of UML Diagrams

The solution presented in the previous section bases on the assumption that we are able to estimate the workload of the computing system caused by an Actor request. Such estimation can be made by the observing of the real system or by estimating of complexity of used algorithms. However, it seams to be desirable to consider the influence of the information gathered in the *timing* diagrams (describing Actors timing behavior) on the final model of the developed software system.

In all methodologies using UML, the *use case* diagrams (and *class* diagrams – for illustration of Domain Model) are the first diagrams generated during the system modeling. Here, we assume that the *timing* diagrams associated with Actors activities are generated at the *use case* level to express the time relations among the elements of the system structure associated with the periodical character of the system functions. The vertical relation AR, introduced earlier in second section, help us to do that. Using AR relation for each Actor's request **r** we able to designate:

- The set of classes modeling the algorithms used during its service (AR(r,CBL)),
- The set of object that are responsible for the servicing of the request r (AR(r,OBL),
- The deployment of the mentioned in the previous point objects ((AR(o,DL)).

Thus we are able to estimate the workload of the software and the hardware components in the following way. Let, for each $r \in$ n_set $(R|_{UL})$, TM(r,t) represents *timing* diagram associated with r (more formally TM(r,t)=AR(r,TML)(t)). Having defined TM for requirements we can calculate it for methods, class, objects and hardware nodes.

For any $m \in$ n_set (R|CML) $TM(m,t) = \bigcup_{r \in AR(m,UL)} TM(r,t)$

For any $c \in$ n_set (R|CBL) $TM(c,t) = \bigcup_{r \in AR(c,UL)} TM(r,t)$

For any $o \in$ n_set (R|OBL) $TM(o,t) = \bigcup_{r \in AR(o,UL)} TM(r,t)$

For any $h \in$ n_set (R|HL) $TM(h,t) = \bigcup_{o \in AR(h,OBL)} TM(o,t)$

where $\cup$ means the logical sum.

Timing diagrams generated for methods and classes help us to better understand the modeled system structure and can be very useful in finding the system elements that should be refactored (Flower, Beck, Brant, Opdyke, & Roberts, 1999; Kotulski & Dymek, 2007).

Timing diagrams generated for Hardware Layer give us information about the time of the hardware nodes activity, triggered by the execution of processes corresponding with objects allocated at it.

Let's notice that the timing diagrams generated for the object can be used to estimate the level of utilization of the hardware equipment. Let's assume that:

- We are able to estimate the (average, periodical) performance of the object components (described as per(o)); this estimation should be associated with the computational complexity of algorithms used inside the object.
- We know the computing power of the hardware nodes (described as cp(h))

Then the function

$$EF(h,t) = \frac{\sum_{o \in AR(h,OBL)} (TRA(o,t) * per(o))}{cp(h)}$$

shows us the efficiency of the hardware nodes utilization in time. It can be used to indicate the periods of time in which the hardware equipment is almost not used or is very close to overloading. Brief analysis of presented function shows us that we have three ways of influence on its value:

1. We can reschedule the user requirements by changing business processes schedule,
2. We can decrease performance demanded by the object's processes by rewriting software modules
3. We can increase the hardware computing power.

More detail analysis of these possibilities we present below, in next section.

EXPRESSION OF TIME CHARACTERISTIC OF THE REPORTING SYSTEMS

In this section we show how the AR function, based on the vertical relation concept, can be used to system workload estimations. For cleaner explanation we consider the real Reporting Data Mart based on the Data Warehouse system in commercial bank. Firstly, we briefly describe the architecture of the Reporting System and some environmental limitations. Next, we show how the ULM *timing* diagrams can be used to express the timing characteristic of the system workload on different levels: from a single process to a hardware node. At the end, we present how to use this characteristic for a system refine by workload balancing.

Business Reporting Data Marts

Every business organization has to prepare many reports for some external organizations based on country's law regulation. In case of Poland, commercial banks have to submit obligatory reports inter alia to the National Bank of Poland (WEBIS reports), the Ministry of Finance (MF reports) and the Warsaw Stock Exchange (SAB reports)[3]. Beside external obligatory reports, each business organization generates large amount of internal reports. Depending of the frequency of their generation we are able to divide them into a few categories. We can distinguish daily, weekly, decadal, monthly, quarterly, half-yearly or annual reports and additionally we have some number of ad-hoc reports, which have no periodical characteristic. In most cases, these reports base on almost the same kind of source data, but various external and internal requirements on format and content cause that different software applications (based on assorted algorithms) are needed. To simplify the example we skip the organization of the Extraction, Transformation and Loading (ETL) processes and assume that all necessary information are maintained by the Data Warehouse Repository. It's ease to realize that for different Data Marts the set of used DW processes can be different. Analyzing the information content of reports we can divide them into a few categories, based on kind of source data and the way of their processing. Each of those categories, regardless of periodical character, is generated by different processes. Their results are integrated on the level of the user interface depending on period and organizational requirements. The schema of data flow for Reporting Data Mart (Dymek & Kotulski, 2007a) is presented in Figure 4.1

Each User Application represents functionality associated with the single period and with the single type of obligatory reports. Because of that, we can treat these applications as user requirements (use cases in terms of UML), defining Data Mart functionality.

To simplify this example we can take a simple Reporting Data Mart with functionality restricted to only two types of reports. First type consists of three periodical reports: weekly, decadal and monthly ones. The second type of the reports consists of ad hoc reports generated by consultants and verification of the hypothesis prepared by them (Kotulski & Dymek, 2008). These activities are represented at *use case* diagram presented in Figure 4.2.

To estimate the system workload, first we have to get the time characteristic for each single type of processes. In next steps we assign the number of processes and generated by them workload.

Time Characteristic of Processes

As it was mentioned above, some reports have the periodical character. It means that processes associated with these reports category have also the periodical character. They are executed only in the given period of time. This period is strictly connected with the organizational process of drawing up the given type of reports. Let us notice that the obligatory reports e.g. these for the National Bank of Poland, have to fulfill

Figure 4.1. General schema of the Reporting Data Mart

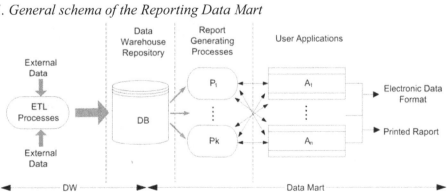

Figure 4.2. Schema for Reports Generation activities

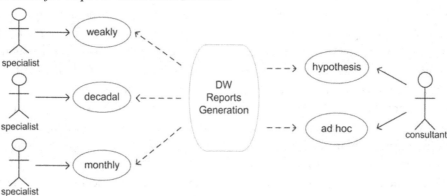

many control rules, before they can be send out. In practice, it means that those reports are not generated in a single execution of the proper software processes. Instead of this, we have the organizational process which can progress even a few days, during which the software process is executed many times after each data correction. As a result, if we analyzing the time of the availability of system functionality connected with those reports, we must take into account the larger time of the readiness of the hardware environment than in the case of the single process execution. We assume that processes associated with weekly, decadal and monthly reports generation are started appropriately 2, 3 or 4 days before of the reports delivery time.

In case of obligatory reports, time of their readiness is set by external factories. In case of reports for National Bank we have e.g. the following limitations:

- Weekly reports have to be ready before Thursday,
- Decadal reports have to be ready in five workdays,
- Monthly reports have to be ready till 20 day of the next month.

Reflecting, mentioned earlier, lasting time of processes associated with each kind of periodical reports generation, we can expressed the time characteristic of these processes in a form of the *timing* diagrams. At Figure 4.3, there are three *timing* diagrams, presenting the process activity respectively for weekly, decadal and monthly reports generation processes. We distinguish only two states on or off (on diagrams it is 1 or 0 respectively).

Knowing the time characteristics for each single periodical reports generation process we can calculate the aggregated time characteristic for all of them together. In this case, the information about state of processes (on/of) is not enough. Also information about number of concurrently running processes, which we can get by simple aggregation of single *timing* diagrams, is not enough. We need information about workload generated by each kind of process in particular hardware environment. This information we can get by observing a real system or on early stage of system development by making some estimation.

Let's assume, for simplifying the example, that each process of periodical reports preparation generate the same level of workload and one process generates "weak" workload, two processes generate "medium" workload and three processes generate "strong" workload. In such case the aggregated *timing* diagram for these processes will look as follow (Figure 4.4):

Figure 4.3. Timing diagrams for periodical reports generation

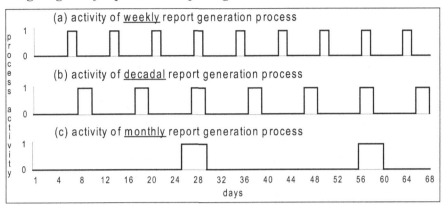

Figure 4.4. Aggregated system workload for periodical processes

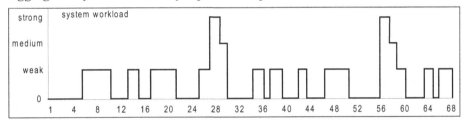

Later we will show how to deal with the system workload level more precisely. But even this brief analysis let us realize, that the system workload is on "strong" level only for a short time and a little rescheduling (if possible) can lower the requirement for computing power of hardware environment.

System Workload Estimation

In previous subsection we considered the case of periodical reports generations and processes linked with them. Each of these processes is running as single process (e.g. there are no two processes of monthly reports generation running concurrently). More complicated situation is in case of a consultant activity and processes connected with ad hoc reports and hypothesis verification (Kotulski & Dymek, 2008). We can have many consultants working concurrently and each

consultant can execute a few processes in the same time. So besides the characteristic of processes we must have information about the number of consultants and their typical behavior. When we have this information we are able to calculate the possible number and type of concurrently running processes starting by them. Next, based on time characteristic of these processes we will be able to estimate the system workload.

Because we have two kinds of different processes we will need two *timing* diagrams for their characteristic. Firstly, analyzing the consultant activity we can realize that:

- Process activity connected with ad hoc reports, which is linked with continues analytical jobs driven by consultant, occurs during work time,
- Much more complicated (in terms of complexity and amount of processed data)

processes of hypothesis verifications are executed in the background, with breaks on non working days.

The *timing* diagrams depicting activity of these processes are shown on Figure 4.5.

Presented *timing* diagrams show us only the activity of given processes in time. As in previous presented *timing* diagrams, we distinguish only two states on or off (on diagrams it is 1 or 0 respectively). But for system workload estimation we must take into account information about number of these processes and the workload linked with each kind of these processes. In usual situation we have many consultants and each of them can execute few processes of the report generation or hypothesis verification.

The method of evaluation of the number of processes depending on number of users and kind of their activity is presented by Dymek and Kotulski (2008). This method, based on some kind of calculus defining on *timing* diagram gives us the new kind of the *timing* diagram, where Y-axis shows not the process status (on/off) but the number of running processes. Let assume that we have 10 processes of hypothesis verification and 20 processes of ad hoc report generation, running concurrently. In such a situation the aggregated *timing* diagram for consultants' activities will look as follow (Figure 4.6). This information can be useful for the characteristic of the overloading of the files system or swapping management.

In this case, we will concentrate only on the computational properties of the system. Information about the number of running processes and their kinds is one of the inputs for the system workload estimation. To make this estimation we also need information about the workload generated by these processes.

Figure 4.5. Timing diagrams for consultant activities

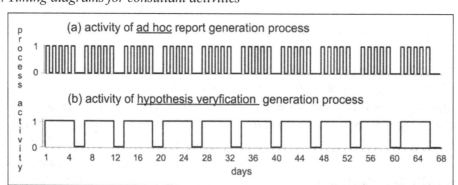

Figure 4.6. Aggregated timing diagrams for consultants' activities

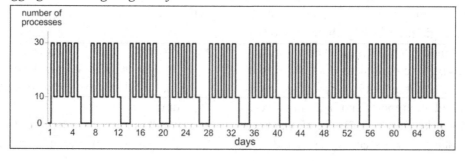

On the early stages of the system design we can assess the workload of given type of process based on its algorithm computational complexity. Aggregating this with the number of processes we are able to estimate the needed efficiency of hardware equipments. Estimated maximum of workload, where workload is a function of time based on *timing* diagrams analysis, gives us the minimum efficiency of hardware demanded by the designed system. Let's realize that in environment with many hardware computing nodes, using AR function, we are able to assign every single process to particular hardware node, as it was shown in the previous section. As a consequence, we can estimate the workload of every single hardware node.

On the late stages of system designing (integration or implementation stages) or for the existing system we can gather real data about the workload generated by particular processes. In similar manner as described above we get the

Table 4.1. Workload generated by single process of different kind

weakly report	30%
decadal report	30%
monthly report	30%
ad hoc report	1,5%
hypothesis verification	4,5%

system workload characteristic as a function of time expressed as a *timing* diagram.

In presented example of the reporting Data Mart we assume that for a given hardware environment the workload generated by particular types of processes looks like at table 4.1. The generated workload is expressed in percentage of hardware environment utilizations. By this we can easily show the system workload characteristic on a single *timing* diagram (see Figure 4.7).

System Workload Balancing

Previously made the estimation of the system workload allows us to conduct a more detail analysis of potential system overloading. *Timing* diagram, representing the system workload as a function of time (Figure 4.7), makes easy to point out the periods of time in which the system is overloaded or is almost unused. Based on this information we are able to take some actions. In case of system overloading we can:

- Reschedule some processes (long term scheduling),
- Reallocate some software applications (to other hardware nodes),
- or distribute processes to few hardware nodes.

In each case we have to collect information for each hardware node about software applications

Figure 4.7. System workload characteristic

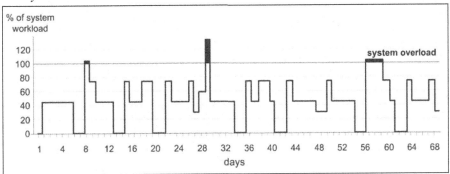

and processes allocated on them, their connections, time dependences and time scheduling. Base on this we can work out the solution of possible overloading of some hardware nodes. The first two cases are generally independent from the structure of software applications. In the last case, the possibility of distributing of processes belonging to one software application depends on its structure; this application must be ready for distributed processing. Setting out such a requirement for all used software applications is economically disadvantageous – such a software application is more complicated and costs more. So it's necessary to work out the method that allows us to point out subsystems which should be ready for distributed processing on early designing phase of software application. This information can be also used in the process of the system refactoring (Kotulski & Dymek, 2007).

Get back to our example and consider the possibility of the long term rescheduling. Analyzing the *timing* diagram shown at Figure 4.6, we can observe that user demand exceeds computing power of the system at 9-th, 30-th and from 57-th to 60-th day of system observation. Fortunately, data for monthly and decadal reports generation usually are prepared by ETL process a few days earlier so we can start: decadal reports evaluation on 7-th and 29-th day, monthly reports on 25-th and 54-th days. Figure 4.8 represents the overloading evaluation in such a case.

System Workload Characteristic after Process Rescheduling

As we can see, in this case rescheduling of some processes allows us to balance the system workload without changes in the hardware environment or the software system structure. In the presented example, for a single process we consider the only two states on/off assuming that workload generated by a process is constant in this process lasting time. This assumption was made for simplifying the example but in real case, especially

for long lasting and complex processes, workload generated by the single process can differ in time. Using the previously defined AR function we can reflect it in presented estimation. Let's trace it in case of weekly reports.

Starting from the set of requirements associated with weakly reports (decadal or monthly appropriately) we can designate set of object *OS* that supports these requirements (using *AR(r,OBL)* function, where $r \in UL$ reflects functionality linked with weekly reports generation). Next we estimate the time of the object activities; for this we should consider the structure of class from which this object has been generated. Moreover, the object activities are made in a some succession path so we should check the *timing* diagrams associated with the classes from which these objects have been generated, designated as follows

$$\bigcup_{i \ \in \ AR(o,CL)} AR(i, TDL) \ o \in OS$$

We have to analyze the *timing* diagrams due to the fact that the time of activity of the cooperating objects is the sum of its executions in the interaction path, but generated by them workload can differ. In such a case the timing diagram for the weekly reports generation process can look like below (Figure 4.9).

In brief estimation we take a maximum of generated workload (30%) as a constant workload generated by this process. But in same cases we should make more detail analysis, especially when maximum workload is achieved only in very short period and the whole process is long. Next steps of system workload estimation are the same as in case of brief analysis.

CONCLUSIONS

The problem of load balancing integrates many different aspects of a software system design. Some

Figure 4.9. Detail timing diagram for the weekly reports generation

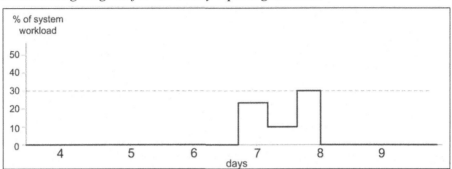

decisions must be taken on the very early design phase and their results have to be embedded into the system software structure. The recent release of UML 2.0, supporting software modeling, has corrected a lot of design difficulties encountered in the 1.x revision. One of the new introduced capabilities is the possibility of characterization of the timing behavior for some components of the modeled system (with help of *timing diagrams*). Unfortunately still actual is Engel's observation that a general consistency of UML model is still missing (Engels & Groenewegen, 2000). The vertical consistency is supported neither by CASE tools nor by the modeling methodologies like RUP or ICONIC.

In the paper the idea of the formal remembering (as a kind of vertical relations) the associations between elements belonging to the different kinds of the UML diagrams was presented. Those associations appear during the reasoning process, while system modeling. However, this formal approach has a specific context; it means that the mentioned associations are remembered as a graph structures (equivalent to the UML Interchange standard (Object Management Group, 2006)), so their maintenance and/or evaluation is possible with help of the graph transformation. In such a meaning this approach differs from other formal approaches supporting UML modeling with such formalisms as SCP (Engels, Küster, Heckel, & Groenewegen, 2001) or B language (Snook & Butler, 2006).

Graph Repository content, called UML(VR) (Kotulski & Dymek, 2008), covers both UML diagrams and vertical relations joining the elements of different diagrams, and is in general used for assuring the vertical consistency of the modeled system. In this chapter, we argue that in a consistent model the timing properties can be inherited from high abstraction level to the lover one. We also suggest of using *timing* diagrams as a tool for description of Actors timing behavior was shown. The mentioned diagrams and vertical associations can be arguments for calculation of the *timing* diagrams associated with objects and classes, and next for deployment diagrams. We use these timing characteristic of the system for high level scheduling made at the level of user requirements (some permanent processes are executed earlier) to achieve satisfactory system overloading of the Reporting Systems in a Data Warehouse environment. The deeper analysis (not covered in the paper) can points out the part of the system that should be consider for possible refactoring (Kotulski & Dymek, 2007). All the more, it is important because the refactoring techniques in general are based on the system developer intuition (who discovers "bad smells" part of program (Flower et al., 1999)).

We would like to ascertain that the estimation of the system overloading is made from the modeling system perspective, and has a form of preliminary estimation of some its properties, especially in case when not all the decisions on the modeled system structure have been undertaken. When the detailed structure of the system is already defined we suggest using well formed optimization methodology based on Markov Chains. The useful examples of such an approach are presented by Hanna and Mouaddib (2002) (see also Abdallah & Lesser, 2005) in context of agents systems and by Lindemann, Lohmann and Thümmler (2004) for the quality assurance of service in the CDMA cellular networks.

REFERENCES

Abdallah, S., & Lesser, V. (2005). Modeling task allocation using a decision theoretic model. In *Proceedings of the Fourth international Joint Conference on Autonomous Agents and Multiagent Systems* (The Netherlands, July 25 - 29, 2005). AAMAS '05. ACM, New York, NY, (pp. 719-726).

Dymek, D., & Kotulski, L. (2006). Evaluation of Risk Attributes Driven by Periodically Changing System Functionality. *Transaction on Engineering, Computing and Technology*, vol.16 November 2006, ISSN 1305-5313, (pp. 315-320).

Dymek, D., & Kotulski, L. (2007a). On the load balancing of Business Intelligence Reporting Systems. *Proceedings of the AIS SIGSAND European Symposium on Systems Analysis and Design,* University of Gdansk, (pp. 121-125).

Dymek, D., & Kotulski, L. (2007b). On the hierarchical composition of the risk management evaluation in computer information systems. *Proceedings of the Second International Conference DepCoS - RELCOMEX,* Szklarska Poreba, 14-16 June, 2007, ISBN-0-7695-2850-3, IEEE Computer Society (pp. 35- 42).

Dymek, D., & Kotulski, L. (2008). Estimation of System Workload Time Characteristic using UML Timing Diagrams. *Proceedings of the Third International Conference DepCoS – RELCOMEX 2008,* IEEE Computer Society No. P3178, (pp. 9-14).

Ehrig, H., Engels, G., Kreowski, H.-J., & Rozenberg, G. (1999a). *Handbook of Graph Grammars and Computing By Graph Transformation: Volume II, Application, Languages and Tools.* World Scientific Publishing Co., NJ.

Ehrig, H., Kreowski, H.-J., Montanari, U. & Rozenberg, G. (1999b). *Handbook of Graph Grammars and Computing By Graph Transformation: Volume III, Concurrency, Parallelism , and Distribution*, World Scientific Publishing Co., NJ.

Engels, G., & Groenewegen, L. (2000). Object-Oriented modeling: A road map. In A. Finkelstein (Eds) *Future of Software Engineering 2000.* ACM, (pp.105-116).

Engels, G., Küster, J. M., Heckel, R., & Groenewegen, L. (2001). A methodology for specifying and analyzing consistency of object-oriented behavioral models. *The 8th European Software Engineering Conference held jointly with ESEC/ FSE-9.* ACM, New York, (pp.186-195).

Flower, M., Beck, K., Brant, J., Opdyke, W., & Roberts, D. (1999). *Refactoring: Improving the Design of Existing Code.* Addison-Wesley.

Hanna, H., & Mouaddib, A. (2002). Task selection problem under uncertainty as decision-making. In *Proceedings of the First international Joint Conference on Autonomous Agents and Multiagent Systems: Part 3* (Bologna, Italy, July 15 - 19, 2002). AAMAS '02. ACM, New York, NY, (pp. 1303-1308).

Kotulski, L. (2000). *Model wspomagania generacji oprogramowania w środowisku rozproszonym za pomocą gramatyk grafowych.* Wydawnictwo Uniwersytetu Jagiellońskiego, Kraków, ISBN 83-233-1391-1.

IBM Rational Unified Process, Retrieved November 05, 2008, from http://www-01.ibm.com/ software/awdtools/rup/

Kotulski, L.(2006). Nested Software Structure Maintained by aedNLC graph grammar. *Proceedings of the 24th IASTED International Multi-Conference Software Engineering,* (pp. 335-339).

Kotulski, L., & Dymek, D. (2007). On the Evaluation of the Refactoring in UML Environment, *Information Systems Architecture and Technology - Information Technology and WEB Engineering: Models, Concepts and Challenging,* Wydawnictwo Politechniki Wrocławskiej, ISBN 978-83-7493-345-2, (pp.185-193).

Kotulski, L., & Dymek, D.(2008). On the modeling timing behavior of the system with UML(VR). In M. Bubak, et al. (Eds), *ICCS 2008, part I, LNCS 5101,* (pp. 386-395).

Kuźniarz L., Reggio, G., Sourrooille, J., & Huzar, Z. (2002). Workshop on "Consistency in UML-based Software Development", Retrieved November 05, 2008, from http://www.ipd.bth.se/uml2002/RR-2002-06.pdf

Lindemann, C., Lohmann, M., & Thümmler, A. (2004). Adaptive call admission control for QoS/revenue optimization in CDMA cellular networks. *Wireless Network.* 10, 4 (Jul. 2004), (pp. 457-472).

Object Management Group (2007a). UML Infrastructure Specification v.2.1.2, OMG document number: formal/2007-11-04, Retrieved November 05, 2008, from http://www.omg.org/spec/UML/2.1.2/

Object Management Group (2007b). UML Superstructure Specification v.2.1.2, OMG document number: formal/2007-11-02, Retrieved November 05, 2008, from http://www.omg.org/spec/UML/2.1.2/

Object Management Group (2006). UML Diagram Interchange v.1.0 OMG document number: formal/2006-04-04, Retrieved November 05, 2008, from http://www.omg.org/technology/documents/formal/diagram.htm

Rozenberg, G. (1997). Handbook *of Graph Grammars and Computing By Graph Trans-formation: Volume I, Foundations.* Ed. World Scientific Publishing Co., NJ.

Rozenberg, D., & Scott, K. (2001). *Applying Use Case Driven Object Modeling with UML: An Annotated e-Commerce Example.* Addison Wesley.

Snook, C. & Butler, M.(2006). UML-B: Formal modeling and design aided by UML. *ACM Transaction on Software Engineering Methodology, 15*(1), 92-122.

Valiente, M., Genova, G., & Cerretero, J. (2005). UML 2.0 Notation for Modeling Real-Time Task Scheduling. *Journal of Object technology, 5*(4), 91-105.

ENDNOTES

[1]   These limits are not as sharp and crucial as for OLTP systems, but they are important and have to be pointed out.

[2]   Packages introduce some sub-layers structure inside this layer.

[3]   Structure and information contents of those reports are based in international standards so the same situation we can meet in other countries.

Chapter V
Information Systems Development:
Understanding User Participation as a Social Network

Angela Mattia
Virginia Commonwealth University, USA

Heinz Roland Weistroffer
Virginia Commonwealth University, USA

ABSTRACT

Conventional wisdom has it that user participation in information systems development (ISD) is essential for systems success. Though the significance of user participation to systems success has been much discussed in the literature, results from empirical studies are inconsistent and suggest, that perhaps new avenues need to be explored. One approach may be viewing user participation as a social network that is, looking at the emergence of social structures and their technological expressions during the user participation process. In this chapter, a framework is presented that organizes user participation approaches that emerge from the different worldviews existing within organizations. This user participation approach (UPA) framework is used as the structure for the systematic arrangement of user participation approaches into a fourfold taxonomy based on extrinsic information attributed to them in the literature. In addition, a categorical analysis and social network analysis (SNA) are used to map and visualize the relationships between analyst and users, thus providing a conceptual and visual representation of the relational structures.

INTRODUCTION

A critical factor in successful information systems (IS) development is generally assumed to be user participation. Interestingly enough, empirical studies have been unable to conclusively link user participation to systems success. Indeed, attempts to organize and synthesize past empirical studies on user participation have resulted in conflicting results (Cavaye, 1995; Hwang & Thorn, 1999; Olson & Ives, 1981). This may not be totally surprising, due to the dynamic nature of organizations (Doherty & King, 2005) and the inability to capture many of the *everyday* social interactions that occur as users participate. Everyday user participation may or may not be public and therefore has been difficult to assess in the past.

However, in today's world, online communication is becoming an increasingly important part of how users participate in information systems development (ISD). Project participants go online to look for information, keep in touch with co-workers and other professional contacts, conduct business, talk about the project, track progress, discuss new developments, and look for answers to problems. Most of these interactions leave behind records of some sort of social interaction: exchanged email messages, discussion forums, instant messaging (IM) logs, newsgroup postings, blog entries, wikis, etc. Hidden in these growing archives of interactions are useful social patterns that, if more easily recognized and understood, could greatly improve the outcome of an ISD project. This chapter looks at how social interaction may be visualized and how such representations may help organizations understand the mediated environments they inhabit, the worldviews they exhibit, and the relationships of these factors to information systems outcome or success. Indeed, information visualization offers a method of observing the unobservable (Shneiderman, 1998).

The Internet has produced a new way to identify "social networks". Indeed, these networks support social interaction and user participation on an unprecedented scale. Social networks are changing the user participation context, as millions of people around the world come together in online public spaces and exchange ideas, ask questions, and comment on daily life events. In-

deed, individuals and organizations are *evolving* in their interactions as they recognize and learn to appreciate how they can stay in touch by e-mail or in online discussion forums with hundreds of people all over the globe. These social networks, which may be public or private, are about collaboration and empowerment for individuals, organizations, and societies (Shneiderman, 2002). They leave behind copious evidence of the evolving social networks and the *revolutionary* ways users are participating. Yet, this evidence is largely undefined and thus so far has been unusable in the context of ISD user participation research. The objective of the current research is to provide a framework that will facilitate visualizing the cues and patterns that are present in social networks, in order to help users, analysts, managers, and other stakeholders participating in ISD, better understand the worldviews they exhibit and their relationship to systems outcomes.

In a sense, we undertake making the intangible aspects of user participation in ISD tangible. In doing so, an issue to contemplate is whether the process of "how users participate" is evolutionary, or are we experiencing a *revolution* with respect to "how users participate?" Disclosing the worldviews and patterns of "how users participate" may help illuminate these issues and others about user participation in ISD. Indeed, it may be a step towards conclusively showing a link between user participation and system success.

This chapter is organized as follows. After providing and discussing some basic terminology, we present and extend the *user participation approach (UPA)* framework (Mattia and Weistroffer, 2008) and justify its use as a means to better understand user participation as a social network. Based on a survey of the literature, we provide and summarize a categorization of user participation approaches using the UPA framework. The chapter concludes with a discussion on how the proposed framework can be better understood as a social network.

THE USER PARTICIPATION APPROACH FRAMEWORK

Basically, this research involves extracting, analyzing, and categorizing information retrieved from available data. The concept of organizing data for better comprehension is not new, and indeed, has an extensive history in the user participation literature (Cavaye, 1995; Hwang & Thorn, 1999; Olson & Ives, 1981; Ware, 2000). What is different in our research is the *what, how,* and *why* in organizing, analyzing, and understanding user participation during ISD, viewed as a social network.

Definitions of Terms

User participation has been discussed in the literature from many theoretical perspectives, but attempts at organizing and synthesizing the literature have proven difficult. First, to properly organize the user participation process in ISD we must define several ambiguous terms. Barki and Hartwick (1989) suggest that the term *user participation* should be used "when referring to the set of operations and activities in the systems development process that users participate in", and the term *user involvement* "should be used to refer to a subjective psychological state which influences user perceptions of the system."

Development-related activities performed by users during ISD include activities that may pertain to either the management of the ISD project or to the analysis, design, and implementation of the system itself (Cavaye, 1995). Therefore, participation reflects what specific behaviors are performed, how many of these behaviors are performed, and how often they are performed. These behaviors can be measured by asking users to indicate the extent to which they have participated in specific assignments, activities, and tasks (Hartwick & Barki, 2001).

Due to the diverse use of the terms user participation and user involvement, the term *user*

engagement has emerged, referring to either user participation or user involvement or both (Hwang & Thorn, 1999). In addition, recent research also looks at *user attitudes* as a separate term and defines it as affective or evaluative judgment (e.g., good or bad) towards an object or behavior (Barki & Hartwick, 1989). Simply said, it is a psychological state that reflects the user's feelings about IS. This is important because recent research has suggested that user participation, user involvement, and user attitude exert different impacts on system outcomes. Indeed, a circular relationship is suggested (Lin & Shao, 2000), because when user's perform participatory activities, they can help users get more involved, which may improve the user's attitude and make them feel more satisfied with the IS.

A *social network* is defined in this research as a social structure consisting of nodes (which are generally individuals or organizations) that are tied by one or more specific worldviews. Consequentially, persistent data to be investigated and visualized need to be collected from different social networks. Thus, these collections of data deal with user participants and with the spaces and the people they encounter during ISD. Rather than visualizing information systems as a technological phenomenon, we are visualizing the social fabric of the user participation process: the relationship between the roles of analysts and users. User roles in this research are sub-classified as user (in the narrow sense), stakeholder, and manager. This role distinctness is necessary to more accurately model the attributes and relationships of the worldview in which the user role exists. Thus the role of a user (in the wider sense) is flexible; it may range in its definition as solely using the system, to designing and managing the user participation process. We are visualizing the ordinary activities of analyst and users participating in ISD and their worldviews that have an impact on these activities. In so doing, we are not limiting this research to one kind of environment, but instead, explore a variety of online spaces and social networks. Every ISD project is fundamentally different from every other, dealing with different social networks, and online architectures. This approach allows us to explore how social networks may affect distinct user and organizational worldviews, synchronous and asynchronous user participant environments, conversation-based and artifact-based ISD communities. Consequently, this research shows how a user's worldview and social networks can impact user participation in ISD and the resulting system outcomes.

The Proposed Framework

Typically in academic research, a research question is first identified, and then ways are investigated to explore and answer this question. In contrast, creators of social networks often begin with, first, the purpose they are interested in pursuing and, second, the raw dimensions present in the data. To these two parameters, the work presented here adds a third one: empirical findings

from information systems research and a variety of social science research – ranging from sociology and psychology to communication research. Whenever possible, the choice of which dimensions to visualize in this research has been guided by the theories and empirical results from these fields. Communication research in particular, can be of great value to designers of social networks because they highlight the kinds of cues users of online spaces utilize as they interact. These studies spell out some of the inner workings of social processes such as online impression formation and the impact that different cues have on interpersonal communications processes (Carroll, 2002). Furthermore, this research explores social network analysis as one analytic approach to better understand user participation.

Adapted from Cavaye (1995) and Mattia and Weistroffer (2008), Figure 1 depicts the various dimensions that have been used in previous user participation research, but extends the model by synthesizing numerous other ideas put forward

Figure 1. User participation approach (UPA) framework

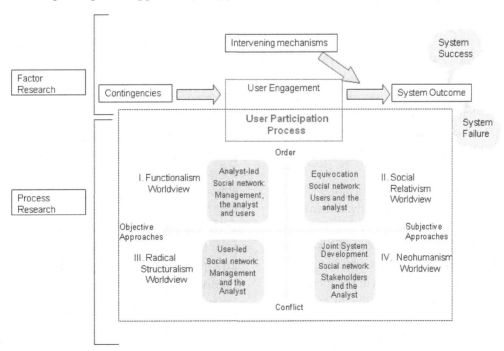

in the literature, including the four paradigms of information systems development proposed by Hirschheim and Klein (1989). This user participation approach (UPA) framework is designed to present a more complete visualization of a complex phenomenon that is frequently marked by gradual changes through a series of states. In addition, this extension will help organize existing research findings and continue the cumulative research tradition on user participation.

Burrell and Morgan (Burrell & Morgan, 1979) use epistemological assumptions (how you obtain knowledge) and ontological assumptions (your social and technical worldview) to yield two dimensions: a subjectivist-objectivist dimension and an order-conflict dimension. The subjectivist position seeks to understand the basis of human life by exploring the depths of the subjective experience of individuals.

The main concern is with understanding the way in which an individual creates, modifies, and interprets the world. The objectivist position applies models and methods resulting from the natural sciences to the study of human affairs. The objectivist thinks of the social world as being the same as the natural world (Burrell & Morgan, 1979). The conflict-order dimension is described as where an order or integrationist worldview emphasizes a social world characterized by order, stability, integration, consensus, and functional coordination. The conflict or coercion worldview emphasizes change, conflict, disintegration, and coercion (Burrell & Morgan, 1979). The dimensions are offered as a theoretical schema for analyzing organizational theory.

Following Burrell and Morgan (1979), Hirschheim and Klein (1989) map the dimensions onto one another to yield the four paradigms of information systems development. These four paradigms are sets of assumptions about ISD which reflect different worldviews about the physical and social world (Hirschheim & Klein, 1989; Hirschheim, Klein, & Lyytinen, 1995). Different worldviews tend to be reflected in dif-

ferent theories. Indeed, all approaches are located in a frame of reference (worldview) of one kind or another. Iivari, Hirschheim and Klein (2001) extended this line of research by supplying a four-tiered framework for classifying and understanding ISD approaches and methodologies that have been proposed in the literature. The UPA framework proposed in this chapter is a frame of reference for the user participation process in ISD. This provides a comprehensive schema for analysis of user participation outcomes (issues and problems) within ISD and in particular, the user participation domain.

The UPA framework recognizes contingencies, which refer to the variables that enable or inhibit user participation. Intervening mechanisms are included to illustrate that the system outcome may have variables that moderate the user participation effect (Cavaye, 1995). It is important to recognize these, so that the user participation process is viewed in the context of the larger picture.

Categorical Analysis of the User Participation Process

A categorical analysis of the user participation process is used to analyze the UPAs in the context of *information system development approaches (ISDA)*. First, we classify and map the list of user participation items into different process model elements. In a similar manner we characterize the ISDAs. Finally, heuristics are used to investigate how the approaches translate into manager, analyst, stakeholder, and user actions. In this study, this analysis technique helps clarify the story that the UPA tells us. In addition, we use the UPA framework and social network analysis to infer from the whole ISD structure to the user participation part; from organizational structure to individual user participant; from behavior to worldview. Consequentially, this allows us to study whole social networks, all the ties containing specific relations in the defined user participation population, and the personal social networks of user participants and the ties that specific users have, such as their *individual communities.*

A categorical analysis of the user participation process produces four generalized categories. Each category consists of typical classes of behavior that follow from the assumptions of a particular worldview. The worldviews that the ISDAs are derived from are archetypes that represent highly simplified but paramount conceptions.

Elements of the Categorical Analysis:

- The definition of the UPA indicates the overarching concept explicitly defined in the approach.
- The definition of the ISDA indicates the worldview concept explicitly defined in the approach.

- The *management rationale* indicates which justifications are provided for the use of the approach and specific goals that managers should pursue.
- Social *relationships* exemplify the established leadership in the user participation process.
- An *episode* is a set of participatory activities.
- Users, managers, stakeholders, and analysts form social networks that have encounters. It is important to note that encounters mark the beginning and end of an episode, i.e. they separate episodes.
- The heuristics indicate how the participatory activities and the UPA are related. The four main view elements are organization, practice, requirements, and functionality.

Table 1.

User Participation Approach (UPA) Taxonomy		
Worldview	**I. The analyst as the user participation leader**	**II. The analyst as a facilitator**
UPA:	User participation as a rational process in a social network.	User participation as a sense making process in a social network.
Worldview:	Functionalism (objective-order) focuses mostly on technical change.	Social relativism (subjective-order) focuses on social interaction.
ISDA:	Typically these approaches to ISD share a number of common features that drive interpretations and actions. Examples: Structured, information modeling, decision support system, socio-technical design, object-oriented.	Interactionist, soft systems methodology, professional work practice.
Management rationale:	The ideal of profit maximization.	None are apparent. As the social worldview is continuously changing, no particular, rationale can be provided to 'explain' the user participation state.
Social Network:	Management, the analyst and users.	Users and the analyst.
Social Relationships:	Analyst-led.	Equivocation.
Episode's Guiding Principles:	Information systems are developed to support rational, organizational operation and effective and efficient project management.	Information systems development creates new meaning.
Heuristic:	This UPA is technical in nature and significantly focused on the requirements element. Functionality, practice, and organizational elements follow in its analyst-led, technical to social focus. Significant emphasis on design and requirements model a worldview that turns a system into a useful tool for management to achieve its goals.	Interrogative activities that enable debate. This UPA focuses on social interaction and thus, is significantly focused on the functionality element. Through interaction, objectives emerge and become legitimate by continuously developing or adding functionality to the information system. The technical communicator role, with its increased emphasis on listening to users and advocating their needs and desires, also can be used to increase and enhance communication during the user participation process and reduce the pain of these changes.

continued on the following page

Table 1. continued

Worldview	III. The user as the user participation manager in a social network.	IV. The analyst and stakeholders as partners in a social network.
UPA:	User participation as a process of empowerment.	User participation as an equal opportunity process.
Worldview:	Radical structuralism (objective-conflict) focuses on radical change.	Neohumanism (subjective-conflict) focuses on social change.
ISDA:	Participation supports democracy at work and quality of work. Example: Trade unionist.	Models communicative action in organizations. Example: Speech act-based.
Management rationale:	The ideal of an evolution from capitalist market economy to a collectively planned and managed economy. This evolution empowers users to meet their own needs.	The ideal of emancipation. Information systems should lead to freedom from all unwarranted constraints and compulsions (e.g., distorted communication) toward a state of well-being for all.
Social Network:	Management and the analyst.	Stakeholders and the analyst.
Social Relationships:	User-led.	Joint system development.
Episode's Guiding Principles:	Information systems are developed to support managerial control because management is the user.	Information systems are developed to remove distorting influences and other barriers.
Heuristic:	This UPA focuses on radical changes that allow users to meet their own needs (User-friendly ISD tools) thus, is significantly focused on the practice element. Craftsmanship and productivity are thought to improve when the users' daily practices are enhanced.	This UPA is social in nature and significantly focused on the organizational element. Practice, functionality, and the requirements elements follow in its social to technical focus. Significant emphasis on organizational design and adaptation should lead to an ideal environment for joint system development.

The worldviews are arranged in groups (categorized) according to the relationship identified in the UPA framework. Therefore, the categorical analysis provides us with a cognitive map (Table 1) that conceptualizes the attributes, whereby nodes (actors) or individuals can be distinguished.

SOCIAL NETWORK ANALYSIS OF THE USER PARTICIPATION PROCESS

The general form of this analysis views the user participation process as a social network that emerges from the UPA chosen. Actors (nodes) participate in social systems; therefore social network analysis is used to make the relationships between actors explicit. The theoretical and methodological focus of social network analysis is identifying, measuring, and testing hypotheses about the structural forms and relations among actors, making this type of analysis well suited

for use with the UPA framework, in contrast to factor research which has an individualistic and variable-centric focus (Knoke & Yang, 2008) (see Figure 1). Basic units of analysis are relations (ties). Other measures of social network structure include range, density, centrality, groups, and positions (for a review, see (Wasserman & Faust, 1994)).

As a point of departure we offer the following research question: *What enables certain groups of users participating in ISD to contribute to system success?* A traditional approach to this question has been to focus on the analysts and their ability to manage the process of user participation. This is because analysts have traditionally played a pivotal role in designing and coordinating collective actions. This traditional (objective) leader-centered worldview has provided valuable insights into the relationship between leadership and group performance. Today, user led approaches exist that are also consistent with an objective, leader-centered worldview. All of these objective, leader-centered worldviews assume that there is only one leader in a group, and view leadership as an exclusively top-down process between one leader and the other users (Figure 2).

A newer, more subjective approach to managing the user participation process is to have multiple leaders. This approach has proven effective because groups often have more than one leader. Even when there is a formally assigned analyst or user as the group leader, other, informal, leaders may emerge. Users often choose informal leaders of their own, leaders who are separate from the analyst designated as leader by the organization. The subjective, multiple-leader worldviews assume that there is a need for more than one leader in a group. These worldviews view leadership as an emergent process between multiple leaders and the other users (Figure 3).

Basic units of analysis here are relations (ties) measured by visualizing formal social structures of the type "reports to".

The purpose of this section was to give a brief explanation and a corresponding visualization of the social relations indentified in the categorical analysis. We have briefly outlined how social network analysis can enhance the research agenda set forth in the UPA framework. User Participa-

tion during ISD until now has remained mostly untouched by social network analysis. In all four worldviews of the UPA framework, we argue that the network perspective combined with the categorical analysis has the potential to supply a cross-level analysis, generally incorporating more macro-level constructs (such as management rationale) into micro-level research (such as user participation leadership). As we continue to analyze user participation during ISD using the UPA framework, we expect social network analysis to supply many more interesting explanations about the user participation process.

CONCLUSION

The research-in-progress reported in this chapter is focused on organizing and analyzing user participation by viewing it as a social network. Though people are quite adept in participating in social networks in new and ever-more detailed and persistent ways, they often lack the ability to see the relationship in intelligible, useful, and business oriented ways. And yet, it is clear that the

Figure 2. Objective, leader-centered social network

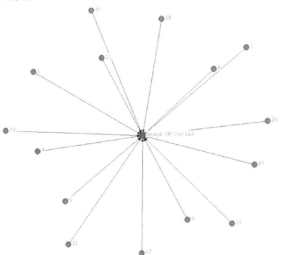

Figure 3. Subjective, emergent-leader social network

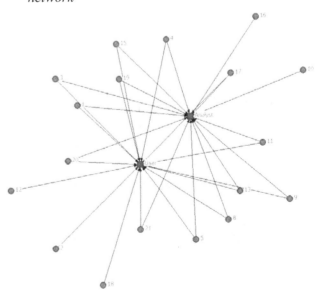

use of social networks can be an important source of information about the people that create them and the worldviews they exhibit. Worldviews play a critical role in determining the way problems are solved, organizations are run, and the degree to which individuals succeed in achieving their goals. Existing social networks supply persistent datasets on how users participate, and a social network analysis may present the cues and patterns that allow us to better understand the relationship of user participation in ISD to systems outcomes. In addition, visual representations of social networks help us understand the dataset and convey the results of the analysis. Social network analysis tools can change the layout, colors, size and many other elements of the social network representation. Indeed, a picture can say a thousand words.

The refinement of the categorical analysis on user participation leads to a more organized taxonomy and therefore a more useful understanding of a user's worldview and the user participation approaches most congruent to the worldview identified. The next logical step is to analyze the social networks and the ties that bind them as a source of persistent data on user participation. This will open new avenues of making tangible what is now obscured and intangible. In addition, social networks should be investigated as a new (evolutionary or revolutionary) approach that managers, analysts, users, and stakeholders can utilize in accordance with the appropriate worldview that they exhibit. As simple as this approach may sound, it is a clear departure from how user participation in ISD has traditionally occurred. Most user participation during ISD is disconnected from the organizational and individual worldviews and the social networks available to the participants. By categorizing user participation approaches according to validated aspects of each worldview and exploring social network structures, this research expands our knowledge of how visualizations of the user participation social network can be used and what impact these UPAs have on systems outcome.

REFERENCES

Barki, H., & Hartwick, J. (1989). Rethinking the concept of user involvement. *MIS Quarterly 13*(1), 53-64.

Burrell, G., & Morgan, G. (1979). *Sociological Paradigms and Organisational Analysis: Elements of the Sociology of Corporate Life.* Heinemann.

Carroll, J. M. (2002). *Human-computer Interaction in the New Millennium.* ACM Press, Addison-Wesley.

Cavaye, A. L. M. (1995). User participation in system development revisited. *Information and Management 28*(5), 311-323.

Doherty, N. F., & King, M. (2005). From technical to socio-technical change: tackling the human and organizational aspects of systems development projects. *European Journal of Information Systems 14*(1), 1-5.

Hartwick, J., & Barki, H. (2001). Communication as a dimension of user participation. *IEEE Transactions on Professional Communication 44*(1), 21-36.

Hirschheim, R., & Klein, H. K. (1989). Four paradigms of information systems development *Communications of the ACM 32*(10), 1199-1216.

Hirschheim, R. A., Klein, H.-K., & Lyytinen, K. (1995). *Information Systems Development and Data Modeling: Conceptual and Philosophical Foundations.* Cambridge University Press.

Hwang, M. I., & Thorn, R. G. (1999). The effect of user engagement on system success: A meta-analytical integration of research findings. *Information and Management 35*(4), 229-236.

Iivari, J., Hirschheim, R., & Klein, K. (2001). Dynamic framework for classifying information systems development: Methodologies and approaches. *Journal of Management Information Systems 17*(3), 179-218.

Knoke, D., & Yang, S. (2008). *Social Network Analysis* (2nd ed.) Sage Publications.

Lin, L. T., & Shao, B. M. (2000). The relationship between user participation and system success: A simultaneous contingency approach. *Information and Management 37*(6), 283-295.

Mattia, A.M., & Weistroffer, H.R. (2008). Information systems development: A categorical analyis of user participation approaches. *Proceedings of the 41st Hawaii International Conference on System Sciences.*

Olson, M. H., & Ives, B. (1981). User involvement in system design: An empirical test of alternative approaches. *Information and Management 4*(4), 183-195.

Shneiderman, B. (1998). *Designing the User Interface: Strategies for Effective Human-Computer-Interaction* (3rd ed.) Addison Wesley Longman.

Shneiderman, B. (2002). *Leonardo's Laptop: Human Needs and the New Computing Technologies.* MIT Press.

Ware, C. (2000). *Information Visualization: Perception for Design.* Morgan Kaufman.

Wasserman, S., & Faust, K. (1994). *Social Network Analysis: Methods and Applications.* Cambridge University Press.

Chapter VI
Solutions to Challenges of Teaching "Systems Analysis and Design" for Undergraduate Software Engineers

Özlem Albayrak
Bilkent University, Turkey

ABSTRACT

This study is an enhancement of previous research presented at the 2nd AIS SIGSAND European Symposium on Systems Analysis and Design and its improved version presented at the 3rd National Software Engineering Symposium (UYMS) 2007. The AIS-SIGSAND 2007 study, the first phase, was part of on-going research by which systems analysis and design-teaching experiences related to course evaluation items were enlightened. This study summarizes previous studies and introduces new findings suggested by those studies that relate to teaching challenges on systems analysis and design in software engineering. The first challenge studied is to decide a suitable evaluation item set in undergraduate level system analysis and design courses for software engineers. The second challenge relates to implicit assumptions made by software engineers during the analysis phase. Based on pre-interview, test, and post-interview data, the study presents a snapshot of an analysis in software engineering regarding implicit assumptions made by analysts. Related to these challenges, the study concludes with proposals on systems analysis and design education.

INTRODUCTION

"Software engineering education" is an important and a challenging arena that involves certain myths and human interaction (Ghezzi and Madrioli, 2005; Hawthorne and Perry, 2005; Hillburn and Watts, 2002; Morrogh, 2000; Vliet, 2005; Hazzan and Tomayko, 2005). Due to this importance, there have been many studies conducted in this area. Several guidelines for software engineering education were prepared (Albayrak, 2003; Bagert, Hilburn, Hislop and Mengel, 1998; Thomas, Semeczko, Morarji and Mohay, 1994; Vliet, 2006). Some studies concentrated on pre-graduation challenges and studied software engineering curricula (Cifuentes and Hughes, 1994; Pullan and Oliver, 1994; Bagert 1998; Parnas, 1999; Schneider, Johnston and Joyce, 2005). Other studies were conducted to prepare software engineers for real life by suggesting industry and university collaboration (Clark, 2005; Ellis, Mead, Moreno and Seidman, 2003; Dawson and Newsham, 1997; Dawson, 2000; Yamaura and Onoma, 2002) or via software engineering projects (Aizamil, 2005; Liu, 2005; Morgan and Lear, 1994; Mohay, Morarji, Thomas, 1994; Oudshoom and Maciunas, 1994). A great deal has been written on the future of software engineering education (Boehm, 2006; Cianciarini, 2005; Bagert, et. al., 1998).

Software engineering is an integrated discipline. Systems analysis and design are two main elements of software development. For today's software engineers, understanding the problem correctly (analysis) and solving it in the best possible way (design) are very important. Thus, special emphasis must be given to teaching systems analysis and design to software engineers.

Studies on teaching systems analysis and design courses were conducted long before Hunter's research on attributes of excellent systems analysts (Hunter, 1994). System Analysis and Design (SAD) in a computer science curriculum was suggested by Spence and Grout in 1978 (Spence and Grout, 1978). Several aspects of SAD course development were studied (Golden, 1982; Goroff, 1982; McLeod, 1996; Larmour, 1997). Archer proposed a realistic approach to teaching SAD (Archer, 1985), while Olfman and Bostrom analyzed innovative teaching for SAD (Olfman and Bolstrom, 1992). Osborne proposed the use of a CASE tool for teaching systems analysis and design (Osborne, 1992), and Dick suggested the

use of student interviews (Dick, 2005). During the 1990s, human factors related to SAD were investigated, and teamwork and the human factor in SAD teaching were studied (Fellers, 1993; Omland, 1999). Following the previous studies, Misic and Russo aimed to identify the importance of the educators' role in various systems development tasks, activities, and approaches and to compare educators' perceptions to those of practicing systems analysts (Misic and Russo, 1999).

Systems analysis and design are important phases in software engineering; hence, importance should be given to both of them. A software engineer should be armed with systems analysis and design related knowledge, not in a classical way but in a comprehensive way similar to that proposed in this chapter, so that software engineers are able to apply what they learn at universities to real-life, practical problems.

This study shares the experiences of preparing undergraduate software engineering students for SAD related subjects applicable to real-life, practical problems. The study is performed in three phases: The fist phase constructs the background for the AISSIGSAND paper and is mostly related to challenge of using different evaluation items to measure software engineers' success in systems analysis and design subjects. The first phase studies the challenges of applying different types of evaluation items in an SAD related undergraduate course. It can be utilized to help academicians who search for an appropriate combination of evaluation means for a course teaching SAD to undergraduate software engineering students. The second phase includes analysis related tests conducted to observe implicit assumptions embedded in analysis studies. Both the second and the third phase of the study deal with challenges related to implicit assumptions made by analysts during analysis. In the third phase of the research, experiments and pre and post interviews were conducted. The results of the second and the third phase of the experiments can be utilized by academicians who aim to avoid, or at least minimize, implicit assumptions during a systems (especially software systems) analysis phase.

This chapter is organized as follows: First, it summarizes the previous phases of the current research study in the Previous Studies' Summary section. It then presents the sample characteristics, study method, and results of the last phase in the Phase III Current Study section. The study concludes with a consideration of future study enhancements of the main subject in the Future Studies and Conclusions section.

SUMMARY OF PREVIOUS STUDIES

This section of the chapter summarizes the previous two phases of the current research. The first phase was conducted at Izmir University of Economics (IUE), Faculty of Computer Sciences and presented at the 2nd AISSIGSAND Symposium (Albayrak, 2007a). By the time the first phase was published, it was on-going research. Some notes collected during the first phase were compiled in the second phase of the study, and the results were published in UYMS 07 (Albayrak, 2007b).

Phase I: Evaluation Items

The Study

The first part of the study is composed of experiences gathered from teaching SAD subjects to undergraduate software engineering students. The goal is to observe whether or not SAD exam results are related to the type of evaluation used. The study is based on the teaching experiences of two sections of an undergraduate course, called "SE303—Principles of Software Engineering" at IUE, Faculty of Computer Sciences. This course, for which there are no prerequisite courses, is mandatory for third year students. Of the students, 97% had successfully completed two semester courses on "Programming Languages (C/C++)" and one semester course, "Systems Analysis and

Design" before enrolling in this course. The major goal of this course, rather than teaching programming or analysis and design alone, is to provide a learning environment in which knowledge gained from these phases is successfully utilized in the real-life experiences demanded from software engineers. The major learning objectives of the course include both practical application and theoretical modeling knowledge.

The total number of students, enrolled on the course, is 58. Fifty-six of the students have prior knowledge related to data-oriented and object-oriented methodologies for analysis and design phases. The students also have prior experience in using UML. In this course, both data-oriented and object-oriented analysis and design were utilized as needed. In addition, agent-oriented and service-oriented analysis and design methodologies were briefly introduced. This study deals only with data and object-oriented analysis and design methodologies. Two different CASE tools were utilized, and different process models varying from waterfall to agile development were studied.

Throughout the semester, different evaluation methods as measures of knowledge were developed and utilized. The list of evaluation items used in the course and their percentage values are presented in Table 1. Observations and experiments were used as study methods, and statistical analysis of data gathered from the students' evaluation means was conducted.

In addition to midterm and final exams, homework and group projects are used for a more comprehensive evaluation of students' knowledge. Initial groups, composed of two students, were formed by the students themselves. The final project was implemented by groups of four, formed by the instructor. The items of evaluation and their characteristics are designated by Table 2.

The students were all aware of the differences between a software engineer and a programmer, yet when it came to developing systems, all acted as programmers rather than as software engineers

Table 1. Evaluation item percentages

Evaluation Item	Percentage (%)
Midterm (4 different parts)	30
Homework (6 integrated assignment)	35
Final	35

responsible for analysis and design studies. The reason for this behavior can be traced back to students' prior education experiences. According to the current curriculum, students need to have completed two programming courses, in which they are trained to accept a given problem as valid, rather than analyze it. Furthermore, during these programming courses, students are not trained in regard to design. Therefore, they start writing the code without analysis and a good design. Students do not conduct analysis unless it is explicitly stated.

H1 was given after three weeks of studying systems analysis. The request was simply to calculate the entered prices of purchased goods in order to obtain the total amount due. A brief and formal explanation was provided to the students, who were also informed that the user, the general manager, was in fact the instructor, and the instructor was available via e-mail, phone, regular office hours, or appointment.

In H2, students formed self-chosen groups of two. Some modifications to the existing program were requested. It was requested that the program would operate in both Turkish and English. The cashier was designated as the program user; students were allowed to ask questions during the analysis.

The midterm exam was composed of four different parts. The first part of the exam, M1, was closed book, and the students were not allowed to ask questions. The second part of the exam, M2, was given after the first-part exam papers were collected. The M2 was closed book, and the students were not allowed to ask questions. The same question was asked in the exam, in a different way: In M1, the definition and elements of a system defined by software engineering were asked. In M2, the students were asked to generate a context diagram for the system defined by software engineering. In other words, the questions in M1 and M2 were identical.

In M3, one question was the same as one of the M2 parts: the object-oriented analysis of a student dormitory system. In M2, the students were asked to prepare individually a use case diagram for that system. In M3, students were given the same question, during which they were allowed to ask questions of the other students, but not to share their work. The time allowed for the question in

Table 2. Evaluation items used

Item	Group Size	Explanation (Hi: Homework i, Mi: Midterm part i)
H1	1	A simple program to add item prices to create total $ due
H2	2	Same program with a Multilanguage support
M1	0	Closed book part
M2	0	Open book, asking questions not allowed part
M3	No limit	Open book, asking questions is allowed part
M4	4	Groups of 4 students formed
H3	2	A menu, help, barcode, and multiplicity are added to H1
H5	2	A database access for price is added to H2
H6	4	Integrate H3 and H5 that they studied previously
Final	0	Closed book

M2 was less than that in M3; M3 questions were delivered after collecting M2 exam papers.

M4 required the students to answer one question in M3 and allowed the students to form groups and to submit group work as answers.

H3 was given after design studies were completed. A menu, help file, and barcode were added to the previous homework given for H2. In addition, the program was changed slightly; it not only obtained the prices but also the amount purchased so that a bill was generated.

H5 concerned a database access from a program in order to read the prices using the barcode entered. The complete database design and a prototype for implementation were given to the students. H6 involved integrating H5 and H3, and students were given four complete source codes as starting points.

The final exam covered the whole course and was a closed book exam during which communication among the students was forbidden.

All evaluation items were read by the same instructor. To grade the evaluation items objectively, the instructor read each question individually.

As can be understood from the above explanations, evaluation items are closely related. The interrelations between these items reflect a more "comprehensive" evaluation than a classical one, in which unrelated items are considered. Having briefly mentioned the evaluation items, it is now time to present the findings of the study, based on evaluations of these items. The results are summarized in Table 3.

Results

According to the results of the study, composed of observations and tests from one semester, the way software analysis and design knowledge is measured has a strong impact on the result of the evaluation process. Students who are successful at defining and utilizing key concepts

Table 3. Brief analysis of evaluation item results

Item	Subject	Results
H1	Analysis	97% failed to ask questions to the user
		99% failed to gather complete requirements and to test the program with alphanumeric data
		90% failed to display the output sentences as given
H2	Analysis/Design	20% made wrong assumption that it was necessary to build a calculator
M1	Analysis	75% were successful in solving analysis problems
M2	Analysis/Design	88% failed to solve the same problem in Midterm part 1, M1
M3	Analysis	35% failed to ask questions during the exam
		73% were less successful in group study
H3	Design	Failed to realize design concepts: flexibility, modularity, multi-lingual support, etc.
H5	Implementation	Initial response: 100% of students claimed they had not learned this previously
		Produced (unnecessary) analysis and design document
		Some designs did not match their implementation
		Past homework response: 78% believed that they had the ability to do the task
H6	Test	95% of groups evaluated others' work, good test cases were determined. Students were successful at testing other groups' projects, but not very effective at testing their own
H7	Maintenance	85% of comments were insufficient
Final	All	Analysis has not yet been completed

and tools related to system analysis and design in a closed book written exam were found to be unable to apply them to solve practical problems in an open book exam. A project that requires an implementation phase means that most of the students fail to conduct the required analysis and design studies.

This section presents the analysis of evaluation item data, homework, and exam results, and provides further observations gathered during the course. Table 3 summarizes the statistical analysis of the evaluation item scores.

When asked in a written exam about the most important step in analysis, almost all of the students chose the analysis of user requirements; yet when it came to satisfying the customer, they neglected to ask the customer questions, an important step in system analysis. Of the students, 89% know what validation means in a software system, yet in practice, they failed to validate solutions because of a lack of proper analysis studies; thus the students assumed that the information given was adequate in itself for analysis studies.

It was also observed that when the students were given homework and questions that did not include implementation (as in M1 and M2), they mostly produced correct answers regarding analysis and design questions. On the other hand, when implementation was included in the assigned homework (as in H1–H6), the students did not pay enough attention to the systems analysis and design phases; instead, they directly worked with the software implementation, causing them to fail.

Having summarized the results of the evaluation items used throughout the study, the next stage is to present observations derived from these results.

Derived Observations

According to this study, it can be said that the way SAD studies are tested does matter, and it may be a challenge of teaching SAD to determine an evaluation items set. It was observed that when analysis and design related subjects are measured by written exams, especially by closed book exams like M1, when directly questioned, most students answer correctly. Yet when it comes to using this knowledge in an open book exam and in a project with an implementation section, the students do not utilize their knowledge of analysis and design in solutions.

Thus, if classical or traditional ways are used as evaluation items for analysis and design problems, the results of the items (exams) might be misleading. In this study, it was observed that in exams (midterm and final), questions on analysis and design were answered correctly. Thus, the majority of the students correctly responded to analysis and design related subjects when the questions were asked in traditional ways.

An analysis of M3 and M4 shows that when the students were asked to answer analysis questions individually, they achieved higher grades than when they were allowed to work in groups. Exams M3 and M4 have two questions in common. According the results of these parts, the students who were successful in individual studies were found to be unsuccessful when working in groups. In other words, according to M3 and M4 analysis, teamwork decreased performance. Considering communication overload, the students were given more time on M4 than M3. Group synergy resulted in a negative impact on the success of the students during the exam.

Between M1 and M2, there was a common question. In M1, students were asked to use structured English as a tool; in M2, they were asked to use a UML use case diagram to solve the same problem. Exam M1 was closed book, and part two was open book. For 88% of the students, answers for the closed book exam were better than for the open book exam. Despite the fact that the students were given more time than for M1, the students performed less well in M2. The weaker performance was not related to the inability to utilize UML, rather to the fact that the students unnecessarily changed their answer to the question. Later interviews with the student revealed the fact that they had expected a more difficult question in an open book exam; thus, they did not trust their initial, but correct answers and changed them. Later, an extra quiz was conducted to make sure that the students were able to convert written cases to UML use cases. Thus, the difference between students' performances in M1 and M2 were not based on any UML conversion/utilization problem.

When the students are tested based on projects, they respond to questions differently. From H1 to H6, most of the students failed to respond to analysis and design related topics. Initially, the students did not conduct any further analysis and design studies, although this was actually required. Furthermore, they conducted analysis in H5 and H6 where, in fact, no analysis studies were required.

If exams are used as the only evaluation means, most of the students will appear to be successful in answering analysis and design related problems. If only projects (or project-like homework) are given, most of the students will appear unsuccessful. Therefore, utilization of both exams and projects (homework) should be applied in order to obtain an overall picture. The utilization of both written exams and projects can therefore be a comprehensive way of measuring students' ability set regarding analysis and design subjects.

Soon after the first midterm, the students were interviewed about the exam. This exam was the only one for which students were allowed to ask questions. According to the interviews, students found asking questions during the exam strange; it was only done by those who understood the importance of user feedback during analysis studies. Experiencing such an exam helped students to remember the importance of user involvement during the analysis phase. After the exam, most of the students stated that they would never forget to involve customers during analysis.

The findings of the first phase are related to the challenges of using different types of evaluation in teaching SAD. To help derive general statements, future studies conducting similar study constructs were suggested by the first phase of the study. The second phase of the study concentrated on implicit assumptions taken by the analyst during software systems analysis.

In this phase, the student grades were found to be very sensitive to the type of evaluation items. This sensitivity may not directly relate to the differences in the evaluation items only. SAD is neither a trivial subject to teach nor, hence, to evaluate. Many variables, most of which are interrelated, are involved in teaching SAD. These variables make teaching and evaluating SAD an intricate process. Some of these variables were controlled by the study, because all the different parts of the midterm exam were delivered as part of the same exam. There were no significant differences in variables related to the students themselves, such as mood, during the exam.

The variables related to the instructor are the same in the study sample. Two sections were taught by the same instructor, who followed exactly the same material in both sections. The instructor, i.e. the author, graded all evaluation means in the study.

One of the variables can be related to the students' assumptions about the evaluation means. Most of the students believed that open book exams were more difficult than closed book exams. With this assumption, some answered the same question differently in a closed and open book exam.

Another variable observed in the study is about creating limits that do not exist. Due to such limits, most students failed to became successful in SAD in M3. The fact that some students did not ask questions of the users during the exam can partially be explained by this variable. There was no restriction on students asking other students questions in the exam. Instructions for M3 stated that only students who spoke would be recorded.

This recording was made to give additional points to those conducting analysis.

The past experiences of the students can be considered another variable. Most students attempted to solve and/or implement problems without conducting analysis and design studies. This may be because of previous experience in programming courses. For more than a year, they were trained to solve problems given to them. During the previously taken, one-semester analysis course, students were given only descriptive sentences and were asked to generate analysis diagrams related to certain technologies, without being asked to conduct complete analysis and design studies.

During the first phase of the study, a test to measure implicit assumptions during software systems analysis was developed. In the second phase, this test was conducted.

Phase II: Assumptions in Analysis

The Study

People make assumptions about things they do not know for certain. Assumptions made by software analysts may be harmful and costly when made implicitly. Implicit assumptions are those that are not shared with and verified by the system's end users. One danger of making an implicit assumption during systems analysis is that it may be wrong. When wrong assumptions become part of system analysis, they can be carried to design and to further implementation phases. As a result, the cost of systems development and the probability of systems failure increase. Thus, dealing with implicit assumptions during the analysis phase is one of the challenges of SAD.

One of the goals of teaching SAD should be to train students not to make implicit assumptions and to avoid reflecting these assumptions to design and implementation phases. This study searched for the impact of SAD education and software development experiences on a number of implicit assumptions made by software developers during the analysis phase.

The second phase of the study is composed of tests and interviews conducted to examine implicit assumption failures during software systems analysis. This phase is conducted at IUE, Faculty of Computer Sciences, Department of Software Engineering. Fifty-four students took the SE303—Principles of Software Engineering course. During this phase, we asked the following question to the students:

"For the following software requirement, do one of the following 3 alternatives:

1. Draw prototype screens for at least two inputs you enter,
2. Write source code in any programming language you know (C/C#, Java, …),
3. Write pseudo code ".

For any positive number entered by the user, the program should display a list of even numbers less than input.

PLEASE LIST ANY QUESTIONS/ASSUMPTIONS YOU HAVE FOR YOUR SOLUTION.

The students were free to choose from developing prototype screens, writing pseudo code, or writing source code in any programming language. Students were forbidden to ask questions while answering this question. The last sentence in the question stated that students should list any questions and/or assumptions they had for their solutions. By that, we wanted to make students' implicit assumptions explicit, by being written on paper.

To respond to the question, the students first conducted an analysis. After the test, we counted the number of assumptions and questions of the students, which were written on paper. Those students who did not write explicit assumptions implicitly reflected their assumptions to their design and implementation studies.

During the test, the students' cumulative grade point averages (CGPA), letter grades for programming language, and SE303 course grades were collected to analyze possible relationships between these grades and the student's choice to answer the question.

The given requirement is vague: It does not explicitly state requirements related to input data type, prompts to display, type of application (Web, console, Windows-based GUI), end of list, order of list (whether ascending or descending), error messages (type and contents), and format of listing (all numbers in one line, or one number per line, or divided into columns). Table 4 shows subjects that an analyst should ask about before design and implementation.

Results

A total of 54 students answered the question, and 54 valid responses were collected. All students passed one programming course, and 34 students took the SE303 Principles of Software Engineering course in addition to the Systems Analysis and Design course.

Thirty-four students preferred to use coding, while 20 selected prototype screens. We counted the number of explicit assumptions (NEA) for each student. We assumed that a total of five explicit assumptions was a sign of good analysis. None

Table 4. Given requirement related subjects for making possible assumptions

Subject	Question
Input type	Is the number integer, double, float,...?
Prompts	What will be displayed to user as text?
Order	Is it ascending or descending?
Format	What is the format of the list?
Application type	Will it be a console, windows, or Web application?
Error messages	Which errors will be displayed, and how?
Stopping condition	What will be the stopping condition?
Language	In which language should the program run?

of the students stated more than five explicit assumptions. We observed that students with lower grades from programming courses preferred to use prototyping and that those who did not enroll in SE303 preferred coding. Students who had above average grades from the programming language (C++) course were able to state more explicit assumptions than those who had lower grades. Figure 1 presents the distribution of NEA values for students grouped by above and below average scores received from the programming language course.

Figure 2 plots the NEA versus the number of students who answered using prototyping and

Figure 1. Number of explicit assumptions versus number of students based on programming course grade

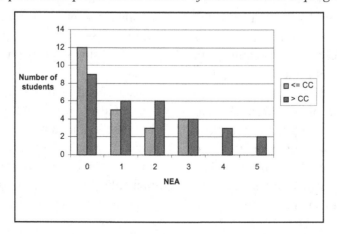

source code. None of the students using proto-typing were able to state more than three explicit assumptions. While most of the students using coding (16) did not make any explicit assumptions, only students who used coding were able to state more than three explicit assumptions.

The majority of the students using prototyp-ing (40%) made two explicit assumptions. None of the students using prototyping had more than three explicit assumptions (Figure 3).

Most of the students using coding (46%) did not make any explicit assumptions. Six percent of the students using coding were able to state five assumptions explicitly. Figure 4 depicts the percentages of students using coding grouped by the NEA made by the students.

It was observed that the development method (using prototyping or coding in a programming language) selected by the students may have impacted the number of explicit, hence, implicit assumptions made during the analysis phase.

In this study, only one requirement was given to the students; for future studies more requirements of different complexity levels may be given to see if the complexity of requirements has an effect on the number of implicit requirements taken by the analysts. The advantage of this study is that it was simple and conducted for a homogenous

Figure 2. Number of explicit assumptions versus number of students based on students' preferences

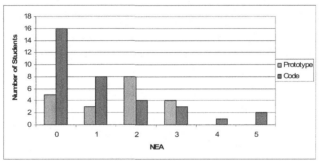

Figure 3. Percentages of students and number of explicit assumptions made in prototyping

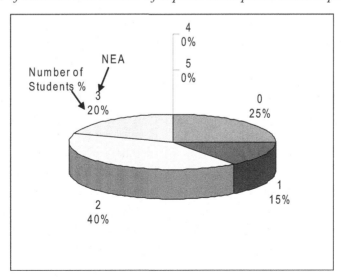

Figure 4. Percentages of number of explicit assumptions made in coding

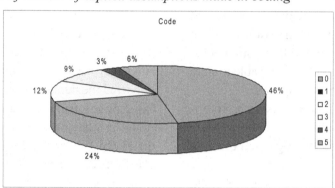

set, composed of students from the same class. It is further suggested that similar studies should be conducted on different samples composed of other students and analysts. Avoiding implicit assumptions during analysis should be a concern of people teaching SAD. Ways to decrease the number of implicit assumptions that are made should be applied during undergraduate training. How to deal with or avoid making implicit assumptions may be one of the major concerns of systems analysts. The second phase of this study can be considered an attempt to observe whether or not the methods used during software design and development have an effect on the number of implicit assumptions during analysis. Based on the results of the second phase, it is not possible to make strong statements about assumptions made during the analysis studies and the methods used in software design and development. For that reason, a similar study was conducted at a different university. The following section explains the third phase of this study in detail.

PHASE III: CURRENT STUDY

The second phase suggested conducting the study in different environments. Based on this suggestion, the current study, the final phase, was developed. This phase uses the same research question developed in the first phase and tested in the second phase. It checks if the number of explicit assumptions during software analysis is related to the method preferred during design and development. It also tests whether or not previously taking SAD related courses and experience has an impact on the number of explicit assumptions made.

Method

The same method used in the second phase was applied in the third phase of the study. Before conducting the study with a student sample, we conducted the study with CTIS Faculty members. Ten CTIS faculty members tested the question and commented on the validity of the study. Experienced faculty members were able to identify all explicit assumptions. They verified that the question was valid and could be used for its intended purpose. Within this small sample, it was observed that instructors who did not teach programming language courses mostly preferred developing prototype screens to coding. Faculty members who selected using prototypes had a tendency to make fewer explicit assumptions than the other faculty members who selected coding. When interviewed, the faculty members using prototypes claimed that developing prototypes was less expensive than developing a program. They further stated that they used prototypes because they believed that it was a less expensive and more effective means of communicating with the users, which is important, due to the determination of systems requirements.

The student sample of the second phase was composed of third year students only. In the third phase, undergraduate students of all levels were included in the sample. Not all of the classes have the same degree of experience related to SAD. The first year and second year students had never taken a course on SAD, while the third and the forth year students had completed SAD courses successfully. The most experienced student group, the senior students, was interviewed before and after the test. In addition to the SAD related courses, during the course CTIS494 Software Quality Assurance, the senior students learned specifications of high quality requirements as a by-product of thorough analysis. This group was more informed about SAD than the other groups.

Sample

The sample was composed of undergraduate students of the Bilkent University Computer Technology and Information Systems (CTIS) department. Although IUE and Bilkent are different universities, there are some similarities between them: Both are private universities in Turkey. At both Bilkent and IUE, the language of instruction is English. Regarding SAD related courses, the CTIS department curriculum is very similar to that of the IUE software engineering curriculum. Furthermore, both use the same textbook in the

software engineering principles course, in which the students learn more about SAD. IUE students of the second phase had completed an extra SAD course, while CTIS students learned analysis and design in a software engineering principles course and applied their knowledge in the CTIS459 Applied Software Engineering course.

The study was conducted with students of all levels, ranging from freshman to senior. The third year students were familiar with SAD concepts from one course they took, CTIS359, on software engineering. The senior students took the CTIS359 and CTIS459 Applied Software Engineering and the CTIS494 Software Quality Assurance courses. The samples used in the study were given SAD experience levels based on the number of SAD courses they had enrolled in. Freshman and second-year students had never taken SAD before, thus their SAD experience level was assigned to 0. The third year students having one course on SAD were assigned to 1, and the forth year students' SAD experience level was assigned to 3, correspondingly.

Hardcopy questions were delivered to the students except for the third year students, who were performing their industrial training at some companies. E-mails were sent to the third year students, and their responses were also collected via e-mail. Hard copy questions were delivered in class with responses collected in class. It took about 10 minutes, on average, and a maximum of 17 minutes for the students to answer the questions in class. While all in-class responses were collected, not all of the third class students who were contacted via e-mail answered the question.

Table 5. Third phase student sample characteristics

Class	Way to collect response	Sample Size	Valid Responses	SAD related courses taken	SAD Level
1	Hard copy	26	22	None	0
2	Hard copy	21	21	None	0
3	e-mail	78	26	CTIS359	1
4	Hard copy	29	29	CTIS359, CTIS459, CTIS494	3

Table 5 lists the characteristics of the student sample used in the third phase.

Descriptive statistics measures were calculated, and the results were used to compare different groups in the study, especially groups with SAD training vs. group without SAD training. We also researched to learn the types of areas that are more likely to be assumed implicitly.

Results

In this section, findings of the third phase are presented. Whenever possible, the results obtained in the third phase will be compared with that of the second phase. Based on their similarities regarding SAD field related experience and training, the first and second year students were considered one group, and the third and forth year students were considered another group. Characteristics of the CTIS third and forth year students are very similar and hence, comparable to the sample of the second phase, third year students of IUE. Both samples have a similar background and training set related to SAD.

The majority of the students failed to state any explicit assumptions needed during analysis. None of the first year students made explicit assumptions. The majority of the first year students (90%)

Figure 5. Number of explicit assumptions versus number of first and second year students based on their preferences

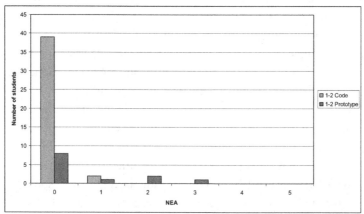

Figure 6. Number of explicit assumptions versus number of third and forth year students based on their preferences

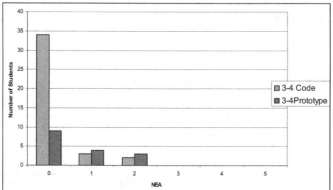

Figure 7. Percentages of number of explicit asssumptions made by the third and forth year students in prototyping

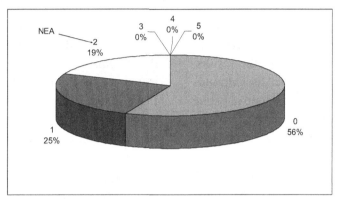

used coding to respond to the questions. Of the second year students, 57% used coding.

It was observed that the students with SAD training (3rd and 4th year students) made more explicit assumptions than the students without SAD training. On average, the NEA made by the 3rd and 4th year students are twice those made by the 1st and 2nd year students.

According to the data in Table 6, we can say that students with SAD training (3rd and 4th year students) achieved more explicit (hence

less implicit) assumptions, on average, than the students without any SAD training (1st and 2nd year students).

Based on data collected, it can be said that students who preferred using prototyping made, on average, more explicit assumptions than the students who preferred coding. Among the 1st and 2nd year students, the average NEA made by the students who selected prototyping was found to be 10 times that of those who used coding. The ratio of the NEA made by the 3rd and 4th year

Table 6. Descriptive statistics for NEA of third phase sample

	All Students		1st–2nd Year Students		3th– 4th Year Students	
	1st–2nd Year	3rd–4th Year	Code	Prototype	Code	Prototype
Mean	.19	.31	.05	.67	.18	.6
Standard Error	.08	.09	.03	.31	.08	.20
Median	0	0	0	0	0	0
Mode	0	0	0	0	0	0
Standard Deviation	.59	.63	.22	1.07	.51	.81
Sample Variance	.35	.40	.05	1.15	.26	.65
Kurtosis	12	2.30	17.79	.43	7.70	-.84
Skewness	3.44	1.90	4.35	1.33	2.89	.85
Range	3	2	1	3	2	2
Minimum	0	0	0	0	0	0
Maximum	3	2	1	3	2	2
Sum	10	17	2	8	7	10
Count	53	55	41	12	39	16

students who preferred prototyping to the NEA made by students who selected coding was found to be 3.

We made a possible classification of assumptions that can be made during analysis of the given problem, in Table 4. According to the results, the students made the most explicit assumptions related to the stopping condition (none negative numbers in the list) of the requirement. The least NEA made were in the subject of prompts used in the program or prototype.

We conducted post interviews with some of the students who were involved in the above study. The third year students contacted via e-mail were not interviewed. Half of the first and the second year students and all of the forth year students were interviewed after they answered the question. Students from the first two years said that they had never faced such conditions in which a tricky question asked by the instructor was incomplete and vague. They claimed that whenever a question was asked to them, they considered it their responsibility to provide an answer, not to judge whether the question was incomplete or vague. Approximately half of the students interviewed stated that the question was so simple that they did not need to ask further questions related to undetermined parts in the question, and thus, they made assumptions that were implicit and reflected these assumptions in their answers.

When we asked the students why they made implicit assumptions rather than writing the assumptions explicitly, the students replied differently. The majority of the first and second year students replied that they did not even realize that they had made assumptions. These students stated that they thought they solved exactly what the problem asked. Some students stated that they did not need to write assumptions explicitly regarding some subjects, because they believed that they should implement the default behavior. According to those students, creating a list in ascending order or listing only positive numbers, for example, are default behaviors of software. A minority (21%) of the forth year students stated that they were aware of their assumptions but instead of writing them explicitly, as stated by the question, they reflected their assumptions in their answers. Those students further claimed that asking questions to the users or making explicit assumptions are time-consuming processes. Instead, these students said that having a solution to show to the user was better than writing explicit assumptions and waiting for approval of the user for these assumptions. They also stated that it was not easy to come up with assumptions related to all subjects and suggested that a solution that included some implicit assumptions was better than a list of questions and no solution at hand.

Figure 8. Percentages of NEA made in related subjects

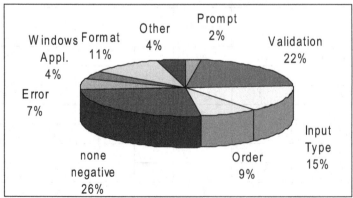

After the post interviews, we gave a one-hour lecture about requirements quality to the forth year students. They learned what made up a good quality software requirement. We then gave the same requirement to the students to analyze. Most of the students replied correctly and were able to write all explicit assumptions related to the requirement.

FUTURE STUDIES AND CONCLUSION

Each of the three phases of this study presents some challenges of teaching SAD to undergraduate software engineering students. The first challenge pointed out by the first phase of this study is on the selection of the evaluation item set used in systems analysis and design courses in undergraduate software engineering education. The second challenge, related to implicit assumptions made during analysis studies is the center of the second and third phases of the study.

The type (closed or open book exams, homework, projects) and set of evaluation items used may have a strong impact on the success of students. Using evaluation sets composed of similar types may be biased. Academicians should be informed about the pros and cons of applied evaluation items. Deciding the set of evaluation means is a problem of education in general, and it is also important in SAD education. In an SAD course, the selection of a wrong set of evaluation items may cause students to succeed when they should actually fail, or visa versa. We observed that to the same questions, students replied differently during closed book and open book sessions of the same exam. Thus, we found that the way that was used to test SAD students' knowledge had a strong impact on their success. We suggest that the use of a single type of evaluation item may not be good enough to test students' ability and knowledge that will be utilized during SAD studies. For a better assessment of student learning, a mix of different measures is suggested, with special emphasis given to open book exams and projects.

We noticed that during an open book exam, students may fail to apply what they already know about systems analysis and design. Open book exams are similar to real-life conditions in which the analyst or the designer has access to some resources and has a limited time to solve problems. The fact that most students who succeed during the closed book part failed in the open book part may be a sign of unsuccessful analysis and design studies after graduation. Either the most appropriate evaluation means set should be found, or students should be trained in such a way that they are able to perform equally under all evaluation means. The findings of the first phase indicate that SAD educators should be careful in selecting the evaluation means set used or should be better at finding ways to help students apply their knowledge to the problems, regardless of the type of evaluation. When a question about implementation was asked, students failed to conduct the analysis and design phases, which contradicted what they learned in systems analysis and design related courses. Most students focus on only the end products of questions. Only with proper training, can students' awareness related to SAD steps be created and students' ignorance of analysis and design steps be removed.

During the exam, students were allowed to form groups. We further observed that students' performance decreased when they worked in groups. To the same question in the same exam, individual answers were better than answers given by groups. There may be several reasons behind this decrease in performance. However, they are beyond the scope of this study. Nevertheless, this study should increase attention given to the importance of group performance related to SAD education. Software engineers mostly work in groups. Students should be trained more in group work. Assigning group projects may help students to practice and learn how to work effectively in groups. Ways to create group synergy should be provided to undergraduate software engineering students so that they will be able to apply what they learn to the real-life SAD of projects.

To cope with the challenge of determining an appropriate type and set of evaluation means used in SAD education, we suggest that creative means that allow similarities to real-life conditions should be used. We consider that asking the same question in the same exam in both the closed and open book part and allowing students to form groups during an open book exam are creative ways of evaluating students. We also suggest supporting such exams with individual and group homework and projects.

Like all other human beings, software engineers make assumptions. However, professional analysts should be careful when working on software systems. A system is only as good as its requirements identified during analysis studies. If analysis of a software system is conducted in isolation from the user, then the requirements may stay incomplete, not valid, and even ambiguous. Explicit assumptions are communicated with the user and requirements are correctly reflected to design and implementation phases. Any assumption taken implicitly during the analysis phase may be costly in later phases, thus assumptions made during the analysis phase should be stated explicitly. An implicit assumption is one that is not taken by a user but is reflected in the analysis study. This situation may result in invalid systems requirements. Implicit assumptions made during analysis studies are further reflected to design and implementation. We observed that students have a tendency to assume that any given requirement to them is valid, and they start design and implementation with their implicit assumptions, which later may be difficult and expensive to communicate to the user.

According to the current curricula of both departments investigated by this study, programming language courses are delivered in the first year; SAD courses are taught in the following years. Thus, the students are better trained in solving implementation related problems than in solving analysis and design related problems. Moreover, in the early years of their education, the students use questions that are clear and valid. They are trained to solve valid problems, but not to make problems valid. Thus, they do not need to explore if a given problem needs further analysis. Currently, in both departments, tools and methods are taught first. How to conduct analysis and design is taught later in the third and fourth years. As a result, during the first two years, students assume that a given requirement or problem is a valid, high quality requirement, and they try to solve it using their own ideas.

Students with SAD training made fewer implicit assumptions and hence more NEA on average than the students without SAD training. This result is parallel to the expected result, and the ratio of the average NEA of students with SAD training to that of students without SAD training was found to be 1,63. This ratio may reflect the impact of SAD training on better analysis studies; hence, ways should be researched to increase this ratio.

It was found that the average NEA is more when prototyping is preferred than when coding is used. Further studies may concentrate on the relationship between prototype development and the number of explicit assumptions made during the analysis studies. As future research, it may be worthy to test if prototype development causes the software systems analyst to make fewer implicit assumptions. Based on the findings of this study, it cannot be inferred that using prototyping causes an analyst to make fewer implicit assumptions.

According to the collected data, the second and the third phases were found to be similar. The third phase of the study has shown that in dealing with implicit assumptions made during analysis, students with SAD training are better than students with no SAD background. Unless implicit assumptions are avoided, users will continue to ask corrections, which will be considered change requests. Different ways to deal with the second challenge of software systems development should be researched. One way is effective training.

Teaching SAD for software engineering students remains an area for further research. Future research may involve gathering data and conducting theoretical studies to model SAD teaching for software engineering, as in this study. The challenges studied may be searched for not only in university environments, as in this study, but also in the industry, in order to compare if they present some similarities.

ACKNOWLEDGMENT

We thank all who voluntarily contributed to the study.

REFERENCES

Aizamil, Z. (2005). Towards an effective software engineering course project, *ICSE'05*, St. Louis, Missouri, USA, 631–632.

Albayrak, O. (2007a). Experiences of teaching systems analysis and design to undergraduate software engineers, A*ISSIGSAND* 2007, (pp. 109–115), Sopot, Poland.

Albayrak, O. (2007b). Software engineering education: Experience and applications of requirements determination and analysis phases (in Turkish) *Proceedings of the third National Software Engineering Symposium, UYMS 2007*, (pp. 15–18), Ankara, Turkey.

Albayrak, O. (2003). Proposals to contribute computer engineers education (in Turkish), *Proceedings of the first. Elektrik Elektronik Bilgisayar Mühendislikleri Eğitimi Sempozyumu ve Sergisi (pp. 220-221)*, Ankara, Turkey.

Archer, C. B. (1985). A realistic approach to teaching systems analysis at the small or medium-sized college, *ACM SIGCSE Bulletin, Proceedings of the sixteenth SIGCSE technical symposium on Computer science education SIGCSE '85*, 17,1, 105–108.

Bagert, D. J. (1998). The challenge of curriculum modeling for an emerging discipline: software engineering, *Frontiers in Education Conference, FIE '98. 28th Annual, 2*, 910–915.

Boehm, B. (2006). A view of 20th and 21st Century Software Engineering, *ICSE'06*, Shanghai, China, (pp. 12–29).

Bagert, D. J., Hilburn, T. B., Hislop, G. W., & Mengel, S. A. (1998). Guidelines for software education: meeting the needs of the 21st Century, *Frontiers in Education Conference, 1998. FIE '98. 28th Annual, 2*, 909.

Ciancarini, P. (2005). On the Education of Future Software Engineers, *ICSE'05*, St. Louis, Missouri, USA, (pp. 649–650).

Cifuentes, C., & Hughes, J. (1994). SE curriculum design: methodologies, formal methods, and life cycle models, *Proceedings of II. Formal methods Software Education Conference*, (pp. 344–346).

Clark, N. (2005). Evaluating student teams developing unique industry projects, *Australian Computing Education Conference*, Newcastle, Australia, *42*, 21–30.

Dawson, R., & Newsham R. (1997). Introducing Software Engineers to the Real World, *IEEE Software, 14*(6), 37–43.

Dawson, R. (2000). Twenty Dirty Tricks to Train Software Engineers, *Proc. 22nd Int'l Conf. Software Eng. (ICSE 00)*, IEEE CS Press, (pp. 209–218).

Dick, M. (2005). Student interviews as a tool for assessment and learning in a systems analysis and design course, *ACM SIGCSE Bulletin, Proceedings of the 10th annual SIGCSE conference on Innovation and technology in computer science education ITiCSE '05, 37*(3), 24–28.

Ellis, H. J. C., Mead, N. R., Moreno, A. M., & Seidman, S. B. (2003). Industry/University software engineering collaborations for the successful reeducation of non-software professionals. *Software Engineering Education and Training, Proceedings. 16th Conference,* (pp. 44–51).

Fellers, J. W. (1996). Teaching teamwork: exploring the use of cooperative learning teams in information systems education, *ACM SIGMIS Database, 27*(2), 44–60.

Ghezzi, C., & Mandrioli, D. (2005). The challenges of software engineering education, *Software Engineering, 2005. ICSE 2005. Proceedings. 27th International Conference,* (pp. 637–638).

Golden, D. G. (1982). Development of a systems analysis and design course, *ACM SIGCE Bulletin, Proceedings of the thirteenth SIGCSE technical symposium on Computer science education SIGCSE '82, 14*(1), 110–113.

Goroff, I. (1982). A systems analysis and design course sequence, *ACM SIGCE Bulletin, Proceedings of the thirteenth SIGCSE technical symposium on Computer science education SIGCSE '82, 14*(1), 123–127.

Hawthorne, M. J., & Perry D. E. (2005). Software Engineering Education in the Era of Outsourcing, Distributed Development, and Open Source Software: Challenges and Opportunities, *ICSE '05*, St. Louis, Missouri, USA, (pp. 643–644).

Hazzan, O., & Tomayko J. (2005). Teaching Human Aspects of Software Engineering, *ICSE '05*, St. Louis, Missouri, USA, 647–648.

Hilburn, T. B. W., & Watts S. (2002). The Impending Changes in Software Education. *IEEE Software, 19*(5), 22–25.

Hunter, M. G. (1994). Excellent Systems Analyst: Key Audience Perceptions. *Computer Personnel,* (pp. 15–31).

IEEE (2004). *SWEBOK, Guide to the Software Engineering Body of Knowledge*. Los Alamitos, California.

Larmour, R. (1997). A survey into the relevance and adequacy of training in systems analysis and design. *ACM SIGCSE Bulletin, 29*(2) , 54–64.

Liu, C. (2005). Enriching Software Engineering Courses with Service-Learning Projects and the Open-Source Approach, *ICSE '05*, St. Louis, Missouri, (pp. 613–614).

McLeod, R. (1996). Comparing undergraduate courses in systems analysis and design. *Communication of the ACM*, 39–5, (pp. 113–121).

Misic, M. M., & Russo, N. L. (1999). An assessment of systems analysis and design courses. *The Journal of Systems and Software, 45*, 197–202.

Mohay, G., Morarji, H., & Thomas, R. (1994). Undergraduate, graduate and professional education in software engineering in the '90s: a case study, *Software Education Conference Proceedings,* (pp. 22–25, 103–110).

Morgan, G. W., & Lear, F. A. (1994). The role of a software engineering project within an undergraduate applied computing degree, *Software Education Conference Proceedings,* (pp. 230–236).

Morrogh, P. (2000). Is software education narrow-minded?—A position paper, *Software Engineering, 2000. Proceedings of the 2000 International Conference,* (pp. 545–546).

Olfman, L. and Bostrom, R.P. (1992). Innovative teaching materials and methods for systems analysis and design, *ACM SIGMIS Database,* 23,2, 7–12.

Omland, H. O. (1999). Educating systems analyst emphasizing the human factor, *ACM SIGCSE*

Bulletin, Proceedings of the 4th annual SIGCSE/ SIGCUE ITiCSE conference on Innovation and technology in computer science education ITiCSE '99, 31(3), 44–47.

Osborne, M. (1992). APPGEN: a tool for teaching systems analysis and design, *ACM SIGCSE Bulletin, Proceedings of the twenty-third SIGCSE technical symposium on Computer science education SIGCSE '92*, *24*(1), 259–263.

Oudshoorn, M.J. and Maciunas, K.J. (1994). Experience with a project-based approach to teaching software engineering, *Software Education Conference, 1994. Proceedings.* (pp. 220–225).

Parnas, D. (1999). Software Engineering Programs Are Not Computer Science Programs, *IEEE Software, 16*(6), 19–30.

Pullan, W. and Oliver, D. (1994). Development of an undergraduate software engineering degree, *Software Education Conference, 1994. Proceedings,* (pp. 111–117).

Schneider, J.-G.; Johnston, L., & Joyce, P. (2005). Curriculum development in educating under-graduate software engineers—Are students being prepared for the profession?, *Software Engineering Conference, 2005. Proceedings.* Australian, (pp. 314–323).

Spence, J. W., & Grout, J. C. (1978). Systems analysis and design in a computer science curriculum, *ACM SIGCSE Bulletin, 10*(4), 24–27.

Thomas, R., Semeczko, G., Morarji, H., & Mohay, G. (1994). Core software engineering subjects: a case study ('86–'94), *Software Education Conference Proceedings*, (pp. 24–31).

Vliet, H. (2005). Some Myths of Software Engineering Education, *ICSE'05*, St. Louis, Missouri, USA, (pp. 621–622).

Vliet, H. (2006). Reflections on software engineering education. *Software, IEEE, 23*(3), 55–61.

Yamaura, T., & Onoma, A. K. (2002). University software education matched to social requests, *Cyber Worlds, Proceedings. First International Symposium,* (pp. 331–336).

Chapter VII
Systems Analysis and Design in Polish Universities Curricula:
Structured or Object–Oriented

Przemyslaw Polak
Warsaw School of Economics, Poland

ABSTRACT

Nowadays, there are two main information systems modeling methods: structured and object-oriented. The structured methods have been widely used since the 1970s, whereas recently the object-oriented methods have attracted more attention. This chapter analyses the methods that are taught on the courses of information systems analysis and design. The curricula of information systems and computer science studies in Polish higher education institutions are compared to the Association for Computing Machinery curricula recommendations. In both cases none of the methods is prevailing. Also, the program of introducing, at the Warsaw School of Economics, Poland, all management and business administration students to the basics of systems analysis and design is presented. Thus, students majoring in information systems learn both modeling methods, whereas only structured methods are introduced to all management students.

INTRODUCTION

In modern systems analysis and design two general group of methods can be distinguished: structured and object-oriented. Structured methods were first introduced in nineteen seventies (DeMarco, 1978; Gene & Sarson, 1979). Since then, they have dominated systems analysis and design for decades, being a subject of only gradual changes including the introduction of event-driven approach and the increased importance of logical models (McMenamin and Palmer, 1984; Yourdon, 1989). Object oriented methods were introduced in the late 80s and early 90s (Coad & Yourdon,

1990; Rumbaugh, Blaha, Premerlani, Eddy, & Lorensen, 1991). Since then, they have gained more attention in research and practice than structured methods.

There is not clear answer to which methods are better, whether their usefulness depends on the area of application, or possibly it's just a case of popularity often accompanying new ideas and technologies, what particularly can be observed in the rapidly changing world of computer science and information systems (e.g. Rickman, 2000; Rob, 2004; Ward, 1989; Weisert, 2006). The purpose of this article is not to answer such a general question but to study which method is taught at business schools and economic universities with a special concentration on Polish higher education institutions.

SYSTEMS ANALYSIS AND DESIGN IN CURRICULA

Courses concerning the methods of information systems modeling are the core of the management information systems curriculum. Usually, they include one mandatory course on systems analysis and design or two separate courses: information systems analysis and information systems design. At specific educational institutions, slightly different names might be used. In 1990s, syllabuses of these courses reached usually high level of maturity and stability, resulting from the popularity and widespread acceptance of the structured modeling methods. Their superiority over describing system logic using natural language which is often imprecise and subject to misinterpretation, what was common practice before the introduction of structured methods, was never contested (Matthies, 1977). However, this standstill was disturbed by the dissemination of object oriented modeling methods, preceded by the development of object oriented programming languages, e.g. Ada, Smalltalk, C++ or Java.

Under these circumstances, teaching staff was faced with the dilemma which of these approaches should have been preferred. Naturally, an ideal solution would include comprehensive courses including both methods. However in reality, most of university curricula are tight, and time limits for particular courses are imposed by independent bodies, where proposals to radically increased one course limit would not be given a lot of support. Different curricula solving that dilemma are presented as follows.

TEACHING STANDARDS OF THE POLISH MINISTRY OF SCIENCE AND HIGHER EDUCATION

The teaching standards published in 2002 by the Minister of National Education and Sport (pol. *Minister Edukacji Narodowej i Sportu - MENiS*)[1] for unified first and second degree[2] Informatics and Econometrics[3] studies (MENiS 1st & 2nd I&E) among majors include a course on information systems design. Its suggested syllabus includes: "Elements of theory of information systems. Types of information systems. Design, implementation and maintenance of information systems. Economical and organizational aspects on information systems. Computer laboratory: information system analysis – case study" (Decree of the Minister of National Education and Sport ..., 2002). The syllabus does not mention any particular modeling methods. The syllabus of IS design suggests doing analysis of information system. It can be assumed that the course was intended to include both analysis and design, but it is not clearly stated, whereas phases of implementation and maintenance are mentioned in the syllabus.

The same ministerial document contains a curriculum of the first degree studies in Informatics and Econometrics (MENiS 1st I&E) which, on the contrary, includes two courses: Information systems analysis, and Information systems design.

The syllabus of the first one consists of: "General characteristics of management information systems. Systems information resources. Searching for information requirements. Systematic information systems analysis. Methods of system examination. Analysis of system structure and behavior. Structured analysis. Modeling methods. Object-oriented analysis, methods and tools. Organization of analysis. Cost and benefit analysis." (Decree of the Minister of National Education and Sport ..., 2002). Thus, the ministry suggests that both methods should be presented. However, it is hard to imagine in a 30-hour course to exercise preparing systems requirements using both methods. The syllabus rather suggests presenting briefly different aspects and methods related to information systems analysis.

The ministerial syllabus of Information systems design in the first degree studies includes: "Characteristics of management information systems. Classification of information systems. Life cycle of information systems. Fundamental project approaches. Organizational and economic aspects of developing information systems. Rules, methods and techniques of information systems design. Selected issues of information systems implementation. Scope, rules and methods of information systems improvement" (Decree of the Minister of National Education and Sport ..., 2002). This course is set for 60 hours. It is an exception because standard course in Polish educational system lasts 30 hours. Therefore, despite the fact that it is not openly stated, it is probably expected to be divided into two equal 30-hour blocks of lecture and class or computer laboratory. The syllabus does not suggest anything about design methods. It is surprising that the life cycle of information systems should be discussed during this course, whereas this topic is not mentioned in syllabuses of other courses in the curriculum, e.g. Information systems analysis or Computer programming. It seems to be reasonable to introduce information systems lifecycle earlier, during the course on Introduction to informatics.

However, its syllabus includes only topics related to information technology alone with no reference to information systems as a comprehensive, functional solution aimed on the fulfillment of users' requirements.

In both cases of the unified first and second degree as well as the first degree studies ministerial curricula leave certain level of freedom for narrow specialty courses. Thanks to this it is possible to expand or add courses related to systems analysis and design and, thereby, introduce students to both structured and object-oriented methods.

Differences in approaches to systems analysis and design can be shown by comparison to the curriculum of computer science studies (MENiS CS). In the ministerial curriculum, there is no course named analysis or design. However, the syllabus of a course Applications - Software Engineering apparently includes systems design, and contains following topics: "Software Engineering. Cycle of designing and life cycle of software. Object-oriented design method. Languages for specification and design. Software testing. Selected supporting tools." (Decree of the Minister of National Education and Sport ..., 2003). So here there is a direct recommendation of object-oriented methods. However, analysis phase is not explicitly mentioned in the syllabus.

In 2007, in Polish tertiary education, the system of unified first and second degree studies was abandoned following the adoption of the Bologna declaration. New teaching standards for separate undergraduate and graduate studies were published by the Ministry of Science and Higher Education. Required content of the first degree studies in Informatics and Econometrics (MNiSW 1st I&E) includes a topic on Information systems design. Both methods are represented in this topic: "Methods and techniques of information systems design – entity-relation diagrams, data flow diagrams, data vocabularies, decision techniques, structure diagrams. Structured design of information systems. Object-oriented systems: basic object model, design based on object-oriented model. Unified Modeling Language." (Decree of the Minister of Science and Higher Education ..., 2007).

On the other hand, the teaching standards of the second degree studies in Informatics and Econometrics do not contain any course on systems analysis and design.

Ministerial standards of the first degree studies in computer science (MNiSW 1st CS) within a field of Software Engineering state that a graduate should have a competence: "to design software in accordance with structured or object-oriented methodology" (Decree of the Minister of Science and Higher Education ..., 2007). It is a significant change in comparison with the curriculum from 2002 which imposed teaching object-oriented methods. A curriculum of the second degree studies in computer science (MNiSW 2st CS) contains a topic on Modeling and analysis of information systems, but none reference to any particular method was included.

ACM CURRICULA RECOMMENDATIONS

IS 2002 (Information Systems) and MSIS 2000 (Master of Science in Information Systems) are model curricula for undergraduate and graduate degree programs in Information Systems. They were developed as a collaborative effort of Association for Computing Machinery (ACM), Association for Information Systems (AIS), Association of Information Technology Professionals (AITP), and International Federation for Information Processing (IFIP). They were created as a consensus of many circles and organizations dealing with information systems and, therefore, are widely acclaimed around the world. They are a source and reference point to many curricula in academic institutions in the United States and other countries (Kobylinski, 2004).

The curriculum of the first degree studies IS 2002 in a presentation area Information Systems

Development embodies Analysis and Logical Design. The scope of this course includes: "Structured and object oriented analysis and design, use of modeling tools, adherence to methodological life cycle and project management standards." (Gorgone, Davis, Valacich, Topi, Feinstein and Longenecker, 2002). The program suggests that students should design a project of limited scope during this course, but again no methods are preferred. The syllabus of another course in this presentation area of the curriculum Physical Design and Implementation with DBMS also recommends both methods: "Conceptual, logical, and physical data models, and modeling tools; structured and object design approaches; models for databases: relational and object oriented; design tools; data dictionaries, repositories, warehousing, and data mining; database implementation including user interface and reports; multi-tier planning and implementation; data conversion and post implementation review." (Gorgone et al., 2002).

The core courses in the second degree MSIS 2000 curriculum include Analysis, modeling, and design. Its syllabus contains "Object-oriented analysis and design" (Gorgone, Gray, Feinstein, Kasper, Luftman, Stohr, Valacich, & Wigand, 1999), but does not mention openly structured methods. Moreover, one of suggested career tracks Systems Analysis & Design includes: "Advanced Design Methodologies (e.g., Object-Oriented Analysis and Design, RAD, prototyping)" (Gorgone et al., 1999). It is worth of noticing that MSIS 2000 curriculum was designed about two years earlier than IS 2002.

Another model curriculum was developed by ACM for undergraduate programs in computer science (CC 2001). The Software engineering area in this curriculum contains the course on Software design. The authors proposed among learning objectives of this course: "Compare and contrast object-oriented analysis and design with structured analysis and design" and "Create and specify the software design for a medium-size software product using a software requirement specification, an accepted program design methodology (e.g., structured or object-oriented), and appropriate design notation." (Computing Curricula ..., 2001).

SYSTEMS ANALYSIS AND DESIGN IN POLISH ACADEMIC INSTITUTIONS

All students of the Warsaw School of Economics (WSE) studying all kinds of economic and business administration majors are introduced to the basics of structured modeling during the compulsory course of Introduction to information systems. The syllabus of this course is significantly different than programs described in equivalent ministerial proposals for respective majors related to business and economics (Decree of the Minister of National Education and Sport ..., 2002). The traditional program of computer laboratories at the WSE was consistent with ministerial suggestion and concentrated on using word processors, spreadsheets and occasionally database systems. The new syllabus was introduced in 2001. Changes were triggered by gradually increasing computer proficiency of enrolled students. The aim of the project was to introduce all management and business administration students to the methods of modeling information systems. These skills might be useful for future users of management information systems participating in defining systems requirements. However, considering that those students do not require thoroughly master developing information systems, the syllabus was limited to structured methods, which are easier to understand for business users (Polak and Polak, 2006).

Analogous approach was taken at the Wroclaw University of Economics (WUE). The syllabus of Introduction to information systems also contains elements of structured modeling. However, in this case, it is 120-hour course allowing authors to incorporate in the syllabus traditional top-ics, according to ministerial proposal, as well as introduction to systems analysis and design (Dyczkowski & Wójtowicz, 2003).

On Economic Universities in Poland and at the Warsaw School of Economics curricula of Informatics and Econometrics[4] include 60 or 90-hour course of Information systems design, following the ministerial standards. None of them has a separate course on systems analysis. However, the faculties of management on the Gdansk, Szczecin and Warsaw Universities offer such 30 or 60-hour course (Dyczkowski & Skwarnik, 2004).

The syllabus of Information systems design at the Warsaw School of Economics does not state preferred modeling methods. In practice, both methods are discussed and the choice of method for a final student project depends on preferences of a lecturer. However, object-oriented methods have been recently preferred since students introduced earlier to structured methods during Introduction to information systems have started to enroll to this course. Additionally, one of the elective courses Business process modeling allows students to increase their knowledge of structured methods in analysis. Similarly, the syllabus of Information systems design on Wroclaw University of Economics suggests presenting both methods but does not specify which should be used in a final project.

Additionally, special studies in Management information systems, carried at the Warsaw School of Economics in cooperation with Microsoft, offer courses on systems analysis and design using both methods and students make their choice of preferred method for final project. Comparable special studies carried at the WSE in cooperation with Oracle are concentrated on Case*Method which is proprietary structured method.

Following the compulsory introduction of independent first and second degree studies in Polish tertiary education, the Warsaw School of Economics also prepared a new curriculum. The introductory course syllabus was not changed and includes elements of structured modeling.

Whereas, the course of Information systems design is in practice dedicated to object-oriented methods. However, new course called Business Applications Development (BAD) was proposed for graduate studies. It is strongly oriented on systems analysis based on identification of business processes followed by the object-oriented application designing fulfilling the requirements of the processes. This solution is analogous to approach suggested in service oriented architecture.

SUMMARY

The study of syllabuses clearly shows that in case of information systems curricula object-oriented methods do not supersede structured modeling methods in systems analysis and design. On the contrary, computer science studies were at some point dominated by object oriented methods, but structured methods regained some attention.

Table 1. Reference to structured and object oriented modeling methods in selected curricula

Syllabus	structured methods	object-oriented methods
IS 2002	+	+
MSIS 2000	-	+
CC 2001	+	+
MENiS 1st & 2nd I&E	-	-
MENiS 1st I&E – Analysis	+	+
MENiS 1st I&E – Design	-	-
MENiS CS	-	+
MNiSW 1st I&E	+	+
MNiSW 1st CS	+	+
MNiSW 2nd CS	-	-
WSE – Introduction to IS	+	-
WSE 1st & 2nd – Design	+	+
WSE 1st – Design	-	+
WSE 2nd – BAD	+	+
WUE – Introduction to IS	+	-
WUE – Design	+	+

There is no data suggesting that Polish curricula in discussed area differ substantially from international model programs. The summary of references to object oriented and structured approaches in syllabuses is shown in Table 1.

Observations indicate that current research in systems analysis and design concentrates on object-oriented methods. However, information systems curricula do not reflect it. Apparently, academic staff finds both methods valuable. It is possible, as well, that stable academic curricula do not keep pace with rapidly changing information technologies. Structured methods also better reflect managerial approach towards business processes, therefore these methods might be preferred in systems analysis on business and management studies. Whereas, object-oriented modeling, better related to contemporary programming languages and methods of building applications, might dominate systems design methods. This trend confirms evolution of CASE tools towards object-oriented methods and concurrent popularity of structured methods used by business process modeling tools, what is conformable to the principles of service oriented architecture (Kaminski, Polak, & Wieczorkowski, 2005).

The research presented in the chapter is limited to the model ACM curricula, the standards of the Polish Ministry of Science and Higher Education and the curricula of some leading Polish academic institutions. Further research might not only compare other curricula but also investigate opinion of academic staff towards both discussed methods of systems analysis and design.

REFERENCES

Computing Curricula 2001. Computer Science. Final Report. (2001) The Joint Task Force on Computing Curricula, IEEE Computer Society, Association for Computing Machinery. Retrieved April 23, 2006 from http://acm.org/education/curric_vols/cc2001.pdf

Coad, P., & Yourdon, E. (1990). *Object-oriented analysis*. Englewood Cliffs: Yourdon Press.

Decree of the Minister of National Education and Sport from April 18th 2002 on designation of teaching standards for respective studies and levels of education [in Polish - Rozporządzenie Ministra Edukacji Narodowej i Sportu z dnia 18 kwietnia 2002 r. w sprawie określenia standardów nauczania dla poszczególnych kierunków studiów i poziomów kształcenia]. (2002). *Dziennik Ustaw*, 116, 1004.

Decree of the Minister of National Education and Sport from June 13th 2003 changing decree on designation of teaching standards for respective studies and levels of education [in Polish - Rozporządzenie Ministra Edukacji Narodowej i Sportu z dnia 13 czerwca 2003 r. zmieniające rozporządzenie w sprawie określenia standardów nauczania dla poszczególnych kierunków studiów i poziomów kształcenia]. (2003). *Dziennik Ustaw*, 144, 1401.

Decree of the Minister of Science and Higher Education from July 12th 2007 on designation of teaching standards for respective studies and levels of education, as well as a procedure of creating and conditions which should be satisfy in order to run cross-field and macro-field studies [in Polish - Rozporządzenie Ministra Edukacji i Szkolnictwa Wyższego z dnia 12 lipca 2007 r. w sprawie określenia standardów kształcenia dla poszczególnych kierunków studiów i poziomów kształcenia, a także trybu tworzenia i warunków, jakie musi spełniać uczelnia, by prowadzić studia międzykierunkowe oraz makrokierunki]. (2007). *Dziennik Ustaw, 164*, 1166.

DeMarco, T. (1978). *Structured analysis and system specification*. Englewood Cliffs: Prentice Hall.

Dyczkowski, M., & Skwarnik, M. (2004). National Academic Institutions Curricula Review [in Polish - Prezentacja programów kształcenia w uczelniach krajowych]. In A. Nowicki (Ed.), *Doskonalenie kształcenia informatycznego na kierunku Informatyka i Ekonometria na wydziale Zarządzania i Informatyki Akademii Ekonomicznej we Wrocławiu. Część 1. Identyfikacja kształcenia w obszarze informatyki* (pp. 46-66). Wrocław: Akademia Ekonomiczna we Wrocławiu.

Dyczkowski, M., & Wójtowicz, R. (2003). The concept of computer laboratory courses for non information systems students, example of business informatics [in Polish - Koncepcja prowadzenia zajęć laboratoryjnych dla studentów kierunków nieinformatycznych na przykładzie przedmiotu informatyka ekonomiczna]. In A. Nowicki, W. Olejniczak (Eds.). *Dydaktyka informatyki ekonomicznej – kształcenie dla społeczeństwa informacyjnego* (pp. 133-138). Wrocław: Akademia Ekonomiczna we Wrocławiu.

Gane, C., & Sarson, T. (1979). *Structured systems analysis: Tools and techniques*. Englewood Cliffs: Prentice-Hall.

Gorgone, J. T., Davis, G. B., Valacich, J. S., Topi, H., Feinstein, D. L., & Longenecker, H. E. Jr. (2002). *IS 2002. Model curriculum and guidelines for undergraduate degree programs in information systems*. Association for Computing Machinery (ACM), Association for Information Systems (AIS), Association of Information Technology Professionals (AITP). Retrieved April 23, 2006 from http://www.acm.org/education/is2002.pdf

Gorgone, J. T., Gray, P., Feinstein, D. L., Kasper, G. M., Luftman, J. N., Stohr, E. A., Valacich, J. S., & Wigand, R. T. (1999). *MSIS 2000. Model Curriculum and Guidelines for Graduate Degree Programs in Information Systems*. Association for Computing Machinery (ACM), Association for Information Systems (AIS). Retrieved April 23, 2006 from http://cis.bentley.edu/isa/pages/documents/msis2000jan00.pdf

Kaminski, A., Polak, P., & Wieczorkowski, J. (2005). Process approach in MIS implementation – business process modeling tools [in Polish - Podejście procesowe we wdrażaniu SIZ – narzędzia modelowania procesów biznesowych]. In E. Niedzielska, H. Dudycz & M. Dyczkowski (Eds.), Nowoczesne technologie informacyjne w zarządzaniu, *Prace Naukowe Akademii Ekonomicznej we Wrocławiu, 1081*, 278-287.

Kobylinski, A. (2004). The comparison of business informatics curriculum at the Warsaw School of Economics with model IS 2002 curriculum [in Polish - Porównanie programu nauczania informatyki gospodarczej w Szkole Głównej Handlowej w Warszawie z modelowym curriculum IS 2002]. In J. Goliński, D. Jelonek, A. Nowicki (eds.), Informatyka ekonomiczna. Przegląd naukowo-dydaktyczny, *Prace Naukowe Akademii Ekonomicznej we Wrocławiu, 1027*, 270-279.

Matthies, L. (1977). *The new playscript procedure*. Stamford: Office Publications Inc.

McMenamin, S. M., & Palmer, J. F. (1984). *Essential systems analysis*. New York: Yourdon Press.

Polak, P., & Polak, D. (2006). The changes in curriculum of business informatics computer laboratories in economic universities [in Polish - Zmiany w programie laboratorium z informatyki gospodarczej na uczelniach ekonomicznych]. In A. Szewczyk (Ed.), *Dydaktyka informatyki i informatyka w dydaktyce* (pp. 188-191). Szczecin: Uniwersytet Szczeciński.

Rickman, D. M. (2000). *A Process for Combining Object Oriented and Structured Analysis and Design*. 3rd Annual Systems Engineering & Supportability Conference. Retrieved February 14, 2007 from http://www.dtic.mil/ndia/systems/Rickman2.pdf

Rob, M. A. (2004). Issues of structured vs. object-oriented methodology of systems analysis and design. *Issues in Information Systems, 5*, 275-280.

Rumbaugh, J., Blaha, M., Premerlani, W., Eddy, F., & Lorensen, W. (1991). *Object-oriented modeling and design*. Englewood Cliffs: Prentice Hall.

Ward, P. T. (1989). How to integrate object orientation with structured analysis and design. *IEEE Software, 6*(2), 74-82.

Weisert, T. (2006). *Systems Analysis Methodology Sliding Backwards*, Chicago: Information Disciplines Inc. Retrieved January 15, 2007 from http://www.idinews.com/story.html

Yourdon, E. (1989). *Modern structured analysis*. Englewood Cliffs: Yourdon Press.

ENDNOTES

[1] Currently tertiary education is a domain of the Ministry of Science and Higher Education (pol. *Ministerstwo Nauki i Szkolnictwa Wyższego - MNiSW*).

[2] This form of 5-6 year studies was dominant in Polish tertiary education. Recently independent undergraduate and postgraduate studies has been introduced to Polish higher education.

[3] "Informatics and Econometrics" is a direct translation of the Polish Ministry of Science and Higher Education official name for information systems and quantitative methods studies.

[4] At the Warsaw School of Economics an equivalent major of Informatics and Econometrics is named Quantitative methods in economy and information systems.

Chapter VIII
Systems Engineering Modeling and Design

Kumar Saurabh
Satyam Computer Services Ltd., India

ABSTRACT

System theories, analysis and design have been deployed within every corporate function and within a broad section of businesses and markets. Systems thinking involve changing paradigms about the way the world works, the way corporations function, and the human role in each. In systems thinking, analysis and design we look for interrelationships among the elements of a system. The chapter reflects the core insights of system modeling. This chapter addresses the core issues of system engineering, analysis, design, Simulation and modeling of real-world objects. It tells everything one needs to know to be a successful system thinker, modeler, technical manager and forecaster. The chapter focuses on: the real-world goals for, services provided by, and constraints on systems; the precise specification of system structure and behavior, and the implementation of specifications; the activities required in order to develop an assurance that the specifications and real-world goals have been met; the evolution of systems over time and across system families. It is also concerned with the processes, methods and tools for the development of systems in an economic and timely manner.

1. INTRODUCTION

This widespread acceptance and deployment of system theories means System engineering, analysis and design and modeling are now more on the critical path than ever before.

This chapter should be an interesting source of information both for people who want to experi-
ment with their thinking and simulating the real world who face the need to deal with the inner levels of system engineering concepts. We hope this chapter is useful as a starting point for people who want to become system analyst and architect but don't know where to start.

On the technical side, this text should offer a hands-on approach to understanding the system theory and thinking, modeling, simulation, knowledge management, system analysis and design, system forecasting and different types of real world modeling techniques like techno-socio-economic modeling and some of the design choices made by the system developers for auditing and output designs from scratch.

The first part of the chapter deals system engineering, analysis, design theories and thinking concepts. This part visualizes an interdisciplinary approach and means to enable the realization of successful systems. It focuses on defining customer needs and required functionality early in the development cycle, documenting requirements, and then proceeding with design synthesis and system validation while considering the complete problem. Second part works with the system analysis design modeling concepts and its types. It reflects that computer model, as used in modeling and simulation science, is a mathematical representation of something—a person, a building, a vehicle, a tree—any object and a model also can be a representation of a process. Third part will give the inputs to understand the dynamics of the system. This chapter is based on system dynamics that is a computer-based simulation modeling methodology tool for managers to analyze complex problems. Using system dynamics simulations allows us to see not just events, but also patterns of behaviour over time. The behaviour of a system often arises out of the structure of the system itself, and behaviour usually changes over time.

This chapter will give you the knowledge of important sections from the scratch, step-by-step procedures, and the skills necessary to effectively system thinker, modeler, Analyst, technical and solution architect.

2. SYSTEM THEORY AND THINKING

One of the biggest breakthroughs in how we understand and guide change in organizations is systems theory and systems thinking. To understand how they are used in organizations, we first must understand a system. Many of us have an intuitive understanding of the term. However, we need to make the understanding explicit in order to use systems thinking and systems tools in organizations.

Simply put, a system is an organized collection of parts (or subsystems) that are highly integrated to accomplish an overall goal. The system has various inputs, which go through certain processes to produce certain outputs, which together, accomplish the overall desired goal for the system. So a system is usually made up of many smaller systems, or subsystems. For example, an organization is made up of many administrative and management functions, products, services, groups and individuals. If one part of the system is changed, the nature of the overall system is often changed, as well -- by definition then, the system is systemic, meaning relating to, or affecting, the entire system. (This is not to be confused with systematic, which can mean merely that something is methodological. Thus, methodological thinking -- systematic thinking -- does not necessarily mean systems thinking.)

2.1 System Theory

History and Orientation

Hegel developed in the 19th century a theory to explain historical development as a dynamic process. Marx and Darwin used this theory in their work. System theory (as we know it) was used by L. von Bertalanffy, a biologist, as the basis for the field of study known as 'general system theory', a multidisciplinary field (1968). Some influences from the contingency approach can be found in system theory.

Core Assumptions and Statements

System theory is the trans-disciplinary study of the abstract organization of phenomena, independent of their substance, type, or spatial or temporal scale of existence. It investigates both the principles common to all complex entities, and the (usually mathematical) models which can be used to describe them.

Most systems share the same *common characteristics*. These common characteristics include the following:

1. Systems have a **structure** that is defined by its parts and processes.
2. Systems are **generalizations** of **reality**.
3. Systems tend to **function** in the same way. This involves the **inputs** and **outputs** of **material** (**energy** and/or **matter**) that is then processed causing it to change in some way.
4. The various parts of a system have **functional** as well as **structural relationships** between each other.
5. The fact that functional relationships exist between the parts suggests the **flow** and **transfer** of some type of **energy** and/or **matter**.
6. Systems often exchange energy and/or matter beyond their defined boundary with the outside environment, and other systems, through various **input** and **output** processes.
7. Functional relationships can only occur because of the presence of a **driving force**.
8. The parts that make up a system show some degree of **integration** - in other words the parts work well together.

Within the boundary of a system we can find three kinds of *properties*:

- **Elements:** Are the kinds of parts (things or substances) that make up a system. These parts may be atoms or molecules, or larger bodies of matter like sand grains, rain drops, plants, animals, etc.

- **Attributes:** Are characteristics of the elements that may be perceived and measured. For example: quantity, size, color, volume, temperature, and mass.
- **Relationships:** Are the associations that occur between elements and attributes. These associations are based on cause and effect.

We can define the state of the system by determining the value of its *properties* (the elements, attributes, and/or relationships).

Scientists have examined and *classified* many types of systems. Some of the classified types include:

- **Isolated system:** A system that has no interactions beyond its boundary layer. Many controlled laboratory experiments are this type of system.
- **Closed system:** Is a system that transfers energy, but not matter, across its boundary to the surrounding environment. Our planet is often viewed as a closed system.
- **Open system:** Is a system that transfers both matter and energy can cross its boundary to the surrounding environment. Most ecosystems are example of open systems.
- **Morphological system:** This is a system where we understand the relationships between elements and their attributes in a vague sense based only on measured features or correlations. In other words, we understand the form or morphology a system has based on the connections between its elements. We do not understand exactly how the processes work to transfer energy and/or matter through the connections between the elements.

2.2 Systems Engineering

A management technology involving the interactions of science, an organization, and its environment as well as the information and knowledge bases that support each. The purpose of systems engineering is to support organizations that desire improved performance. This improvement is generally obtained through the definition, development, and deployment of technological products, services, or processes that support functional objectives and fulfill needs. It is a comprehensive, iterative technical management process that includes translating operational requirements into configured systems, integrating the technical inputs of the entire design team, managing interfaces, characterizing and managing technical risk, transitioning technology from the technology base into program specific efforts, and verifying that designs meet operational needs. It is a life cycle activity that demands a concurrent approach to both product and process development.

Systems engineering has triple bases: a physical (natural) science basis, an organizational and social science basis, and an information science and knowledge basis. The natural science basis involves primarily matter and energy processing. The organizational and social science basis involves human, behavioral, economic, and enterprise concerns. The information science and knowledge basis is derived from the structure and organization inherent in the natural sciences and in the organizational and social sciences.

2.3 The Scope of System Engineering Activities

One way to understand the motivation behind systems engineering is to see it as a method, or practice, to identify and improve common rules that exist within a wide variety of systems.

At times a systems engineer must assess the existence of feasible solutions, and rarely will customer inputs arrive at only one. Some customer requirements will produce no feasible solution. Constraints must be traded to find one or more feasible solutions. The customers' wants become the most valuable input to such a trade

and cannot be assumed. Those wants/desires may only be discovered by the customer once the customer finds that he has over constrained the problem. Most commonly, many feasible solutions can be found, and a sufficient set of constraints must be defined to produce an optimal solution. This situation is at times advantageous because one can present an opportunity to improve the design towards one or many ends, such as cost or schedule. Various modeling methods can be used to solve the problem including constraints and a cost function.

Systems engineering encourages the use of modeling and simulation to validate assumptions or theories on systems and the interactions within them. Use of methods that allow early detection of possible failures are integrated into the design process. At the same time, decisions made at the beginning of a project whose consequences are not clearly understood can have enormous implications later in the life of a system, and it is the task of the modern systems engineer to explore these issues and make critical decisions. There is no method which guarantees that decisions made today will still be valid when a system goes into service years or decades after it is first conceived but there are techniques to support the process of systems engineering. Examples include the use of soft systems methodology, Jay Wright Forrester's System Dynamics method is currently being explored, evaluated and developed to support the engineering decision making process.

Initially, when the primary purpose of a systems engineer is to comprehend a complex problem, graphic representations of a system are used to communicate a system's functional and data requirements

3. INTRODUCTION TO SYSTEM DYNAMICS

System dynamics is a computer-based simulation modeling methodology developed at the Massachusetts Institute of Technology (MIT) in the 1950s as a tool for managers to analyze complex problems. Its primary audience is still managers, although it has spread widely in academia, where professors and students use it to model systems from every conceivable discipline ranging from history and literature to biology, physics, and economics.

The word "dynamic" implies continuous change and that is what dynamic systems do – they continuously change over time. Their position, or state, is not the same today as it was yesterday and tomorrow it would have changed yet again.

Using system dynamics simulations allows us to see not just events, but also patterns of behaviour over time. The behaviour of a system often arises out of the structure of the system itself, and behaviour usually changes over time. Sometimes the simulation looks backward, to historical results. At other times it looks forward into the future, to predict possible future results. Understanding patterns of behaviour, instead of focusing on day-to-day events, can offer a radical change in perspective. It shows how a system's own structure is the cause of its successes and failures. This structure is represented by a series of causally linked relationships. The implication is that decisions made within an organization have consequences, some of which are intentional and some are not. Some of these consequences will be seen immediately while others might not be seen for several years.

System dynamics simulations are good at communicating not just what might happen, but also why. This is because system dynamics simulations are designed to correspond to what is, or might be happening, in the real world.

3.1 System Dynamics as Simulation Modeling

System dynamics is a subset of the field of simulation modeling. Simulation modeling is widely practiced in many traditional disciplines such as engineering, economics, and ecology. Since the formulation of differential equations to simulate the progression of systems through time is nearly a free-form exercise, with very few paradigmatic constraints, simulation modeling is usually shaped by the paradigm of discipline more than by the modeling technique. The concept of simulating a system is too general and unstructured to be in itself a paradigm that helps one organize questions and observations about the world.

System dynamics, however, includes not only the basic idea of simulation, but also a set of concepts, representational techniques, and beliefs that make it into a definite modeling paradigm. It shapes the world view of its practitioners.

3.2 System Simulation Analysis and Design

System development can generally be thought of having two major components: systems simulation & analysis and systems design. In System simulation & analysis more emphasis is given to understanding the details of an existing system or a proposed one and then deciding whether the proposed system is desirable or not and whether the existing system needs improvements. Thus, system analysis is the process of investigating a system, identifying problems, and using the information to recommend improvements to the system.

System design is the process of planning a new business system or one to replace or complement an existing system. Analysis specifies what the system should do. Design states how to accomplish the objective. After the proposed system is analyzed and designed, the actual implementation of the system occurs. After implementation, working system is available and it requires timely maintenance.

System dynamicists are not primarily concerned with forecasting specific values of system variables in specific years. They are much more interested in general dynamic tendencies; under

Figure 1. The various stages involved in building an improved system

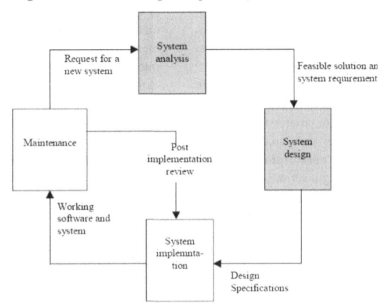

what conditions the system as a whole is stable or unstable, oscillating, growing, declining, self-correcting, or in equilibrium.

The primary assumption of the system dynamics paradigm is that the persistent dynamic tendencies of any complex system arise from its internal causal structure - from the pattern of physical constraints and social goals, rewards, and pressures that cause people to behave the way they do and to generate cumulatively the dominant dynamic tendencies of the total system. A system dynamicist is likely to look for explanations of recurring long-term social problems within this internal structure rather than in external disturbances, small maladjustments, or random events.

The central concept that system dynamicists use to understand system structure is the idea of two-way causation or feedback. It is assumed that social or individual decisions are made on the basis of information about the state of the system or environment surrounding the decision-makers. The decisions lead to actions that are intended to change (or maintain) the state of the system. New

information about the system state then produces further decisions and changes Each such closed chain of causal relationships forms a feedback loop. System dynamics models are made up of many such loops linked together. They are basically closed-system representations; most of the variables occur in feedback relationships and are endogenous. When some factor is believed to influence the system from the outside without being influenced itself, however, it is represented as an exogenous variable in the model.

3.3 Solving Problems

When confronted with problems or new situations, we can react to them in several possible ways. The approach we select is based on prior experience and our knowledge of the problem at hand. The most common approach to new problems and situations is to take them apart and examine their pieces. We do this in the hope that by understanding the pieces we will also be able to understand the entire problem or situation at hand. We are taught this method in our youth and it is reinforced almost daily. This approach helps us to manage the incredible amount of data, stress, problems, and chaos that bombards us every day. If we didn't have this ability, all but the simplest problems would appear overwhelming.

Although this method is a good approach in some situations, it can be inappropriate or even dangerous under different circumstances. More sophisticated approaches are usually required when investigating corporate problems. If a company is experiencing a serious threat to its survival, be it declining market shares or disagreements with the labor union, resources are mobilized to deal with the problem. The company might already be divided into "parts", such as the accounting department, the sales department, and so on. Problems affecting the entire company are often blamed on a department, as when a loss in market shares causes executives to target the sales department for investigation or punishment. The reason for the problem might seem obvious. The company must be losing market shares because the salespeople are not selling the product. What is often lost in the picture is the fact that the sales department depends on many other departments to do its job.

Deficiencies may be in any or all of them. Perhaps the management information services department has not provided the salespeople with the computer support they need. Or maybe manufacturing has been suffering from poor scheduling of orders and a backlog has developed. This will in turn make it harder for the salespeople to sell the product to customers who want an immediate delivery. A number of factors may be the cause of the problem, which may come to light only when the interactions among all parts of the corporation, and not just the parts themselves, are examined.

3.4 Connecting the Pieces

We are viewing a system when we look at a group of individual parts, as well as the connections or interactions among these parts. A corporation is an example of such a system, composed of many departments that in turn act as systems themselves. When we study the parts and the interactions between them, we in fact study the entire system.

The study of systems is not new. It dates back to the 1920s when researchers from different disciplines began to see that many patterns were common to all fields. A new field, general systems theory, developed around the notion that no matter how different the parts of individual systems were, they were put together using a set of rules common to all.

Systems theory suggests that knowledge of one type of system can be applied to many other types. By studying interactions and connections between the pieces of a system, we can gain knowledge that can be useful when confronted with other problems. Systems theory expands further to include two major fields in management science: systems thinking and system dynamics.

3.5 Systems Thinking and System Dynamics

The ideas we have presented thus far are important in both systems thinking and system dynamics. Systems thinking involve changing paradigms about the way the world works, the way corporations function, and the human role in each. In systems thinking we look for interrelationships among the elements of a system. We do this to avoid placing blame in favor of finding the true, long-term solution to a problem. Seeing the interrelationships can also help us find leverage points within a system (places where a slight change will have a tremendous effect on the system's behaviour). Gaining awareness about how the system is built up and how it works can also help us to avoid solutions that only treat the symptoms of an underlying problem without curing the problem itself. System thinking is powerful because it helps us to see our own mental models and how these models color our perception of the world. In many cases, it is difficult for us to alter our mental models. There are always some beliefs or viewpoints that we are not willing to change, no matter what evidence is presented against it. This causes a certain resistance to new concepts. Problems can occur, however, when a rigid mental model stands in the way of a solution that might solve a problem. In such situations, adherence to mental models can be dangerous to the health of the organization. We all use mental models every day. Our minds do not contain real economic or social systems. Instead, they contain representations - models - of reality. We use these models in all aspects of decision-making. Being explicitly aware of our mental models can help us in understanding why we make the decisions we do and how we can improve our decision-making processes. If everyone's mental models are brought to light in the context of an organization, we can begin to see where, how, and why the models diverge. This is the first step in building a shared understanding within an organization. As long as mental models remain hidden, they constitute an obstacle to building shared understanding.

System dynamics is closely related to systems thinking. System dynamics was invented to give managers a tool to understand the complex systems that they were charged with controlling. The methodology uses computer simulation models to relate the structure of a system to its behaviour over time. Viewed in this way, system dynamics can translate the understanding gained by systems thinking into a computer simulation model. By experimenting with this prototype of the system at hand, we can gain further knowledge about the system. System dynamics is capable of creating a learning environment - a laboratory that acts like the system in miniature. Even if building a learning organization - an organization with a high degree of shared understanding and knowledge about how the organization works - isn't the goal, systems thinking can be a very valuable tool at the outset of a system dynamics study. It helps bring

together the people necessary to the success of the system dynamics study, and get them in a frame of mind that is open to new ideas, and allow an evolution of mental models. For change to be successfully implemented people must be motivated to learn and able to act on what they've learned, and they must be in an environment of open and honest exchange. Systems thinking, by helping people in an organization see what the problems are and how their mental models contribute to the problems, set the stage for a successful system dynamics study.

When we conduct a systems thinking or system dynamics study, we must base it on existing information. The information we can use exists on several levels. The largest and most complete information available to us is our mental information; everything we carry in our heads. In sheer size, this information database is the largest and most complete available to us. Next is the written database, which may be smaller by a factor of a hundred or even a thousand. It represents all the information we have on thesis or stored electronically. Finally, we have a numerical database, representing all information that is stored as numbers and constituting another hundred- or thousand fold loss in the amount and richness of the information. Obviously, the place to find the most complete information about a situation is in the mental database. What we do with that information is another matter. The human mind is a brilliant storage device, but we do have trouble relating cause and effect, especially when they are not close in time. In such cases, we cannot reliably predict the outcome of any but the simplest situations with the simplest inputs. This is one of the reasons why computer simulation can be a useful addition to the method of systems thinking. A systems thinking study usually produces causal-loop diagrams to map the feedback structure of a system, and generic structures to illustrate common behaviour. System dynamics takes the information about a system's structure that normally remains hidden in mental models and formalizes it into a computer model. The behaviour generated by that particular structure is revealed when the model is simulated. It constitutes a powerful tool for understanding complex problems. Instead of trying to relate pieces of information in our heads, we can use the computers to formalize our ideas and assumptions and then simulate them through time. That is the beauty and power of system dynamics models.

3.6 The Tools and Rules of System Dynamics

System dynamics simulations are based on the principle of cause and effect, feedback, and delay. Some simple simulations will incorporate only one or two of these principles. More sophisticated simulations will use all three to produce the kind of behaviour we encounter in the real world.

3.6.1 Cause and Effect

Cause and effect is a simple idea, but some simulations based on methodologies other than system dynamics don't use it. The idea is that actions and decisions have consequences. Price affects sales. Births affect the size of a population. Advertising affects market awareness. If we examine these cause and effect relationships isolated, they are usually very easy to understand. However, when they are combined into long chains of cause and effect, they can become complex. This is one reason for using simulations. The human mind is good at developing intuition around complex problems, but poor at keeping track of dozens, hundreds, or even thousands of interconnections and cause and effect relationships.

We can create causal-loop diagrams, as are often used in systems thinking to illustrate cause and effect relationships. In such diagrams we use arrows to indicate the relationships. Sometimes, information about the way in which the relationship works is also included in the diagram. A mark "o" or "–" on the diagram implies a "change in

Figure 2. A simple causal-loop diagram illustrating connections between price, sales, and unit costs

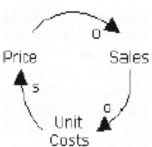

the opposite direction." The relationship between price and sales is such a relationship, where an increase in price leads to a decrease in sales. The relationship between births and population is of another type. When births increase, so does the population. This is a situation where a change leads to a "change in the same direction". It is shown by marking "s" or "+" on the arrow in the diagram.

Figure 2 shows a simple causal-loop diagram. In this diagram, which we will discuss closer in the next section, price has a negative effect on sales, which in turn has a negative effect on unit costs, which in turn has a positive effect on price.

3.6.2 Feedback

Feedback is a concept that most people associate with microphones and speakers. A microphone that isn't properly set up will pick up the sound coming from its own speaker. This sound gets amplified further by the speaker and picked up by the microphone again. This process keeps going until the speaker is producing the loudest sound it can or the microphone cannot pick up any louder sound. If the microphone and the speaker were set up correctly, the system would work linearly. The loudness of the sound going into the microphone would only affect the loudness of the sound coming out of the speaker. Because of the misplacement of the microphone, however, the loudness of sound coming out of the speaker also affects the loudness of sound going into the microphone. Cause and effect feed back on each other. This is the general principle of feedback - that some causal chains are linked together so that cause and effect feed back to each other. This happens everywhere in real world in all kinds of systems, though people are often not aware of it.

Epidemic is another example. Viruses spread when a member of an infected population comes into contact with someone, who is uninfected, but susceptible. This person then becomes part of the infected population, and can spread the virus to others. The larger the infected population, the more contacts, the larger the infected population.

The simple causal-loop diagram illustrates feedback as seen in a price and sales example. If we used a cost-based pricing strategy, then we could show that as sales increase, the unit costs for the product goes down. As the unit costs go down, the price can go down. As the price goes down, the sales go up. The causal-loop diagram of Figure 2 shows that the price we charge today will affect what we charge in the future. A low price will increase sales and reduce unit costs, making it possible to further reduce price in the future. A high price will reduce sales and increase

unit costs, making it necessary to increase price in the future. This is obviously not the whole story. This structure is only one part of a larger system and the level of price and sales are also subject to influences from other variables in the system. But still, this isolated feedback loop is easy to understand. Feedback relationships can produce a variety of behaviours in real systems and in simulations of real systems. Figure 3 illustrates four common behaviours created by various feedback loops.

3.6.3 Building Blocks in System Dynamics

Simulation tools is a modeling environment based on the science of system dynamics. Simulation tool allows us to model systems - with all their cause and effect relationships, feedback loops, and delays - in an intuitive graphical manner. Symbols representing levels, flows, and "helper" variables (so called auxiliaries) are used to create graphical representations of the system in constructor diagrams. Flows and information links represent relationships and interconnections. The entire structure of a system, no matter how complex, can be represented in Simulation tool by the use of these variables and connections.

- **LEVELS AND FLOWS**

In a system dynamics model, the structure of the system is represented mathematically. A level

Figure 3. Four common behaviours created by various feedback loops

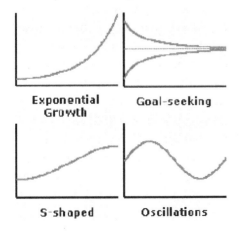

Figure 4. Integrating a function measures the area underneath the function

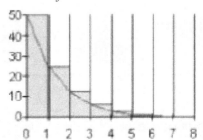

is the accumulation (or integration) of the flows that causes the level to change. In integrating a function, we are simply measuring the area underneath the function by dividing it into equal-width partitions and then summing up the area of all the partitions. This is illustrated in Figure 4.

When creating a simulation model graphically in Simulation tool, connecting the variable symbols generates the integral (flow) equations. Every variable in the model is defined by an equation, in the same way as cells in a spreadsheet are defined. In Simulation tool, boxes represent levels. Double arrows represent the flows, and that is controlled by a flow rate. The flow rate is defined in the same way as auxiliaries. Figure 5 shows a simple model when created graphically in Simulation tool.

The cloud-like symbol to the left of the first flows and to the right of the second flow represents source and sink of the structure, respectively. The cloud symbol indicates infinity and marks the boundary of the model. For instance, in the simple structure illustrated in the Figure 5, the level is the 'Workforce', measured in people, which is increased by the 'Hiring Rate' (flow) and decreased by the 'Firing Rate' (flow). The clouds tell us that in this model we are not concerned with where the hired people come from or where the fired people go. That information is beyond the model boundaries. If we were interested in including this information, we could add another level to the left of the hiring rate and one to the right of the firing rate extending the model boundary. This is shown in Figure 6, where we have the hiring rate

Figure 5 A simple model created in the graphical modeling language

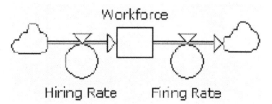

Figure 6. The model with extended model boundaries

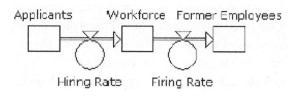

Figure 7. Auxiliary

draining a level of applicants, and the firing rate adding to a level of former employees.

• AUXILIARIES

While it is possible to create an entire model with only levels and flows, Simulation tool has a few more tools to help us to capture real-world phenomena in a model. To achieve a certain level of detail or to aid in the formulation of flow rate equations, it is sometimes necessary to model a variable as an auxiliary. In Simulation tool, a circle represents auxiliaries, as shown in Figure 7.

An auxiliary is used to combine or reformulate information. It has no standard form; it is an algebraic computation of any combination of levels, flow rates, or other auxiliaries. Although auxiliary variables may appear to be accumulations, they have no memory, unlike levels. Auxiliaries are used to model information, not the physical flow of goods, so they change with no delay, instantaneously. They can be inputs to flows, but never directly to levels, because flows are the only variables that change their associated levels. Levels, however, can be inputs to auxiliaries. Note that flow rates and auxiliaries are defined in exactly

Figure. 8 Constant

the same manner. The difference is that the flow rate is connected to the flow valve, and thereby controls the flow directly.

• CONSTANTS

Constants are, unlike ordinary auxiliaries, constant over the time period of the simulation. A diamond represents these constants, as shown in Figure 8.

A constant is defined by an initial value, and maintains this value throughout the simulation, unless the user changes the value manually (by using a slider bar, for example). For instance, in a one-year simulation, a company may have an essentially fixed workforce that can be represented as a constant auxiliary. If the simulation were to expand to 20 years, however, workforce would most likely become a level and be allowed to vary over time. Sometimes we find ourselves confused about whether an element of the system should be included as a constant or auxiliary or as a level. In these situations we should try to rethink the problem. We should think of the time period of the problematic behaviour and whether or not it is reasonable to expect the element to change over that period. We will then be in a better position to decide what elements should be constants and what elements should be allowed to vary during the simulation.

• INFORMATION LINKS

Connections are made among constants, auxiliaries, and levels by means of information links. These links appear as thin connectors in the constructor diagram, as shown in Figure 9.

Figure 9. Information links connects various variables

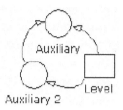

Figure. 10 A closed feedback loop representing the interest earned from an account in a bank

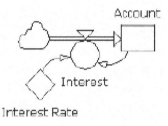

Information links show how the individual elements of the system are put together. In a sense they close the feedback loops. We have already seen how flows change the levels by filling them or draining them. Information links can transfer the value of the level back to the flow, indicating a dependence of the flow on the level, as well as the obvious dependence of the level on the flow, as seen in Figure 10.

3.7 Decisions and Policies

Many people intuitively understand the difference between decisions and policies. However, we often do not realize that every decision we make is somehow governed by a policy. Even the system of a swinging pendulum can be described in terms of its "decisions" in the face of governing policies (the rules of physics). Within corporations, the distinction between the two is extremely important. Managers must often make decisions based on limited information and their own previous experience. They may have little or no control over what information they receive, what form it is in, when they receive it, or how much they receive. When their decisions turn out to be wrong, they are often blamed for misinterpreting the data. Sometimes the conclusion is that the manager simply didn't have enough information to make the correct choice. Unfortunately, the actual problem is usually much deeper. As mentioned earlier, the behaviour of a system is a consequence of its structure. Therefore, the only real changes we can make to a system are changes to the structure. Other changes to the system will soon be canceled out through the actions of negative feedback loops. Providing the managers with more and more information is not necessarily the correct solution, since too much detail or complexity might do more harm than good. It is often a better idea to examine the structure of the organization. This way we can gain knowledge and insight about the policies of the company; the rules of the organization, spoken or unspoken, implicit or explicit, that provides the setting for decisions.

3.7.1 Decision-Making Process

Decisions must always be based on observable variables. In a system dynamics model, this means that decisions must be based entirely upon levels, as flows are never instantaneously observable and therefore can never affect instantaneous decision-making. In the aforementioned example, the decision on how much inventory to order must be based on the present value of the level of inventory. Levels can represent the actual state of the system at a given point in time (current inventory) or the desired state of the system (desired inventory). When there is discrepancy between actual and desired conditions, corrective actions are usually taken to move the actual state closer to the desired state. The first attempt to solve a complex problem rarely succeeds. This is not surprising, given the complex cause and effect relationships

and feedback loops that exist in most systems we are in contact with. Usually, corrections change the system and lead to a total redefinition of the problem. Decisions are attempts to move the system toward our goals. Actual conditions are continuously compared to the desired conditions and action is taken according to the discrepancy between them. This is an iterative process. In the context of a corporate model, decisions could be how many orders to submit to the supplier to replace inventory, how many workers to hire, or when to replace capital equipment. A decision to replenish inventory should be based on the present level of inventory (a level) and not on the rate of sales (a flow). Levels should be the only inputs to decisions; decisions control the flows to and from levels, and the flows determine the change in the levels. As Forrester states "Only rates [flows] resulting from decisions change levels. Only levels control decisions and rates of flows. In other words, decisions control all processes of change". Decisions are governed by policies. Therefore, the way decisions control change is through policies. Flows are defined by equations, and these equations are statements of system policy. Policies describe how and why decisions are made. Specifically, it is the policy statement that attempts to move the system toward a goal. It provides the connection between information inputs and the resulting decisions stream.

Policies may be informal, such as a consequence of habit, intuition, personal interest, and social pressures and power within the organization. They can also be explicit, with a formal awareness of the reasons of action. In the latter case, participants know exactly what policies are guiding their decisions and are able to anticipate the actions of others in a similar situation. Informal policies can be hazy, but the system dynamics model attempts to make them explicit. In such a model, informal policies are treated with as much concern as explicit policies. They are considered equally important in understanding the behaviour of a complex system. To truly capture the problematic behaviour of a system, a system dynamics model must represent the basic policy structure of that system. The model can then be used to try out various policies before implementing them in the real system. In this way, effective policies can be developed to provide a proper guiding framework for the average manager .

The ultimate goal, if real change is sought, is to find the optimal mix of policies that create the desired behaviour (smooth growth of revenue, constant inventory, etc.), no matter who is in the decision- making process.

3.8 Building the Models

The system dynamics provides a new way of viewing the world around us. We can formalize the concepts and views of the world into a computer simulation model. Let us take a closer look at the stages of the modeling process. Although we will go through these in a certain order, we should always keep in mind that creating simulation models is an iterative process. Usually, when creating a model, we will not create it in a linear fashion. Instead, we will advance one step, then take three steps back and reevaluate everything we've already done. This is the art of modeling: it is subjective, frustrating at times, and in the end we can never say that the model is "correct" or even finished. It is simply one representation of reality, built to explain a particular problem. We may find that we learn more in the process of creating the model than in manipulating it after it is finished.

3.8.1 Problem Definition

The modeling process begins with defining a problem. The problem definition is the keystone of the entire activity. Although it might sound like the easiest part, it is not enough to have a vague notion about the problem behaviour. Defining the problem is essentially defining the purpose of the model. The problem should therefore be

defined as precisely as possible. This definition is the basis of all our future efforts and our guide in decisions concerning boundaries and validity of our model. The narrower our focus, the easier it will be to resist the temptation to overdo the structure.

Numbers are useful tools in this stage of the process. If we can use numbers to define the problems, such as real inventory data to illustrate the problem of inventory fluctuations, we will be better equipped to define the problem. If no real data are available, it is extremely useful to draw the shape of the behaviour against time. If the problem concerns the interactions of variables, such as the effect of seasonal fluctuations in demand on the level of inventory, it is necessary to map the relevant variables against each other. This way we can build an understanding of how each of the various variables affects each other. We should always keep in mind that system dynamics models are not concerned with the behaviour of individual variables. The main focus is on how each variable interacts with the other variables to produce the system's behaviour.

3.8.2 Identification of Variables

The problem definition helps us to structure our information, and to start generating names and units of measurement for variables. The list of variables usually becomes very long. From this list, we should identify primary system variables. We can throw out the variables that are irrelevant to the purpose of the model and set aside the variables that we are not sure of. The latter ones might become helpful later, when we arrive at the stage of model design.

3.8.3 Model Boundaries

Given the problem definition, we can start to set the boundaries of the model. Creating boundary diagrams can be useful at this stage of the process. Such diagrams will also help us to identify the variables to be included in the model, and whether these variables will be endogenous or exogenous.

3.8.4 Simulation

We are now ready for the simulation stage of the system dynamics modeling. When we have put our conceptual model into the computer, and all the variables and equations are well defined, we can simulate the model and view its behaviour over time. It is often useful to try a few "mental simulation" exercises before simulating the model. We should try to imagine what the model should do when it is simulated. When the model is simulated, we will see whether the actual behaviour differs from our expectations - it most probably will - and thereby has a starting point in figuring out why. It could be that the structure of the model is in error. It could be that we forgot to take certain variables into account and that our expectations of the behaviour were wrong. When we simulate the computer model, we must set up appropriate simulation settings for the model.

The two most important are the time horizon and the time step. The time horizon represents the period of time we want our model to simulate. It is specified by a start and stop time given relative to the selected calendar. The time horizon will vary from model to model, and we will usually select it so it matches the time frame of the problem behaviour. The time step represents the time interval that the simulation progresses for each calculation. The shorter the time step, the more calculations tool will perform, and the slower the model will run.

Once we have determined the time horizon and time step of the simulation, we will be able to simulate our model under different conditions and observe the results. To truly understand the model, we must relate the structure we have created to the behaviour that results from simulating the model. If we cannot get the behaviour we want we must go back and reexamine the structure of the

model and try to determine why it is creating the unwanted behaviour. The causal-loop diagram is often useful in this regard. When we understand why the model generates certain behaviour, we can experiment with changes in the structure to generate the actual problem behaviour as we described it in the early stages of the model creation. When the model adequately represents the real problem, we can use it for policy analysis and experimentation. We now have a mini-labouratory in which to simulate the effects of various policy changes before implementing them in the real system.

3.9 A Sample System Dynamics Model- Sdmodel

Software Marketing Management (SMM) is the business discipline focused on the practical application of marketing techniques and the management of a firm's marketing resources and activities. Software Marketing managers are often responsible for influencing the level, timing, and composition of customer demand in a manner that will achieve the company's objectives. Software marketing management is the art and science of choosing target markets and getting, keeping and growing customers through creating, delivering, and communicating superior customer value. This case study gives the insights of diffusion of new software product and its adoption in the market. We will model the diffusion and adoption of the new software strategy and will suggest the scenarios through simulation result.

3.9.1 Case Introduction

In order to make fact-based decisions regarding software marketing strategy and design effective, cost-efficient implementation programs, and firms must possess a detailed, objective understanding of their own business and the market in which they operate. In analyzing these issues, the discipline of software marketing management often overlaps with the related discipline of strategic planning.

3.9.2 Software Marketing Research and Analysis

Traditionally, software marketing analysis was structured into three areas: Customer analysis, Company analysis, and Competitor analysis (so-called "3Cs" analysis). More recently, it has become fashionable in some software marketing circles to divide these further into five "Cs": Customer analysis, Company analysis, Collaborator analysis, Competitor analysis, and analysis of the industry Context.

The focus of customer analysis is to develop a scheme for market segmentation, breaking down the market into various constituent groups of customers, which are called customer segments or market segments. Software marketing managers work to develop detailed profiles of each segment, focusing on any number of variables that may differ among the segments: demographic, psychographic, geographic, behavioral, needs-benefit, and other factors may all be examined. Marketers also attempt to track these segments' perceptions of the various products in the market using tools such as perceptual mapping.

The firm's collaborators may also be profiled, which may include various suppliers, distributors and other channel partners, joint venture partners, and others. An analysis of complementary products may also be performed if such products exist.

Software marketing management employs various tools from economics and competitive strategy to analyze the industry context in which the firm operates. These include five forces analysis of strategic groups of competitors, value chain analysis and others. Depending on the industry, the regulatory context may also be important to examine in detail.

In Competitor analysis, marketers build detailed profiles of each competitor in the market, focusing especially on their relative competitive strengths and weaknesses using SWOT analysis. Software marketing managers will examine each competitor's cost structure, sources of profits, resources and competencies, competitive positioning and product differentiation, degree of vertical integration, historical responses to industry developments, and other factors.

Once the company has obtained an adequate understanding of the customer base and its own competitive position in the industry, software marketing managers are able to make key strategic decisions and develop a software marketing strategy designed to maximize the revenues and profits of the firm. The selected strategy may aim for any of a variety of specific objectives, including optimizing short-term unit margins, revenue growth, market share, long-term profitability, or other goals.

To achieve the desired objectives, marketers typically identify one or more target customer segments which they intend to pursue. Customer segments are often selected as targets because they score highly on two dimensions: 1) The segment is attractive to serve because it is large, growing, makes frequent purchases, is not price sensitive (i.e. is willing to pay high prices), or other factors; and 2) The company has the resources and capabilities to compete for the segment's business, can meet their needs better than the competition, and can do so profitably. In fact, a commonly cited definition of software marketing is simply "meeting needs profitably."

3.9.3 Software Marketing Strategy and Implement Planning

Once the company has obtained an adequate understanding of the customer base and its own competitive position in the industry, software marketing managers are able to make key strategic decisions and develop a software marketing strategy designed to maximize the revenues and profits of the firm. The selected strategy may aim for any of a variety of specific objectives, including optimizing short-term unit margins, revenue growth, market share, long-term profitability, or other goals.

After the firm's strategic objectives have been identified, the target market selected, and the desired positioning for the company, product or brand has been determined, software marketing managers focus on how to best implement the chosen strategy. Traditionally, this has involved implementation planning across the "4Ps" of software marketing: Product management, Pricing, Place (i.e. sales and distribution channels), and Promotion.

3.9.4 Project, Process, and Vendor Management

Once the key implementation initiatives have been identified, software marketing managers work to oversee the execution of the software marketing plan. Software marketing executives may therefore manage any number of specific projects, such as sales force management initiatives, product development efforts, channel software marketing programs and the execution of public relations and advertising campaigns. Marketers use a variety of project management techniques to ensure projects achieve their objectives while keeping to established schedules and budgets.

3.9.5 Causal Loop Diagram and Stock Flow Diagram

The causal loop diagram of the new product introduction may look as follows:

There are two feedback loops in this diagram. The positive reinforcement loop on the right indicates that the more people have already adopted the new product, the stronger the word-of-mouth impact. There will be more references to the product, more demonstrations, and more reviews. This positive feedback should generate sales that continue to grow. Figure 11 shows the causal loop diagram of the new product production.

The second feedback loop on the left is negative reinforcement. Clearly growth can not continue forever, because as more and more people adopt, there remain fewer and fewer potential adopters.

Both feedback loops act simultaneously, but at different times they may have different strengths. Thus one would expect growing sales in the initial years, and then declining sales in the later years.

Figure 11. Causal loop diagram of new product adoption

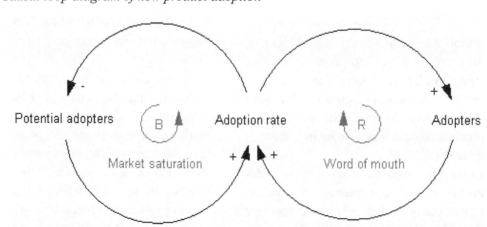

Figure 12. Stock and flow diagram of new product adoption

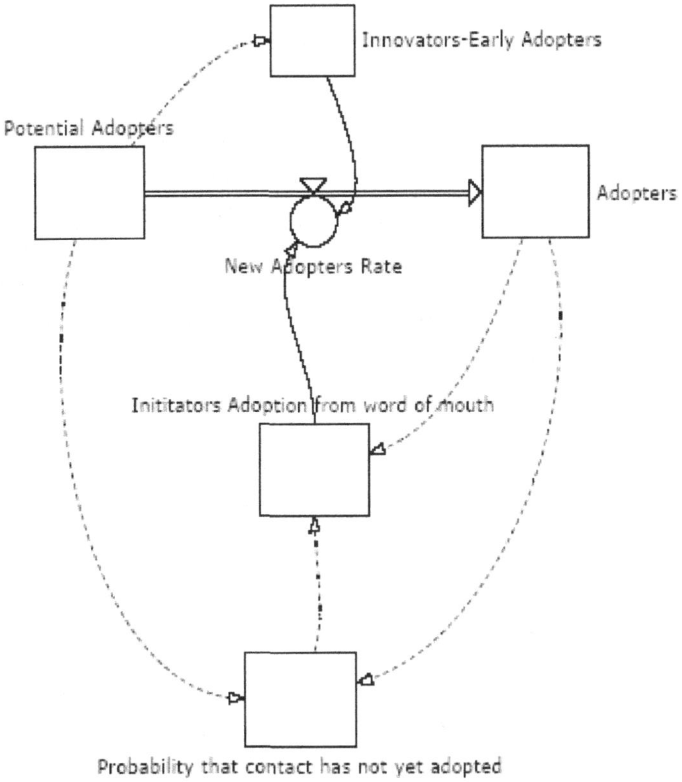

3.9.6 Stock Flow Diagram

In our example, there are two basic stocks: Potential adopters and Adopters. There is one flow: New adopters. For every new adopter, the stock of potential adopters declines by one, and the stock of adopters increases by one. Figure 12 depicts the stock and flow diagram of the new product production based on the causal loop diagram discussed before.

3.9.7 Equations Of The Models

The equations for the causal loop example are:

Adopters =

$$\int_0^t New\ adopters\ dt$$

Potential adopters =

$$\int_0^t -New\ adopters\ dt$$

New adopters = Innovators + Imitators

Innovators = p * Potential adopters

Imitators = q * Adopters * Probability that contact has not yet adopted

Probability that contact has not yet adopted =

$$\frac{\textbf{Potential adopters}}{\textbf{Potential adopters + Adopters}}$$

p = 0.03
q = 0.4

Figure 13. Simulation graph of adoption of new product

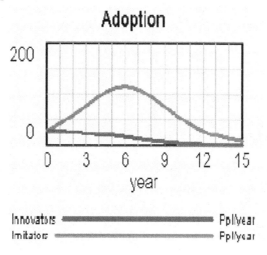

Figure 14. Simulation graph of adopter population

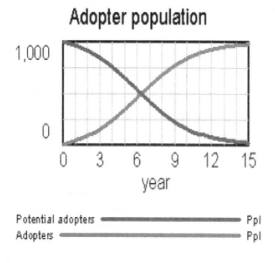

3.9.8 Simulation Results

The simulation results show that the behaviour of the system would be to have growth in adopters that follows a classical s-curve shape. The increase in adopters is very slow initially, then exponential growth for a period, followed ultimately by saturation

3.9.9 Case Summary

Facing new pressures from a global, web-driven economy characterized by greater competition, companies need smart, customer-centric marketing strategies. The case study provides system dynamics modeling simulation for developing an effective marketing strategy by examining how firms create and sustain customer value. Here we are focused on alignment, growing businesses, delivering key performance indicators, innovation, customer and channel penetration, reliable technology and communication tools, and subject matter sales and marketing experts.

3.10 Conclusion

System Engineering modeling and design is a technique that aims to allow understanding and modeling of complex systems. A system in this sense is any organization of people, items and capabilities that work together to achieve goals. The models provide a holistic view of the system. This is done by showing causal relationships between different elements of the system graphically, and describing the nature of the relationship through equations. Another key element of the system dynamics approach is the time evolutionary view. This allows the representation of the behavior of the system as it evolves through time, giving a dynamic rather than a static view of the system.

REFERENCES

Forrester, J. W. (1958). Industrial Dynamics: A Major Breakthrough for Decision Makers. *Harvard Business Review, 38*(4), 37-66.

Forrester, J. W. (1961). *Industrial Dynamics.* Pegasus Communications, Waltham, MA.

Wolstenholme, E. F. (1990). *System Enquiry: a System Dynamics Approach.* John Wiley & Sons, New York.

Chapter IX

UML 2.0 in the Modelling of the Complex Business Processes of Reporting and Control of Financial Information System

Sebastian Kwapisz
University of Gdansk, Poland

ABSTRACT

*The General Inspectorate of Financial Information is instituted under the Ministry of Finance. Its duty is to counteract bringing into financial circulation pecuniary assets derived from illegal sources and to intercept any possible signs of money laundering. The procedure requires institutions such as banks and insurance companies to forward information of "over-the-limit" transactions in which the amounts involved exceeds the value specified by the Ministry. The efficiency of collecting information about these transactions is actually working, and is determined to a large extent by the speed and efficiency of the information systems in particular institutions responsible for those issues. The chapter discusses and analyses problems associated with the sending information about such transactions by the institution under such obligation. It lays out the range of possibilities opened up by the **Unified Modeling Language (UML)**, which constitutes a universal tool for exchanging information within IT groups and specifying complex business processes. The potential of the language lies in its numerous extensibility mechanisms, which allow the application of various stereotypes, depending on the area given. The chapter also emphasizes significance of the **CASE tool**, which makes it possible to control and create **UML diagrams**. Programs of the CASE type are also able to generate a skeleton code used subsequently by programmers during implementation. This chapter includes an analysis and design of a system with a task of improving the efficiency of the information forwarding process by the institutions under obligation so that the criteria laid down by law are met. The description of the system has been created in accordance with the specifications of **UML 2.0** and - based on many diagram types and the architecture - the business processes that it extends to and the database structure required to collect* *information about transactions are set forth. Thanks to the application of use cases the main functionality of the system is defined: searching for and bringing together particular transactions followed by transformation and the dispatching of reports. Complex business processes are presented by corresponding activity and interaction diagrams. The architecture and the placement of the system within the structure of the organization, however, are depicted with the help of structure diagrams such as class, component and deployment diagrams. The use made of the extensibility mechanisms of UML merits attention here. The database stereotype presented in the work made it possible for the database to be designed at the level of implementation, and the functionality of the CASE tool enabled the complete software script to be compiled on this basis.*

1 INTRODUCTION

Unified Modeling Language(UML) is a successor of object- oriented methodologies of analysis and design of informatics systems which was invented at the turn of the 80ties and 90ties. Conception of UML was elaborated in Rational Corporation as the result of cooperation so-called 'three musketeers': Grady Booch, Jim Rumbaugh, Ivar Jacobson (1999). UML is graphical notation which is applying to present varied problems into models and assuring good communication in IT teams with sharing ideas. Natural language can not be precise and cause lack of understanding in complicated problems. UML is irreplaceable in designing large systems and helps in illustrating its elements and correlations (Wrycza S., Marcinkowski B., & Wyrzykowski K., 2005).

UML has become primary standard in specification of projects and architectures of object- oriented systems and still receives wide recognition in IT professionals. Although initially conceived as a language for software development, UML may be used to model a wide range or real world domains. For example, UML can be used to model many real world Processes (in business, science, industry, education and elsewhere), Organizational Hierarchies, Deployment maps and much more.

Modeling informatics systems requires different view of analyzing problem, because many people are included in project (users, programmers, analysts or specialist of integration). Each of mentioned above group of people uses different perspective of system and is interested in different stage of its life time. Specification of UML 2.0 provides many possibilities in presenting systems with emphasizing each main element. Therefore multi-perspective nature of UML could help controlling iterative and evolutionary development of system (Maciaszek L., 2005). Usefulness of UML is also common in modern software methodologies (RUP, Agile, XP).

This chapter also emphasizes the use of tools for object modeling, which give abilities to produce fragments of skeleton programming code and facilitate communication in IT team.

All diagrams which define system of reporting and control presented in this article are created in Enterprise Architect. EA has comprehensive support for UML 2.0 standard. It has all 13 UML 2.0 diagrams in the tool. Intuitive visualization of UML is a part of strength of EA. Thanks to modeling tools often called CASE programs (Computer Aided Systems Engineering), designing such solution and improve use of UML become more effective (Maciaszek L., 2005).

Using UML Profiles, UML Patterns and other extensions, UML with EA may be tailored to address a particular modeling Domain not explicitly covered in the original UML specification. EA makes extending the UML simple and straightforward, and best of all, the extension mechanism is still part of the UML Specification (Enterprise Architect Home Page). The UML database profile presented in this chapter enables defining in the model such elements as keys on tables (primary, foreign), indexes or even users of database. Additionally CASE tools help in converting such models into SQL code with compatibility of database type (e.g. SQL Server 2000, Oracle, InterBase etc.) (Muller, R. J., 2000).

The aim of this article is to show great functionality of UML 2.0 which is a best practice for communicating, modeling, specifying and defining business and software systems. At the beginning there is introduction of institution of The General Inspectorate of Financial Information and requirements of reporting and control system. Then moving from analysis to design system functionalities, processes and architecture are illustrated on the UML diagrams.

2 THE CHALLENGE OF INTEGRATION OF CORPORATE INFORMATION SYSTEMS WITH INSPECTION OF FINANCIAL INFORMATION SYSTEMS

The General Inspection of Financial Information is a non-police body of the state administration, having access to bank, broker, treasury, and notary secrets. Its head is an Undersecretary of State at the Ministry of Finance, appointed at a motion of the Prime Minister. It is his duty to carry out analytical investigation after having been informed by institutions under obligation to do so about suspicious transactions that have occurred.

The tasks of the General Inspection include obtaining, storing, processing, and analyzing financial information and taking steps in order to counteract bringing into circulation pecuniary values coming from illegal or undisclosed sources.

Under the legal acts mentioned above, "institutions under obligation' (IUO) should supply information about registered transactions to the General Inspection in an electronic form. The term 'transactions' means cash and non-cash deposits and drawings, including transfers among various accounts belonging to the same account holder.

An IUO taking a client's instruction or order for carrying out a transaction in excess of 15,000 EURO or the equivalent is obliged to register such a transaction, even if it is carried out through more than one operation when circumstances show that these transactions are interrelated.

The issue of 'money laundering' mentioned above more and more often affects the Polish financial system as well. In order to counteract this phenomenon, the Parliament passed an act imposing the duty of collection and registration of all the financial transactions carried out by the so-called IUOs'.

The system's task is to collect information about 'above-threshold' transactions the value of which exceeds a certain value fixed by the Ministry in order to identify possible signs of money laundering. Both the scope and format of data transferred to the General Inspection must comply with the requirements of this institution.

Regulations issued by the Ministry of Finance impose on the institutions the duty and responsibility of registration of such transaction on financial markets when the organization acts upon a client's instruction. This makes the IUO undertake appropriate steps in order to meet the Ministry's requirements. The process of transferring information requires appropriate IT infrastructure enabling efficient detection of such operations and integration with the Ministry's system. Figure 1 shows a general flowchart of the system:

In order to collect data for reports efficiently, the system takes required information automatically from the databases of the subsidiaries of the organization. The Controllers' responsibility is to verify the validity of registered transactions and to key them in case of suspected offence. The General Controller is responsible for creating a 'batch' of the transactions for a given month, saved as an XML file, and transferring it to the Ministry.

The system will be compiled as a web application, which means that the user will communicate with the application server through an

Figure 1. The flowchart of the system

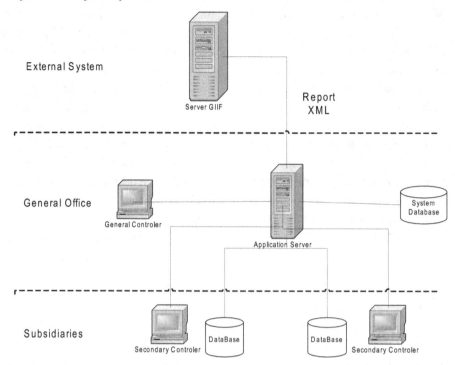

Internet browser. This will make it possible for a dispersed group of units to work within one institution, with simultaneous data saving on the central database server.

The system will be implemented in the institution's internal network, using its architecture in order to communicate between components of the system. Communication with the Ministry's external systems will be limited to report sending and validation.

3 BUSINESS PROCESSES MODELING

The first stage of creating an **IT system** in conformity with the UML is identification of an objective domain. Before starting the deployment of the system it is necessary to identify the needs of the future user as precisely as possible. It is important to obtain profound understanding of

business processes, their initiation and flow. This stage is so important because it is responsible for displaying a fragment of real world which is a foundation for further development of the application from the programmer's point of view.

The flowchart above shows the context of processes for the system under design, which is helpful during the identification of its functionality. The flowchart includes an abstract *User* who may initiate the events: *Appearance of Suspicion* or *Generating Report*. *Appearance of Suspicion* is an event executed when suspicious transaction is spotted and it starts a process of *Registry of Transaction*. This process aims at *Registration of Transaction* labeled by a stereotyped *<<goal>>*. The input data of the process are labeled as stereotyped *<<input>>* and they may be entered through a component, i.e. *Web Page of Transaction* or by using the system's object *Automatic Import*. The process ends in saving the output data *<output>>* in the database labeled in the flowchart as *Database*.

Figure 2. Flowchart of business processes

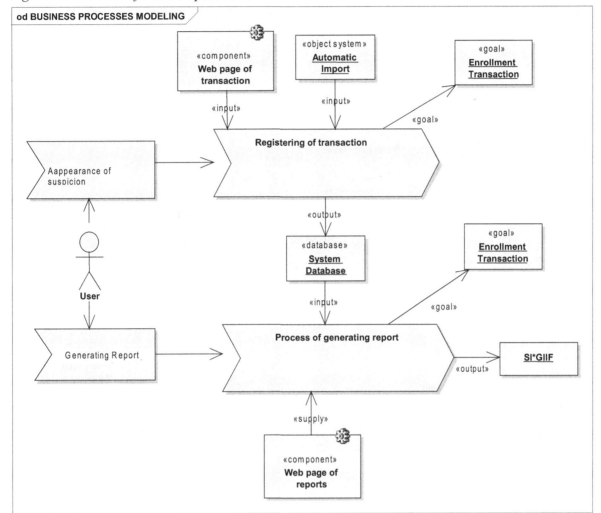

The other event which may occur is *Generating Report* which takes place when the user wants to report to the General Inspection. This event starts up a *Generating Report* process aimed at *Report Generation*. The input data for the process come from the database and the report generation is supported (<<*supply*>>) by a component of the system – *Web Page of Report*. The process ends with transferring data to the Ministerial system SI*GIFI.

4 FUNCTIONALITIES OF THE SYSTEM IN THE FORM OF USE CASE DIAGRAM

Using the flowchart *Use Case Diagram* it is possible to identify correctly the requirements of the designed system and identify users with the functions they perform within the system. Each use case is described with the major scenario and, if necessary, by an alternative scenario. The

Figure 3. Use case diagram

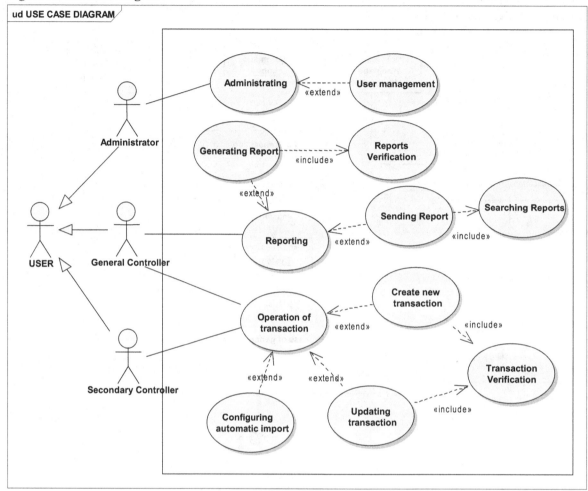

scenarios describe how the software is used by the individual user.

The use case diagram presented in Figure 3 includes three players, i.e. *Administrator*, *General Controller* and *Secondary Controller* as an expansion of the abstract player *User*.

The execution of the use case *Administrating* is ascribed to the player *Administrator*. He can tune the application to proper operation. Additionally, this case is extended (<<*extend*>>) by the case *User Management* which allows for full management of the users and their roles. This relation is optional.

The user *General Controller* may utilize full functionality of the system. He has authorization

to perform the use cases *Reporting* and *Operation of Transaction*. The tasks of *Secondary Controller*, however, are less complex and they focus only on the use case *Operation of Transaction*.

The use case *Operation of Transaction* allows for registering of transaction and it is extended by the following cases: *Create New Transaction*, *Updating Transaction* and *Configuring Automatic Import*. By initiating *Creating New Transaction* or *Updating Transaction,* the user is obliged to verify the validity of the input data. He carries out the included case (<<*include*>>) of using *Transaction Verification.*

The player *General Controller* uses the functionality of report generating consisting in downloading specific data from the set of registered transactions. The use case *Reporting* is extended by the cases *Sending Report* and *Generating Reports*. The use case *Generating Report* requires verification of the validity of the report. This is done through initiating the included use case (*<<include>>*) *Report Verification*. After generating the report and positive validation, it is registered in the database. At that moment the *General Controller* may carry out *Sending Report* which includes use case *Searching Reports* aimed at exact identification of the report which is to be sent to the Ministerial system SI*GIFI.

In Figure 3 three main modules of the system are specified:

- Administrative module – makes it possible to create users and assign authorization to them. Users are subdivided into system administrators, General Controllers and Secondary Controllers. The Local Controller has a possibility of putting in and updating data, and verifying the validity of registered transactions from a given subsidiary; he also enters on a current basis data concerning "emergency drawings". The General Controller can enter corrections, edit and report the operations of all the units and create reports for the General Inspection;
- Reporting module – enables data operations: editing, browsing, sorting out, report generating and sending to the SI*GIFI. The possibilities of editing and reporting are available depending on the authorization conferred upon the user;
- Operation of transaction module – enables importing, inputting and updating transactions. The system checks on-line the validity of entered transactions. The process of automatic import of data is launched by an authorized user in order to detect suspicious financial transactions in any of the subsidiaries.

When starting to work with the system, the user has to go positively through the process of authorization and authentication, which means a necessity of correct logging into the system. Only a registered user with the ascribed role may use the functionalities of the system.

5 TRANSACTION PROCESSING

The process of transaction registration may be carried out in two ways. The first one – the authorized user is connected to the transaction processing interface and enters the data manually. Then the keyed-in data are validated, and, if the process runs positively, the data are stored in the database.

The Sequence Diagram presented in Figure 4 presents the interaction of the process of registering a new transaction. In order to start the process, the user employs *Transaction Processing*. Then the control is taken over by *ITransaction interface*, to which the user feeds the transaction data and issues the message *addTrans*. Instance of the *ITransaction* classifier triggers an operation on the tables *Owner*, *Dispatcher*, *Beneficiary* in order to download *id* number of a given identity. This operation is performed as a *program loop* and allows to search all the registered identities. If the input data of the transaction are positively verified, the interface *validateTrans* of *ITransaction* executes component procedure *addTrans* at the table *Transaction*. If the process ends positively, a *message (Saved)* is sent; otherwise the *error message (Error)* is displayed.

Another way of registration is based on automatic import of transaction. The system downloads information about daily transactions from existing transaction database and places them in the system's database. All the transactions are saved because there is a possibility of error occurrence during importing. If the validation of the import proves unsuccessful, it is assigned a

Figure 4. Transaction processing

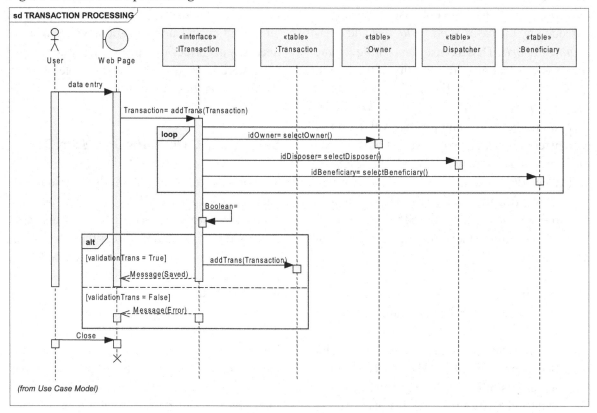

parameter value of *Validation = False,* otherwise the value is *Validation = True.* Thanks to this solution users can easily identify transactions that need corrections. All the data can, if necessary, be upgraded or corrected by the users.

Transaction import is carried out after defining search options. It is possible to define the following search options:

- A set of options for identifying transactions of a value higher then the current 15,000 EURO;
- A set of options for identifying suspicious transactions. These options can be defined as automatic options, performed each time after importing a transaction, or as manual options initiated by the user at any time.

Figure 5 displays activities performed during import of transaction to display the logic of data-

flow through two partitions: *User* and *Import.* The first activity is performed by the user while *Setting Import Parameters.* By initiating import process – *Start Import* – the dataflow is directed to an *Import* classifier. The import information is downloaded – *Get Import Parameters.* Then operations of connecting to the database and searching for transactions follow. If a transaction meeting the parameter *valueTrans >1,500 EURO* is not found,, the data flow is directed to the *User* with the information that there are no transactions above the 'threshold' level. Otherwise the transaction is downloaded, validated, and saved in the database of the system. Finally the User is informed about the imported transactions.

Sequence diagram presented in Figure 6 shows interactions of the transaction import. To start the process, the User engages *Process of Transaction Import.* Then, control is taken over by the ITransaction interface, by the use of

Figure 5. Transaction import chart

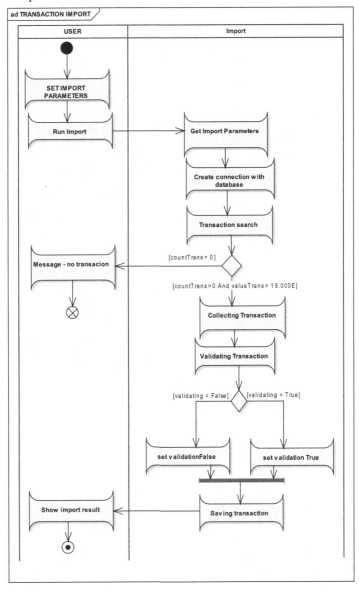

which the User defines import parameters, such as Transaction Value, Database, Table, login and password. This information is necessary to initiate correctly a connection with the database which contains importable data. Thus the instance of ITransaction generates operation *setimport* of the *Import* classifier. After initiating import by the User, parameters of import are downloaded, and then a search for transactions in the indicated database is launched. This operation is carried out as a programmed loop. If the message *select=0* is received, the system informs the user that there are no transactions. However, if at least a single transaction is found, the validation '*validatingTrans*' is started, and then it is saved in the database. Finally the user is informed about the effects of the import.

Figure 6. Sequence diagram of the transaction import

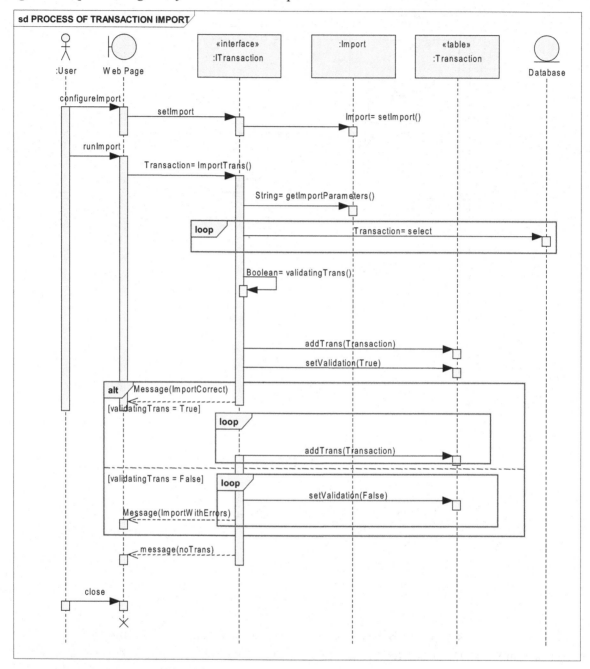

6 GENERATING REPORTS

All the transactions saved in the system must be sent to the General Inspection. Exporting periodical reports generates an XML document. The document is saved to a file with an appropriate name, e.g. 14022006.xml. Exported positions of the registry are labeled with a common identifier.

The process of generating reports is initiated by the user authorized as the General Controller. First, a transaction saved in the database of the

Figure 7. The process of generating reports

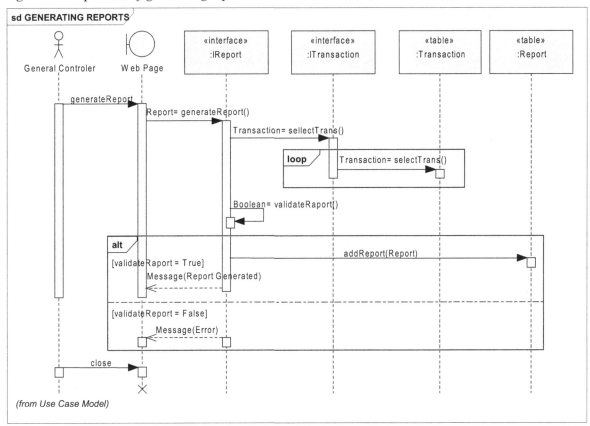

sd GENERATING REPORTS

system in the specific time interval is downloaded. After successful validation of the report, an XML document created in this way may be saved.

The sequence diagram in Figure 7 demonstrates the interactions in the process of generating reports. To initiate this process, the user engages *Generating Reports*, which evokes the message *generateReport* on the *IReport* interface. Then, using the message *selectTrans* of the *ITransaction* interface, aided by component procedure *select-Trans* the user imports transactions registered in the table *Transaction* for the month relevant for the report. If *validateReport =True,* the component procedure *addReport* allows for saving data in the table *Report*. Then the user receives the message *Report Generated*.

The process of sending the report to the SI*GIFI system may take place immediately

after it has been created or later, but it needs the interference of the General Controller of the Organization.

The process of posting the report demonstrated in Figure 8 starts when the *General Controller*, using the page *Generating Reports* executes the message *sendReport* on the *IReport* interface. The report data are imported from the *Report* table with the message *selectReport*. Then the *IReport* interface transfers the report (with the message *sendReport)* to the boundary object, i.e. the Ministerial SI*GIFI system. The *IReport* interface classifier waits for a feedback message after the report has been processed at the Ministry. Depending on the verification run by the Ministerial system, on the page *Generating Reports* a message *correct* or *rejected* will be displayed.

*Figure 8. The process of posting reports to the SI*GIFI*

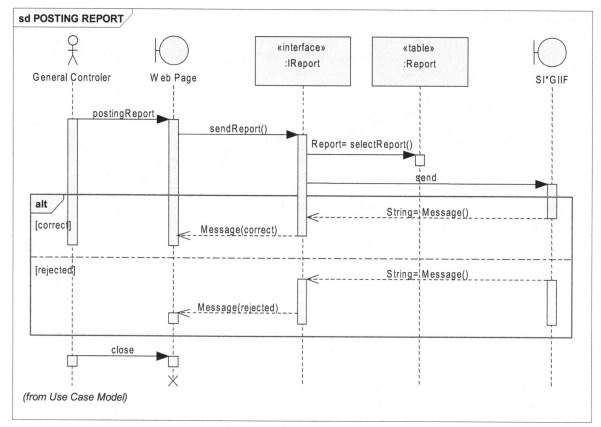

The diagram of the finite state machine shown in Figure 9 shows the states of the report after being sent to the Ministerial system. *Processing in SI*GIFI* is a complex state which contains finite state submachines. The states presented in the diagram mean:

- Registered – the file has been accepted by the GIFI system. In the case of sending files by email this status will be displayed after decoding of the file which, depending on the number of files queuing up, may last several hours. The procedure is so long because identification of a transmitted file and its assignment to a specific institution may happen only after positive verification of electronic signature and decoding of the file,

- Signature is waiting for verification – the IT system of GIFI is waiting for verification of the signature's authenticity. Time needed for checking authenticity is 1 hour. This time results from the Electronic Signature Act. During that time authorized certification offices verify the authenticity of the signature,

- Signature correct – the signature has been verified as authentic and the file is waiting for decoding,

- Signature incorrect – the signature has been verified as incorrect and the file will not be decoded, and its status will change into "To be clarified",

- Transaction read – the IT system found correct data referring to transactions in the decoded file, and the transactions have been read into the GIFI IT system. The process of file transfer has been correctly completed.,

- Incorrect – in the decoded file, the GIFI IT system found data saved and sent by the IUO in breach of the relevant ordinance of the Ministry of Finance on the transmitted data formats. The IUO should verify the correctness of the data sent in terms of their compliance with the format provided for by the ordinance, and after identification of the error the corrected data should be sent once again.

The timing diagram presented by Figure 10 specifies the order of occurrence of classifier of instance states in terms of time change. It presents states of *Report Generating* and their duration through the definition of their time limits. The break of the state alteration line means the oc-

currence of a new state of this instance. For the states *generatingReports, SavingReports, PostingReports* and *ReadingReports,* the time scale clearly defines their duration. It is impossible, however, to define precisely the duration of the following states:

- verificationSignature – {1 hour}
- verificationReport – {a few hours}
- enrolmentReport – {10 minutes}

7 DATA MODEL OF TRANSACTION AND REPORTING MODULE

By the use of UML available in the database profile, it is possible to apply in the diagrams classes stereotypes, tables, relations, views or component procedures:

Figure 9. The diagram of finite state machine of sending reports to the SI*GIFI

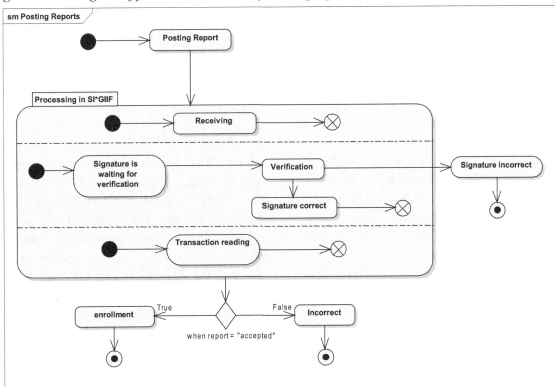

Figure 10. The timing diagram of the process of generating and posting reports to the SI*GIFI

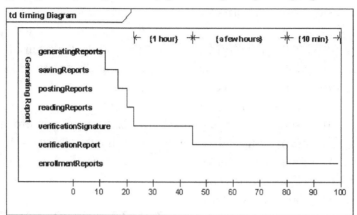

- Labeling tables with stereotype *<<Table>>*, columns - *<<Column>>* and views - *<<View>>*,
- Keys defined according to the stereotype *<<PK>>* - Primary Key, and *<<FK>>* - Foreign Key,
- Unique values - *<<Unique>>*.

Database profile of UML contains all the elements needed for modeling database structure. By applying specific stereotypes we can easily design a database. By using the CASE software it is possible to obtain more detailed specification of created diagrams and generate on their basis ready-made scripts, such as SQL. Table spaces are also an important element, as they are used to aggregate and decompose tables. They constitute clear, hierarchic structure which enhances better understanding of the database by the project team. It is of significant importance in a situation, when we want to use the database once again or introduce some modifications.

The system's database consists of the following table spaces *(<<Tablespace>>)* which are identical to the system's modules:

- Transaction handling, created by tables: *Transaction, Dispatcher, Owner, Beneficiary;*

- Reporting, consisting of both *Report* and *Transaction* tables.

Since the modules of transaction handling and reporting overlap, the structure of this segment of the database may be considered on a single diagram. Figure 11 includes tables *Report, Transaction, Dispatcher, Owner* and *Beneficiary.* From the system functionality point of view, the central point of this segment of the database are two tables: *Transaction* and *Report.*

The table *Transaction* consists of the primary key *PK IdTransaction* and four foreign keys *idReport, idBeneficiary, idOwner,* and *idDispatcher,* which represent primary keys of their own tables. The other columns describe transaction data. The column *Validation* is an important element, since it can take *False* and *True* values depending on verification of data correctness during the transaction's import. Size of associations points to relation between tables. Each transaction must have one *Owner, Dispatcher,* and *Beneficiary* assigned. The *Report,* however is an element that aggregates transactions from a given month, and in order to generate it we must have at least one transaction. Partial aggregation applied here shows that shared objects or *Transactions* may function independent of the aggregate.

Figure 11. Data structure of the transaction handling and reporting module

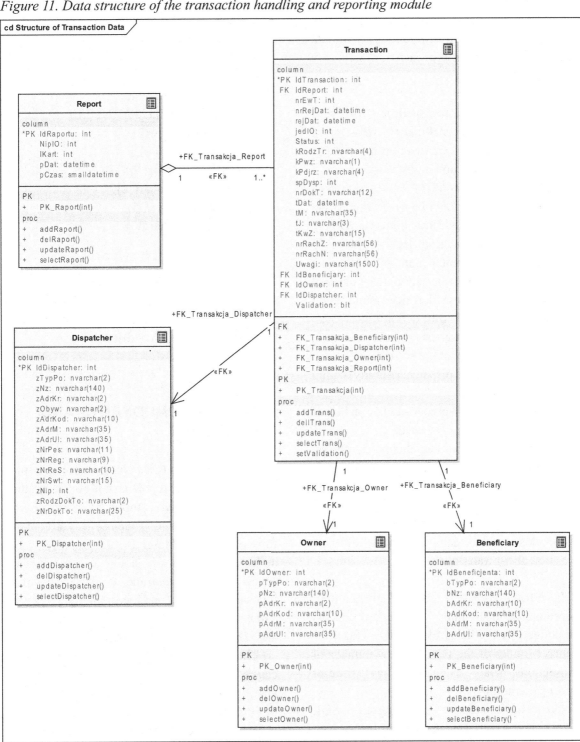

The Ordinance of the Minister of Finance exactly specifies the structure of a transaction, defining all the required fields and types of data specific to them. Elements of each transaction are grouped as follows [15]:

- Identification of transaction – nrEwt – evidence number, nrRejDat – registration number, rejDat – registration date, jedIO – organizational unit and status;
- Transaction – kRodzTr – transaction type code, kPwz – transaction association code, kPdjrz – suspicious transaction code, spDysp – mode of dispatching decision, nrDokT- transaction document number, tDat- date of completion of transaction, tM – place of completion of transaction, tKw- total amount of transaction, tJ- transaction unit, tKwZ- total amount of transaction after revision, tJZ – transaction unit after revision;
- Information about dispatcher – entity issuing transaction note;
- Information about owner – entity on behalf of which the order is issued;
- Information about beneficiary – person benefiting from completed transaction;
- Account of parties to the transaction – nrRachZ – Number of Source Account, and - nrRachN – number of target account;
- Fields of notes – include additional information about transaction.

Each transaction registered in a given month contributes to the monthly XML report. Reports are defined by the fields like NipIO – Tax Reference Number of the IUO, lKart – number of transactions, pDat – date, and pCzas – time of report generation.

On the basis of the presented diagram, a SQL script has been generated. Excerpt from the script can be seen as follows:

```
-- --------------------------------------------------
-- DBMS      : SQL Server 2000
-- --------------------------------------------------

-- Create Tables
CREATE TABLE Beneficiary (
    IdBeneficiary int NOT NULL,
    bTypPo nvarchar(2),
    bNz nvarchar(140),
    bAdrKr nvarchar(10),
    bAdrKod nvarchar(10),
    bAdrM nvarchar(35),
    bAdrUl nvarchar(35)
)
;
-- Create Primary Key Constraints
ALTER TABLE Beneficiary ADD CON-
STRAINT PK_Beneficiary
    PRIMARY KEY (IdBeneficiary)
;
```

8 SYSTEM COMPONENTS AND DEPLOYMENT

Figure 12 presents three components forming a functionality of the reporting and control system. The *Administration* component stores classes *User, Department* and *Branch Office* and contains three interfaces of *IAdministrator, Autentification,* and *Login* ensuring accessibility. As the very labels suggest, *Autentification* and *Login* interfaces make it possible to verify and log in the User, whereas *IAdministrator* allows for efficient management and configuration of the system.

The component *Report Handling* contains a class *Report* and makes an interface *Ireport* available. It utilises a component *Transaction Handling* through an interface searching *ITransaction* in order to download transactions for reporting.

Transaction Handling is the third component, consisting of classes *Transaction, Import,* and an

Figure 12. Component diagram

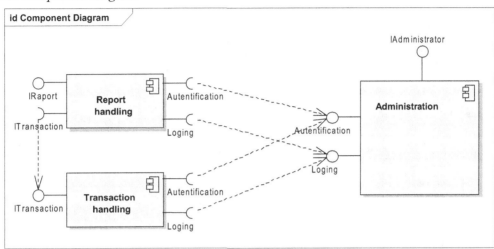

abstract class *Person* and its expansions – *Beneficiary, Dispatcher, Owner*. Performing operations on these classes is possible through the availability interface *ITransaction*.

For appropriate operation, *Transaction Handling* and *Report Handling* need two interfaces: *Login* and *Autentification* components of Administration.

The above deployment diagram has been constructed at a physical level because it contains detailed specifications of node attributes. The system is meant to be implemented in the inner network of the organization. According to this assumption, the Figure 13 diagram demonstrates the arrangement of the system in the network architecture. Specific parameters are presented in three nodes: *the GIFI Application Server, Database Server* and *User Station*. These are the only elements that, in a present situation, may undergo the configuration meant for this system. The other elements, such as network setup or *firewall*, are the parameters which must be accepted by the system.

The *Database Server* and *Application Server* nodes contain detailed information about a processor, RAM, HDD controllers and operating systems. As far as the database is concerned, its type has been defined: *Microsoft SQL Server*.

The user station, however, should have the web browser which will enable the User to utilize the system.

Three artifacts, i.e. *Handling Reports.aspx, Login.aspx*, and *Transaction Handling.aspx* have been located on the server, together with three system components. Because they have been located on the Internet application server *Microsoft IIS(Internet Information Services)* which is a component of the operational system *Windows Server 2003*, they can be utilized by the user through his web browser. The database server, however, will contain the whole structure of the database which is needed for appropriate operation of the system.

SUMMARY

Examples of usage of UML 2.0 language presented in this chapter show its possible wide spectrum of application in various areas of software engineering. Particular attention should be paid to utilization of Unified Modeling Language in the process of reaching and defining functionality of systems in which complex architecture combines numerous objective domains. By applying the

Figure 13. Diagram of system deployment

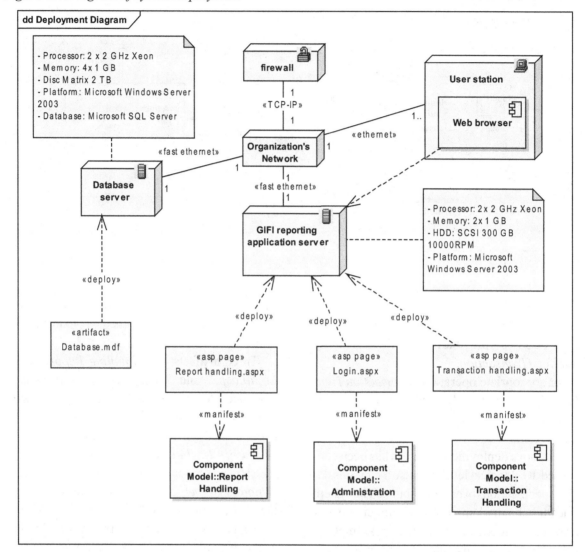

possibilities of UML we can precisely define the functionality, facilitate communication between design teams, and monitor unification of specification of concepts. Thanks to complex UML profiles and multi-perspective nature, the language is applicable in designing various problem areas.

Besides, the chapter presents applicability of UML in the database modeling process. Utilization of the CASE tools comprehensively supports possibilities offered by UML at construction of model multi-level applications and their data structures. It is a major step forward in designing contemporary IT solutions.

The design of the system presented above which facilitates generating and sending reports to GIFI has been constructed in compliance with the specification of UML 2.0. Its coherent and systematic description credibly reflects complex business model and concurrent processes.

REFERENCES

Ambler S. W. (2003). *The Elements of UML Style*. Cambridge: University Press.

Ariadne Training (2001). *UML Applied – Object Oriented Analysis and Design using the UML.* Ariadne Training Limited.

Booch G., Rumbaugh J., & Jacobson I. (1999). *UML user guide.* Addison Wesley.

Enterprise Architect Home Page, *http://www. sparxsystems.com/*

Gamma, E., Helm, R., Johnson, R., & Vlissides, J. (1995). *Design Patterns: Elements of Resuable Object- Oriented Software.* Addison-Wesley.

Gamma, E., Helm, R., Johnson, R., & Vlissides, J. (1995). *Design Patterns: Elements of Resuable Object- Oriented Software.* Addison-Wesley.

Maciaszek, L. (2005). *Requirements Analysis and Systems Design*s. Addison Wesley.

Marcinkowski, B., & Wrycza, S. (2005). Interaction Occurrences and Combined Fragments in System Dynamics Modelling with UML 2 Sequence Diagram art. In G. Nilsson, R. Gustas, W. Wojtkowski, G. Wojtkowski, S. Wrycza, & J. Zupancic (Eds.), *ISD 2005 Proceedings of the Fourteenth International Conference on Information Systems Development,* Karlstad University Studies, s (pp. 59-68), Karlstad.

Martin, J., & Odell, J. J. (1992). *Object- oriented Analysis And Design.* Prentice Hall.

Martin, R. C. (2003). *Agile Software Development.* Pearson Education.

Muller, R. J. (2000). Databases –UML In database modeling. *MIKOM 2000* (in Polish).

Shalloway, A., & Trott, J. R. (2002). *Object oriented design – Design Patterns.* HELION (in Polish).

Śmiałek, M. (2005). *Understanding UML 2.0 Methods of object oriented modeling*, HELION (in Polish).

The Ministry of Finance GIFI. *Counteracting money laundering.*

Wrifs-Brock, R., & McKean, A. (2006). *Object design – Role, responsibility and cooperation,* Helion 2006

Wrycza, S., Marcinkowski, B., & Wyrzykowski, K. (2005). *UML 2.0 in Informatics System Modeling.* Helion.

Wrycza, S., Marcinkowski, B., & Wyrzykowski, K. (2005). UML *2.0 in Information Systems Modeling.* Helion 2005 (in Polish), (pp.1-448).

Wrycza, S., & Marcinkowski, B. (2006). UML 2 Teaching at Postgraduate Studies – Prerequisites and Practice art. In D. Colton, & T. Janicki (Eds.), *The Proceedings of ISECON 2005, Columbus, Ohio, Volume 22, the 22nd Annual Conference foe Informations Systems Educators, AITP Foundation for Information technology Education.*

Chapter X
The UML 2 Academic Teaching Challenge:
An Integrated Approach

Stanisław Wrycza
University of Gdańsk, Poland

ABSTRACT

UML 2.x version has become even more complicated and diverse set of graphical techniques than its predecessors. Therefore, system developers propose preparation of its reduced, limited or minimal version called Light UML. This problem has become also the serious challenge for the UML academic teachers. The goal of this chapter is the study of specifying the UML 2.x Light version content on the basis of the questionnaire survey registering opinions of 180 university students of the University of Gdansk, Poland. After the introduction, the methodological prerequisites of the survey are clarified. Then, the research results are presented and discussed according to seven essential UML diagrams assessment criteria, included in a questionnaire. The final UML 2.x version, resulting from the accomplished survey is exposed in the last section of the chapter.

1 INTRODUCTION

Unified Modeling Language (UML), proposed by G. Booch, I. Jacobson and J. Rumbaugh (2004), has attracted the attention of both academics and practitioners of information systems analysis and design. In the last few years, increasing interest in UML stimulated spreading it across computing curricula at universities. This tendency evoked the exchange of ideas regarding the effective teaching of UML among the language trainers. Version 2.0 (OMG 2005) and the working drafts of future UML versions (OMG 2006) are in fact a diverse and in some parts excessive toolbox, which combined with system development process create a methodological platform for developing a working system.

Most of the UML teachers stress the question of the language complexity and variety of its modeling constructs. They consider this issue as a fundamental problem from a teaching point of view. On the basis of practical projects and teaching experiences it may be stated that only purposefully selected part of the complete UML potential is used. Moreover, a few diagrams and sets of UML notions are known to form the core of a typical system model. There are versatile opinions what specific modeling notions are the most required for teaching and practical aims. Such set of UML diagram types and notions might create its minimal set or – as it is commonly called – UML Light version.

The question of the effective implementation of UML in education, in respect of a UML Light version concept, has already been raised in different papers. Flint, Gardner and Boughton (2004) indicate a number of problems associated with UML teaching. They stress that the use of strict subsets of UML is easier to understand than the full language notation. Burton and Bruhn (2004) generalize their experiences related to use of the UML and underline the role of CASE tools application in UML teaching. In their opinion such tools are important factors, stimulating support of the active students' involvement in teaching process as well as allowing enrichment of system specifications by using stereotypes. The concept of minimal set of UML diagrams was also proposed by DeLooze (2005). Another survey, carried out among 171 practitioners, was directed at the UML version that would have a limited scope as well (Dobing and Parsons, 2006). It seems that the quickness of UML upgrading and implementing modifications as well as potential difficulties in getting familiar with the language by novices are underestimated. The goal of this chapter is the study of specifying the UML 2.x Light version content on the basis of the questionnaire survey of the university students' opinions.

The courses of UML (2.0 and earlier versions) have been given at the University of Gdansk since 2001. The complete UML teaching approach was implemented soon after and then continuously modified and improved with each released UML version. The UML teaching process is discussed in detail in (Wrycza and Marcinkowski, 2005b). The authors identified and analyzed several problems described in (Wrycza and Marcinkowski, 2006). One of the essential conclusions, being in accordance with the opinions expressed by authors cited to follow, is that the students are overwhelmed by the number of different UML diagrams (13 in UML 2.0), complicated interrelationships among them and the extensive number of modeling notions. The following constraints should concern such Light version:

- Light version would only consist of diagrams that are most often used in practice and would include only part of the current, detailed syntax;
- The minimal UML version should support the RUP basic disciplines, i.e. requirements specification as well as analysis and design;
- Light version should be entirely compatible with the "full" version of UML 2.x.

This concept does not limit the UML potential as the system specifications elaborated in the Light version could be subsequently extended towards the full version by the application of complete scope of UML modeling diagrams and constructs.

2 METHODOLOGICAL BACKGROUND

To solve the problem of UML Light version concept, the authors decided to carry out the questionnaire survey among the university students. The target group encompassed 180 students within knowledge of both structured and object-oriented methodologies of systems development. All students taking part in the survey formed a competent target group, as they:

- Participated in the 30 hrs lecture of UML 2.0;
- Have studied the extensive UML manual entitled "UML 2.0 in information systems modeling" (Wrycza, Marcinkowski and Wyrzykowski, 2005a);
- Exercised the fluency in UML diagramming by solving the specified design problems using UML 2 diagrammatic notation with the support of Sparx Systems Enterprise Architect CASE tool;
- Developed small UML projects in 3-4 students groups;
- Had access to extensive e-learning content, supporting the course;
- In many cases the students had practical working experience as programmers or designers (in particular group leaders).

As noted, the appropriate questionnaire containing 17 basic questions was elaborated and handed to 180 students taking part in UML course. The questions were focused around Light version concepts, reciprocal influence of structured and object-oriented approach as well as possible UML extensions. To make the proper assessment of the UML 2.x Light version the following seven crucial issues, raised in questionnaire, were analyzed:

1. UML complexity level,
2. UML diagrams cardinality,
3. Usefulness of the specific diagrams,
4. Choice of diagrams overwhelmed with modeling constructs,
5. Selection of the user-friendly UML diagrams,
6. Use of the UML diagrams for the source code generating,
7. Assessment of the appropriateness of the dynamics diagrams for the Light version support.

The assessment of the aforementioned problems in the synthetic opinions of interviewees is discussed in detail in the next point.

3 SELECTED RESULTS OF THE SURVEY

3.1 UML Complexity Level

The initiating enquiry of the questionnaire regarded UML complexity (Figure 1). It's a basic question for justification the necessity for introducing UML Light version. Classifying UML 2.x as an easy or very easy technique by most of the respondents would in fact deny the concept of the Light version introduction. The students' answers, however, confirmed the authors hypothesis – according to the students' assessment, UML is most frequently classified as moderately difficult (51%), rather difficult (33%) or very difficult (7%). It means that more than 90% of respondents would

Figure 1. UML complexity level

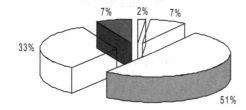

Figure 2. Adequacy of the number of UML diagrams

welcome the more introductory, i.e. the Light version of UML.

3.2 UML Diagrams Cardinality

The students taking part in the survey had a chance to exercise all 13 types of UML diagrams. The number of UML diagrams is in a natural way related to the UML complexity. Majority of interviewees (over 57%) assessed that the UML standard comprises too many types of diagrams, as shown at Figure 2. The remaining respondents accepted all types of diagrams, not assessing however the potential surplus of cardinality of modeling notions that were used in each type of diagram.

3.3 Usefulness of the Specific Diagrams

Since only the part of the formal UML specification is used in practice, the problem of uselessness of the specific diagram types arises. The survey revealed that the future system analysts propose the following diagrams as the most useful ones (Figure 3):

- Class Diagrams (62% of accepting responses),
- Use Case Diagrams (56%),
- Activity Diagrams (26%),
- Sequence Diagrams (21%).

The investigations acknowledged commonly recognized leading role of Class Diagrams and Use Case Diagrams as the basic graphical formal-

isms for object-oriented modeling of the structure and dynamics of information system respectively. Supplementary, Use Case Diagrams initiate iterative- incremental lifecycle in RUP and the other IS object-oriented methodologies. On the other hand, State Machine Diagrams (28%), Timing Diagrams (19%), Deployment Diagrams (13%) and Composite Structure Diagrams (12%) are recognized as the most useless diagrams. In the opinion of teachers, students underestimated the relevance of State Machine Diagram and Deployment Diagram. While the former is semantically rich, but often rejected by novices, the latter is used at the lower, closer to implementation, disciplines of system development process. Therefore, the teaching of these types of diagrams could be transferred to the object-oriented programming courses.

3.4 Diagrams Types and their Modeling Constructs

As concerned the fourth criterion, students were supposed to enumerate diagrams particularly overwhelmed with UML notions (Figure 4). Most interaction diagrams were found on the list. Sequence Diagram was considered overwhelmed or very overwhelmed with specific modeling constructs by 32% of the interviewees, while Interaction Overview Diagram and Communication Diagram by 28% and 27% respectively. Only Timing Diagram was ranked as average. On the other hand, number of UML notions used while creating a diagram was not a problem in the case of Object Diagrams, Use Case Diagrams and Class Diagrams. Only 14%, 18% and 20%

Figure 3. Usefulness of the specific UML diagrams

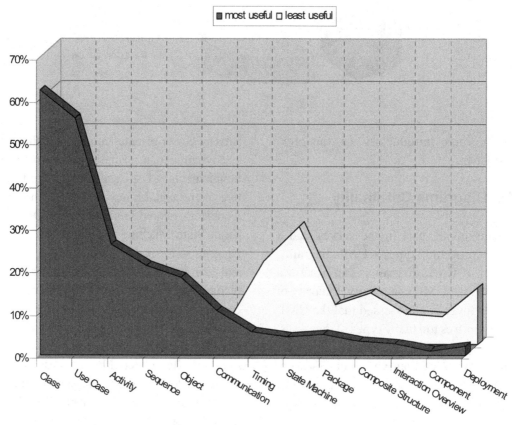

Figure 4. UML diagrams overwhelmed with modeling constructs

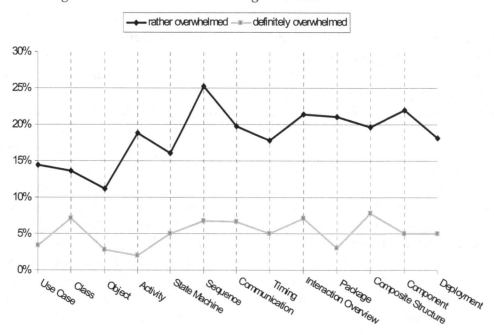

of the respondents respectively mentioned these diagrams as overwhelming. The case of Class Diagrams may be considered as an interesting one. This type of diagram is in fact a complex one, consisting of a relatively large number of modeling constructs. However they are accepted and naturally mastered by students, owing to the awareness of the significance of the classes in contemporary programming languages.

3.5 User-Friendliness of UML Diagrams

User-friendliness is one of the keywords and challenges of Computing field. Assessment of UML diagrams under this angle should facilitate the specification of UML Light version. Definitely the Use Case Diagram was recognized as the most easy to use in the family of 13 UML diagrams

(Figure 5). The survey respondents (74%) confirm this feature, so required at the high level of system specification. This aspect of the system model should be as precise as possible, remaining easy to interpret by all system stakeholders, in particular system owners, managers and future users. Acknowledged user-friendliness of Use Case Diagrams is a good starting point for achieving system specification correctness, precision, consistency and completeness by using the other related UML diagrams, supporting Use Case Diagrams.

Due to the pragmatic role of Class Diagrams for programming, they have also achieved a high rank of acceptance – 66% of the respondents classified this type of diagram as an easy or very easy one. Students appreciated (59%) the significance of Activity Diagrams as a backbone of algorithms and programs. Certain types of UML

Figure 5. Assessment of UML diagrams user-friendliness

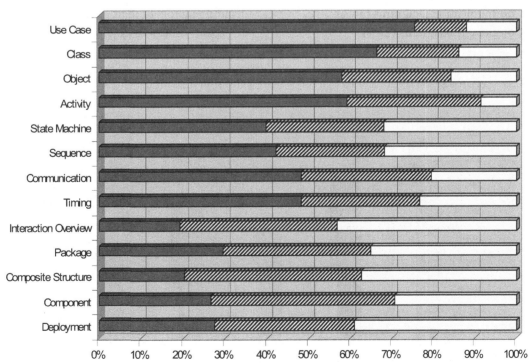

139

diagrams ought to be reconsidered in respect of their "user-friendliness". In particular, Interaction Overview Diagrams were classified as difficult or very difficult to use by 43% of the students. Also Deployment Diagrams (39%) and Composite Structure Diagrams (38%) were found difficult to use. Therefore, the mentioned diagrams are the natural candidates for excluding them from the scope of the UML 2.x Light version.

3.6 UML Diagrams Best-Suited for Source Code Generation

The development of CASE tools inspired the research and works on source code generation on the basics of system documentation. UML diagrams at large give the profound opportunity for code generation on the basis of precise system specifications. The interviewees assessed the following types of diagrams as a particularly good basis for code generation:

- Class Diagrams (66% total);
- Activity Diagrams (42%);
- Sequence Diagrams (34%);
- Communication Diagrams (34%);
- Component Diagrams (23%).

Again the Class Diagrams have been recognized as the most helpful types of UML diagrams while transferring system model into a code (Figure 6). Both the contribution and usefulness of the other UML diagrams in respect of code generation, but not included in the aforementioned group of five types, have been estimated as low.

3.7 Modeling the System Dynamics

Potential UML user has quite a number of UML diagrams types used for describing system dynamics at his/her disposal. Some of them are relatively intuitive and easy to use (eg. Activity Diagrams, Timing Diagrams) while the others are very precise, robust and consequently difficult, but they still remain helpful and are eagerly used by system analysts and designers. In particular, Sequence and Communication Diagrams are not as intuitive as diagrams used for modeling system requirements, by and large because they are addressed to professional and experienced programmers. Precision in developing low-level system dynamics specifications as well as their transferability to the source code should be the deciding factors of their functionality. As shown at Figure 7, besides Interaction Overview Dia-

Figure 6. UML diagrams best-suited for source code generation

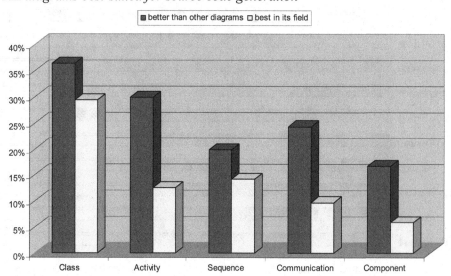

Figure 7. UML diagrams for supporting system dynamics specification

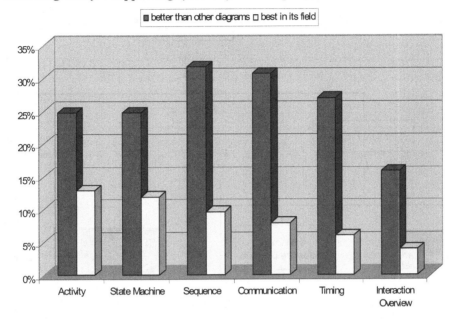

grams, all remaining UML dynamics diagrams are helpful in preparing such specifications. Activity Diagrams were considered the best in this field by as much as 13% of the respondents. Given the fact that Activity Diagrams are rather user-friendly, the closest to the structured methodologies, they remain a good basis for specifying the system logic and source code backbone.

4 SUMMARY

The survey results presented in this chapter are helpful in defining the scope of the UML 2.x Light version. Such version would be extremely stimulating and motivating in effective teaching of UML 2.x. This concept was warmly welcomed by students and still does not limit the UML potential. The system specifications elaborated using the Light version could be subsequently extended towards the complete systems by the implementation of full scope of UML modeling notions and diagrams.

To sum up, the following UML diagrams were selected and indicated in the survey as the components of the proposed UML Light version:

- Use Case Diagrams,
- Class Diagrams,
- Activity Diagrams,
- Sequence Diagrams.

These four types of diagrams (Figure 8) enable modeling of all essential system aspects, i.e. system requirements, analysis and design of system structure and dynamics. This conclusion was revealed by the first criterion analyzed in the reported survey and then consequently supported by six succeeding criteria.

Not all modeling constructs are used while preparing the system specifications according to the UML 2.x Light version. Students are particularly overwhelmed by the number of modeling notions mostly while developing Sequence Diagrams and Activity Diagrams. Therefore, only the most relevant of these diagrams notions should

Figure 8. UML 2.x diagrams selected for the Light version

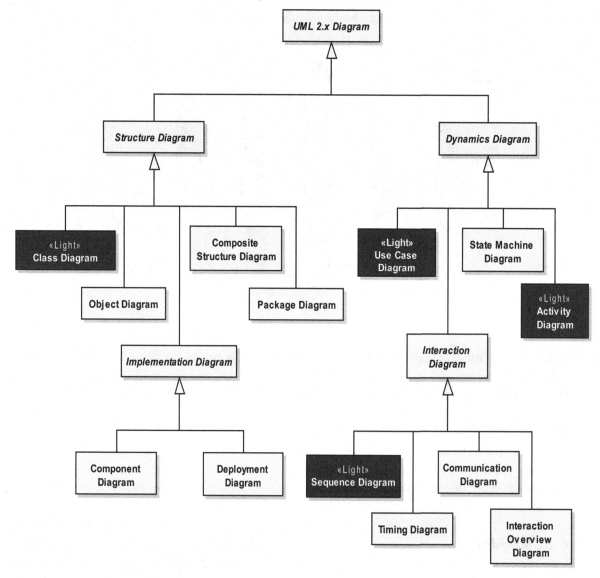

be transferred to the UML 2.x Light version. Wrycza, Marcinkowski, Wyrzykowski (2005a) divided the UML modeling notions into basic and advanced ones. The proposal of the division of the specific modeling constructs adequate for the four selected types of diagrams respectively is presented in Table 1.

Both four selected types of UML diagrams (Class, Use Case, Activity and Sequence Diagrams), shown at Figure 8 as well as respective basic modeling categories of these types of diagrams (Table 1) form the proposed scope of UML 2.x Light version according to the survey accomplished.

Table 1. The basic and advanced modeling constructs in respect of UML 2.x Light version

	Class Diagram	Use Case Diagram	Activity Diagram	Sequence Diagram
Basic notions	Class Attribute Operation Binary association Association name Role name Navigability Multiplicity Aggregation Composition	Use case Actor Binary association	Activity Subactivity Activity Initial Activity Final Control Flow	Actor Class Boundary class Control class Entity class Lifeline Execution specification Synchronous message
Advanced notions	Responsibility Visibility Static attributes/operations N-ary associations Association classes Reflexive associations Multiple associations Qualification Generalization Dependency Realization	«include» dependency «extend» dependency Generalization Types of actors Multiplicity Navigability Realization	Decision Activity edge connector Merge node Action Pin Activity parameter node Weight Signal Central buffer Data store Activity partition Expansion region Interruptible activity region Exception handler	Asynchronous message Return message Lost message Found message Balking message Timeout message Guard condition Message to self Iteration Branching Interaction fragment Interaction occurrence Gate

REFERENCES

Ambler, S. W. (2005). *The Elements of UML 2.0 Style*. Cambridge: Cambridge University Press.

Booch, G., Rumbaugh, J., & Jacobson, I. (2004). *The UML Reference Manual*. 2nd Edition. Boston: Addison-Wesley.

Burton, P. J., & Bruhn, R. E. (2004). Using UML to Facilitate the Teaching of Object-Oriented Systems Analysis & Design. *Journal of Computing Sciences in Colleges, 19*.

DeLooze, L. L. (2005). *Minimal UML Diagrams for a Data-Driven Web Site*. SIGITE.

Dobing, B., & Parsons, J. (2006). How UML is Used. *Communications of ACM, 49*.

Flint, S., Gardner, H., & Boughton, C. (2004). Executable/Translatable UML in Computing Education. In R. Lister & A. Young (Eds.), *Conferences in Research and Practice in Information Technology, 30*.

Jacobson, I., Christerson, M., Jonsson, P., & Overgaard, G. (1992). *Object-Oriented Software Engineering: A Use-Case Driven Approach*. Boston: Addison-Wesley.

Kontio, M. (2005). *Architectural Manifesto: Designing Software Architectures*. Part 5. Introducing the 4+1 View Model. http://www-128.ibm.com/developerworks/wireless/library/wi-arch11.

Kruchten, P. (1995). Architectural Blueprints – the "4+1" View Model of Software Architecture. *IEEE Software, 12*.

OMG (2006). Object Management Group. *The UML 2.1 Superstructure Convenience Document*. http://www.omg.org/cgi-bin/doc?ptc/2006-04-02.

OMG (2005). Object Management Group. *Unified Modeling Language 2.0 Superstructure Specification*. http://www.omg.org/cgi-bin/doc?formal/05-07-04.

Trujillo, J. (2006). A Report on the First International Workshop on Best Practices of UML. *SIGMOD Record, 35.*

Wrycza, S., Marcinkowski, B., & Wyrzykowski, K. (2005a). *Systems Modeling with UML 2* (in Polish). Helion, Gliwice, (pp. 1-456).

Wrycza, S., & Marcinkowski, B. (2005b). UML 2 Teaching at Postgraduate Studies – Prerequisites and Practice. *Proceedings of ISECON 2005, 22, New Orleans. AITP Foundation for Information Technology Education.*

Wrycza, S., & Marcinkowski, B. (2006). UML 2 Academic Course – Methodological Background and Survey Benchmarking. *Proceedings of ISECON 2006, 23, Dallas. AITP Foundation for Information Technology Education.*

Chapter XI
User Interface Generation from the Data Schema

Akhilesh Bajaj
University of Tulsa, USA

Jason Knight
University of Tulsa, USA

ABSTRACT

Traditionally, the data model and the process model have been considered separately when modeling an application for construction purposes. The system analysis and design area has largely ignored the issue of the relationship between the user interface (UI) and the underlying data schema, leaving UI creation within the purview of the human computer interaction (HCI) literature. Traditional HCI methods however, underutilize the information in the data schema when designing user screens. Much of the work on automatic user interface (UI) generation has met with limited success because of the added load on the human designer to use specialized scripts for UI specification. In this research in progress, the authors propose a methodology applicable to database driven systems that a) automatically infers a draft interface directly from an extended entity relationship (EER) model schema and b) lists the interactions that need to take place between the designer and the tool in order to generate the final user schema.

INTRODUCTION

The graphical user interface has become both ubiquitous and relatively uniform in providing access to applications for diverse users (Myers et al., 2000). From the early 1980-s, user interface (UI) management systems focused on providing human designers high-level specification languages such as state transition diagrams or event based representations to specify the interface in response to events (Jacob, 1986, Olsen, 1986). These representations have become progressively richer and model-based interface development tools today range from automatic interface generators to tools that offer advice based on task representations.

This research in progress is important because traditionally, the data model and the process model have been considered separately when modeling an application for construction purposes. The system analysis and design (SA&D) area has largely ignored the issue of the relationship between the user interface (UI) and the underlying data schema, leaving UI creation within the purview of the human computer interaction (HCI) literature. Traditional HCI methods underutilize the information in the data schema when designing user screens. However, business applications are usually database driven, and the UI for most business information systems represents processes that allow users to interact with the data. In this work, we take a first step in bridging this gap between the SA&D and HCI literatures, and propose a generalized methodology to generate a UI that uses the data schema as the foundation.

Figure 1 (Szekely, 1996) describes the model-based interface development process. The model component organizes the specification into three layers. Domain models correspond to the data schema. Examples of task models include data flow diagrams or other activity diagrams. An abstract UI specification provides a set of low level interface tasks such as selecting from a set of elements, information elements selected from the domain model, and how the two should be grouped. The concrete UI specification deals with the actual interface elements such as the windows, buttons, checkboxes and navigation buttons. Based on Figure 1, it is clear that the majority of model-based environments explicitly differentiate between task (process) models and data models.

The very great majority of business applications involve a database back-end with a front-end UI, and hence we utilize the extended entity relationship (EER) model to capture the data schema (Chen, 1976, Smith and Smith, 1977). Our methodology uses a set of rules to map EER objects automatically to provide a first cut user-interface, and then provides an opportunity for a structured dialog with the user to attempt to assuage some of the problems with the data-model-only approach.

A METHODOLOGY TO DERIVE A UI FROM AN EER SCHEMA

Before presenting the methodology, we list the concepts in the EER model that we will map. We

Figure 1. Model-based interface development process (Szekely, 1996)

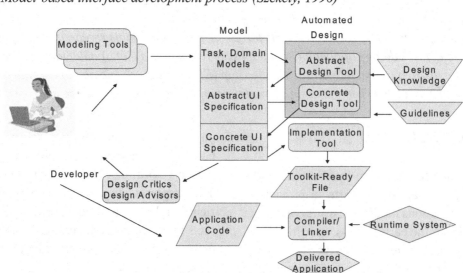

base our list of concepts largely from standard database textbooks like (Korth et al., 2005) and assume an EER schema to consist of the following concepts:

- Entity sets,
- Relationship sets with *0/1* cardinality on at least one side, and any cardinality on the other,
- Relationship sets with *m:n* cardinality and *n*-ary relationships
- Attributes of entity and relationship sets,
- Multi-valued attributes
- Composite attributes
- Entity subclasses that have extra attributes and/or extra relationships, with no multiple inheritance
- Weak entity sets (existence dependencies) with a unique identifier

As summarized in (Szekely, 1996), an automatic interface generation algorithm should specify components at the following levels:

a. *P*: Presentation units (the different windows and a list of their contents)
b. *N*: Navigation between presentation units
c. *A*: abstract interface items (*e.g.,* a drop down list, a check box, etc.)
d. *C*: Concrete interface items (how each abstract item will be implemented, such as a list-of-values for a drop-down list specification)
e. *L*: Window layout (position, font size, and other presentation criteria

Our methodology, described next, consists of two phases: the *automated generation* of the first-cut interface (FCI), followed by the *structured dialog with the human designer* to generate the second-cut interface (SCI).

Generating the First Cut Interface (FCI)

The FCI consists of **primitive** screens that interact with the data, as well as provides for navigation between them. For convenience, we present our methodology for FCI generation in the following format. For **each EER concept**, we list the mapping to a relational schema and to the UI. We will not consider the *C* components of the mapping here, since *C* is system dependent (*e.g.*, different UI systems will implement drop down lists differently). The *L* aspect is described in the end, since it contains common rules that apply to all the screens.

Entity Sets

Relational mapping: Create a table for the entity set. The columns of the table are the attributes of the strong entity set. The primary key of the table is the primary key of the entity set.

UI Mapping
Presentation Units: Create a separate screen with all the attributes of the entity set. Additional buttons labeled CREATE, UPDATE, DELETE, RESET, EXIT are also created for the screen. These allow basic database access operations, as well as allow the user to exit the application.

Navigation: The screen gets links to the screens that correspond to every *m:n* relationship set in which the entity set participates, and to the screens that correspond to every multi-valued attribute of the entity set

Abstract Interface Items
- For enumerated type attributes, provide a fixed list of values.
- For attributes that are dates, currency, strings or numbers, provide a text box.
- For the primary key attribute(s), provide a non-updatable text box (grayed out) with a

drop down list to search for existing rows in the table.

- For attributes that are Boolean, provide a check box
- Primary key fields should be in grey background and non-updateable

Relationship Sets with 0/1 Cardinality on at Least One Side, and Any Cardinality on the Other

Relational mapping: Add a column(s) in the table that corresponds to the entity set that is on the "Any Cardinality" side. The column(s) we add here is the primary key of the entity set that is on the 0/1 side and any other attributes of the relationship set.

UI Mapping

Presentation Units: Use already developed screens say, S1 for the entity set that corresponds to the "Any Cardinality" side, and S2 for the entity set that corresponds to the 0/1 side

Navigation: No additional navigation provided here

Abstract Interface Items

- In S1, provide a drop-down list of values that show the primary key of the entity on the "Any Cardinality" side.
- Follow the same rules for other relationship attributes as described for entity sets.
- In S2, provide a view only drop down list for all entities on the "any cardinality" side that are linked to the entity which is displayed in all of S2.

Relationship Sets with m:n Cardinality and n-ary Relationships

Relational mapping: Create a separate table for the relationship set. The columns of the table are the attributes of the relationship set (if any) + primary keys of all the entity sets that participate

in the relationship set. The primary key of the table is = the primary keys of all the entity sets that participate in the relationship set.

UI Mapping

Presentation Units: Create a separate screen with all the attributes of the relationship set, as well as the primary keys of all participant entity sets. Additional buttons labeled CREATE, UPDATE, DELETE, RESET, EXIT are also created for the screen. These allow basic database access operations, as well as allow the user to exit the application. If the relationship has no attributes then disable the UPDATE button.

Navigation: The screen gets links to the screens that correspond to every participant entity set

Abstract Interface Items

- For enumerated type attributes, provide a fixed list of values.
- For attributes that are dates, currency, strings or numbers, provide a text box.
- For the primary key attributes, provide a drop-down list of relevant values drawn from the participant entity sets
- For attributes that are Boolean, provide a check box
- Primary key fields should be non-updateable (grayed out) and drop down search. If no attributes other than primary keys, then no UPDATE button should be there.

Multi-Valued Attributes

Relational mapping: Create a separate table for the multi-valued attribute. The columns of the table are the primary key of the entity set to which the attribute belongs + a separate column for values of the attribute. The primary key of the table is all the columns of the table.

UI Mapping

Presentation Units: Create a separate screen with the primary key of the entity set and the multi-valued attribute. Additional buttons labeled CREATE, DELETE, RESET, EXIT are also created for the screen. These allow basic database access operations, as well as allow the user to exit the application.

Navigation: The screen gets a link to the screen for the entity set that owns the multi-valued attribute.

Abstract Interface Items

- For enumerated type attributes, provide a fixed list of values.
- For attributes that are dates, currency, strings or numbers, provide a text box.
- For the primary key attributes of the owner entity set, provide a non-updatable text box (grayed out) with a drop down list to search for existing rows in the table.

Composite Attributes

Relational mapping: No separate table is created for composite attributes. Only the leaf attributes are used when transferring to the relational schema. The only effect on the UI is at the L level, where attributes that belong to a composite hierarchy should be grouped together on the screen corresponding to that entity set or relationship set.

Entity Subclasses that have Extra Attributes And/Or Extra Relationships

Relational mapping: Create a separate table for the superclass first, using the rules for mapping entity sets we have seen earlier. For each subclass entity set, create a separate table. The columns of each table = the additional attributes of the corresponding subclass entity set + the primary key of the superclass entity set. The primary key of the subclass table is the primary key of the superclass table.

UI Mapping

Presentation Units: Create a separate screen with all the extra attributes of the subclass, as well as the primary key of the superclass entity set. Additional buttons labeled CREATE, UPDATE, DELETE, RESET, EXIT are also created for the screen. These allow basic database access operations, as well as allow the user to exit the application.

Navigation: The screen gets a link to the screen that corresponds to the superclass entity set

Abstract Interface Items

- For enumerated type attributes, provide a fixed list of values.
- For attributes that are dates, currency, strings or numbers, provide a text box.
- For the primary key attributes, provide a drop-down list of relevant values drawn from the superclass entity sets
- For attributes that are Boolean, provide a check box

Weak Entity Sets (Existence Dependencies) with a Unique Identifier

Relational mapping: Create a separate table for the weak entity set. The columns of the table are the attributes of the weak entity set + the primary key of the corresponding strong entity set. The primary key of the table is the primary key of the corresponding strong entity set + the unique identifier of the weak entity set.

UI Mapping

Presentation Units: Create a separate screen with all the attributes of the weak entity set, as well as the primary key of the strong entity set. Additional buttons labeled CREATE,

UPDATE, DELETE, RESET, EXIT are also created for the screen. These allow basic database access operations, as well as allow the user to exit the application.

Navigation: The screen gets a link to the screen that corresponds to the strong entity set

Abstract Interface Items

- For enumerated type attributes, provide a fixed list of values.
- For attributes that are dates, currency, strings or numbers, provide a text box.
- For the primary key attributes, provide a drop-down list of relevant values drawn from the superclass entity sets as well as a non-updateable field for the unique identifier attributes of the weak entity set.
- For attributes that are Boolean, provide a check box

As shown, the primitive screens in the FCI correspond to tables in the relational schema that is derived from the EER schema. Each screen provides *write* access to one table, and *read* access to multiple tables, as specified in the Presentation Units. Navigation is also provided to other primitive screens as specified. Next we describe the *Layout* guidelines for the screens in the first cut interface, drawing on well known HCI principles.

Layout Guidelines for FCI Screens

Basic layout principles that we utilize include the following:

- Grouping like objects
- Using familiar language
- Using color
- Consistency
- Clearly marked Exits
- Shortcuts
- Easy reversal

These are summarized from classic works such as (Shneiderman, 1998, Nielsen, 1993). Next we describe definite guidelines for incorporating several of these concepts in the first cut interface.

Grouping like Objects

Grouping like objects is useful because it allows the user to create multiple-item chunks. This allows the users' short term memory to manage more items on the screen than the usual 7 +/- 2 items. Grouping can be performed using line boundaries, or spatial proximity. This rule can be applied in many ways on the FCI screens. First, for each screen corresponding to an entity set, weak entity set, subclass and relationship set, the primary key fields used to identify objects in the table that the screen can write to, should be grouped together. Second, attributes that are intrinsic to an entity set or a relationship set should be grouped together. Third, primary keys that allow selection from other tables (as in the case of 1:n relationships) should be grouped together. Fourth primary keys that are view-only should be grouped together. Fifth, attributes that are part of the same composite hierarchy should be grouped together. Sixth, buttons providing database functionality such as CREATE, UPDATE and DELETE should be grouped together. The RESET button should be kept in its own group. Finally, the EXIT button should be kept separate from the others.

Using familiar language: One of the tenets of good data modeling is to use the language of the users in creating the names of objects and attributes. Since the primitive screens are based on the data schema, our methodology provides support for this HCI requirement.

Consistency: Using the FCI generation rules promotes consistency in look and feel. For each screen, the primary key of the table that it writes to should provide a drop down selection. All other primary keys from other tables that are read only from that screen should be select only, but should provide a GO button to be able to jump to the write screen for the corresponding table, so that particular record may be edited from its relevant screen. Buttons that perform the same tasks across screens should be in the same location, and have the same look and feel.

Clearly Marked Exits: This is useful to provide a feeling of user empowerment. Since the first cut interface screens all have clearly marked exits that allow us to exit the application, this HCI requirements is supported in our methodology.

AN ILLUSTRATIVE EXAMPLE OF A FIRST CUT INTERFACE

Figure 2 depicts a simple EER schema, following standard diagramming conventions (Korth et al., 2005). Attributes are next to each entity and relationship set. Figure 3 illustrates the 4 screens

Figure 2. EER schema for application

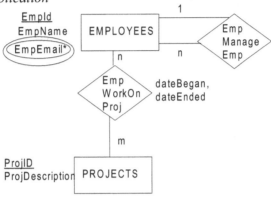

Figure 3. The four first cut UI screens from the EER schema

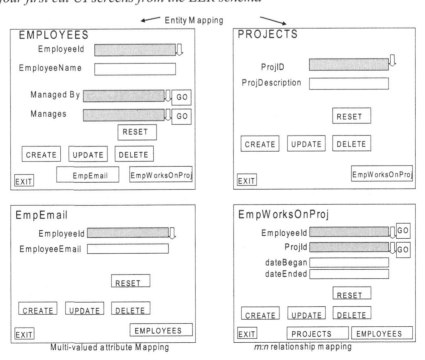

in the FCI, generated using the AIG algorithm outlined before.

After the first cut interface has been generated, using the described guidelines, the primitive screens need to be augmented with a set of navigation screens as well as view only items specific to the application. This is described in brief next, because of space limitations. It will be presented in more detail at the conference.

Generating the Second Cut Interface

The motivation is to overcome some of the earlier disadvantages of AIG toolkits. This step is based on interaction from users, as well as the process diagram for the application. The steps in the SCI can be divided into the following categories:

- Generation of menu screens that perform navigation to the primitive screens
- Bundling of primitive screens into one window if access to more than one table is required for a business process
- Removal of attributes from certain screens (*e.g. salary* from the *employees* screen)
- Addition of specific view-only information that the employee needs to perform the data entry on a screen *E.g.*, a summary for the sales of a particular customer for the last year can be useful view-only information when updating the *customer_category* field on the primitive screen corresponding to the *customers* entity set. customers screen).
- Addition of graphic reports on certain primitive screens
- Addition of intuitive identifiers such as *customer_name* for the *customers* primitive screen that allow for easier human searching in the drop down list for customers and add more intuitive identifiers such as *name* to the primary keys in the drop down lists. In order to simplify the human workload, we do not allow the addition of any updateable fields,

the idea being that each screen provides at most one updateable table, though multiple readable tables. This is similar to the notion of updateable views in the database literature.

CONCLUSION

In this research in progress, we propose a methodology to infer a set of primitive screens from an EER schema, that serves as a foundation for a complete UI. The chief contribution of the methodology is that it focuses on database driven applications, and balances automatic generation of the UI with input from the designer in order to arrive at a final UI. We are testing our methodology with a teaching case that consists of approximately 12 tables. Students or end users familiar with the domain will be provided a user interface generated with the methodology described here and asked to evaluate the interface.

As part of this work, we aim to extend the rules described here to incorporate higher level navigation screens, construct a compiler that automatically generates the first cut schema based on the rules described here, and test the methodology for large scale applications.

REFERENCES

Chen, P. P. (1976). *ACM Transactions on Database Systems, 1,* 9-36.

Jacob, R. J. K. (1986). *ACM Transactions on Graphics, 5,* 283-317.

Korth, H., Silberschatz, A., & Sudarshan, S. (2005). *Database Systems Concepts.* McGraw Hill, New York.

Myers, B., Hudson, S. E., & Pausch, R. (2000). *ACM Transactions on Computer-Human Interaction, 7,* 3-28.

Nielsen, J. (1993). *Usability Engineering,* Academic Press.

Olsen, D. R. (1986). *ACM Transactions on Information Systems, 5,* 318-344.

Shneiderman, B. (1998). *Designing the User Interface.* Addison Wesley Longman.

Smith, J. M., & Smith, D. C. P. (1977). *ACM Transactions on Database Systems, 2,* 105-133.

Szekely, P. A. (1996). In F. Bodart, & J. Vanderdonckt (Eds.), *Design, Specification and Verification of Interactive Systems: Proceedings of the Third International Eurographics Workshop.* Namur, Belgium.

Chapter XII
Decision Rule for Investment in Reusable Code

Roy Gelbard
Bar-Ilan University, Israel

ABSTRACT

Reusable code helps to decrease code errors, code units and therefore development time. It serves to improve quality and productivity frameworks in software development. The question is not HOW to make the code reusable, but WHICH amount of software components would be most beneficial (i.e. cost-effective in terms of reuse), and WHAT method should be used to decide whether to make a component reusable or not. If we had unlimited time and resources, we could write any code unit in a reusable way. In other words, its reusability would be 100%. However, in real life, resources and time are limited. Given these constraints, decisions regarding reusability are not always straightforward. The current chapter focuses on decision-making rules for investing in reusable code. It attempts to determine the parameters, which should be taken into account in decisions relating to degrees of reusability. Two new models are presented for decisions-making relating to reusability: (i) a restricted model, and (ii) a non-restricted model. Decisions made by using these models are then analyzed and discussed.

INTRODUCTION

Software reuse helps decrease code errors, code units and, therefore, development time; thus improving quality and productivity of software development. Reuse is based on the premise that educing a solution from the statement of a problem involves more effort (labor, computa-

tion, etc.) than inducing a solution from a similar problem for which such efforts have already been expended. Therefore, software reuse challenges are structural, organizational and managerial, as well as technical.

Economic considerations and cost-benefit analyses in general must be at the center of any discussion of software reuse; hence, the cost-benefit issue is not HOW to make the code reusable, but

WHICH amount of software components would be most beneficial (i.e. cost-effective for reuse), and WHAT method should be used when deciding whether to make a component reusable or not.

If we had unlimited time and resources, we could write any code unit in a reusable way. In other words, its reusability would be 100% (reusability refers to the degree to which a code unit can be reused). However, in real life, resources and time are limited. Given these constraints, reusability decisions are not always straightforward.

Literature review shows that there are a variety of models used for calculating-evaluating reuse effectiveness, but they are not focused on the issue of the degree to which a code is reusable. Thus the real question is how to make reusability pragmatic and efficient, i.e. a decision rule for investment in reusable code. The current chapter focuses on the parameters, which should be taken into account when making reusability degree decisions. Two new models are presented here for reusability decision-making:

- A Non-Restricted Model, which does not take into account time, resources or investment restrictions.
- A Restricted Model, which takes the aforementioned restrictions into account.

The models are compared, using the same data, to test whether they lead to the same conclusions or whether a contingency approach is preferable.

BACKGROUND

Notwithstanding differences between reuse approaches, it is useful to think of software reuse in terms of attempts to minimize the average cost of a reuse occurrence (Mili et al 1995).

*[Search + (1-p) * (ApproxSearch +q * Adaptation* old *+ (1-q)* Development* new *)]*

Where:

- *Search (ApproxSearch)* is the average cost of formulating a search statement of a library of reusable components and either finding one that matches the requirements exactly (appreciatively), or being convinced that none exists.
- *Adaptation* old is the average cost of adapting a component returned by approximate retrieval.
- *Development* new is the average cost of developing a component that has no match, exact or approximate, in the library.

For reuse to be cost-effective, the aforementioned must be smaller than:

p *Development* exact *+(1-p)* * **q** * *Development* approx *+(1-p)* *(1-q)' Development* new*)

Where:

- *Development* exact and *Development* new represent the average cost of developing custom-tailored versions of components in the library that could be used as is, or adapted, respectively. Note that all these averages are time averages, and not averages of individual components, i.e. a reusable component is counted as many times as it is used.

Developing reusable software aims at maximizing P (probability of finding an exact match) and Q (probability of finding an approximate match), i.e. maximizing the coverage of the application domain, and minimizing adaptation for a set of common mismatches, i.e. packaging components, in such a way that the most common old mismatches are handled easily. Increasing P and Q does not necessarily mean putting more components in the library; it could also mean adding components that are more frequently needed, because adding components not only has its direct expenses (adaptation costs), but also increases search costs.

There are two main approaches to **code adaptation**: (1) Identifying components that are generally useful, and (2) covering the same set of needs with fewer components, which involves two paradigms: (i) abstraction, and (ii) composition. Composition supports the creation of a virtually unlimited number of aggregates from the same set of components, and reduces the risk of combinatorial explosion that would result from enumerating all the possible configurations. In general, the higher the level of abstraction at which composition takes place, the wider the range of systems (and behaviours) that can be obtained. The combination of abstraction and composition provides a powerful paradigm for constructing systems from reusable components (Mili et al. 1995).

Frakes and Terry (1996) describe a wide range of metrics and adaptation models for software reuse. Six types of metrics and models are reviewed: cost-benefit models, maturity assessment models, amount of reuse metrics, failure modes models, reusability assessment models, and reuse library metrics (Frakes & Terry 1996). Other studies (Otso 1995; Henninger 1999; Virtanen 2001; Ye 2002; Ye & Fischer 2002), present additional metrics and methods. These studies evaluate and make comparisons, but as is typical in an emerging discipline such as systematic software reuse, many of these metrics and models still lack formal validation. However, in some cases they are found useful in industrial practice (Ferri et al. 1997; Chaki et al. 2004).

In other cases questions are raised; several researchers identify and address problems that still exist in the framework of reuse (William et al. 2005; Krik et al. 2006; Burkhardt et al. 2007). Garcia et al. (2006) find inconsistency in software measurement terminology. It seems that the factors affecting reuse of software assets, haven't changed much along the last decade, but still they

are quite complicated for implementation (Mellarkod et al. 2007; Spinellis 2007). Mohagheghi et al. (2007) present a review of industrial studies, while Desouza et al. (2006) indicate four dynamics for bringing use back into software reuse.

Empirical works (Virtanen 2001; Ye 2002; Mens & Tourwé 2004; Tomer et al. 2004; Mohagheghi et al. 2007) have analyzed existing reuse metrics and their industrial applicability. These metrics are then applied to a collection of public domain software products, and projects categories to assess the level of correlation between them and other well-known software metrics such as complexity, volume, lines of code, etc.

The current chapter is focused on decision-making rules for investment in reusable code. The well known "Simple Model" and "Development Cost Model" deal with these decisions, but do not take into account restrictions and constraints such as time, budget, resources, or other kinds of investment, such as delivery time that may impact on the decision to reuse.

ANALYZING NEW REUSE MODELS

Assume a software development project contains 3 code components: A, B and C, and we need to determine two things: Which of these components should be reusable? What criteria should be taken into account?

Table 1. Choice alternatives

Alternative	Component A	Component B	Component C
1	-	-	-
2	+	-	-
3	-	+	-
4	+	+	-
5	-	-	+
6	+	-	+
7	-	+	+
8	+	+	+

There are eight combination-choice alternatives for these 3 components, as shown in Table 1 (+ represents "make reusable", - represents "don't make reusable").

A. The Non-Restricted Model

The model contains the following parameters:

C_i Cost of creating component **i** from scratch (without making it reusable).

R_i Cost of making component **i** reusable (extra costs – not included in C_i).

IC_i Cost of implementing reusable component **i** into code.

NR_i Number of reuses of component i. (C, R and NR are in man-hours).

Savings resulting from making component **i** reusable are represented as follows:

$$SAV_i = NR_i *(C_i - IC_i) - (C_i + R_i)$$

Therefore: If $SAV_i > 0$, it is worthwhile to make component **i** reusable.

Suppose a company that employs two kinds of programmers: **M** and **N**. Programmers of type **M** are permanent employees of the firm. Programmers of type **N** are highly qualified consultants who are employed by the company for specific projects. The company is going to write / create / develop a new project, and has to make a decision regarding which components should be reusable.

The following are additional parameters:

C_{im} Hours needed for programmer M to create component **i** from scratch.

R_{im} Hours needed for programmer M to make component **i** reusable.

IC_{im} Hours needed for programmer M to implement reusable component **i** into code.

S_m Costs of programmer M, per 1 hour.

Hence:

C_i $= Min(C_{im}*S_m, C_{in}*S_n)$
IC_i $= Min(IC_{im}*S_m, IC_{in}*S_n)$
R_i $= Min(R_{im}*S_m, R_{in}*S_n)$

Hence:

$$SAV_i = NR_i *(Min(C_{im}*S_m, C_{in}*S_n) - Min(IC_{im}*S_m, IC_{in}*S_n)) - (Min(C_{im}*S_m, C_{in}*S_n) + Min(R_{im}*S_m, R_{in}*S_n))$$

B. The Restricted Model

The Non-Restricted model has the following limitations:

- It requires absolute values
- It is quite difficult to measure parameters such as: C_i, R_i and IC_i
- It does not take into account the most typical situation where time and budget are restricted as well as in-house investment in reuse, i.e. time and resources for reusable code developing.

In order to avoid these limitations, the Restricted Model is based upon the following parameters:

I   Maximal **investment** that can be allocated for writing a reusable code.

T   Maximal calendar **time** that can be allocated for writing a reusable code.

I_i Percent of "**I**" needed to make component **i** reusable.

T_i Percent of "**T**" needed to make component **i** reusable.

C_i Relative **complexity** of creating component **i** from scratch.

F_i **Frequency** (%) of future projects that are likely to reuse component **i**.

P_i Relative **profit** of making component **i** reusable.

R_I Remainder of "**I**", after some reusable components have been written.

R_T **R**emainder of "**T**", after some reusable components have been written.

Assume that: **Pi = Ci * Fi.**

Hence: Component **i** is the next component to be made reusable if:

Pi = Max(P1, P2, ..., Pn-1, Pn)
Ii <= RI
Ti <= RT

C. Illustrative Example - Non-Restricted Model

The following example (Example 1) demonstrates the decision made by the Non-Restricted Model. Assume we want to develop 10 projects, each one containing components A, B and C according to Table 2.

Hence:

NRa = 10,   NRb = 1,   NRc = 4

Table 3 presents illustrative assumptions concerning **Cim** and **Cin** (hours needed for

programmer type M and N to create component **i** from scratch).

Moreover, assume programmers' costs to be: **Sm = 20, Sn = 40**

Hence:

Ca = Min(300*20, 200*40) = 6,000
Cb = Min(20*20, 10*40) = 400
Cc = Min(150*20, 100*40) = 3,000

Table 4 presents illustrative assumptions concerning **Rim** and **Rin** (hours needed for programmers type M and N to make component **i** reusable).

Hence:

Ra = Min(650*20, 300*40) = 12,000
Rb = Min(15*20, 7*40) = 280
Rc = Min(150*20, 80*40) = 3,000

Table 5 presents illustrative assumptions concerning **ICim** and **ICin** (Hours needed for programmers type M /N to implement reusable component **i** into code).

Hence:

Table 2. Example 1, Number of components for future reuse

Project	1	2	3	4	5	6	7	8	9	10
Component A	+	+	+	+	+	+	+	+	+	+
Component B	+									
Component C	+	+	+	+						

Table 3. Example 1, Ci illustrative assumptions

Programmer type	Component A	Component B	Component C
Type M	300	20	150
Type N	200	10	100

Table 4. Example 1, Ri illustrative assumptions

Programmer type	Component A	Component B	Component C
Type M	650	15	150
Type N	300	7	80

Table 5. Example 1, ICi illustrative assumptions

Programmer type	Component A	Component B	Component C
Type M	60	5	50
Type N	15	3	10

ICa = Min(60*20, 15*40) = 600
ICb = Min(5*20, 3*40) = 100
ICc = Min(50*20, 10*40) = 400

Hence:

SAVa = 10 *(6,000 – 600) – (6,000 + 12,000) = 36000 > 0

SAVb = 1 *(400 – 100) – (400 + 280) = -380 < 0

SAVc = 4 *(3000– 400) – (3,000+ 3,000) = 4400 > 0

In light of the aforementioned, the Reuse Decision according to the Non-Restricted Model is to make components A and C reusable (i.e. Alternative 6).

D. Illustrative Example - Restricted Model

The following example (Example 2) demonstrates the decision made by the Restricted Model, based on the previous example (Example 1). Assume the following:

1. **I** 10,000.
2. **T** 150. The available remaining time to make the existing code reusable.
3. **Ci** Assume component B is the easiest one to develop, and requires 10 hours. Assume component A requires 300 hours, and component C requires 150 hours. Hence, complexities are: C_A=30, C_B=1, C_C =15.
4. **Fi** Component A will be reused by 100% of future projects, B by 10% and C by 40%.
5. I_A = 12,000/10,000=120%, I_B = 280/10,000=2.8%, I_C = 3000/10,000=30%.
6. T_A = 300/150=200%,
   T_B = 7/150=4.7%,
   T_C= 150/150=100%.

Hence Example 2 parameters are seen in Table 6.

Table 6. Parameters used by Example 2

Component	Ci	Fi(%)	Pi	Ii(%)	Ti(100%)
A	30	100	30	120	200
B	1	10	0.1	2.8	4.7
C	15	40	0.6	30	100

Taking time and investment restrictions into account, the reuse decision, according to the Restricted Model is to make only component C reusable (i.e. Alternative 5).

CONCLUSION AND FUTURE TRENDS

The current chapter presented two new reuse decision making models: a restricted model and a non-restricted model, which are mainly different in the way they take into account real-life constraint-restrictions such as time, budget, and resources repetition.

The models produced different results from the same data. The decision made by the restricted model pinpointed fewer software components for reuse. It is worth mentioning that different groups of software components were not the issue, but rather different subgroups of the same group, i.e. software components selected by the Restricted Model were subgroups of components selected by the Non-Restricted Model.

Moreover, the parameters of the Restricted Model relate to relative value arguments, by contrast to the parameters of Non-Restricted Model, which relate to absolute values. While absolute values are difficult to measure, relative values are simpler to define. There are a variety of formal methods by which relative values may be defined, methods that are used in other areas of software engineering, such as cost estimation, effort estimation, priority decision and others.

The reusability decision made by the Restricted Model may be biased by the following parameters:

time, resources, component complexity, and number-percent of future projects in which the component would be reused. Further research should be conducted focusing on decision robustness in light of the aforementioned parameters and their possible spectrum.

REFERENCES

Burkhardt, J. M., & Détienne, F., (2007). An empirical study of software reuse by experts in object-oriented design. *arXiv:cs/0702005v1.*

Chaki, S., Clarke E. M., Groce, A., Jha, S., & Veith, H. (2004). Modular Verification of Software Components in C. *IEEE Transactions on Software Engineering, 30*(6), 388-402.

Desouza, K. C., Awazu, Y., & Tiwana, A., (2006). Four dynamics for bringing use back into software reuse. *Communications of the ACM, 49*(1), 96-100.

Frakes, W., & Terry, C. (1996). Software Reuse: Metrics and Models. *ACM Computing Surveys, 28*(2), 415-435.

García, F., Bertoa, M. F., Calero, C., Vallecillo, A., Ruíz, F., Piattini, M., & Genero, M. (2006), "Towards a consistent terminology for software measurement ",*Information and Software Technology, 48*(8), 631-644.

Henninger, S. (1999). An Evolutionary Approach to Constructing Effective Software Reuse Repositories. *ACM Transactions on Software Engineering and Methodology, 6*(2), 111-140.

Kirk, D., Roper, M., & Wood, M., (2006). Identifying and addressing problems in object-oriented framework reuse. *Empirical Software Engineering, 12*(3), 243-274.

Mens, T., & Tourwé, T. (2004). A Survey of Software Refactoring. *IEEE Transactions on Software Engineering, 30*(2), 126-139.

Mellarkod, V., Appan, R., Jones, D. R., & Sherif, K. (2007). A multi-level analysis of factors affecting software developers' intention to reuse software assets: An empirical investigation. *Information & Management*, 2007, *44*(7), 613-625.

Mili, H., Mili, F., & Mili, A. (1995). Reusing Software: Issues and Research Directions. *IEEE Transactions on Software Engineering, 21*(6), 528–562.

Mohagheghi, P., & Conradi, R., (2007). Quality, productivity and economic benefits of software reuse: a review of industrial studies. *Empirical Software Engineering*, May 2007, (pp. 471-516).

Otso, K. J. (1995). A Systematic Process for Reusable Software Component Selection. *Technical Report, University of Maryland.*

Spinellis, D. (2007). Cracking Software Reuse. *IEEE Software, 24*(1), 12-13.

Tomer, A., Goldin, L., Kuflik, T., Kimchi, E., & Schach, S. R. (2004). Evaluating Software Reuse Alternatives: A Model and Its Application to an Industrial Case Study. *IEEE Transactions on Software Engineering, 30*(9), 601-612.

Virtanen, P. (2001). Empirical Study Evaluating Component Reuse Metrics. *Proceedings of the ESCOM*, (pp. 125-136).

William, B., Frakes, W. B., & Kang, K. (2005). Software Reuse Research: Status and Future. *IEEE Transactions on Software Engineering, 31*(7), 529-536.

Ye, Y. (2002). An Empirical User Study of an Active Reuse Repository System. *Proceedings of 7th International Conference on Software Reuse,* (pp. 281-292).

Ye, Y., & Fischer, G., (2002). Supporting Reuse by Delivering Task-Relevant and Personalized Information. *Proceedings of International Conference on Software Engineering*, (pp. 513-523).

Chapter XIII
Web–Based Systems Development:
An Empirically–Grounded Conceptual Framework

Michael Lang
National University of Ireland, Galway, Ireland

ABSTRACT

This chapter encapsulates the main findings of an in-depth study of Web development practices in Ireland. The essential research objective was to build a richer understanding of the modern context of Web development and of how that context influences design practices. At the outset, a conceptual framework was derived through a synthesis of issues in the literature and an analysis of existing models of IS development. Data was then gathered through a dual-mode (Web and postal) quantitative survey which yielded 165 usable responses, and later through a series of 14 semi-structured qualitative interviews in a follow-up field study. Following an interpretive approach, elementary statistics and grounded theory were used to iteratively analyze the data until a reasonably comprehensive and stable explanation emerged. This is presented in the form of an elaborated conceptual framework of Web-based systems development as "situated action."

INTRODUCTION

The latter years of the 1990s saw a frenetic surge in activity on the World Wide Web, driven by improvements in networking and communications technologies, enhanced browser capabilities, more advanced server-side and client-side functionality, increased sophistication of visual user interfaces, and the rise of electronic commerce. This sudden and spectacular growth caused quite a degree of apprehension amongst the academic research community because the apparently "out of control" Internet technological upheaval was progressing at such a chaotic pace that the state-of-theory was left lagging some distance behind the state-of-practice (Cusumano & Yoffie, 1999).

Whereas the Web a few short years previously was predominantly a publishing medium, it was metamorphosing so quickly into an applications development environment that serious doubts hung over the readiness of the incumbent generation of Web designers, many of whom were self-trained and from backgrounds other than "proper" software engineering.

On such a premise, Murugesan & Deshpande (1999) called for a "new concept and discipline of Web Engineering" and affirmed that there was a "pressing need for new methods and tools" (Murugesan, Deshpande, Hansen, & Ginige, 1999). In similar vein, Oinas-Kukkonen et al (2001) claimed that "systematic analysis and design methodologies for developing Web information systems are necessary and urgently needed among practitioners". Speculation was rife of an imminent "Web crisis" on foot of a prevalent view that industry development practices in general were unsystematic and unreliable. Whether these remarks were well-founded or mere "exception reporting" (Glass, 1998) is arguable, for the software industry has supposedly been chronically afflicted by a "crisis" as long as it has existed (Gibbs, 1994; Naur & Randell, 1969).

This research project was initiated at a point (c. 2001) when there was much sensational talk in the academic literature of an imminent "Web crisis". Quite a number of empiricial studies of Web development, mostly of the nature of descriptive surveys or narrow experience reports, were published about that time. Though useful and interesting, those studies are now a little dated. Setting aside general HCI research on the effectiveness/usability of Web sites and the mainly experimental contributions of the Web Engineering community, remarkably few studies of actual industry *practice* have since appeared. Following the post-Y2K implosion of the "dot.com" bubble, the Web design industry went through an upheaval whereby firms engaging in haphazard practices were forced to either reform (if they were capable of so doing) or perish (as very many of them

did). Development technologies have advanced remarkably in recent years, and many Web development firms originally established in the mid- to late-1990s have at this stage settled down and attained process maturity. The objective of this research project was therefore to contribute towards a richer and updated understanding of the "real-world" context of Web-based systems development, and of how that context influences design practices.

Specifically, the research questions were as follows:

R 1. What is the profile of a typical Web-based systems development project?

R 2. What are the main challenges being experienced by Web-based systems designers in practice?

R 3. What development practices are being engaged to address these challenges?

R 4. What situational factors influence the enactment of development practices?

R 5. Where formalised design guidance is in place, what is its nature and from where is it derived?

RESEARCH APPROACH

A three-phase research approach was taken, as shown in Figure 1. At the outset, a number of informal meetings were held with a few experienced Web developers to help solidify the research objectives, assess the salience and relevance of certain aspects raised by the literature, and uncover any major topical issues of which the researcher was unaware.

The second phase consisted of a dual-mode (postal and Web-based) survey of 438 organisations. The sampling frame included organisations engaged in bespoke software application development; those specialising in Web or interactive multimedia systems design; companies from traditional media that had branched into "new media"; and large organisations with internal IT departments. The survey received an overall response rate of 52%, ultimately yielding 165 usable responses.

The third and final phase was a follow-up field study, consisting of semi-structured qualitative interviews with 14 Web developers. The selection of interviewees was theoretically driven, chosen so as to seek out similarities and dissimilarities, looking at both typical and atypical cases. They varied according to organisational size, organisational type, application domains, client location (in-house versus external Web development houses), and the interviewee's professional background. Many of the interviewees had recently won or been nominated for awards at prestigious national ceremonies. It was assumed that award winners would be more forthcoming, knowledgeable and insightful, and also that they exemplify best practice. In most of the organisations visited,

one personal interview was conducted with the team leader, typically convened during the midday break so as not to encroach upon busy work schedules. In one organisation two developers were separately interviewed, and in another the managing director brought five staff members into the meeting room. Where available, secondary data sources were also consulted. Data gathering continued until a point of reasonable "theoretical saturation" was reached.

The survey data was mainly analysed using descriptive and enumerative statistics, such as frequency distributions, averages/medians, and cross-tabulations. Because an interpretive approach was taken in this research project, no formal hypotheses were set out. Instead, some theoretical propositions based on posited relationships in the conceptual framework were explored by means of simple difference/correlation tests. The qualitative data gathered in the field study

Figure 1. Overview of research process

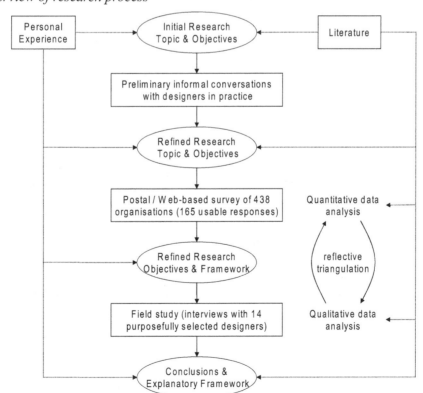

was analysed using a hybrid method, mainly based on the procedures of grounded theory (Glaser & Strauss, 1967; Locke, 2001; Strauss & Corbin, 1998), but also informed by the principles laid down by Miles & Huberman (1994). Although data gathering for the survey and field study phases was done in chronological sequence, data analysis was an iterative and parallel activity, involving both inductive and deductive reasoning in a grounded, reflective process. Through this triangulation of methods and data, the inherent weaknesses of individual methods are reduced, strengthening the validity and reliability of findings.

Limitations of the Survey

The survey element of this research project is limited by a number of shortcomings, some of which relate to the inherent weaknesses of questionnaires and are compensated for by the field study:

- The survey questionnaire comprised mostly fixed-format questions that captured quantitative data, and responses to the few open-ended questions were scant. For this reason, a qualitative follow-up field study was conducted to elucidate upon the survey findings.
- As is generally the case with survey research, there remains the possibility that findings may be skewed because of reliability and validity issues. Numerous measures to counteract and alleviate potential bias were taken, but it is very difficult to fully eradicate the possibility of contamination.
- The survey was conducted in a small geographical region (the island of Ireland), so caution must be exercised in generalising findings to wider international populations. To test for regional bias, the survey could be replicated in another area and it would be interesting to conduct a cross-national comparison of Web development practices. The option of so doing was originally en-

visaged at the outset of this project, but to rigorously and successfully perform such a study would involve considerable procedural and methodological challenges (Lang, 2002), necessitating collaboration between a distributed team of international partners. For that reason, it was decided not to pursue this option for now, but to defer it as a future possibility. Indeed, parts of the questionnaire used in this study have since been replicated in surveys of Web development practices in Korea and in Croatia (Lang, Plantak Vukovac, 2008)).

Limitations of the Field Study

While the combination of a quantitative survey in conjunction with a qualitative field study helps to redress some of the shortcomings of either used in isolation, there remains a number of intractable problems with the field study which mainly have to do with the shortcomings of interpretivism, grounded theory, and qualitative interviews. In brief, these are:

- Interviews can be intrusive and atypical; by his very presence as a "foreigner" in an organisational setting, a researcher may introduce bias into that setting. Though interviewees were generally relaxed, forthcoming, and willing to be recorded by means of a digital audio device, there remains the possibility that some unnatural behaviour was caused by the intrusion of the interviewer.
- With data gathered from field studies, only "analytical" generalisability is possible. Logical inferences can be drawn, but statistical inferences can not. This shortcoming was redressed by the combination of a field study and a large-scale survey in this research.
- Qualitative data is prone to subjective and conflicting interpretations. Because this field study was based on interviews personally

conducted by the author, he has the advantage above all others of having a first-hand "feel" for the data and is therefore best placed to draw conclusions. That said, the opinions of a number of academic colleagues and peers were sought in order to assess the plausibility of interpretations. The author's knowledge of relevant background literature was also an important point of reference in the interpretive process, as was his own professional experience in the area.

- Because the resultant explanatory framework is a deliberate simplification and is grounded in a limited number of observations, it cannot be expected to account for all possible variations that might be encountered. Of course, no explanation can ever be said to be complete so it is necessary to decide when to stop. In the logic of grounded theory this happens at "theoretical saturation", the point of diminishing returns beyond which analysis is necessarily delimited. At this juncture there typically remain data fragments which have not been fully exhausted, but the conceptual model is bounded and deemed to be "good enough" because, while accepted as being incomplete, it accounts for most of the observed variations in the recorded data incidents (Locke, 2001).

- Again, because the field study was based on a restricted sample of interviewees, it is limited to the extent that this sample is broadly representative of the general population. The interviewees in this study were purposefully selected in order that comparisons and differences might be drawn between cases, but it should be noted that they were mainly award-winning companies. As such, they may be argued to be unrepresentative of industry as a whole, but it was decided that it would be preferable to capture a description of best practices (i.e. award winners) rather than general practices.

- For reasons of limited access, just one person was interviewed in most of the organisations visited. For issues where the unit of analysis is the organisation (e.g. the use of processes and procedures) as opposed to the individual (e.g. the influence of one's professional background), the reliance on a single organisational spokesperson is clearly not ideal for it can be prone to rather personal and biased interpretations. It might have been better, for the sake of reliability, to have spoken with a number of persons within each organisation, in different roles and at different levels of the organisational hierarchy. The unfortunate reality is that with small businesses, such access is often difficult to negotiate, particularly in the industry of Web development where pressing deadlines and multiple concurrent projects are the norm. Furthermore, the participants in this field study were distributed geographically across Ireland which placed a constraint on the feasibility of multiple return site visits. As it turned out, there were indeed possible reliability issues with some of the interview data because: (i) at times, the received impression was that the interviewee was self-convinced that initiatives they pushed for are "working"; (ii) some interviewees were a little opinionated; (iii) in a few cases, it seemed that the interviewee was trying to impress the interviewer, either endeavouring to provide the "correct" answer or even veering towards a "sales pitch". Ultimately, it was necessary to use a degree of personal judgement to separate credible statements from the ones which seemed likely to be exaggerated. Where possible, interview transcripts were cross-checked against survey data and other secondary data to look for anomalies which cast doubts over reliability. A few discrepancies were found between survey and interview responses, but these were all readily explained by changes in organisational practices that had been implemented in the interim period between the execution of the survey and the conduct of interviews. In spite of the shortcoming of having interviewed just one person in most of the organisations visited, the researcher is of the opinion that interviewees for the greater part were frank, forthright, and representative of the general views that pertain within their organisations.

OVERVIEW OF THE CONCEPTUAL FRAMEWORK

Anselm Strauss, one of the original advocates of grounded theory (GT), has affirmed that it can be used not merely to build new theories, but also to extend existing theory by filling in gaps (Strauss, 1970). Accordingly, the framework derived by this study used GT to produce an extended variant of the "Method-in-Action" model, given that the application of this model to Web-based systems development has not yet been investigated in depth (Fitzgerald, Russo, & Stolterman, 2002). Elements

were also adapted from other models, including NIMSAD (Jayaratna, 1994), Multiview/WISDM (Avison, Wood-Harper, Vidgen, & Wood, 1998; Vidgen, Avison, Wood, & Wood-Harper, 2002), Kumar & Bjørn-Andersen's model of designer values (Kumar & Bjørn-Andersen, 1990), and Gasson's social action model of ISD (Gasson, 1999). The iterative GT technique of "constant comparison" was used firstly to synthesise the main concepts of these models into a coherent unified framework, and then to mould this initial framework into the empirically-grounded model which emerged as the sense-making tasks of data gathering and analysis progressed. Simply put, the resultant framework came together in a manner that was both top-down and bottom-up. Conceptual categories were initially derived from a review of literature and other models, then the content of these categories was filled in by a grounded analysis of empirical data.

As the research project unfolded and the conceptual framework began to take shape, it became the nucleus of all efforts, providing reference links to the background literature and research questions, informing the research design and

Figure 2. Conceptual framework of Web-based systems development as situated design

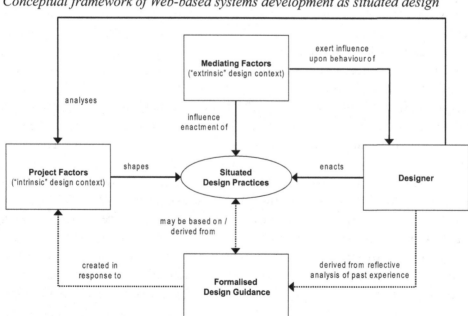

philosophical perspective, and guiding the elicitation and reflective analysis of data. The refined conceptual framework which eventually emerged is presented in Figure 2. At its heart, design practices are regarded as situated actions, purposefully enacted by knowledgable actors who analyse the design context and act accordingly, drawing upon their own experiences to choose an appropriate method. The foundation of the "situated action" view of design is that, "rather than attempting to abstract action away from its circumstances and represent it as a rational plan, the approach is to study how people use their circumstances to achieve intelligent action" (Suchman, 1987). It rejects the "technical rationalist" assertion that formalised design methods can be executed objectively. Rather, design methods must always be uniquely interpreted; as Essinck (1988) puts it, "in a real life project one has to puzzle together one's own specific method, tuned to the problem at hand and the situation the designer is in".

Because of space constraints, it is not possible here to report the full details of empirical findings as they relate to the various categorical headings of the conceptual framework. The following sections therefore briefly explain the elements of the framework as they apply to the practice of Web-based systems development. Further details of this study and the process by which the framework was derived are published in [56-61]. A copy of the survey instrument is available from the author upon request.

Designer-Encapsulated Factors

A designer's professional training and education can shape his problem-solving orientation and world view by indoctrinating certain values and conditioning him to think and behave in certain ways (Sahraoui, 1998). An analogy can be drawn here with Thomas Kuhn's notion of a "scientific community" which he defines as "the practitioners of a particular specialty … [who] have undergone similar educations and professional initiations"

(Kuhn, 1996). Kuhn makes the point that these communities, or "schools", may "approach the same subject from incompatible viewpoints". "Incommensurable" (Kuhn, 1996) or "incongruent" (Orlikowski & Gash, 1994) viewpoints can cause people to work at cross-purposes, which has been seen to lead to disappointing outcomes in ISD projects (Bostrom & Heinen, 1977). A number of authors have mentioned that it would be interesting to investigate the practices of Web designers from backgrounds other than software development, so as to build a broader, richer understanding (Jonasson, 2000; Russo & Graham, 1999). However, this issue has received very little attention thus far. In view of this gap in the literature, a comparison of the methods and approaches used by designers from different professional backgrounds was one of the main concentrations of this study.

In the survey phase of this research, the cover letter attached to the questionnaire simply requested that it be completed by someone in a design role, the rationale being to capture a cross-section of respondents across the various disciplines that contribute to Web-based systems development. As expected, two dominant disciplinary groupings emerged: computer-based systems development (CBSD), and visual design (VD). Differences in priorities and preferences were observed, apparently influenced by the historical practices (e.g. software specifications versus graphic design "briefs") and orientations (e.g. functional/transactional versus informational/ promotional) in each field. For example, the VD group were considerably more lax than the CBSD group as regards requirements documentation, and were also generally very loose concerning the use of "approaches" and "methods". Indeed, the notion of a design "method" seemed to be alien to many of the VD group. On the other hand, the CBSD group were mostly comfortable with the idea of a systematic process for Web-based systems development, such processes mainly being adaptations of traditional software development methods and techniques.

In the follow-up field study, the influence of professional background on design practices was probed in greater depth. Interestingly, a number of different problem-solving perspectives were discovered, each clearly shaped by the various priorities and orientations of the respective disciplines. The perspectives identified were: Web-based systems development as the design of a functional software application (emphasis on back-end functionality); as the design of an interactive tool (emphasis on ergonomics); as the design of a directed communicational dialogue (emphasis on audience engagement); and as an extension of branded graphic design (emphasis on visual presentation). For a more detailed analysis, see Lang, M. (2009) and Lang, M. (2003).

The framework therefore recognises that a designer's professional background and education can shape his "world view" by conditioning him to think and behave in certain ways. While different perspectives and orientations were found to exist, it would seem that, at least in the field of practice, there is a growing degree of pluralism, as

evidenced by a substantial degree of cross-skilling and cross-pollination of techniques.

Though some tasks and stages of Web-based systems development may be formalised and codified, or even automated, there remains a critical need for creative human intervention and the exercise of judgement. Many authors argue that software design is essentially a highly skilled craft (McBreen, 2002; Taylor, 2004; Wroblewski, 1991). It is inaccurate to conceive of design as merely following some pre-defined "cookbook" method; rather, design requires creative thinking and draws upon the skills and experiences of talented individuals (Glass, 1995; Shaw & Garlan, 1996; Stolterman & Russo, 1997). Rumbaugh (1995) puts it as follows:

"You can't expect a method to tell you everything to do. Writing software is a creative process, like painting or writing or architecture. There are principles of painting, for example, that give guidelines on composition, color selection, and perspective, but they won't make you a Picasso … Some methods claim to fully automate the

Figure 3. Conceptual framework: Designer-encapsulated factors

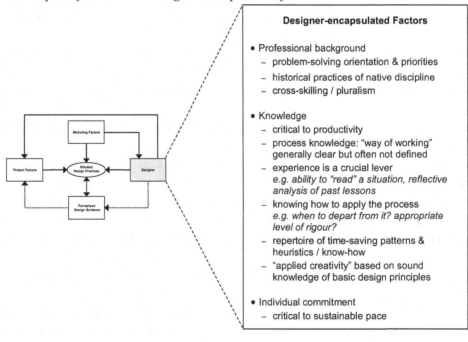

[software development] process, to tell you every step to follow so that software design is painless and faultless. They are wrong. It can't be done. What can be done is to supply a framework that tells you how to go about it and identifies the places where creativity is needed."

Continuing with the analogy between painting and software design, it is interesting to read the following extract from Leonardo da Vinci's *Trattato della Pittura* (Treatise on Painting) of 1651:

"These rules will enable you to possess a free and good judgement, since good judgement is born of good understanding, and good understanding derives from reason expounded through good rules, and good rules are the daughters of good experience – the common mother of all the sciences and arts" (White, 2000).

This relationship between method, understanding, experience and judgement, which of course is not specific to painting, can also be seen in the writings of Schön (1983) and, within the ISD literature, in the work of Introna & Whitley (Introna & Whitley, 1997; Whitley, 1998). Accordingly, like the Method-in-Action model, the conceptual framework derived by this study recognises the vital contribution played by creative, talented individuals in the successful execution of the design process. Designers interpret the design context and use their judgement to decide what actions to take in a particular situation.

A strong theme which emerged from the field study was the role of knowledge and experience as a crucial lever in the determination of how Web development processes and guidelines are tailored to meet the needs of the particular situation at hand. Furthermore, knowledge is a critical asset in a development environment characterised by high-speed work practices because it contributes to productivity. More knowledgeable employees are able to work faster because they are equipped with a repertoire of time-efficient "tricks", heuristics, and patterns acquired along the downward traverse of the learning curve. It was found that most of the award-winning companies interviewed have

mechanisms in place to facilitate and encourage the management of Web design knowledge, with rewards and bonuses accruing to employees who use slack time to gain and exchange useful knowledge. A number of companies schedule regular time slots for innovative research activity, setting aside normal development work.

The other main designer-encapulated factor which emerged in this study was individual commitment. Again, like knowledge, this is critical in order to be able to sustain a continuous pace of high-speed delivery. Such issues as organisational culture, appropriate reward mechanisms, and the adoption of practices to eliminate morale-sapping overtime were found to be important in this regard.

Formalised Design Guidance

Departing slightly from the original Method-in-Action framework, the term "formalised design guidance" is used here in preference to "formalised method" because this study found that, even where Web developers have process documentation in place, it is usually not at the comprehensive level of "method" but more often seems to be simply a collected body of concise procedures, rules of good practice, heuristics and guidelines, or "how-to" memoranda (e.g. intranet-based "Wiki's" and "blogs").

Though 83% of survey respondents have a clearly understood way of working, in very many cases development processes are not explicitly documented. A similar pattern emerged during follow-up interviews. It would seem that design know-how is best transmitted and acquired by working "on the job", rather than from perusal of formalised procedures or attending training programmes. Most organisations use a "home-cooked" in-house development process that is founded on research, experimentation and reflective analysis of past experience. On the basis of interview findings, these in-house "methods" seem not to be complete end-to-end solutions, but more

Figure 4. Conceptual framework: Formalised design guidance

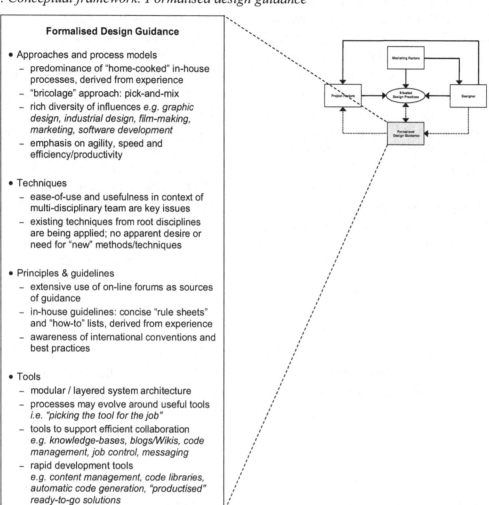

of a high-level process model within which there is a pick-and-mix selection of low-level techniques to support phase tasks. They are mainly hybrids and custom-tailored variants, based on combinations of internally devised guidelines and public domain methods, informed by an awareness of best industry practice as gleaned from handbooks or on-line forums, and supported by or based around useful tools. This is consistent with the concept of "bricolage" whereby Web designers, rather than shunning method, judiciously assemble fragments of methods and distil the most useful elements into a flexible custom-made approach. Though the same high-level process model may be applied across all projects, tailoring occurs at the level of within-phase tasks, depending on the needs of the particular situation at hand.

Ironically, while there is a vast and ever-growing "jungle" of academically-produced Web-based systems development methods in the literature, none of which are being used to any significant extent in actuality (as evidenced by the survey results), the findings of the field study suggest that out in the real world a single generic high-level process dominates, it resembling a derivative of the traditional "Waterfall" software development model wedded to an amalgam of sub-processes inherited from the fields of graphic design, HCI, strategic marketing / brand design, and industrial design. On the basis of the interview data gathered in this research project, it can be concluded that what differentiates one company from the next is not the overall shape or format of their development process, – notwithstanding the fact that many companies do indeed present their process as a unique selling point, – but rather the way in which the finer points of that process are uniquely interpreted by their design team in the specific context of a particular project.

In addition to the form of the generic Web development process model, – which represents a fusion of approaches drawn from a variety of sources, – the influence of multiple disciplinary fields on the practice of Web-based systems development is evidenced by the finding that all interviewees, regardless of their professional backgrounds, found that the same methods and techniques they had formerly used in their "native" discipline transferred across to Web design. This suggests that wholly new methods and techniques for Web-based systems development are neither necessary nor appropriate. It was also generally found that ease-of-use, usefulness and representational capabilities are important factors which affect the choice of conceptual modelling techniques for Web design. Whereas the emphasis of traditional software development techniques was on back-end functionality (e.g. ERDs for database-driven applications), there is now also an essential need for front-end design techniques drawn from the field of visual communications, such as storyboards and "mood boards".

Given the high-speed nature of Web-based systems development, the emphasis of formalised design guidance is very much on agility, speed, efficiency and productivity. Streamlined processes are necessary in order to maximise throughput, and also to sustain a continual pace by eradicating the need for ongoing overtime (which has fatiguing and demoralising effects). Interestingly, the Web developers interviewed have evolved practices that are markedly similar to those of

the "agile" methods family, such as: collective code ownership; an emphasis on simplicity; the use of regular informal team briefings; insistence on a close working relationship with the client; the pursuit of continuous process improvement through reflective evaluation; and a general emphasis on people, communication, and working software over processes, documentation, and adherence to a plan. Processes and procedures are therefore treated as flexible frameworks to guide and assist the essentially creative tasks of analysis and design.

The central role of tools in the formalisation of work practices also emerged as an important factor. For example, the use of automatic code generation, re-usable components (both code and graphical elements), enhanced RAD tools, modular tiered systems architectures, and "productised" software solutions greatly speeds up Web development without subverting cost or quality. Additionally, the store of in-house knowledge, which is an important factor in productivity, can be more effectively leveraged through the advantageous use of collaborative forums such as intranets, "Wiki's", and "blogs".

Project Factors (Intrinsic Design Context)

Whitley (1998) makes the point that "in order to be able to use a method appropriately, it is necessary to have an understanding of the context in which it is being used". There is a significant body of literature on the notion of situation-specific "method engineering" (Brinkkemper, 1996; Gnatz, Marschall, Popp, Rausch, & Schwerin, 2003; Hidding, 1996; Kumar & Welke, 1992; Song, 1997), and while there are considerable issues surrounding the feasibility of such an approach in practice (Fitzgerald, Russo, & O'Kane, 2003; Ter Hofstedt & Verhoef, 1997; Truex & Avison, 2003), it is nevertheless generally accepted that different situations warrant different approaches (Cockburn, 2000; Essinck,

1988; Jackson, 2000; Kraemer & Dutton, 1991; Malouin & Landry, 1983; Ratbe, King, & Kim, 1999). All of the aforementioned conceptual frameworks recognise that design practices may be affected by the specific circumstances of the design context, which is variously referred to as the "problem situation"/"methodology context" (NIMSAD), "situation" (Multiview), "context" (Kumar & Bjørn-Andersen's model), and "business/development context" (Method-in-Action). Here, the design context is represented by the categories labelled "Project Factors: intrinsic design context" and "Mediating Factors: extrinsic design context".

It was found that the duration of a typical Web development project is of the order of 2 to 3 months. Such short delivery cycles, until recently at least, were unprecedented in traditional software development and are made possible in Web-based systems development by a combination of factors. Firstly, the Web is an immediate delivery medium which is not impeded by production, distribution and installation delays. Secondly, as evidence by the interview data, there have been dramatic gains in recent years in developer productivity, coupled with ever more efficient and refined development processes. This has been achieved through the use of high-speed rapid application development tools, templates and wizards for automatic code-generation, plug-and-play database connectivity, and libraries of pre-fabricated components and applets. Web programming is now advanced to a point where most development time is invested into the ongoing evolution of an out-of-the-box solution. Code production for a project has moved from crude cut-and-paste re-use to instant automatic generation, meaning that most of the standard back-end functionality required for any given project can be up and running within a day or two. The visual design of the GUI front-end, like the traditional production process for commercial art, can also be done within a very short timeframe. A fully-proven working prototype can therefore be very quickly launched, which can later be modified and enhanced in such a manner that end-users may be largely oblivious to the ongoing changes. As such, rapid/agile and evolutionary/incremental development approaches are a natural fit to the Web environment.

Consistent with the previous work of Baskerville & Pries-Heje (2001, 2004), this study found, as one would expect, that time pressure is the

Figure 5. Conceptual framework: Project factors

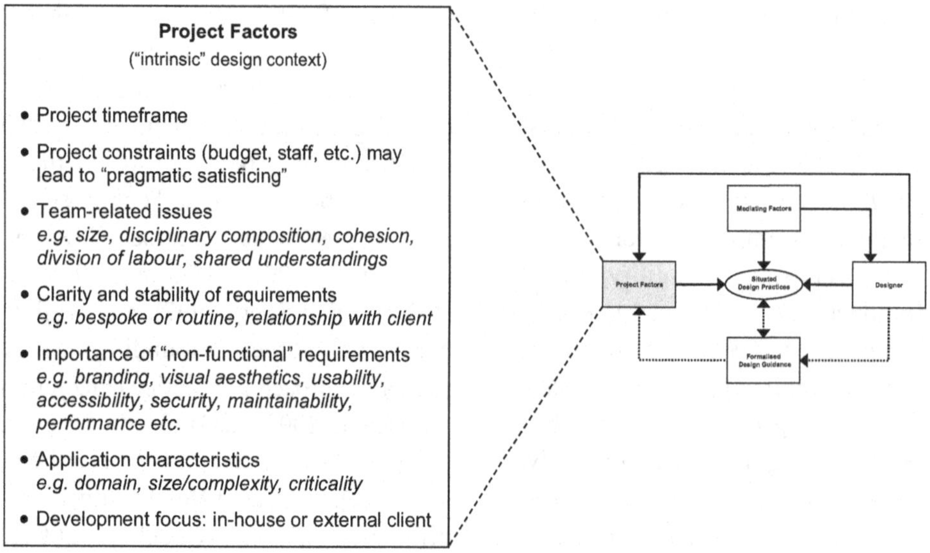
Project Factors
("intrinsic" design context)
• Project timeframe
• Project constraints (budget, staff, etc.) may lead to "pragmatic satisficing"
• Team-related issues
e.g. size, disciplinary composition, cohesion, division of labour, shared understandings
• Clarity and stability of requirements
e.g. bespoke or routine, relationship with client
• Importance of "non-functional" requirements
e.g. branding, visual aesthetics, usability, accessibility, security, maintainability, performance etc.
• Application characteristics
e.g. domain, size/complexity, criticality
• Development focus: in-house or external client
Mediating Factors
Project Factors
Situated Design Practices
Designer
Formalised Design Guidance

central determinant of design practices. However, there are discrepancies between this research and that of Baskerville & Pries-Heje, most notably with their finding that developers may resort to the practices of "coding your way out" and "negotiated quality" because of the pressures of high-speed development environments. Whereas in Baskerville & Pries-Heje's study such practices were endemic, in this research hardly any such incidents were discovered. This can be explained in a number of ways. Firstly, the interviewed companies were mostly award-winners, a likely indicator that they make special efforts to strive for excellence and quality. Secondly, the marketplace has become more competitive in recent years and users are much less tolerant of unprofessional standards of work, meaning that expectation levels have risen. Thirdly, as already mentioned, the use of pre-fabricated "productised" solutions that are already fully tested means that robust systems can be rapidly delivered without compromising cost or quality. Even in the worst case scenario for a development team, where they face the dreaded "backs-to-the-wall" combination of acute time and resource constraints, a tactic herein coined as "pragmatic satisficing" is engaged, meaning that a tried-and-tested solution is re-used, albeit it may not be the best possible outcome.

It was found, initially in the survey and later in the follow-up interviews, that most Web development teams are small, typically comprising about 5 to 10 members for any given project. This affords the advantage that communication problems are minimal and that cohesion can more easily be achieved, both of which are important for timely delivery. As teams grow in size, knowledge becomes fragmented. There consequently arises a need to formalise and standardise working methods (e.g. conventions for collective code ownership) because otherwise wasteful inefficiencies due to "re-inventing the wheel" can occur. In both the survey and the follow-up interviews, it was found that larger teams tend to make more use of documented guidelines and procedures.

Conflict between Web designers from different professional backgrounds was not found to be much of a problem in practice. This is because the once rival factions of software engineering and graphic design have over time come to gain an appreciation of each others' perspectives and priorities (as evidenced by a considerable degree of cross-skilling), and it is now easier to separate front-end and back-end Web design into different layers than it was a few years ago.

The clarity and stability of requirements is an age-old issue in systems development, but in high-speed environments it is important to "nail" a prioritised list as quickly as possible. In comparison with traditional software development, it was found during the field study that a greater weighting of time in Web-based systems development is spent on analysis and design as opposed to coding. Requirements analysis is the most time-consuming phase of all in Web development, whereas coding can actually be very quick. Though most of the functional requirements for a Web-based system are typically standard and can therefore be readily described, the bespoke elements take time to specify, as does a considered analysis of the fine details of the overall package including the "non-functional" requirements (usability, accessibility, security, performance levels, etc.). As initially revealed by the survey and later substantiated by follow-up interviews, it is common practice to produce and sign-off a detailed requirements specification before commencing full scale production, the purpose of which is to keep feature creep in check and compel clients to make firm decisions.

From the interviews, it seems that most organisations use largely the same development process for all types of applications, regardless of delivery platform or application domain. While the general process may be very similar across all projects, the rigour with which its sub-tasks are executed varies, as one would expect, in accordance with application size/complexity and application criticality. Some evidence was found in the survey that in highly specialised areas such as interactive e-learning/CBT applications, a proprietary method might be used, and also that in some sectors (e.g. Financial Services) there is a greater emphasis on processes and documented procedures (e.g. detailed functional specifications, formalised organisational guidelines). However, a shortcoming of this study is that insufficient data was gathered to analyse the influence of specialised application domains on the finer details of Web development processes and procedures (e.g. security is a concern in the development of e-banking systems, but this was only incidentally touched upon in this research).

The focus of systems development activity (i.e. in-house versus external client) was also found to impact development practices. Whereas Web design agencies can agree plans with clients and negotiate with them over who pays for subsequent over-runs, in-house development teams are in a "hands tied" situation, meaning that project planning is necessarily done very differently.

Mediating Factors (Extrinsic Design Context)

Design practices can sometimes be affected by the intervention of extraneous factors, the influence of which may be to cause designers to pursue a course of action they might not otherwise take. For example, it was found during interviews that there may be a mandate by the client that certain procedures are to be rigidly followed (e.g. because of statutory requirements to comply with certain

Figure 6. Conceptual framework: Mediating factors

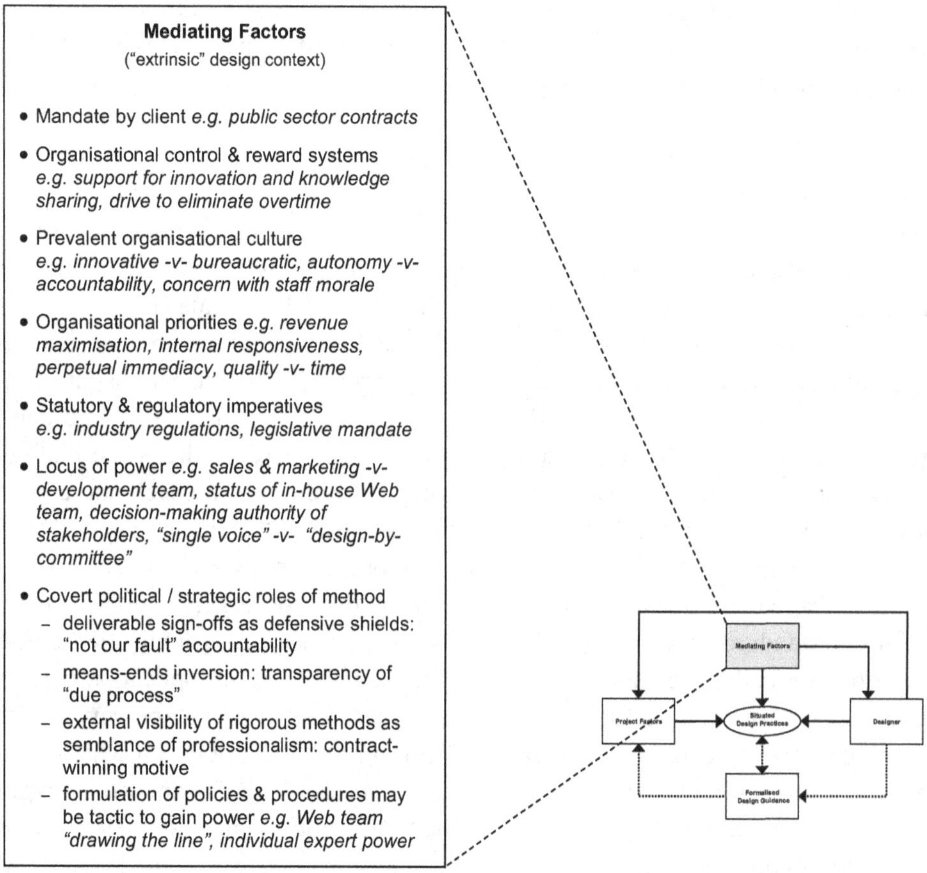
Mediating Factors
("extrinsic" design context)
• Mandate by client e.g. public sector contracts
• Organisational control & reward systems e.g. support for innovation and knowledge sharing, drive to eliminate overtime
• Prevalent organisational culture e.g. innovative -v- bureaucratic, autonomy -v- accountability, concern with staff morale
• Organisational priorities e.g. revenue maximisation, internal responsiveness, perpetual immediacy, quality -v- time
• Statutory & regulatory imperatives e.g. industry regulations, legislative mandate
• Locus of power e.g. sales & marketing -v- development team, status of in-house Web team, decision-making authority of stakeholders, "single voice" -v- "design-by-committee"
• Covert political / strategic roles of method
- deliverable sign-offs as defensive shields: "not our fault" accountability
- means-ends inversion: transparency of "due process"
- external visibility of rigorous methods as semblance of professionalism: contract-winning motive
- formulation of policies & procedures may be tactic to gain power e.g. Web team "drawing the line", individual expert power
Mediating Factors
Project Factors
Situated Design Practices
Designer
Formalised Design Guidance

standards, or the existence of binding protocols for procurement or software testing), or not to be followed (e.g. political pressure to complete, "just do it!").

As was previously observed by Powell et al (1998), this study found that the locus of power within organisations can significantly influence the development approach. For example, fledgling in-house Web development units often have to resort to "pragmatic satisficing" behaviour because they are under-resourced. In Web design agencies, a typical cause of conflict is the competing motives of the sales team (revenue maximisation) and the development team (quality optimisation), – this argument is usually won by the sales team, and programmers might end up being coerced into taking shortcuts to meet targets. The locus of power is also a common issue for client organisations, where the politics, indecision, and communicative difficulties arising from the "design-by-committee" syndrome can frustrate even the best laid project plans.

Associated with the concept of reward and control systems are two closely related other concepts: organisational priorities and organisational culture. Prerogatives such as perpetual immediacy, statutory and regulatory imperatives, a commercial desire to maximise revenue/throughput, a need to be internally flexible with schedules and requirements, or a focus on quality above time and cost considerations can impact development processes by directing priorities. Similarly, the culture of an organisation, as reinforced by control and reward mechanisms, is also a relevant issue (e.g. emphasis on individual *accountability* as opposed to responsible *autonomy*).

As with the original Method-in-Action model, it was again found in this study that development methods may fulfil covert political roles. These included: establishing a power-base for method champions (e.g. the XP, WAI, or BS7799 "expert"), maintaining a transparent and accountable audit trail of the development process as a protective fallback (e.g. the in-house "blame game", or negotiating responsibility for change requests or delays with clients), providing assurance that correct and "proper" practices are being followed (e.g. public-sector tenders), and helping to raise the status of in-house Web development departments (e.g. the creation of internal policies to "legitimise" or "professionalise" operations).

CONCLUSION

The framework presented in this chapter provides a macro-level overview of the context of Web-based systems development and the various inter-related issues therein. A criticism that can be made of much "Web engineering" research, particularly that which concentrates on design methods, is that problems are often investigated in isolation, without due consideration of their "natural" context in the real-world environment of practice. For example, there is a vast array of academically-produced Web/hypermedia design methods in the literature, but very few of these are being used in industry. There are many reasons why this may be so, but the long-standing criticism (Fitzgerald, 1991) remains that many of these methods have only been validated in restricted experimental settings or pilot studies as opposed to industrial-strength projects. The framework is helpful in this regard by providing academic researchers and method developers with a view of the over-arching context of Web-based systems development, thereby encouraging systemic thinking and "big picture" problem-solving, which ultimately should lead to research products that are more attuned and adaptable to the demands of practice.

As regards implications for education, IS/IT graduate programmes historically placed substantial emphasis on formalised design methods and techniques as described in standard textbooks, neglecting or entirely ignoring the factors which impact the use of those methods and techniques in practice. This limited one-dimensional perspective meant that perplexed graduates straight out of college often found themselves at a loss to understand how so much of the material they had diligently studied seemed to be irrelevant in the "real world". The conceptual framework derived by this research is therefore potentially valuable for educators because it constitutes the outline for a revised and extended curriculum which treats Web-based systems development as a situated contextually-sensitive activity.

REFERENCES

Avison, D. E., Wood-Harper, A. T., Vidgen, R. T., & Wood, J. R. G. (1998). A further exploration into information systems development: The evolution of Multiview2. *Information Technology & People, 11*(2), 124-139.

Baskerville, R., & Pries-Heje, J. (2001). Racing the e-bomb: How the internet is redefining information systems development methodology. In N. L. Russo, B. Fitzgerald & J. I. DeGross (Eds.), *Realigning research and practice in information systems development: The social and organizational perspective. IFIP Wg8.2 Conference, Boise, Idaho, USA, 27-29 july 2001* (pp. 49-68). Boston: Kluwer Academic Publishers.

Baskerville, R., & Pries-Heje, J. (2004). Short cycle time systems development. *Information Systems Journal, 14*(3), 237-264.

Bostrom, R. P., & Heinen, J. S. (1977). Mis problems and failures: A socio-technical perspective, part 1: The causes. *MIS Quarterly, 1*(3), 17-32.

Brinkkemper, S. (1996). Method engineering: Engineering of information systems development methods and tools. *Information and Software Technology, 38*(4), 275-280.

Cockburn, A. (2000). Selecting a project's methodology. *IEEE Software, 17*(4), 64-71.

Cusumano, M. A., & Yoffie, D. B. (1999). Software development on internet time. *IEEE Computer, 32*(10), 60-69.

Essinck, L. J. B. (1988). A conceptual framework for information systems development methodologies. In H.-J. Bullinger, E. N. Protonotarios, D. Bouwhuis & F. Reim (Eds.), *Information technology for organisational systems* (pp. 354-362). Amsterdam: North-Holland.

Fitzgerald, B., Russo, N. L., & O'Kane, T. (2003). Software development method tailoring at motorola. *Communications of the ACM, 46*(4), 65-70.

Fitzgerald, B., Russo, N. L., & Stolterman, E. (2002). *Information systems development: Methods in action.* London: McGraw-Hill.

Fitzgerald, G. (1991). Validating new information systems techniques: A retrospective analysis. In H.-E. Nissen, H. K. Klein & R. Hirschheim (Eds.), *Information systems research: Contemporary approaches and emergent traditions* (pp. 657-672): Elsevier Science Publishers B.V. (North-Holland).

Gasson, S. (1999). A social action model of situated information systems design. *DATA BASE (ACM SIGMIS), 30*(2), 82-97.

Gibbs, W. W. (1994, September). Software's chronic crisis. *Scientific American,* 72-81.

Glaser, B. G., & Strauss, A. L. (1967). *The discovery of grounded theory: Strategies for qualitative research.* New York: Aldine de Gruyter.

Glass, R. L. (1995). *Software creativity.* Englewood Cliffs, NJ: Prentice Hall.

Glass, R. L. (1998). Is there really a software crisis? *IEEE Software, 15*(1), 104-105.

Gnatz, M., Marschall, F., Popp, G., Rausch, A., & Schwerin, W. (2003). The living software development process. *Software Quality Professional, 5*(3), 4-16.

Hidding, G. (1996). Method engineering: Experiences in practice. In S. Brinkkemper, K. Lyytinen & R. Welke (Eds.), *Method engineering: Principles of method construction and tool support.* London: Chapman & Hall.

Introna, L. D., & Whitley, E. A. (1997). Against method-ism: Exploring the limits of method. *Information Technology & People, 10*(1), 31-45.

Jackson, M. (2000). The origins of JSP and JSD: A personal recollection. *IEEE Annals of Software Engineering, 22*(2), 61-63.

Jayaratna, N. (1994). *Understanding and evaluating methodologies, NIMSAD: A systemic framework.* London: McGraw-Hill.

Jonasson, I. (2000). *Developing the information systems of tomorrow - competencies and methodologies.* Unpublished M.Sc. Dissertation, University of Skövde, Sweden.

Kraemer, K. L., & Dutton, W. H. (1991). Survey research in the study of management information systems. In K. L. Kraemer (Ed.), *The information systems research challenge: Survey research methods. Volume 3* (pp. 3-58). Boston, Massachusetts: Harvard Business School.

Kuhn, T. S. (1996). *The structure of scientific revolutions* (3rd ed.). Chicago: University of Chicago Press.

Kumar, K., & Bjørn-Andersen, N. (1990). A cross-cultural comparison of IS designer values. *Communications of the ACM, 33*(5), 528-538.

Kumar, K., & Welke, R. J. (1992). Methodology engineering: A proposal for situation-specific methodology construction. In W. W. Cotterman & J. A. Senn (Eds.), *Challenges and strategies for research in systems development* (pp. 257-269): John Wiley & Sons.

Lang, M. (2002, April 29-30). *The use of web-based international surveys in information systems research.* Paper presented at the European Conference on Research Methodology for Business and Management Studies (ECRM 2002), Reading, England.

Lang, M. (2003) Hypermedia Systems Development: A Comparative Study of Software Engineers and Graphic Designers. *Communications of the AIS, 12*(16), 242-257.

Lang, M. (2009) The Influence of Disciplinary Backgrounds on Design Practices in Web-based Systems Development. *Journal of Information and Organizational Sciences*, forthcoming.

Lang, M. & Plantak Vukovac, D. (2008) Web-based Systems Development: Analysis and Comparison of Practices in Croatia and Ireland. In Papadopoulos, G. A. et al. (eds), *Proceedings of 17th International Conference on Information Systems Development*, Paphos, Cyprus, August 2008.

Locke, K. (2001). *Grounded theory in management research.* London: Sage.

Malouin, J.-L., & Landry, M. (1983). The mirage of universal methods in systems design. *Journal of Applied Systems Analysis, 10*, 47-62.

McBreen, P. (2002). *Software craftsmanship: The new imperative.* Boston: Addison Wesley.

Miles, M. B., & Huberman, A. M. (1994). *Qualitative data analysis: An expanded sourcebook* (2nd ed.). Thousand Oaks, CA: Sage.

Murugesan, S., & Deshpande, Y. (1999, May 16-22). *Preface to ICSE 1999 workshop on web engineering.* Paper presented at the 21st International Conference on Software Engineering (ICSE), Los Angeles, California, USA.

Murugesan, S., Deshpande, Y., Hansen, S., & Ginige, A. (1999, May 16-17). *Web engineering: A new discipline for development of web-based systems.* Paper presented at the 1st ICSE Workshop on Web Engineering, Los Angeles, California, USA.

Naur, P., & Randell, B. (Eds.). (1969). *Software engineering: Report on a conference sponsored by the NATO Science Committee, Garmisch, Germany, 7-11 october 1968*.Brussels: Scientific Affairs Division, NATO.

Oinas-Kukkonen, H., Alatalo, T., Kaasila, J., Kivelä, H., & Sivunen, S. (2001). Requirements for web engineering methodologies. In M. Rossi & K. Siau (Eds.), *Information modeling in the new millennium* (pp. 360-382). Hershey, PA: Idea Group Publishing.

Orlikowski, W. J., & Gash, D. C. (1994). Technological frames: Making sense of information technology in organizations. *ACM Transactions on Information Systems, 12*(2), 669-702.

Powell, T. A., Jones, D. L., & Cutts, D. C. (1998). *Web site engineering: Beyond web page design.* Upper Saddle River: Prentice Hall.

Ratbe, D., King, W. R., & Kim, Y.-G. (1999). The fit between project characteristics and application development methodologies: A contingency approach.*Journal of Computer Information Systems, 40*(2), 26-33.

Rumbaugh, J. (1995). What is a method? *Journal of Object Oriented Programming, 8*(6), 10-16;26.

Russo, N. L., & Graham, B. R. (1999). A first step in developing a web application design methodology: Understanding the environment. In A. T. Wood-Harper, N. Jayaratna & J. R. G. Wood (Eds.), *Methodologies for developing and managing emerging technology based information systems: 6th International BCS Information Systems Methodologies Conference* (pp. 24-33). London: Springer.

Sahraoui, S. (1998). Is information systems education value neutral? *Journal of Computer Information Systems, 38*(3), 105-109.

Schön, D. A. (1983). *The reflective practitioner: How professionals think in action*.London: Temple Smith.

Shaw, M., & Garlan, D. (1996). *Software architecture: Perspectives on an emerging discipline*:Prentice Hall.

Song, X. (1997). Systematic integration of design methods. *IEEE Software, 14*(2), 107-117.

Stolterman, E., & Russo, N. (1997). *The paradox of information systems methods: Public and private rationality.* Paper presented at the 5th British Computer Society Conference on Information Systems Methodologies, Lancaster, England.

Strauss, A., & Corbin, J. (1998). *Basics of qualitative research: Techniques and procedures for developing grounded theory* (2nd ed.). Thousand Oaks, CA: Sage.

Strauss, A. L. (1970). Discovering new theory from previous theory. In T. Shibutani (Ed.), *Human nature and collective theory* (pp. 46-53). Englewood Cliffs, NJ: Prentice Hall.

Suchman, L. A. (1987). *Plans and situated actions: The problem of human-machine communication.* Cambridge: Cambridge University Press.

Taylor, P. R. (2004). Vernacularism in software design practice: Does craftmanship have a place in software engineering? *Australasian Journal of Information Systems, 11*(12), 14-25.

Ter Hofstedt, A. H. M., & Verhoef, T. F. (1997). On the feasibility of situational method engineering. *Information Systems, 22*(6-7), 401-422.

Truex, D., & Avison, D. (2003, August 4-6). *Method engineering: Reflections on the past and ways forward.* Paper presented at the 9th Americas Conference on Information Systems (AMCIS), Tampa, Florida, USA.

Vidgen, R., Avison, D., Wood, B., & Wood-Harper, T. (2002). *Developing web information systems: From strategy to implementation*.Oxford: Butterworth Heinemann.

White, M. (2000). *Leonardo: The first scientist.* London: Little, Brown & Company.

Whitley, E. A. (1998, December 13-16). *Methodism in practice: Investigating the relationship between method and understanding in web page design.* Paper presented at the 19th International Conference on Information Systems (ICIS), Helsinki, Finland.

Wroblewski, D. A. (1991). The construction of human-computer interfaces considered as a craft. In J. Karat (Ed.), *Taking software design seriously: Practical techniques for human-computer interaction design* (pp. 1-19): Academic Press.

Chapter XIV
Configurable Reference Modeling Languages

Jan Recker
Queensland University of Technology, Australia

Michael Rosemann
Queensland University of Technology, Australia

Wil M. P. van der Aalst
Queensland University of Technology, Australia, & Eindhoven University of Technology, The Netherlands

Monique Jansen-Vullers
Eindhoven University of Technology, The Netherlands

Alexander Dreiling
SAP Research CEC Brisbane, SAP Australia Pty Ltd., Australia

ABSTRACT

This chapter discusses reference modeling languages for business systems analysis and design. In particular, it reports on reference models in the context of the design-for/by-reuse paradigm, explains how traditional modeling techniques fail to provide adequate conceptual expressiveness to allow for easy model reuse by configuration or adaptation and elaborates on the need for reference modeling languages to be configurable. We discuss requirements for and the development of reference modeling languages that reflect the need for configurability. Exemplarily, we report on the development, definition and configuration of configurable event-driven process chains. We further outline how configurable reference modeling languages and the corresponding design principles can be used in future scenarios such as process mining and data modeling.

INTRODUCTION

Business systems have evolved as computer-based information systems that present themselves as comprehensive commercial packages for the support of business requirements. Being IT-supported software solutions, they presumptively support and enhance organizations in all their business operations. First attempts towards such corporate-wide integrated information systems were developed in the 1960s (Beer, 1966). The huge success of this idea has led to the proliferation of comprehensive business information systems such as enterprise resource planning (ERP) systems or enterprise systems (ES), the current generation of which is known under the label of process-aware information systems (Dumas, van der Aalst, & ter Hofstede, 2005). This label has emerged from an act of "silent revolution" that has embraced the IS discipline over the last decades and which has started to shift the focus of attention from a data perspective towards a process perspective. As a result, an increasing number of business processes are now conducted under the governance of process-aware information systems, with the intention of bridging not only business and IT but also people and software through process-based technology.

The successful implementation of process-aware business systems is, however, dependent on a seamless alignment between the system capabilities and the organizational requirements of the enterprise. The process of aligning organizational requirements and system functionality (Rosemann, Vessey, & Weber, 2004) is known as configuration and rests on the assumption of similarity between enterprises, in the sense that generic business system functionality, with some customization, is assumed to be applicable to all enterprises in a given industry sector. Following the idea of process-orientation, business system vendors often offer their solutions in the form of pre-defined generic business processes for a set of industry sectors. Oracle, for example, offers system-supported business process solutions that cover 19 industrial sectors (Oracle, 2006) while SAP offers business process solutions for 24 industrial sectors (SAP, 2006). These industry-specific process "templates" are introduced to organizations to offer a final implementation of the business system in the form of a configured, enterprise-specific set of business processes that are enabled, enacted and supported by the system.

Yet, the act of aligning generic industry-specific with enterprise-specific business processes that reflect organizational requirements has been shown to imply extensive configuration efforts and may lead to significant implementation costs that exceed the price of software licenses by factors of five to ten (Davenport, 2000). Some instances even indicate that a misalignment may result in severe business failure if conducted badly. Consider the example of FoxMeyer, once a \$5 billion wholesale drug distributor, which filed for bankruptcy in 1996 after Andersen Consulting concluded that the insufficiently aligned SAP installation crippled the firm's distribution (Stein, 1998). Other examples include Mobil Europe and Dow Chemical (Davenport, 1998).

Business systems vendors are aware of these problems and try to increase the manageability of the configuration process of their software solutions. One respective measure is to deliver the products along with extensive documentation and specific implementation and configuration support tools. Conceptual models play a central role within such documentation. They describe functionality and structure of the business systems on a semi-formal level and have become popular under the notion of reference models. Though such reference models for business systems exist in the form of function, data, system organization, object and process models, the latter is by far the most popular model type (Rosemann, 2000) and often forms a constituent part of the documentation of software packages.

While the existence of such reference models as part of the system documentation in general is valuable in software implementation projects (Kesari, Chang, & Seddon, 2003), traditional reference models offer little or no support for configuration (Daneva, 2000) This is mainly due to a lack of conceptual support in the form of a configurable modeling language underlying the reference models (Rosemann & van der Aalst, in press).

Nevertheless, the business system configuration process can significantly benefit from the usage of reference models, for instance, in terms of consistency, completeness, adaptability and communicability. Since most business information systems are quite extensively depicted in their reference models, it motivates the idea of utilizing these reference models for the configuration task. However, the language that is used to formulate reference models for the task of system configuration needs to be configurable to support this delicate task. A configurable reference process model should, for instance, provide rules defining how a generic reference process model can be adapted to suit a specific organizational context.

This chapter provides an introduction to configurable reference modeling languages and their role in the configuration process of business information systems. It covers discussions of current shortcomings of reference modeling languages, the need for configurable reference models and the different stages towards the development and application of configurable reference modeling languages, particularly in the context of business information systems. While we will, during the course of this chapter, address multiple perspectives using the examples of process and data models, our foremost focus lies on the process perspective. We will explicate our argumentations using the example of a configurable reference process modeling language called configurable EPCs (Rosemann & van der Aalst, in press).

Forthcoming from this introduction we will first discuss traditional reference modeling languages. Then, we will present and discuss design principles for the design of configurable reference modeling languages and then apply the principles in the development of EPCs. Next, we will briefly outline future scenarios for configurable reference modeling languages and their design principles. We close this chapter by discussing some conclusions from our work.

REFERENCE MODELING LANGUAGES

Reference models are generic conceptual models that formalize recommended practices for a certain domain (Fettke & Loos, 2003; Misic & Zhao, 2000). Often labeled with the term "best practice," reference models claim to capture reusable state-of-the-art practices (Silverston, 2001a, 2001b). The depicted domains can be very different and range from selected functional areas, such as financial accounting or customer relationship management, to the scope of an entire industry sector (e.g., higher education).

The main objective of reference models is to streamline the design of enterprise-individual (particular) models by providing a generic solution (Rosemann, 2000). The application of reference models is motivated by the "design-for/by-reuse" paradigm, postulating that they should accelerate the modeling process by providing a repository of potentially relevant business processes and structures, ideally in an easy "plug & play" modus. Thus, reference modeling is closely related to the reuse of information models (Wisse, 2000) by providing a generic model solution that can be adapted to a specific model reflecting individual requirements.

Reference models are often used for describing the structure and functionality of business systems. In these cases, a reference model can be interpreted as a structured, semi-formal description of a particular application. Such application reference models correspond to an existing off-the-shelf solution that supports the functionality and structure described in the model (Rosemann, 2002). They can, for example, be used for a better understanding and evaluation of the appropriateness of the software.

One of the most comprehensive models is the SAP reference model (Curran, Keller, & Ladd, 1997). In version 4.6, its data model includes more than 4,000 entity types and the reference process models cover more than 1,000 system processes and inter-organizational business scenarios. Most of the other market leading business systems vendors have alternative or similar approaches toward such reference models.

Foundational conceptual work for the SAP reference model had been conducted by SAP AG and the IDS Scheer AG in a collaborative research project in the years 1990-1992 (Keller, Nüttgens, & Scheer, 1992). The outcome of this project was the process modeling language event-driven process chains (EPCs) (Keller et al., 1992; Scheer, 2000), which has been used for the design of the reference process models in SAP. EPCs have become one of the most popular reference modeling languages overall and have, for instance, been used for the design of many SAP-independent reference models (e.g., Siebel CRM, ITIL, eTOM and PMBOK).

EPCs basically denote directed graphs, which visualize the control flow and consist of events, functions and connectors. Each EPC starts and ends with at least one event. An event triggers a function, which leads to a new event. Three types of connectors (logical AND ∧, logical exclusive OR XOR and logical OR ∨) can be used to specify the logical links that exist between sequences of events and functions in process chains. They model control flow splits and joins. An AND-split activates all outgoing branches in concurrency while an AND-join waits for all incoming branches to synchronize before propagating control to the following EPC element. An OR-split activates one, two or up to all outgoing

branches based on certain conditions while an OR-join synchronizes all incoming branches that are active and then propagates control to the following EPC element. An XOR-split activates one of multiple outgoing branches based on certain conditions while an OR-join propagates control to the following EPC element when the first active incoming branch arrives.

Figure 1 gives an example for an EPC as it potentially can be found as part of a reference model. This model shows an extract of a procurement process. The EPC contains eight events, six functions and three connectors. The events can be seen as pre- and/or post-conditions of functions. For example, the function Verify Invoice can be executed if event Invoice posted is received and the completion of this function will trigger the event Payment to be effected. There are two functions triggering event Invoice arrived. The XOR-connector in the lower half of the diagram shows that there is no need to synchronize these two functions (e.g., the completion of Store Goods directly triggers event Invoice posted). The XOR-connector in the upper half of the diagram splits the control flow in accordance to the condition whether the purchase performed relates to goods (left branch) or services (right branch). The remaining connector denotes an AND-join, meaning that both input events need to be triggered in order to enable function Create Purchase Order.

As can be observed from Figure 1, regular EPCs do not contain any configuration information. Therefore, valuable information is lacking. For example, it is not shown that Record Service (i.e., the scenario in which procured services need to be audited during execution, is only of interest for a subset of all procurement scenarios, namely those where services are being procured instead of goods). There are cases imaginable where enterprises only enact a procurement process for goods but not services. In these cases the accordant part of the reference model is not applicable to the organization and should be eliminated from the enterprise-specific process model. This implies

Figure 1. An example for a potential reference model in EPC notation

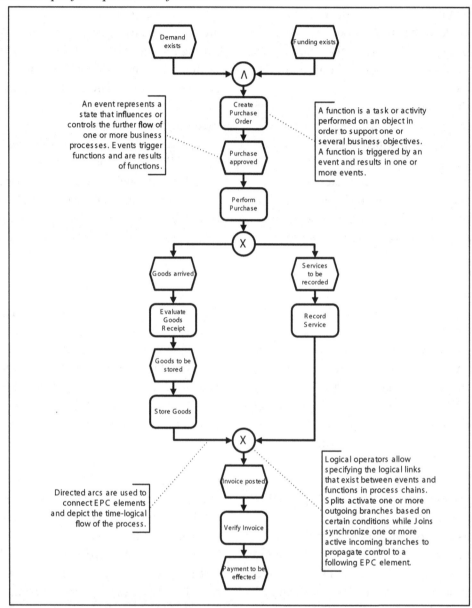

that the XOR connector may be a choice made for the whole process rather than for an individual process instance. Consider a second example. The EPC shown in Figure 1 neither shows that Store Goods is only relevant if Evaluate Goods Receipt is conducted. If organizations opt never to procure goods but only services, there is no need to implement functionality for goods storage. Also, the model neither gives any insights into the necessity or criticality of potential configurations nor into possible inter-dependencies between configuration decisions. Thus, the model expressive power is limited and cannot guide the configuration of a corresponding business system. Hence, a reference model designed using a traditional reference modeling language is only of limited use for the configuration process due to a lack of support on a conceptual level.

DESIGN OF CONFIGURABLE REFERENCE MODELING LANGUAGES

Design Principles for a Configurable Reference Modeling Language

Following the elaborations in the preceding section and the idea of reference modeling (i.e., the streamlined development of individual models through "design-for/by-reuse") we postulate that reference modeling languages ought to be configurable. We can reason our argumentation by introducing a simple reference model lifecycle that depicts the different stages of a reference model, ranging from model design to execution (see Figure 2).

The lifecycle is initiated by ES vendors who depict the functionality of their software packages in reference models (design time). Such a reference model typically does not include merely one proposed alternative for conducting business in a certain domain but a range of often mutually exclusive alternatives. It denotes an "upper-bound" of business system models that may possibly be implemented in a particular enterprise. An organization might merely favor one of the depicted alternatives and thus only to a subset of system functionality to be implemented. Accordingly they only refer to a subset of the reference model. Figure 2 demonstrates this problem in a simple example. The upper-bound reference model depicts two mutually exclusive alternatives of conducting business, either the sequence A-B-C or A-B-D. A particular enterprise has to select one of these two substitutive alternatives of conducting business under the governance of the respective business system. The XOR split in this case represents a decision point that is of relevance during configuration time. Note that a model in this phase cannot necessarily be executed. It rather captures different alternatives for a domain and thus needs to be configured before it can serve as the actual build time model, a template for implementing and executing process instances at run time.

These types of decisions cannot be reflected in traditional reference models due to a lack of conceptual support of the underlying reference modeling language. Existing reference modeling techniques do not support the highlighting and selection of different alternatives. The resulting lack of expressiveness denotes a major issue for model users, as (a) it does not become obvious what configuration alternatives exist during system implementation, and (b) the models do not provide any decision support towards the selection of different alternatives.

Figure 2. Reference model lifecycle

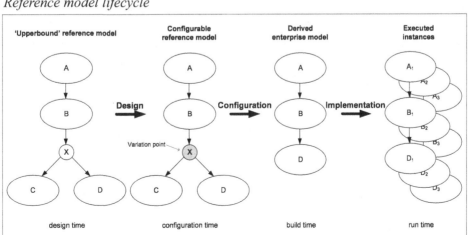

Contemplating the reference model lifecycle and the shortcomings of traditional reference modeling languages, we have identified the following design principles for a configurable reference modeling language:

a. A configurable modeling language is characterized by its capability to support decisions for the transformation of reference models from configuration time to build time (i.e., the model user can individualize the model by selecting from alternative options before instances will be derived from it). Such configuration decisions on a type level have to be clearly differentiated from decisions on an instance level and can be highlighted as variation points in a model (Halmans & Pohl, 2003) that should capture a decision point together with the related possible choices.

b. A configurable modeling language has to support configurations of business systems regarding processes, functions, control flow and data. In terms of processes, configuration should address the active parts of process models (i.e., functionality—functions, tasks, transitions and the like—and control flow). As events (or states), being more passive parts of processes cannot actively be influenced by an organization, these should not be covered by a configurable reference process modeling language.

c. It should be possible to differentiate configuration decisions into mandatory and optional decisions. Mandatory decisions have to be made before the very first instance can be derived from this model. Optional decisions can initially be neglected. It should be possible to maintain defaults for optional configuration decisions. This allows the instantiation of the model even without explicitly making all possible decisions.

d. Configuration should be differentiated into global and local decisions. Global decisions are based on the general context, including factors such as industry, country, size, and so forth. The relevant context factors have to be maintained for every variation point. As soon as information regarding the relevant context has been provided, a first (hidden or background) configuration of the reference model can take place, which would lead to "context-aware models." Local configurations require an explicit study of the relevant reference model as the related decisions may be based on local or individual factors such as available budget, risk profile, time, and so forth.

e. Configuration decisions should be differentiated into critical and non-critical decisions. Critical decisions have significant impact on the use of the system and other business processes, can often not be re-done and should be made by the project team. Non-critical decisions are of minor importance, can be made by individual team members and change over time.

f. Configuration decisions can have interrelationships. Such pre-requisites for a configuration decision should be clearly highlighted. This can include other decisions that have to be made before. Moreover, any impact of one decision on other decisions has to be depicted. This means a logical order between configuration decisions has to be considered. This includes interrelationships within one model, between two process models or even interrelationships between reference process and related data models (Rosemann & Shanks, 2001).

g. Variation points should refer to further related information within the part of the business system it depicts. This may include the system online help and the system configuration module, such as the SAP implementation guide (IMG) (Bancroft, Seip, & Sprengel, 1997). Such information can provide valuable support for the decision maker.

h. The entire configuration process should be guided by recommendations in the form of guidelines. Such information could come as benchmarking data from the outside of the system if a critical mass of system users is willing to provide such data. It may include information such as the processing time of a given process path, the number of times a decision has been made in the same industry or the required investments and implementation time for a certain configuration. Such recommendations may as well assist reference model users in assessing the compliance of their configuration to industry best practices.

i. Reference models can be very comprehensive. Any extension of the underlying modeling languages has to carefully consider the impact on the perceived model complexity. It is advisable to extend existing reference modeling languages rather than developing new ones.

In the following we will apply these design principles in the development of a configurable reference modeling language. As process modeling is key to acquiring, communicating and validating business requirements (Daneva, 2004; Welti, 1999) we will focus the process perspective (i.e., the alignment of IT functionality to the actual business processes of an organization). The following section introduces Configurable EPCs as the representation language of a reference process modeling approach that considers the configurable nature of a business system and reflects the design principles for configurable modeling techniques.

Configurable Event-Driven Process Chains

This section introduces the notion of a Configurable EPC (C-EPC). We start our elaborations by referring back to the procurement example given

before. Figure 1 shows a potential reference model for the process of procurement in the form of a classical EPC. Following this diagram, procurement starts with the creation of a purchase order (function Create Purchase Order) when a demand for services or goods exists (event Demand exists) and (logical AND-connector ∧) when sufficient funding for the procurement exists (event Funding exists). Once the created purchase order has been approved, the procurement can be conducted. The process succeeds with either reception and storage of the arrived goods, or recording of the enactment of the requested service. In either case, an invoice will arrive at some point in time demanding payment for the delivery of goods or services. Then, the invoice needs to be verified, which in turn triggers the effectuation of payment, which ends the process.

However, not all organizations implement procurement the same way. For example, not only goods may be purchased but also services, with the former being in a need for appropriate storage while the latter need to be audited during enactment. A particular organization may only want to implement procurement functionality of a business system for either services or goods. Furthermore, for illustration purposes, let us assume that a purchase may or may not be related to a purchase order. Similarly, the verification of invoices may or may not be essential for the effectuation of payment, for example in cases where long-term contracts to trusted vendors or sophisticated support exists (e.g., in the form of Evaluated Receipt Settlement functionality). None of these potential configuration decisions can be visualized using the traditional EPC reference modeling language. In particular, the model does not express possible configuration alternatives and scenarios with respect to the process it represents.

This section introduces configurable EPCs as an approach to depict variation points in a reference process model as well as further configuration information (Rosemann & van der Aalst, in press).

Adhering to design principle (b), we seek to make the active parts of processes configurable (i.e., functionality and control flow). Accordingly, in a C-EPC, functions and connectors can be configured. As an example, Figure 3 shows the procurement reference process model introduced in the preceding section depicted in C-EPC notation. We will use this example model throughout the remainder of this section to introduce the notion of C-EPCs.

Adhering to design principle (i), C-EPCs extend regular EPCs with the specification of variation points (configurable functions and connectors), configuration requirements and configuration guidelines.

Configurable functions may be included (ON), excluded (OFF) or conditionally skipped (OPT). To be more specific, a decision has to be made whether to perform such a function in every process instance during run time (ON), whether

Figure 3. Potential configurable reference model for the procurement process, depicted in C-EPC notation

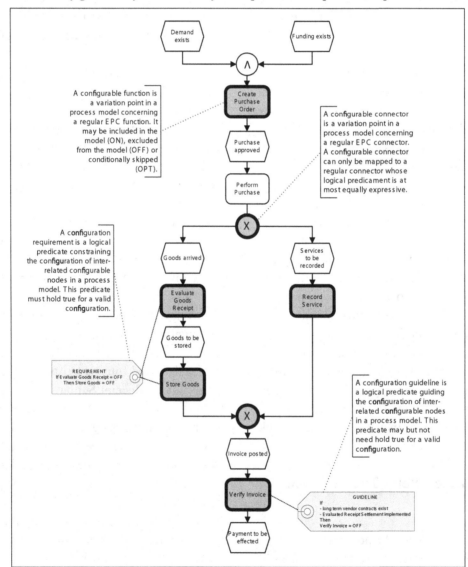

to exclude this function permanently (i.e., it will not be executed in any process instance (OFF) or whether to defer this decision to run time, i.e., for each process instance it has to be decided whether or not to execute the function (OPT)). Referring to the example given in Figure 3, it is possible, for instance, to configure the procurement process in a way that Create Purchase Order and Verify Invoice are not to be implemented; therefore, they are to be excluded from the enterprise-individual process model. Reflecting this decision in the configurable reference process model, the accordant configurable functions can be switched OFF.

Configurable connectors subsume possible build time connectors that are less or equally expressive. Hence, a configurable connector can only be mapped to a connector type that restricts its behavior. A configurable OR-connector may be mapped to a regular OR-, XOR- or AND-connector. Or, the OR-connector may be mapped to a single sequence of events and functions (indicated by SEQ_n for some process path starting with node n). That is, out of the incoming/outgoing branches of a configurable OR-connector, a single branch is chosen that is to be included in the individual model while the remaining branches are to be excluded from the model. A configurable AND-connector may only be mapped to a regular AND-connector with a decision being made as to how many of n available process paths are to be executed in synchronization. A configurable XOR-connector may be mapped to a regular XOR-connector, or the XOR-connector may be mapped to a single process sequence SEQ_n. Table 1 summarizes these mapping constraints.

Referring back to the example given in Figure 3, consider the decision that a particular enterprise does not want to implement procurement for both goods and services but instead only for goods. The assessment and recording of services would then be deemed unnecessary. In the reference process model, such a decision can be reflected by mapping the configurable XOR-connector to a single sequence $SEQ_{Goods\ arrived}$ specifying the process branch containing the handling of received goods.

In order to depict inter-dependencies between configurable EPC nodes, configuration requirements can be introduced to limit the configuration possibilities between inter-related configurable nodes. These constraints are best defined via logical expressions in the form of If-Then statements and denote predicates for a set of configurable nodes that must hold true for a valid configuration. Consider again the example given in Figure 3. If the goods receipt sub-process is deemed unnecessary, there is no need for the storage of goods, as services cannot be physically stored. A configuration constraint could be that if Evaluate Goods Receipt is switched OFF, so must be function Store Goods.

In order to provide input in terms of recommendations and proposed best practices, configuration guidelines may be depicted (also in the form of logical expressions) to guide the configuration process semantically. They, too, may be expressed in the form of If-Then statements. They denote logical predicates for a set of configurable nodes that may but not need hold true for a given configuration. Again, consider

Table 1. Constraints for the configuration of connectors

Configurable connector	Mapping to OR	Mapping to XOR	Mapping to AND	Mapping to SEQ_n
OR				
XOR				
AND				

Figure 3. Verify invoice may be an unnecessary task if long-term procurement contracts with trusted vendors or advanced Evaluated Receipt Settlement functionality exists that automatically settles invoices based on goods issued. For these scenarios a configuration guideline suggests switching Verify Invoice OFF.

In summation, the notion of a C-EPC potentially facilitates a selection and modification of process flows and process activities within a reference process model. As can be seen from Figure 3, configurable nodes are denoted as usual EPC nodes shaped by thick circles, while both configuration requirements and guidelines are depicted as notes-like boxes attached to a number of configurable nodes.

Configuration Using Configurable EPCs

According to the reference model lifecycle (see Figure 2), at configuration time a configurable reference process model can be configured in the sense that configuration alternatives within the model are selected in a way that a configuration scenario is created which is deemed desirable for the particular organization. Such a configuration maps all configurable nodes to concrete values (i.e., regular EPC nodes) while adhering to configuration requirements (and possibly also configuration guidelines). Figure 4 shows two possible regular EPCs resulting from a configuration of the C-EPC shown in Figure 3.

Consider the EPC depicted in the left part of Figure 4: In this case, the particular enterprise decided to relate purchase requests to purchase orders, hence, the function Create Purchase Order is included. Similarly, as the organization only purchases from long-known, trusted vendors, an extra invoice verification activity was deemed unnecessary. Hence, the accordant function Verify Invoice was excluded from the model. Furthermore, procurement in this case has to cater to either physical goods or services.

Hence, the configurable XOR-connector has been mapped to a regular XOR-connector, allowing for the procurement of either services or goods at run time, for both of which accordant activities have been included as well. In the left part of Figure 4, Configuration (a) shows the process model resulting from the configuration {(Create Purchase Order,ON),(XOR,XOR),(Evaluate Goods Receipt,ON),(Store Goods,ON),(Record Service,ON),(XOR,XOR),(Verify Invoice,OFF)}.

Configuration (b) shows an EPC resulting from the configuration {(Create Purchase Order,OFF),(XOR,SEQ$_{Services\ to\ be\ recorded}$),(Goods Receipt,OFF),(Storage,OFF),(Service recording,ON),(XOR,SEQ$_{Services\ to\ be\ recorded}$),(Verify Invoice,ON)}. As both EPC models do not conflict against the configuration requirements depicted in Figure 3, both configurations are valid. Note here that a valid configuration is also suitable if it further satisfies all configuration guidelines.

Strictly speaking, deriving a correct build time EPC from a configured C-EPC involves three kinds of tasks: (a) derivation of a partial EPC model for each configured function, (b) derivation of a partial EPC model for each configured connector and (c) recalculation of the complete EPC process graph by excluding unnecessary paths. The calculation of the build time EPC should be governed by the minimality criterion: if elements have to be added by configuration, add as few elements as possible; if elements have to be removed by configuration, remove as many as possible, and optimize the graph so as to include no unnecessary paths (Mendling, Recker, Rosemann, & van der Aalst, 2006; Recker, Rosemann, van der Aalst, & Mendling, 2006).

Theoretically, there are four constellations in which a configured function may appear in a C-EPC (Dreiling, Chiang, Rosemann, & van der Aalst, 2005; Recker, Rosemann, van der Aalst, & Mendling, 2006): (a) between two events, (b) between a connector and an event, (c) between an event and a connector and (d) between two connectors. Figure 5 illustrates the derivation rules for these four cases (connectors labeled with any indicate that any connector type is allowed to make the rule applicable). In case (a) a configurable function mapped to OPT generates two additional XOR-connectors. This mapping is proposed in accordance to the minimality criterion as it introduces a minimal set of additional elements. In case (b) the configurable function mapped to OPT generates an additional function and two XOR-connectors. This additional function allows for the XOR-split decision, otherwise there

would have been a split connector subsequent to a join connector, which is not lawful. Case (c) is similar to case (a)—instead of the succeeding event a successor split connector (any) is given. In Case (d) the configurable function mapped to OFF may not simply be excluded. As the any join may be the last connector in a chain of several connectors, the exclusion of the configurable function may not be possible in every case (if the connector chain is composed of join connectors only, events preceding the connector chain can be eliminated together with the function. If the

Figure 4. Two possible configurations of the C-EPC shown in Figure 3

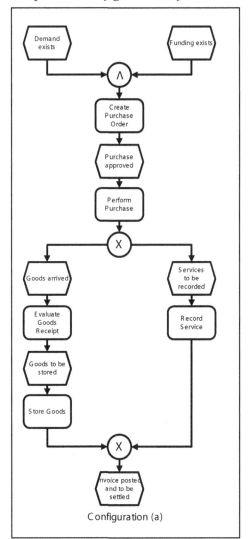

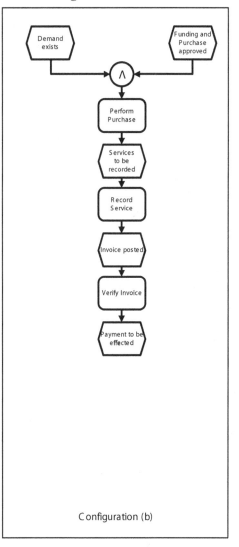

connector chain also includes split connectors, there are further functions at the end of the chain that require the events in order to comply with the EPC alternation rule). The optional function follows a similar idea as applied in case (b). All of these derivation rules preserve the correctness of the model.

Configured connectors can mostly be derived in a straightforward manner. If a configurable connector is not configured to a sequence, only its label has to be adopted. If a connector is configured to a sequence SEQ_n, those succeeding paths that are not to be included in the build time model have to be eliminated. This means that all subsequent elements are to be excluded from the model until a join connector is reached. If there are no more paths to be eliminated, it must further be checked whether there are join connectors in the model that do not link to any incoming arc. Paths starting with these joins have to be eliminated, too, and the check must be repeated. This procedure is iterated until there are no more connectors without incoming arcs. Figure 6 illustrates this procedure by presenting the case of a split connector whose outgoing paths are eliminated. Following our argumentation, this connector and its successor path must be eliminated until a join connector is reached. Again, these derivation rules preserve the correctness of the model.

After deriving configured functions and configured connectors, the resulting EPC may still include unnecessary process graph structures. Functions that are switched OFF and connectors that are configured to SEQ_n may lead to empty paths or connectors with only one incoming and one outgoing arc (for instance the XOR connector in the resulting model shown in Figure 6). In order to comply with the minimality criterion, certain graph reduction rules have to be applied. Figure 7 gives five reduction rules that are sufficient to derive EPCs that comply with the minimality criterion. Rule (a) eliminates arcs a from an AND-split to an AND-join if there is a path from the split to the join that does not pass a. Rule (b) deletes a path

of concurrency if that path only includes an event and no function. Rule (c) eliminates connectors that only have one incoming and one outgoing arc. Rule (d) deletes an arc between an OR split or an XOR split and a join connector if there is another arc between them. Rule (e) merges two events if they both are successors of an OR split or an XOR split and predecessor of the same join connector. These reduction rules preserve a minimal process graph structure that represents the control flow of the configured process flow variant.

The previous derivation rules can be summarized in the definition of a respective derivation algorithm. The algorithm includes the steps 1-4 for connector configuration, 5-6 for graph reduction, 7 for function configuration and 8-9 for graph reduction. We start with the configuration of connectors as sequence configurations might already reduce the model; in particular, it may lead to the exclusion of configurable functions. Furthermore, connector configuration may result in unnecessary connectors. The graph is reduced in steps 5-6, as the removal of unnecessary connectors before handling configurable functions

Figure 5. Derivation rules for configured functions

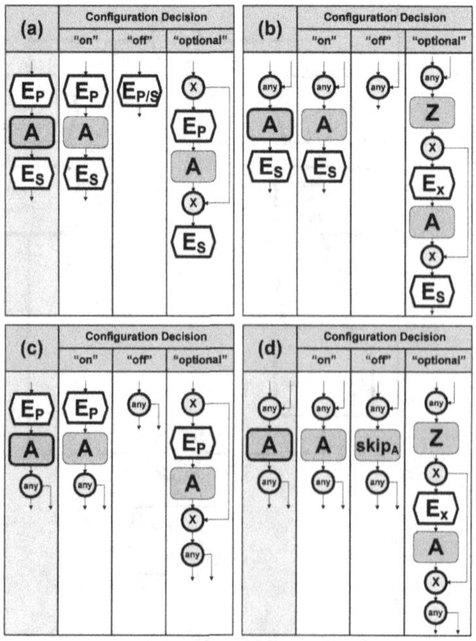

allows applying the derivation rules (a) and (c) of Figure 7, which in turn result in a smaller graph than rules (b) and (d). Still, function configuration may also result in unnecessary connectors that have to be removed in steps 8-9.

1. Map configured connectors to regular connectors in adherence to the configuration value.

2. If the configuration value is SEQ_n eliminate paths (including all nodes) $i \neq n$, until a join connector or an end node is reached.

3. Check whether there is a connector c without any incoming arcs. If yes, go to 4. If no, go to 5.

4. Eliminate all paths starting with connector c until a join connector or an end node is reached. Go to 3.

Figure 6. Example: Connector configured to SEQ_{E2}

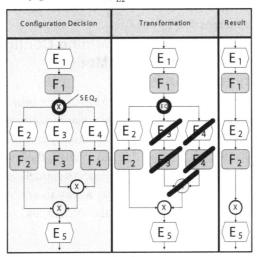

Figure 7. Reduction rules to derive minimal EPCs

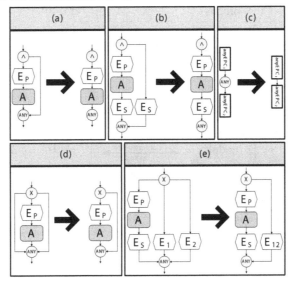

5. Check whether one of the reduction rules shown in Figure 7 is applicable. If yes, go to 6. If no, go to 7.
6. Apply one reduction rule and go to 5.
7. Configure functions according to the rules shown in Figure 5.
8. Check whether one of the reduction rules shown in Figure 7 is applicable. If yes, go to 9. If no, end.
9. Apply one reduction rule and go to 7.

Steps 1 to 9 ensure that all configurable nodes in a C-EPC are either deleted from the model or mapped to regular EPC counterparts. At this stage, we can ensure that the resulting process graph neither contains semantically ambiguous process paths nor unnecessary ones. What we cannot ensure is a formal semantics of the resulting EPC (Kindler, 2005; van der Aalst, 1999). Yet, our extension (and the respective reduction) approach allows for the application of existing formalization approaches (e.g., Kindler, 2005; van der Aalst, 1999) as a semantic foundation for (derived) EPCs.

The algorithm as shown here rests on the specification of C-EPCs in XML (Mendling, Recker, Rosemann, & van der Aalst, 2005; Recker, Rosemann, van der Aalst, & Mendling, 2006) using the interchange format EPML (Mendling & Nüttgens, 2006) and can be implemented using the object-oriented scripting language XOTcl (Neumann & Zdun, 2000) (the prototype program and the EPML specifications can be downloaded from http://wi.wu-wien.ac.at/~mendling/EPML).

FUTURE TRENDS

Mining Configurable Reference Models

Most of the work reported in this Chapter discusses the use of configurable process models as a way to actually configure an ES (i.e., the model is used to realize the system). However, configurable process models (e.g., C-EPCs) can also be used as a way to analyze the processes supported by the system and to "discover" the actual system

Figure 8. Relation between reference models and process mining

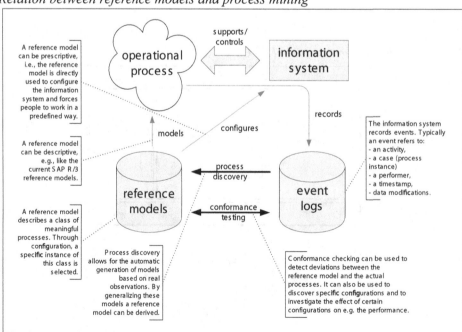

configuration. As a starting point for such types of analysis, one can use audit trails (also known as event or transaction logs) and apply process mining techniques.

The goal of process mining is to extract information about processes from event logs (van der Aalst et al., 2003). Process mining techniques such as the alpha algorithm (van der Aalst, Weijters, & Maruster, 2004) typically assume that it is possible to sequentially record events such that (a) each event refers to an activity (i.e., a well-defined step in the process), and (b) each event refers to a case (i.e., a process instance). Moreover, there are other techniques explicitly using additional information such as (c) the performer also referred to as originator of the event (i.e., the person/resource executing or initiating the activity), (d) the timestamp of the event or (e) data elements recorded with the event (e.g., the size of an order). This information can be used to automatically construct process models. For example, the Multi-Phase Mining approach (van Dongen & van der Aalst, 2004) can be used to construct an EPC describing the behavior observed in the log. There are mature tools such as the ProM framework (van Dongen, Alves de Medeiros, Verbeek, Weijters, & van der Aalst, 2005) available to construct different types of models based on process executions.

There are several ways to use event logs in the context of configurable reference models (see Figure 8). Reference models can be descriptive or prescriptive (i.e., they are used to describe a process or control to respectively guide the system). The SAP reference models are expressed in terms of EPCs describing how people should/could use the SAP system. In reality, however, the real process may deviate from the modeled process (e.g., the implementation is not consistent with the specification, or people use a SAP solution in a way not modeled in any of the EPCs). Even if reference models are more of a prescriptive nature, it is still interesting to investigate how people really use the system.

Figure 8 shows that reference models can be used to configure an information system (prescriptive) or to merely model the desired process (descriptive). Independent of the way the reference model is used, most information systems log events in the form of audit trails or transaction logs. The information can be used for process discovery and conformance testing. Process discovery aims at the construction of models based on the logs without explicitly using some apriori reference model. This approach is used to construct models that can be used for comparison with existing reference models, or to generate input for the construction of new reference models. Conformance testing can be used to compare real processes with some a priori knowledge represented in the form of a reference model. It may be used to see if some descriptive reference model is actually followed in reality. Note that system users may deviate from the procedure prescribed in the reference models. Such information can be used for auditing or process improvement. Moreover, the configuration itself can be investigated (e.g., analyzing which configuration is used, what is the effect of using a specific configuration, etc.).

Process mining is far from trivial. Knowledge of the many ways in which a system may be used can assist process mining techniques, as illustrated by Jansen-Vullers, van der Aalst, and Rosemann (2006). Based on inspecting the event logs, it is relatively easy to discover the particular configuration being used. Moreover, event logs can be used to "diagnose" a configuration. For example, using process mining it is possible to automatically locate the bottlenecks and present them in the context of the configurable process model (e.g., a function in the C-EPC). This may assist the reconfiguration of the system. Furthermore, process mining techniques can be used to compare different configurations and their effects on the performance of the resulting process, which supports an "evidence-based" approach towards business process management.

Configurable Data Modeling Languages

So far, we have covered the configurability of reference process models. Yet, given that reference models are often used in the context of business systems, there are more perspectives to consider. Business systems are not only popular, since they provide process-oriented support for typical functional areas such as Procurement or Materials Management, but also since they provide integrated data repositories across the whole enterprise. Accordingly, available reference models not only depict business processes but also the data structure of business systems. As an example, in version 4.6, the SAP reference data model covers more than 230 business objects clustering more than 4,000 entity types. A configuration approach needs to place emphasis on the configuration of reference data models as well. Consider an organizational perspective: Reference data models are of particular importance to the configuration of system organizational units as they precisely depict the given opportunities of a business system. A subset of the SAP reference data model (approximately 30-40 entity types) allows for a complete description of the interrelations between system organizational units such as company, factory or distribution channel, which facilitates configuration decisions as to the system organizational structure.

Similar to the process perspective, current reference data models are typically based on traditional modeling techniques such as the Entity-Relationship Modeling (ERM) notation (Chen, 1976). Entity types are used to group and depict distinct subjects of interest (e.g., customers, organizations, sales order items, etc.). These entities may possess various attributes for further specification. Relationships between such elements of interest are depicted using relationship types that specify the type of association between distinct entities. Cardinalities can further be used to specify the extent of dependency between associated entity types.

Classical data modeling techniques do not allow for the depiction of configuration information, such as variation points or configuration requirements (Rosemann & Shanks, 2001). In the following, we discuss some configuration decisions that can be made and how they could be depicted in reference data models. Extracts of the SAP reference data model are used as an example. The structure of this analysis follows the main constructs of Entity-Relationship-Models (i.e., entity and relationship types, Chen, 1976). Note that the variant used here is called SAP-Structured ERM; refer, for instance, to Seubert, Schäfer, Schorr, and Wagner (1994).

Transparent examples for model configurations related to optional entity types can be found in Enterprise Systems in the definition of system organizational structures. The Sales & Distribution solution in SAP, for example, requires a decision whether shipping points of an enterprise are to be subdivided into loading points. The IMG (Bancroft et al., 1997) marks this decision as optional. This variation point, however, cannot be reflected in the available reference data model (see Figure 9) as the data structure is statically fixed.

In a configurable reference data model, optional entity types such as Loading Point could be highlighted with a dotted line, thereby indicating that such organizational structure may (a) or may not be (b) implemented.

The configuration of optional relationship types includes two decisions. First, if the relationship type is required at all. If the relationship is required, a second decision is related to what cardinalities the relationship should have. Again, consider an organizational perspective: The IMG allows for the decision whether or not to assign a purchasing organization to a company code (i.e., whether procurement may be effectuated company-specific for all plants assigned to that company, Figure 10, configuration (a)), or whether procurement may be effectuated plant-specific for all the plants assigned to the purchasing organization (Figure 10, configuration (b)), irrespective

Figure 9. Configuration of reference data models: Entity types

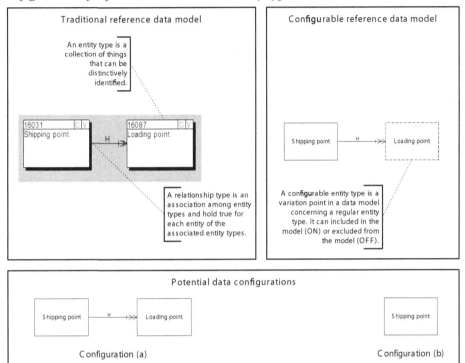

of the super-ordinate company code. Again, the available reference data model cannot reflect this decision as the relationship between the entity types Company Code and Purchasing Organization is fixed.

A configurable reference data model could highlight this variation point by using a dotted line for the connection between these entity types.

There is a need to further explore configurability of reference data models. We only presented a brief outline of a proposed conceptual extension to existing reference data modeling techniques. Our short discussion revealed that, following the idea of configurable reference process modeling, the design principles that led to the development of C-EPCs may also be used to extend or refine other reference modeling techniques towards configurability (leading for example to C-ERMs). Exemplarily, we elaborated on the conceptual development of a configurable data modeling technique that allows for the modeling

of optional entity types and optional relationship types. Clearly, this has to be considered a work-in-progress but nevertheless denotes an important and interesting research facet in the future of (configurable) reference modeling.

CONCLUSION

This chapter discussed and introduced extensions to conceptual modeling languages in order to facilitate the configuration of reference models. These modeling languages have been developed in light of a number of critical design principles which are of relevance following the paradigm of information model reuse. We used an extension of the event-driven process chain to demonstrate the design of a configurable reference process modeling language. Furthermore, we gave first insights into how configurable models can be derived via process mining from executed business system-

Figure 10. Configuration of reference data models: Relationship types

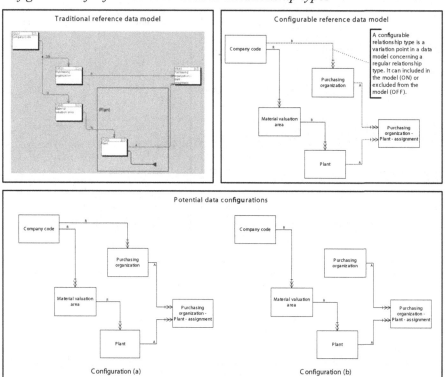

supported processes. In principle, other modeling languages could be extended in similar ways. It has been discussed how the idea of configuring process models can be applied to other views, such as the data perspective. We briefly reported on the development of a configurable data modeling language as an example.

We expect research on configurable reference modeling to give a stimulating input to both academic and practical work around reference models in the future. The development of generic, configurable languages such as the C-EPC and the establishment of tool-neutral interchange formats such as EPML (Mendling & Nüttgens, 2006) or the XML metadata interchange (XMI) format (OMG, 2005) provide promising prototype examples that strive for practical adoption in the form of commercial solutions. Configurable reference models may be used to facilitate a model-driven implementation process of business systems (Recker,

Mendling, van der Aalst, & Rosemann, 2006), or the usage of configurable reference models can lead to the cross-organizational consolidation of previous process configurations, thereby accumulating an evidence-based body of knowledge as to the configuration and enactment of business processes across multiple industry sectors, regions and cultures. These are just a few ideas, but they already indicate that reference modeling and model configurability continue to emerge as a vibrant and influential research discipline in the future.

REFERENCES

Bancroft, N. H., Seip, H., & Sprengel, A. (1997). *Implementing Sap R/3: How to introduce a large system into a large organization* (2nd ed.). Englewood Cliffs, NJ: Prentice Hall.

Beer, S. (1966). *Decision and control: The meaning of operational research and management cybernetics.* London: John Wiley & Sons.

Chen, P. P.-S. (1976). The entity relationship model: Toward a unified view of data. *ACM Transactions on Database Systems, 1*(1), 9-36.

Curran, T., Keller, G., & Ladd, A. (1997). *SAP R/3 business blueprint: Understanding the business process reference model.* Upper Saddle River, NJ: Prentice Hall.

Daneva, M. (2000). Practical reuse measurement in ERP requirements engineering. In B. Wangler & L. Bergmann (Eds.), *Advanced information systems engineering: 12th International Conference* (Vol. 1789, pp. 309-324). Stockholm, Sweden: Springer.

Daneva, M. (2004). ERP requirements engineering practice: Lessons learned. *IEEE Software, 21*(2), 26-33.

Davenport, T. H. (1998). Putting the enterprise into the enterprise system. *Harvard Business Review, 76*(4), 121-131.

Davenport, T. H. (2000). *Mission critical: Realizing the promise of enterprise systems.* Boston: Harvard Business School Press.

Dreiling, A., Chiang, M., Rosemann, M., & van der Aalst, W. M. P. (2005). Towards an understanding of model-driven process configuration and its support at large. In N. C. Romano (Ed.), *2005 Americas Conference on Information Systems* (pp. 2084-2092). Omaha, NE: Association for Information Systems.

Dumas, M., van der Aalst, W. M. P., & ter Hofstede, A. H. M. (Eds.). (2005). *Process aware information systems: Bridging people and software through process technology.* Hoboken, NJ: John Wiley & Sons.

Fettke, P., & Loos, P. (2003). Classification of reference models: A methodology and its application. *Information Systems and E-Business Management, 1*(1), 35-53.

Halmans, G., & Pohl, K. (2003). Communicating the variability of a software-product family to customers. *Software and System Modeling, 2*(1), 15-36.

Jansen-Vullers, M. H., van der Aalst, W. M. P., & Rosemann, M. (2006). Mining configurable enterprise information systems. *Data & Knowledge Engineering, 56*(3), 195-244.

Keller, G., Nüttgens, M., & Scheer, A.-W. (1992). *Semantische Prozessmodellierung auf der Grundlage "Ereignisgesteuerter Prozessketten (EPK)"* (Working Paper No. 89). Saarbrücken, Germany: Institut für Wirtschaftsinformatik, Universität Saarbrücken. [in German]

Kesari, M., Chang, S., & Seddon, P. B. (2003). A content-analytic study of the advantages and disadvantages of process modelling. In J. Ang & S.-A. Knight (Eds.), *14th Australasian Conference on Information Systems* [CD-ROM]. Perth, Australia: School of Management Information Systems.

Kindler, E. (2005). On the semantics of EPCs: Resolving the vicious circle. *Data & Knowledge Engineering, 56*(1), 23-40.

Mendling, J., & Nüttgens, M. (2006). EPC markup language (EPML): An XML-based interchange format for event-driven process chains (EPC). *Information Systems and E-Business Management, 4*(3), 245-263.

Mendling, J., Recker, J., Rosemann, M., & van der Aalst, W. M. P. (2005). Towards the interchange of configurable EPCs: An XML-based approach for reference model configuration. In U. Frank & J. Desel (Eds.), *Enterprise modelling and information systems architectures 2005* (Vol. P-75, pp. 8-21). Klagenfurt, Germany: German Computer Society.

Mendling, J., Recker, J., Rosemann, M., & van der Aalst, W. M. P. (2006). Generating correct EPCs from configured CEPCs. In H. M. Haddad (Ed.), *2006 ACM Symposium on Applied Computing* (pp. 1505-1510). Dijon, France: ACM.

Misic, V. B., & Zhao, J. L. (2000). Evaluating the quality of reference models. In A. H. F. Laender, S. W. Liddle, & V. C. Storey (Eds.), *Conceptual modeling—ER 2000* (Vol. 1920, pp. 484-498). Salt Lake City, UT: Springer.

Neumann, G., & Zdun, U. (2000). XOTcl: An object-oriented scripting language. In *7th USENIX Tcl/Tk Conference* (pp. 163-174). Austin, TX.

OMG. (2005). *MOF 2.0/XMI mapping specification, v2.1*. Retrieved January 17, 2006, from http://www.omg.org/docs/formal/05-09-01.pdf

Oracle. (2006). *Oracle consulting business solutions*. Retrieved January 13, 2006, from http://www.oracle.com/consulting/solutions/index.html

Recker, J., Mendling, J., van der Aalst, W. M. P., & Rosemann, M. (2006). Model-driven enterprise systems configuration. In E. Dubois & K. Pohl (Eds.), *Advanced information systems engineering—CAiSE 2006* (Vol. 4001, pp. 369-383). Luxembourg, Grand-Duchy of Luxembourg: Springer.

Recker, J., Rosemann, M., van der Aalst, W. M. P., & Mendling, J. (2006). On the syntax of reference model configuration. Transforming the C-EPC into lawful EPC models. In C. Bussler & A. Haller (Eds.), *Business process management workshops* (Vol. 3812, pp. 497-511). Berlin, Germany: Springer.

Rosemann, M. (2000). Using reference models within the enterprise resource planning lifecycle. *Australian Accounting Review, 10*(3), 19-30.

Rosemann, M. (2002). Application reference models and building blocks for management and control (ERP Systems). In P. Bernus, L. Nemes,

& G. Schmidt (Eds.), *Handbook of enterprise architecture* (pp. 595-616). Berlin, Germany: Springer.

Rosemann, M., & Shanks, G. (2001). Extension and configuration of reference models for enterprise resource planning systems. In G. Finnie, D. Cecez-Kecmanovic, & B. Lo (Eds.), *12th Australasian Conference on Information Systems* (pp. 537-546). Coffs Harbour, Australia: School of Multimedia and Information Technology.

Rosemann, M., & van der Aalst, W. M. P. (in press). A configurable reference modelling language. *Information Systems,* (forthcoming).

Rosemann, M., Vessey, I., & Weber, R. (2004). Alignment in enterprise systems implementations: The role of ontological distance. In *25th International Conference on Information Systems* (pp. 439-448). Washington, DC: Association for Information Systems.

SAP. (2006). *SAP business maps: Solution composer*. Retrieved January 13, 2006, from http://www.sap.com/solutions/businessmaps/composer/

Scheer, A.-W. (2000). *ARIS: Business process modeling* (3rd ed.). Berlin, Germany: Springer.

Seubert, M., Schäfer, T., Schorr, M., & Wagner, J. (1994). Praxisorientierte datenmodellierung mit der SAP-SERM-Methode. *EMISA Forum, 4*(2), 71-79. [in German]

Silverston, L. (2001a). *The data model resource book, Volume 1: A library of universal data models for all enterprises.* New York: John Wiley & Sons.

Silverston, L. (2001b). *The data model resource book, Volume 2: A library of data models for specific industries* (2nd ed.). New York: John Wiley & Sons.

Stein, T. (1998, August 31). SAP sued over R/3. *Information Week,* p. 134.

van der Aalst, W. M. P. (1999). Formalization and verification of event-driven process chains. *Information and Software Technology, 41*(10), 639-650.

van der Aalst, W. M. P., van Dongen, B. F., Herbst, J., Maruster, L., Schimm, G., & Weijters, A. J. M. M. (2003). Workflow mining: A survey of issues and approaches. *Data & Knowledge Engineering, 47*(2), 237-267.

van der Aalst, W. M. P., Weijters, A. J. M. M., & Maruster, L. (2004). Workflow mining: Discovering process models from event logs. *IEEE Transactions on Knowledge and Data Engineering, 16*(9), 1128-1142.

van Dongen, B. F., Alves de Medeiros, A. K., Verbeek, M., Weijters, A. J. M. M., & van der Aalst, W. (2005). The ProM framework: A new era in process mining tool support. In G. Ciardo & P. Darondeau (Eds.), *Applications and theory of Petri Nets 2005* (Vol. 3536, pp. 444-454). Berlin, Germany: Springer.

van Dongen, B. F., & van der Aalst, W. M. P. (2004). Multi-phase process mining: Building instance graphs. In P. Atzeni, W. W. Chu, H. Lu, S. Zhou, & T. W. Ling (Eds.), *Conceptual modeling: ER 2004* (pp. 362-376). Shanghai, China: Springer.

Welti, N. (1999). *Successful SAP R/3 implementation: Practical management of ERP projects*. Reading, MA: Addison-Wesley.

Wisse, P. (2000). *Metapattern: Context and time in information models*. Boston: Addison-Wesley.

This work was previously published in Reference Modeling for Business Systems Analysis, edited by P. Fettke; P. Loos, pp. 22-46, copyright 2007 by IGI Publishing (an imprint of IGI Global).

Chapter XV
Designing Reputation and Trust Management Systems

Roman Beck
Johann Wolfgang Goethe University, Germany

Jochen Franke
Johann Wolfgang Goethe University, Germany

ABSTRACT

This article analyzes the handling of customer complaints after shipping ordered goods by applying automated reputation and trust accounts as decision support. Customer complaints are cost intensive and difficult to standardize. A game theory based analysis of the process yields insights into unfavorable interactions between both business partners. Trust and reputation mechanisms have been found useful in addressing these types of interactions. A reputation and trust management system (RTMS) is proposed based on design theory guidelines as an IS artifact to prevent customers from issuing false complaints. A generic simulation setting for analysis of the mechanism is presented to evaluate the applicability of the RTMS. The findings suggest that the RTMS performs best in market environments where transaction frequency is high, individual complaint-handling costs are high compared to product revenues, and the market has a high fraction of potentially cheating customers.

INTRODUCTION

The continued demand for automated interorganizational business processes to reduce transaction costs in supply chains has provided a strong demand for extensive information systems (IS) support. While areas for the application of IS in supply chain management are growing rapidly, the management and automation of personal relationships in impersonal electronic business relations is still an area that has not been adequately served by existing IS research and development. In this article, we describe how a reputation and trust management system (RTMS) for an automated evaluation of business relationships in supply chains can be designed and implemented. As

RTMS research domain, we have chosen the management of customer complaints since it is also a largely unexplored, yet promising application area. While empirical research and data are limited in this area, two cases provide an indication of how much money can be saved by an improved complaint-handling process: Eastman Chemicals saved $2 million after improving its business processes associated with investigating and responding to complaints by cutting expenses for waste removal and rework caused by off-quality products or incorrect paperwork (Hallen & Latino, 2003). The second example provides a more accurate view on the de facto costs of handling customer complaints manually: According to Schilling and Sobotta (1999), a medium-sized enterprise with approximately €5 million annual revenue calculated the average processing costs as €837.47 for each complaint handling process in 1997.

The need for human interaction and decision (e.g., to check complaints or to prevent opportunistic customer behavior) historically has been a major impediment to increasing the degree of automation. Since handling of complaints is costly for both suppliers and customers, only 5% to 10% of all dissatisfied customers decide to complain at all (Tax & Brown 1998). Dissatisfied customers are likely to switch providers, which usually leads to future revenue losses higher than the costs caused by complaints in the first place (Fornell & Wernerfelt, 1987). Therefore, suppliers face two dilemmas: First, they cannot automate or standardize the complaint-handling process, since opportunistic customers may benefit from this lack of human diligence. Second, dissatisfied customers, having switched to another supplier, may never notify the errant supplier, since the manual complaint-handling process is too expensive in comparison to the value of the defective or missing delivery.

This article proposes an RTMS-based complaint-handling solution, not only to provide benefits from the efficiency of computer-based customer complaint management but also to prevent opportunistic behavior and customer losses in relevant market environments. We provide a mechanism that allows increasing the role of automated business processes while concurrently mitigating incentives for opportunistic behavior in business-to- business as well as business-to-consumer relationships. We believe that this approach is a contribution to IS literature, since reputation and trust management research from behavioral science has not yet been expatiated adequately in existing IS research.

After describing the problem relevance, the theoretical background of the article presents foundations of reputation and trust as well as transaction cost theory. Since we strive to contribute to knowledge by following a design science approach, the guidelines provided by Hevner, March, and Park (2004) and further IS design science contributions are related to this research in the theoretical section. Next, we detail the (predominantly) existing defective product handling or customer complaint process after receiving defective articles or failing to receive articles. A game-theoretical model of supplier and customer motivations is introduced providing the formal representation and logic for process redesign. Afterward, we modify the customer complaint-handling process by introducing RTMS to minimize the number of manual interactions. To evaluate our solution, results of a simulation model are provided for demonstrating the utility and efficacy of the proposed design artifact. The validity of the sociotechnical approach is discussed and scenarios are identified where this IT artifact may yield higher benefits for suppliers. The article closes with a short summary of our findings and a discussion of the design problems.

THEORETICAL BACKGROUND

The need for efficient relationship management arises whenever independent business partners have to coordinate interdependent activities (Malone & Crowston, 1994). When engineering a rigorous RTMS that meets design science requirements, we must consider reputation and trust as well as economic demands. Both will provide the theoretical foundation upon which this research rests. Before digging deeper into the theoretical foundations, basic guidelines for engineering artifacts according to design science requirements are given.

Design Science and Artifact Engineering

According to Walls, Widmeyer, and El Sawy (1992), design theory is different from grand theories (e.g., as propagated by Popper). Serving human purposes by improving process performance, building and evaluating constructs, models, methods, and instantiations are typical design science research activities (March & Smith, 1995). This differentiates design theory from, for example, grounded theory (Eisenhardt, 1989; Glaser & Strauss, 1967), which uses an empirical inductive approach and qualifies design theory to be part of middle-range theories (Merton, 1968). Nevertheless, design theory is suggested to utilize grand theories deductively as kernel theories. In this article, reputation and trust, as well as economic theories, serve as these so-called kernel theories. According to Merton (1968), emerging disciplines should develop special theories with limited conceptual ranges that function as stepping stones or middle-range theories on the way toward a total conceptualization or grand theory. In this epistemological context of middle-range theorizing, Walls et al. (1992) postulated that "the IS discipline needs to articulate and develop a class of 'design theories' and provide examples where goal-oriented theorizing has successfully led to executive information systems (EIS), management information systems (MIS), decision support systems (DSS) (Walls et al., 1992), or emergent knowledge process systems (EKPS)

(Markus, Majchrzak, & Gasser, 2002)." Inspired by the idea of developing theories unique to the IS discipline, Hevner et al. (2004) articulated seven guidelines on how to evaluate and present rigorous design science research. We use these guidelines to create a purposeful RTMS artifact and, more specifically, a method (guideline 1) for the trust and reputation management in customer complaint handling, which, as outlined before, represents a relevant organizational problem (guideline 2). The RTMS was evaluated by applying a simulation approach (guideline 3) to reengineer and automate the customer complaint handling to contribute to a more effective and efficient customer complaint process (guideline 4). Regarding research rigor (guideline 5), the RTMS has been informed by kernel theories, such as theories on reputation and trust and transaction cost economics, and subsequently defined and formally represented as a game theoretical problem. Simulated artificial market scenarios are developed to find the limitations of the RTMS artifact (guideline 6). Finally, the solution is communicated in this article to allow for a thorough discussion in the scientific community (guideline 7). In the following sections, the kernel theories applied in this research to comply with Hevner's fifth guideline are introduced.

Reputation and Trust

In the business world, a supplier's reputation reflects an aggregate ratio incorporating multiple factors: quality of merchandise, reliability of financial transactions, and/or level of customer service. It is often observed that reputation and trust acquire fundamental importance in long-term business-to-business (B2B) relations. According to Mui, Mohtashemi, and Halberstadt (2002), reputation is a "perception that an agent creates through past actions about its intentions and norms" and trust is a "subjective expectation an agent has about another's future behavior based on the history of their encounters." It has been shown that reputation reduces the complexity of the decision process (Wigand, Picot,& Reichwald, 1997) by better estimating the likelihood of failed orders and through a reduction in the number of quality tests needed for a product (Marsh, 1992).

It is important to distinguish between the individual and social dimensions of reputation (Sabater & Sierra, 2002). This article focuses on the individual dimension of reputation relevant for direct interactions between two business partners. Experience of transactions with a partner is directly reflected in an assigned reputation value. The social dimension of reputation relies on intermediaries to propagate common reputation assessments and must be aggregated through standardized processes. Due to the specific setting of bilateral supplier-customer relationships, the social aspect of reputation can be neglected because, typically, only two partners are involved in the complaint-handling process at hand.

Models of reputation and trust have been developed extensively in agent-based computational economics. A broad overview of approaches to the use of reputation in multiagent systems is provided by Mui, Halberstadt, and Mohtashemi (2002). Sabater and Sierra (2001) introduced a reputation model, taking the individual and social dimension of reputation into account for a multiagent society. Others propose a formalization of reputation for multiagent systems, applying the sociological concept of role fulfillment for establishing a positive reputation and for examining the link between reputation and trust (Carter, Bitting, & Ghorbani, 2002). The role of trust in supply relationships and the underlying implications were addressed by Lane and Bachmann (1996) in an empirical study of business relationships in Germany and U.K. (Lane & Bachmann, 1996). As they pointed out, trust relations are highly dependent on stable social, institutional, and legal structures. Moorman, Zaltman, and Deshpande (1992) investigated the specific relationship between providers and users of market research reports, providing a reasonable

introduction to the role of trust in relationships (Moorman et al., 1992).

Das and Teng (1998) argued that trust and control are the two pivotal sources of confidence in the cooperative behavior of business partners in strategic alliances. Both sources of confidence are highly interdependent. A large amount of control reflects a low amount of trust and vice versa. Without any control, the trusting party assumes the risk of the trustee's opportunistic behavior. As described, trust and control are inherently different approaches to business relationships. The costs to control the behavior of business partners can be extremely high. If reputation or trust is not established and the threshold to behave in an undesirable manner is low, the defrauded partner's control costs can be higher than the value of the goods, and consequently one may accept—to a certain degree—some fading in deliveries. Business partners are anticipating that control is difficult (e.g., in the case of defective, low-value goods, where shipping them back to the vendor is more expensive than accepting to discard them by the customer). Such behavior is more likely in new business relations and more anonymous markets, such as electronic marketplaces, where no face-to-face contact is established.

Reputation Mechanisms and Transaction Costs

Increasing the level of control by establishing contracts or mechanisms to prevent opportunistic behavior can result in higher transaction costs so that, in the worst case, the handling of an order might be more costly than the expected benefit. In the context of reputation and trust, ex-post transaction costs are of particular importance (Williamson, 1975, 1985). Ex-post transaction costs refer to costs that emerge after the order has been shipped and before the transaction cycle is completed. Ex-post transaction costs will increase if the trust level decreases. In other words, the monitoring and enforcement costs to prevent ex-post bargaining will be higher if the incentive for opportunistic behavior increases (Dahlstrom & Nygaard, 1999). For suppliers, such costly uncertainties are based on unanticipated changes in the behavior of business partners (Noordewier, George, & Nevin, 1990). The greater the level of uncertainty, the more difficult it is to formulate, negotiate, and enforce a contract to reduce the risk of being a victim of opportunistic behavior. In long-term relations, expensive tracking and monitoring instruments may be replaced by mutual trust; however, trust and reputation must be effectively managed in an automated way when the number of business partners increases.

A REPUTATION AND TRUST MANAGEMENT SYSTEM FOR CUSTOMER COMPLAINT-HANDLING PROCESSES: DESIGNING AN ARTIFACT

In our RTMS, extensive control in the customer complaint-handling process is replaced by trust to reduce costs for suppliers and customers. A supplier utilizing RTMS assigns individual reputation values to its customers and tracks past actions in complaint issues to assess the probability of future opportunistic behaviors. The supplier can use this reputation measure to decide whether to trust the customer and accept the complaint without validating the claim, or to pursue a detailed investigation. In the following sections, we will elaborate on the proposed automated system in detail and introduce the artifact, referring to Hevner's first guideline for design science.

Customer Complaint Alternatives and Implications

Many business processes are not yet fully automated. In order to discuss the complaint process, both on the customer and supplier sides in more detail, the alternatives and relevant business cases are depicted in the following. Drawing from the *exit, voice, and loyalty* model provided by Hirschman (1970), and the customers *problem impact tree* framework of Rust, Subramanian, and Wells (1992), a problem tree of *voice a complaint or exit without making a complaint* is utilized. According to Hirschman, customers have two potential feedback options: (1) to voice complaints and thereby express the dissatisfaction directly to the supplier or (2) to stop buying and exit the relation. Both options have different but always unfavorable impacts on suppliers, who must respond with adequate defensive strategies to overcome those problems. To elaborate, all possible customer complaints scenarios are first described briefly: After submitting an order and receiving a delivery note from the supplier, the incoming orders are checked by the customer's receiving department. In the case of a faultless shipment, one expects that customers have no reason to complain (see the upper branch of Figure 1). This is true in nearly all cases: Customers receiving correct deliveries will be satisfied, continue with the supplier, and will not place any complaints. The situation is slightly different if complaints are not too costly and the supplier does not ask for the defective items to be sent back in order to validate the complaint. If customers do not perceive the recall of defective items as a credible threat, then they might be tempted to cheat and complain about faultless shipments. Avoiding such an incentive is a pivotal element when designing an automated customer complaint-handling solution.

In the case of defective or partially missing items in the shipment (see the lower branch of Figure 1), the supplier must be contacted and/or the broken parts sent back. Afterward, the supplier sends the defective parts again and the customer tracks the complaint until all replacement parts are received. If the supplier handles the complaint satisfactorily, the customer will buy again. If this is not the case and the customer is dissatisfied with the process management, then the exit strategy might be chosen. In the latter case, the supplier has

Figure 1. Customer action alternatives

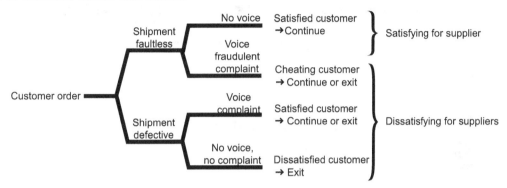

no chance to contact the dissatisfied customer if a defective shipment is delivered and the customer decides not to complain. This can be the case if the complaint process is more costly then the value of the defective products. Dissatisfied with the delivered quality, it is likely that such a customer will discontinue the business relationship.

As Figure 1 reveals, dissatisfying scenarios can emerge for suppliers, even when the shipment was faultless. A solution to the dissatisfying results for customers and suppliers might be offered by an automated reputation-based system where customers do not have to prove that parts of a shipment are damaged or missing. Instead, the supplier simply believes the customer based on the reputation the customer has acquired in past transactions and trusts him or her in the case of complaints.

Designing an RTMS-Based Automated Customer Complaint-Handling Solution

In this section, a simplified customer complaint process is described to reduce the handling costs for suppliers and customers. It will be shown that from a game-theoretical point of view, the simplified customer complaint-handling process dominates the conventional process if customers are always truthful. If truthful customers cannot be assumed, a reputation mechanism is introduced to inhibit cheating. Before digging deeper into the conventional and the simplified complaint-handling process from a game-theoretic perspective, the assumptions our model is based on are delimited:

- Neither supplier nor customer knows the exact value of the defective ratio d.
- The exact quality of the products en route is not known (e.g., due to unknown conditions during the shipment).
- There is a long-term recurring business relationship between supplier and customer. Products are exchanged frequently between both of them.
- The value of a single order is relatively low, as can be observed for raw materials or office supplies.
- The customer complaint-handling costs of the new simplified process are ignored. In the simplified process, the customer only has to send an electronic notification to the supplier without shipping the defective items; the supplier does not have to perform a manual check of the incoming goods and thus is assumed to cause no relevant costs compared to the conventional scenario, where the customer has to process the defective shipment for physically returning it to the supplier.

Table 1. Conventional customer complaint process cost matrix

		Customer complains?	
		Yes	No
Shipment defect?	Yes (d)	Customer: complaint costs (c_C^C) Supplier: {0; fraction of defective shipment (v)+} complaint costs (c_S^C)	Customer: {0; fraction of defective shipment (v)} Supplier: 0
	No (1-d)	Customer: complaint costs (c_C^C) Supplier: complaint costs (c_S^C)	Customer: 0 Supplier: 0

- There are no limitations referring to legal issues.

We use a game-theoretical design approach to analyze the trade situation for the conventional and the simplified complaint-handling process. In a conventional complaint-handling process, the customer checks the shipment, and if there are defects, the defective parts of the shipment are sent back freight forward to the supplier. The supplier checks whether the complaint is justified. Both partners have expenses due to the manual processing and shipment of products. Table 1 depicts the cost matrix in a game with a conventional customer complaint process.

If the shipment is indeed defective and the customer decides to reclaim (see the upper left cell in Table 1), both customer and supplier pay for manual handling of the customer complaints c_C^C and c_S^C, respectively. Additionally, the supplier will not be paid for its defective products, and the value v (ranging from 0 to the total value of the shipment if all parts are defective) of these parts is lost. When the customer decides not to reclaim the defective products (see the upper right cell in Table 1), his or her loss equals the value of the defective

shipped products v. If the shipped products have only minor defects, the consumer may be able to use the products partially, thereby reducing his or her loss to a fraction of v, indicating the shipment's remaining utility. Nevertheless, compared to flawless products, the consumer encounters loss ranging from a cost of 0 for minor defects to the value of the shipment v for major defects. If the shipment is not defective and the customer decides to issue a complaint (see the lower left cell in Table 1), both partners will have to pay complaint costs c_C^C and c_S^C. After the order is sent back, the supplier checks the products and finds them nondefective and may reship them or sell them to another customer. Thus, there are no further costs, despite the complaint processing costs. In cases where the shipment is not defective and the customer does not decide to reclaim (see the lower right cell in Table 1), the transaction is completed as originally intended with no additional cost outside the regular transaction process.

Now an RTMS-supported, simplified customer complaint-handling process is implemented, reducing complaint costs for both partners. In cases when the customer decides to complain about a shipment, the supplier trusts the customer, as-

Table 2. Simplified customer complaint process cost matrix

		Customer complains?	
		Yes	No
Shipment defect?	Yes (d)	Customer: 0 Supplier: fraction of defective shipment (*v*)	Customer: {0; fraction of defective shipment (*v*)} Supplier: 0
	No (1-d)	Customer: - fraction of defective shipment (-*v*) Supplier: fraction of defective shipment (*v*)	Customer: 0 Supplier: 0

suming the products are indeed defective without the need for validation. The customer subtracts the invoice accordingly or a new shipment is immediately scheduled and the supplier does not audit the complaint further. This new setting is described in Table 2.

If the shipment is not defective and the customer decides not to reclaim (see the lower right cell in Table 2), the situation is unchanged. In cases where the products are defective and the customer does not complain (see the upper right cell in Table 2), the situation is unchanged, despite the lack of complaint costs. The critical case is a cheating customer who lodges a complaint for a shipment that is not defective at all (see the lower left cell in Table 2). In this case, the customer does not pay for the faultless products. She/he immediately *earns* the value of the products ("negative loss costs (-*v*)"). On the other hand, the supplier loses the value of the products shipped.

Comparing both situations reveals that for defective product shipments, the second scenario with a simplified customer complaint process is advantageous. If supplier-side complaint costs are less than the value of the shipment, only the lower left quadrant of the cost-matrix is disadvan-

tageous. This outcome, which implies a cheating customer, should be avoided.

As we have seen, the costs of shipping and handling complaints in a specific market are important for the viability of the simplified customer complaint process. In the case of low or negligible shipping and complaint-handling costs, it might be rational to always return defective shipments, depending on the relationship of total complaint costs to the individual value of a shipment. However, if total complaint costs are high in relation to the shipment's value, the simplified complaint process can realize substantial cost savings.

The Reputation and Trust Management System to Inhibit Fraudulent Behavior

In the case of accurate shipments, there is a significant difference between the conventional and simplified scenario. If the customer decides to complain for faultless shipment, then she/he will not have to pay for the faultless products and immediately gains the value *v*. Concurrently, the supplier loses the equivalent value because it trusts the customer and does not perform a quality check on the reclaimed products that would expose a cheating customer. If there is no additional monitoring or control structure, the customer will always reclaim the delivered shipments, regardless of the actual status (whether it is indeed defective or not) in the scenario with the new system. It is a weakly dominant strategy for the customer always to complain. Thus, the supplier always loses the equivalent value of the shipment if no mechanism is applied to counter cheating behavior.

In an idealized world, customers would always tell the truth to reduce transaction costs. Both partners could improve their respective position in all cases, because only the upper left and lower right sections in Table 2 would be relevant. Assuming a customer who is always telling the truth reveals that the conventional complaint-handling mechanism is dominated by the simplified automated complaint handling. Both parties benefit from the reduction of transaction costs when processing complaints. Nevertheless, the world is not ideal, and the customer might be tempted to complain about defective products even if it is not justified. The pivotal question here is how to assure that the customer has no interest in cheating. One solution is to apply an inexpensive incentive mechanism enforced by a RTMS.

Reputation in this context is based on business transactions with a certain customer in the past. The more orders successfully processed in the past, the higher the reputation account (and the higher the level of trust). Otherwise, the customer withdraws from hid or her reputation account on the supplier side if transactions failed in the past. In the simplest case, the supplier could estimate the defection rate d of its products r and adjust the customer's reputation account if his or her complaint rate significantly differs from the estimated quality (e.g., by applying a χ^2 test).

The supplier's credible threat is to switch back to the conventional customer complaint-handling mechanism, imposing complaint-processing costs on future transactions. This threat only works

for infinitely repeated games, as are assumed in this model. This assumption seems appropriate for our setting, since B2B relationships are often characterized as long-term relationships with frequently recurring transactions. The supplier can implement several strategies to ensure that the customer is truthful. The following strategies can be applied, if the supplier knows the defection rate d with reasonably high accuracy:

- The supplier can randomly select reclaimed shipments and request the customer to return the products for an intensive test. If the products are faultless, the customer cannot be trusted and is removed from the simplified customer complaint-handling process. The process is immediately switched back to the traditional handling process. This *grim trigger* strategy is potentially suboptimal if the customer accidentally complains about products that are not defective.
- The supplier can switch back to the conventional complaint-handling process if the ratio of complained products significantly exceeds the defectiveness ratio d. This mechanism only works if the supplier knows the defectiveness ratio d with high accuracy.
- Each customer receives a reputation account for a given period, calculated as the product of the mean ordered value and the quality parameter d. If a customer reclaims a shipment, the shipment's value is subtracted from this account and if the account is exhausted, the customer has to justify his or her behavior. This mechanism also relies strongly on the accuracy of the parameter d.

The threshold for identifying cheating behavior on the part of a customer should be chosen according to the accuracy with which d is known. If d is not known and is subject to change, this threshold should be increased and vice versa.

If the supplier does not know the defectiveness ratio d, it can improve the reputation mechanism by taking into account the responses of all other customers for each product. Each customer has individual reputation values for each product. If a customer reclaims a shipment, the value of this shipment is subtracted from his or her reputation account for the product in question. Afterward, the reputation values of all customers receive a bonus. This bonus for product r and customer i is calculated as an adjusted ratio of the mean quantity ordered by the customer. This value can be regularly recalculated for all orders of a given period (e.g., monthly). The following equation calculates the reputation bonus for each customer i and product r.

$$bonus_r^i = \frac{q_r^i}{\sum_{j-1}^{n} q_r^j} * p_r q_r^d$$

p_r: price of product r

q_r^i: aggregated quantity of product r ordered by customer i in a given period

q_r^j: aggregated quantity of product r ordered by customer j in a given period

n: number of customers with reputation accounts

q_r^d: quantity of defective product r that is reclaimed

The RTMS works as follows: If all customers are acting truthfully, the individual reputation accounts for every product will be zero on average. A simple example should illustrate the mechanism: A defectiveness ratio d of 10%, a price of 1 for a given product r and three customers are assumed. The first customer regularly orders 1,000 units, customer 2 orders 50 units and customer 3 orders 200 units. Each customer reclaims truthfully 10% of the shipments. When the first customer reclaims 100 units, his or her reputation account is immediately reduced by 100, equivalent to the total value of the complaint. Afterwards, all customers' reputation accounts are given a bonus (including the customer initiating the claim), resulting in 80

bonus points for customer 1, 4 bonus points for customer 2, and 16 bonus points for customer 3. This process is also applied for the complaints of the other customers, leading to neutral reputation accounts at the end of the selected period.

If one of the customers decides to cheat and complains with a higher ratio (e.g., 15%), then his or her reputation account will be negative while the accounts of the other customers will be positive. If the first customer complains 15% of his or her shipments and the other customers complain 10%, their respective reputation accounts for the illustrative example will be -10, +2, and +7.2. Customers with a higher complaint ratio than other customers can be identified by their negative reputation accounts. The first cheating customer will put him- or herself into an inferior position compared to truthful customers. This system can only be cheated if all customers collude to produce a consistent and artificially inflated complaint ratio. Furthermore, the mechanism does not work with a small number of customers. If there were only one customer, then the reputation value would never deviate.

EXPERIMENTAL EVALUATION OF THE PROPOSED REPUTATION AND TRUST MANAGEMENT SYSTEM

To evaluate the developed solution as suggested in Hevner's third guideline regarding design science, we constructed a simulation to conduct sensitivity analyses for different transaction frequencies and fractions of potential cheaters in the market. For simplification and computational reasons, we assume that the structure of relationships remains unchanged within each simulation run—customers are always able to correctly assess the quality of the delivered products (faultless or defective), and that the production capacities of the suppliers' facilities are not limited. Further, we assume that there are no shortages and arbitrary amounts of products ordered may be delivered.

The following section describes the dynamic behavior of the simulation and explains the core processes performed by the simulated agents. In the subsequent section, specific simulation settings are described and the results are discussed.

Model Evaluation and Simulation Setting

The simulation implements the proposed IS-based reputation model and assesses environmental conditions where suppliers using the proposed solution would outperform comparable suppliers without it. For the simulation, an idealized trading situation between suppliers and customers is assumed. An arbitrary number of suppliers and customers can be simulated, including truthful acting, as well as cheating customers. The transaction starts with the customer who generates an order. The receiving supplier executes and ships the ordered goods to the customer who is checking the incoming delivery. A random percentage of products in the suppliers' shipments is defective. The customers check the shipments and decide whether to complain or not. All suppliers receive identical orders in order to compare different parameterizations of the reputation mechanism.

If the specified supplier implements the reputation system, a new shipment will be scheduled immediately after a customer complaint is lodged—if the customer's reputation value is high enough (in accordance with the reputation mechanism outlined in section 0). Furthermore, the system will also update reputation values of all customers. If a customer exceeds a prespecified reputation threshold on the lower bound, the supplier will switch back to conventional mode and check all complained products. Although we assume every supplier is deploying a quality management program to ensure high standards in production, a small but unavoidable ratio d of defective products leaves every company unnoticed. For our study, this defective ratio follows a normal distribution but can be freely configured in the model. The performance of each supplier is assessed by the operating profit resulting from the difference between revenues and costs. Revenues are calculated for faultless shipped and paid products that do not result in a customer complaint. Occurring costs are (1) variable costs for each product shipped (independent of faultless or defective) and (2) costs imposed by processing customer complaints if no RTMS is in place. Customers in our simulation approach randomly issue identical orders to all suppliers. They also check all shipments arriving from the suppliers. If they are truthful customers, they will only complain if the shipment is indeed defective. Cheating customers, in contrast, may also reject a fraction of shipments that are not defective. Simulation time is discrete and a fixed number of processes are executed for all agents in every simulated period (see Figure 2).

As an initial condition, all suppliers will designate all customers as *trusted*. If a customer exceeds his or her reputation threshold, she/he will be removed from *trusted* status, requiring him or her to resend the shipment, thus generating complaint handling costs.

At the beginning of a period, each customer randomly decides with a prespecified probability whether she/he issues an order in this period or not (1). By varying the order likelihood of a customer, the transaction frequency between supplier and customer can be adjusted. If the customer decides to order in this period, she/he calculates an order quantity drawn randomly from a normal distribution and issues identical orders to all suppliers (2). Mean and standard deviation are prespecified in the simulation setting. After receiving orders from all customers, suppliers process orders and ship goods according to the quantities requested. A randomly drawn fraction of products shipped is defective. The defective ratio is normally distributed; the mean defective ratio and the standard deviation are input parameters of the simulation (3). After all goods have been shipped, customers check the received shipments

Figure 2. Course of action of a simulated period

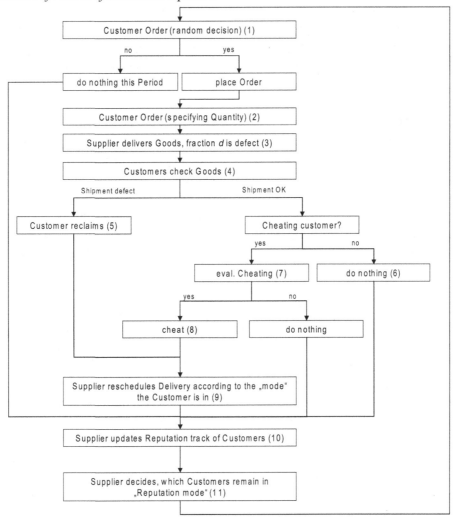

to determine whether they have received defective products (4). If defective products are included in the shipment, the customer immediately issues a complaint message to the supplier specifying the amount of defective products (5). If the shipment is faultless and the customer is configured to act truthfully, nothing happens (6). If the shipment is faultless but the customer is configured as a potential cheater, she/he decides whether to cheat or not (7). If she/he decides to cheat, a complaint message is issued (8). In the next step, suppliers process all complaints received and act according to the trust status of the customer. If the customer is in trusted mode, the shipment is rescheduled

without further checks and the reputation value of the customer is adjusted. If the customer is not in trusted mode, the shipment must be sent back by the customer to allow the supplier to verify the claim. If there are indeed defective products in the shipment, a new shipment is scheduled containing faultless products; otherwise nothing happens (9). Finally, all suppliers update the reputation values of all customers who are in trusted mode (10) and decide which customers to keep in trusted mode for the next period (11). Step 11 marks the conclusion of the simulation period after which a new period begins with customers deciding whether to order.

To compare the different simulation runs, some settings are kept constant throughout all simulation runs. Each market simulation consists of 1,000 consumers and four suppliers each, trading for 1,000 periods. Each simulation run is repeated 50 times. Furthermore, all suppliers produce with an equal ratio of defective products (mean 0.02, standard deviation 0.05) in all simulations. The four simulated suppliers differ in terms of (1) reputation account thresholds and (2) usage of the reputation account mechanism:

- Suppliers 1, 2, and 3 differ in their threshold for determining whether a consumer regularly cheats or not.
- Supplier 1 applies a very high threshold, which means that she/he will apply the reputation account all the time (all customers will always be in trusted mode).
- Supplier 2 applies a medium threshold.
- Supplier 3 applies a low threshold.
- Supplier 4 does not apply the reputation account at all and marks the "bottom line" of a supplier without the proposed mechanism.
- Therefore, Suppliers 1 and 4 will mark the two extremes of the scale, with 1 always trusting all consumers and 4 never using reputation accounts (and therefore literally distrusting all consumers).

The 1,000 consumers share consistent overall parameters, differing only in their attitude toward "cheating". A fraction of the 1,000 consumers will never cheat, while others will consider cheating, the proportion of whom will be varied in the simulation runs. When placing an order, all consumers share the same normal distribution of order quantity (mean = 100, SD = 75). They also will always complain if there is at least one defective item in a given shipment. If a consumer belongs to the group of cheating consumers, she/he will try to cheat with a likelihood of 15%. If she/he decides to cheat, she/he will always try to complain 20% of the original (faultless) shipment.

To assess in which market settings the RTMS will be advantageous, different idealized markets are simulated. In the following, the impact of transaction frequency and the impact of different fractions of cheating consumers on the reputation system will be investigated (cf. Table 3).

Sensitivity Analysis of the RTMS

To analyze the results, the average number of cheated products per 1,000 items shipped was calculated. Figure 3 provides the results for the four simulated market scenarios. The headers depict the type of market scenario (e.g., HFHC stands for *high frequency of transactions, and high fraction of cheating consumers*; see also Table 3).

As expected, Supplier 4, who always distrusts all customers and does not apply the reputation mechanism, does not experience loss through cheating customers since, even if there is complaint, it will always check whether the claim was valid. On the other hand, Supplier 1, who always trusts everyone and employs the new system, has a ratio of approximately 12 cheated items per 1,000 shipped in the scenarios with a high fraction of cheating consumers, and 3 cheated items per 1,000 shipped in the low cheating scenario. For the other suppliers, the fraction of cheated products not detected ranges between those extremes. Therefore, it can be stated that for the given settings, the reputation account system is able to identify cheating customers and to eliminate them from the trusted mode system (cp. Suppliers 2 and 3). In the case of markets with low transaction frequency, Supplier 2 is unable to achieve a better result than Supplier 1. In these cases, the reputation account system takes more time to identify the cheating customers. The system works best in markets with a high transaction frequency. In markets with low transaction frequency, the system will fail. In low-transaction-frequency scenarios, the threshold ratios must be set lower to ensure that cheating consumers are identified. In scenarios with a low transaction frequency and a low frac-

Table 3. Parameterization of different market scenarios

		Low transaction frequency, low fraction of cheating consumers (LFLC)	Low transaction frequency, high fraction of cheating consumers (LFHC)	High transaction frequency, low fraction of cheating consumers (HFLC)	High transaction frequency, high fraction of cheating consumers (HFHC)
		Parameterization			
Transaction frequency (order probability)	Market scenarios	5%	5%	30%	30%
Fraction of cheating consumers		5%	25%	5%	25%

tion of cheating customers (cp. LFLC), the effect of the reputation account system is small.

Profitability Analysis of the RTMS

We now look at the profits of suppliers depending on the customer complaint-handling costs. The absolute number of complaints is independent of the costs associated with the complaint. Based on the mean values of the simulation runs, it is feasible to calculate the financial flows in each market scenario. For the HFHC market scenario, the results for different complaint-handlings costs levels are depicted in Figure 4. The main tendency can also be found in the other scenarios, but it is most clearly visible in this scenario. If customer complaint-handling costs are high compared to variable production costs, the reputation account solution is always advantageous (cp. Supplier 4 without deploying a reputation account solution has the highest losses of all suppliers in the upper two diagrams of Figure 4). Not until customer complaint handling costs nearly equal product revenues (see Figure 4, lower left diagram) or are below product revenues (see Figure 4, lower right

diagram), does the supplier without the reputation account mechanism become profitable. In these scenarios depicted in the lower two diagrams, the reputation account mechanism is not always the best solution, especially the "always trust" strategy of Supplier 1 should not be applied.

In summary, the proposed reputation account mechanism is especially advantageous in settings where (a) the transaction frequency is high, (b) the individual complaint-handling costs are high compared to product revenues, and (c) the market has a high fraction of potentially cheating consumers. In markets where complaint-handling costs are low compared to the individual production costs, the reputation account mechanism should not be deployed.

SUMMARY AND CONCLUSIONS

The combination of information systems and game-theory inspired reputation and trust accounts in a RTMS establishes new solutions to automate business transactions where human decisions were formerly necessary. Through

Figure 3. Simulation results

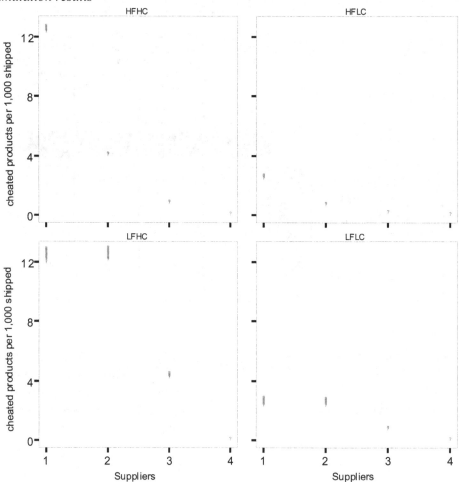

the reduction of manual handling and shipping costs, quality of the complaint-handling process may be increased both for customers and suppliers, resulting in higher customer retention. A game-theoretic analysis of the order and customer complaint process has yielded insights into undesired outcomes of the interaction of suppliers and customers. While faulty deliveries will always remain a problem, costs associated with customer complaint-handling can be reduced significantly if substituting human decision competence with an automated information system. Thus, we believe that an economic interpretation of existing information systems may help to uncover as-yet unrealized potential for computer-mediated ap-

plications and offer the RTMS as an example for this claim. The RTMS allows firms to deploy a simplified customer complaint-handling process while preventing customers from acting opportunistically. The RTMS has been developed according to the guidelines put forward for design science approaches and has been tested in an agent-based artificial setting, indicating its strength in specific market environments. In more detail, the RTMS has been found applicable in market environments where (a) the transaction frequency is high, (b) the individual complaint-handling costs are high compared to product revenues, and (c) the market has a high fraction of potentially cheating consumers.

REFERENCES

Carter, J., Bitting, E., & Ghorbani, A. A. (2002). Reputation formalization within information sharing multiagent architectures. *Computational Intelligence, 18*(4), 515-534.

Dahlstrom, R., & Nygaard, A. (1999). An Empirical investigation of ex post transaction costs in franchised distribution channels. *Journal of Marketing Research, 36*(2), 160-171.

Das, T. K., & Teng, B.-S. (1998). Between trust and control: Developing confidence in partner cooperation in alliances. *Academy of Management Review, 23*(3), 491-512.

Eisenhardt, K. M. (1989). Building theories from case study research. *Academy of Management Review, 14*(4),532-550.

Fornell, C., & Wernerfelt, B. (1987). Defensive marketing strategy by customer complaint management: A theoretical analysis. *Journal of Marketing Research, 24*(4), 337-346.

Glaser, B. G., & Strauss, A. L. (1967). *The discovery of grounded theory: Strategies for qualitative research.* New York: Aldien de Gruyter,.

Hallen, G., & Latino, R. J. (2003, June). Eastman Chemical's success story. *Quality Progres,* 50-54.

Hevner, A. R., March, S. T., & Park, J. (2004). Design science in information systems research. *MIS Quarterly, 28*(1), 75-105.

Hirschman, A. O. (1970). *Exit voice and loyalty: Responses to decline in firms, organizations, and states.* Cambridge, MA: Harvard University Press.

Lane, C., & Bachmann, R. (1996). The social constitution of trust: Supplier relations in Britain and Germany. *Organization Studies, 17*(3), 365-395.

Malone, T. W., & Crowston, K. (1994). The interdisciplinary study of coordination. *ACM Computing Survey, 26*(1), 87-119.

March, S. T., & Smith, G. F. (1995). Design and natural science research on information technology. *Decision Support Systems, 15*(4), 251-266.

Markus, L. M., Majchrzak, A., & Gasser, L. (2002). A design theory for systems that support emergent knowledge processes. *MIS Quarterly, 26*(3), 179-212.

Marsh, S. (1992). *Trust and reliance in multiagent-systems: A preliminary report.* University of Stirling, Department of Computer Science and Mathematics,.

Merton, R. K. (1968). *Social theory and social structure.* New York: The Free Press.

Moorman, C., Zaltman, G., & Deshpande, R. (1992). Relationships between providers and users of market research: The dynamics of trust within and between organizations. *Journal of Marketing Research, 29*(3), 314-328.

Mui, L., Halberstadt, A., & Mohtashemi, M. (2002). Notions of reputation in multiagents systems: A review. In *Proceedings of the First International Joint Conference on Autonomous Agents and Multiagent Systems* (pp. 280-287)l New York: ACM Press.

Mui, L., Mohtashemi, M., & Halberstadt, A. (2002). A computational model of trust and reputation. In *Proceedings of the 35th Hawaii International Conference on System Science (HICSS)* (p. 188). Big Island, HI:

Noordewier, T. G., George, J., & Nevin, J. R. (1990). Performance outcomes of purchasing arrangements in industrial buy-vendor relationships. *Journal of Marketing Research, 54,* 80-93.

Rust, R. T., Subramanian, B., & Wells, M. (1992). Making complaints a management tool. *Marketing Management, 1*(3), 40-45.

Sabater, J., & Sierra, C. (2001). REGRET: A reputation model for gregarious societies. In *Proceedings of the Fourth Workshop on Deception*

Fraud and Trust in Agent Societies (pp. 61-70). Montreal, Canada:

Sabater, J., & Sierra, C. (2002). Reputation and social network analysis in multiagent systems. In *Proceedings of the First International Joint Conference on Autonomous Agents and Multiagent Systems* (pp. 475-482). New York: ACM Press.

Schilling, V., & Sobotta, A. (1999). Prozesskostenrechnung der mittelständischen industrie. *Betriebswirtschaftliches Forschungszentrum für Fragen der mittelständischen Wirtschaft e.V.* Bayreuth, Germany.

Tax, S. S., & Brown, S. W. (1998). Recovering and learning from service failure. *Sloan Management Review, 40*(1), 75-88.

Walls, J. G., Widmeyer, G. R., & El Sawy, O. A. (1992). Building an information system design theory for Vigiliant EIS. *Information Systems Research, 3*(1), 36-59.

Wigand, R. T., Picot, A., & Reichwald, R. (1997). *Information, organization and management: Expanding markets and corporate boundaries.* Chichester, England: Wiley.

Williamson, O. E. (1975). *Markets and hierarchies: Analysis and antitrust implications. A Study in the economics of internal organization.* New York: The Free Press.

Williamson, O. E. (1985). *The economic institutions of capitalism: Firms, markets, relational contracting.* New York: The Free Press.

This work was previously published in Journal of Electronic Commerce in Organizations, Vol. 6, Issue 4, edited by M. Khosrow-Pour, pp. 8-29, copyright 2008 by IGI Publishing (an imprint of IGI Global).

Chapter XVI
SEACON:
An Integrated Approach to the Analysis and Design of Secure Enterprise Architecture–Based Computer Networks

Surya B. Yadav
Texas Tech University, USA

ABSTRACT

The extent methods largely ignore the importance of integrating security requirements with business requirements and providing built-in steps for dealing with these requirements seamlessly. To address this problem, a new approach to secure network analysis and design is presented. The proposed method, called the SEACON method, provides an integrated approach to use existing principles of information systems analysis and design with the unique requirements of distributed secure network systems. We introduce several concepts including security adequacy level, process-location-security matrix, data-location-security matrix, and secure location model to provide built-in mechanisms to capture security needs and use them seamlessly throughout the steps of analyzing and designing secure networks. This method is illustrated and compared to other secure network design methods. The SEACON method is found to be a useful and effective method.

INTRODUCTION

Designing and implementing a secure computer network has become a necessity for companies big or small. Network security is no longer just a technical issue anymore (Sarbanes-Oxley Compliance Journal, 2005). It has also become an economic and legal issue for most companies. According to

an IT security management survey, "Two-thirds of those who took part in the survey acknowledged that the wide range of government regulations, such as Sarbanes-Oxley, HIPAA, and GLBA, has affected their company's handling of IT security issues" (Sarbanes-Oxley Compliance Journal, 2005). According to CSI/FBI's Tenth Annual Computer Crime Security Survey, unauthorized access to information and theft of proprietary information showed significant increases in average loss per respondent (CSI/FBI, 2005). Hackers have also moved to new areas such as identity theft (McMillan, 2005). As a consequence, the cost of information theft has jumped considerably. These surveys indicate that a better computer network design method is needed for designing a more secure computer network.

There has been increased activity in various aspects of security, network system security, and secure network design in the last several years. There are several good articles (Cisco Systems, 2001; Fisch & White, 2001; Ghosh, 2001; Oppenheimer, 2004; Southwick, 2003; Whitman & Mattord, 2005; Whitmore, 2001) that deal with secure network design. For example, Fisch and White (2001) discuss security models and various kinds of security measures in detail. Ghosh (2001) discusses principles of secure network design and an in-depth analysis of ATM networks and their security. Oppenheimer (2004) uses a top-down network design methodology to design an enterprise computer network. The emphasis is on the technical analysis and design of networks. Whitman and Mattord (2005) present a Security Systems Development Life Cycle (SecSDLC) methodology paralleling the basic system development life cycle (SDLC) methodology. There are sophisticated network simulation and performance tools such as OPNET (OPNET, 2005). Most of the existing work on secure network design, however, tends to lean more toward technical details. There is very little research that addresses the issue of security and business requirements of a computer network simultaneously. It is very important to understand an organization's business requirements to design an effective network (Oppenheimer, 2004). It is equally important to understand the organization's security requirements as well. To our knowledge, there is no published design method that integrates secure network requirements with business requirements to develop a

secure network. In this article, we address the following research questions:

1. How can we identify security and business requirements of a network system seamlessly?
2. How can we identify all possible assets and resources, including business processes and data that need to be protected in a network system?
3. How can we incorporate and document security requirements into conceptual and logical network diagrams?

This article follows the DEACON method (Shaw & Yadav, 2001) and presents a new method that provides built-in mechanisms to carry secure network requirements along with business requirements seamlessly throughout the process of analyzing and designing secure network architecture. We have developed, as part of the method, several new concepts such as the security adequacy level, process-location-security matrix, data-location-security matrix, and secure location model to achieve a good interplay between network security requirements and business requirements.

CURRENT WORK ON DEVELOPING SECURE COMPUTER NETWORKS

Computer networking and its security is a vast area of research and study. The topics cover network security concepts, principles, frameworks, techniques, methods, laws, and practices. This article draws from research on several of the topics mentioned above; however, it is not practical for this article to review even a fraction of the literature covering those topics. Interested readers are kindly referred to Ghosh (2001), Kizza (2005), and Whitman and Mattord (2005) for a good review of topics related to secure computer networks. Here, we limit our literature discussion to research that deals with secure network design methods.

Paul Innella (Innella, 2001) presents a design method based upon the software process model. This is an interesting method but it is, in its current form, too general and too brief to be of any practical use.

Cisco Systems (2001) has developed a secure blueprint for enterprise networks (SAFE) to provide best practice information on designing and implementing secure networks. SAFE is not a design method in the sense of providing specific steps for designing a secure network. Instead, it is a set of design and configuration guidelines that should be followed to design a secure network.

James J. Whitmore presents a method for designing secure solutions. He describes "a systematic approach for defining, modeling, and documenting security functions within a structured design process in order to facilitate greater trust in the operation of resulting IT solutions" (Whitmore, 2001). Using Common Criteria as a basis, he proposes five interrelated security subsystems. These are (Whitmore, 2001):

1. Security audit subsystem
2. Solution integrity subsystem
3. Access control subsystem
4. Information flow control subsystem
5. Identity or credential subsystem

Whitmore's approach develops network security architectures. Once the security requirements have been identified, they can be mapped to the above mentioned security subsystems to develop a security architecture for the system. This is a very important step to designing secure solutions. However, its focus is more on the technical side of the network solution and does not address the identification and determination of security requirements. It also lacks in providing steps for integrating security requirements with business requirements in designing secure network solutions.

Priscilla Oppenheimer presents a top-down network design method consisting of the following major steps (Oppenheimer, 2004):

1. Identifying customer needs and goals
2. Logical network design
3. Physical network design
4. Testing, optimizing, and documenting network design

It is obvious that the top-down network design method parallels the structured systems analysis method for software development. The method provides a detailed discussion of various topics related to computer network design including security. However, the method does not have built-in steps and mechanisms to explicitly address security requirements in addition to business requirements. Also, the method has more focus on technical details of network design. It does not address the issue of network modeling and simulation.

Whitman and Mattord (2005) present a Security Systems Development Life Cycle (SecSDLC) which is based upon the Systems Development Life Cycle (SDLC) waterfall methodology. The SecSDLC methodology consists of investigation, analysis, logical design, physical design, implementation, and maintenance phases (Whitman & Mattord, 2005). The SecSDLC has steps for documenting security policies, analyzing threats, and examining legal issues. However, the SecDLC does not have steps to identify security or business requirements. There is very little support in the form of guidelines and techniques for designing and documenting secure network models and architectures based upon the security and business requirements of an organization.

There is a very limited literature on design methods that provide mechanisms to incorporate security requirements along with business requirements in designing a secure computer network. The next section discusses a new method to analyze and design a secure network and shows how to use these two requirements seamlessly.

AN INTEGRATED APPROACH TO SECURE NETWORK ANALYSIS AND DESIGN

To deal with current security challenges, designing a secure computer network must be an integral part of the overall approach to design a computer network. Security of computer networks cannot be an afterthought anymore. This section discusses the proposed integrated method to analyze and design secure computer networks. The proposed method has been named SEACON (design of Secure Enterprise Architecture-based Computer Networks). The SEACON method has built-in mechanisms to capture a firm's network security needs from the analysis stage and carry them to the implementation stage. Figure 1 shows the detailed steps of the SEACON method. The following paragraphs discuss the SEACON method in detail.

Figure 1. The SEACON method

1. Problem Definition
a. Define organizational goals, objectives, and security policies using SVPSS framework b   . Define IS goals, objectives, and security policies c   . Define network goals, objectives, and security policies
2. Requirement Specification

a. Model business processes and their security requirements (process model)
        b. Model organizational data and their security requirements (data model)
        c. Identify physical locations to be connected within the network
        d. Identify information domains at each location using data-location-security and process-location-security matrices
        e. Construct secure location model (secure extended location connectivity diagram) with security annotation
        f. Perform the assessment of security risks for each asset such as process, data, and network components and determine appropriate security requirements and mechanisms

3. Secure Network Architecture

a. Identify enclaves and boundary controllers under each information domain
        b. Specify security requirements and mechanisms for each enclave based upon the security risk assessment conducted in step 3
        c. Assign enclaves and boundary controllers to appropriate nodes
        d. Create a secure network architecture diagram
        e. Match available technology with specifications on architecture diagram

4. Secure Network Performance Evaluation

a. Simulate secure network operation (e.g. using software such as OPNET)
        b. Identify performance bottlenecks and optimize network
        c. Identify security holes and correct them
        d. Refine secure network architecture

5. Implementation
a   . Implement the secure network architecture b   . Prepare a conversion plan c   . Convert to the new secure network system

Problem Definition

The first step in the method requires the establishment of goals, objectives, and security policies at three levels, firm, information system (IS), and computer network. The establishment of goals, objectives, and security policies helps determine the context and scope of the problem at hand. Hopefully, the organizational and IS level goals, objectives, and security policies have already been established. If not, then these organizational an IS policies should be defined along with the goals, objectives, and security policies for the network under consideration. Network security policies are determined using the Six-View Perspective of System Security (SVPSS) framework (Yadav, 2006). The SVPSS framework enables an analyst to determine a comprehensive set of security policies by providing a multiview look at system security. Network security policies should be defined under each security view, Threat, Resource, Process, Management, Legal, and Assessment. A firm's security policies act as the bedrock on which secure network and secure information systems are designed and built. Network security policies should be stated as precisely as possible. Access rules and security requirements for internal as well as external entities should be clearly stated. Security risks should be assessed after the initial set of network security policies has been identified. There are several risk assessment methods (GAO, 1999; ASIS, 2003; Verdon & McGraw, 2004) proposed in the literature. All of these methods are quite similar to one another and any of them can be used to assess risks in conjunction with the SVPSS framework.

Requirement Specification

This step involves determining network security needs in addition to traditional business and data modeling activities. We used a process model, data model, network model, and security risk register as major tools to document security requirements and mechanisms that should be included in a network system. We discuss an extended version of these tools below.

The modeling of business activities presented by Shaw and Yadav (2001) and other researchers do not address the integration of security activity modeling with business activity modeling. Security has become too critical to leave it as an afterthought when developing a secure network. Security requirements should be modeled along with business requirements simultaneously. Security requirements modeling can be easily handled by adopting certain conventions as part of existing process and data modeling techniques. For example, a data flow diagram can be easily adapted to capture process security requirements. The entity-relationship data modeling (ERD) can be adapted to capture data security requirements. A business process detailed in a Data Flow Diagram (DFD) must have with it an appropriate security level required to secure the business process. We need to identify and specify security for each process and for each data object-entity. One way to state security for processes and entities is to attach a security classification level as a property of an entity or process. We propose a concept of the Security Adequacy Level (SAL) to easily state the nature of security in a data model. SAL refers to the degree of security-strength needed to adequately protect a process or an entity (a data object). The definition of the SAL concept is based on the work on Strength of Mechanism Level (Arber, Cooley, Hirsh, Mahan, & OSterritter, 1999) and four hierarchical divisions of security protection under the trusted computer system evaluation criteria (Department of Defense, 1985). We define six levels of SAL—Low, Basic, Medium, High, and Very High—of security adequacy. The SAL levels are hierarchical in nature, meaning that a given security adequacy level subsumes all the lower level security requirements, Low being the lowest level and Very High being the highest level of security adequacy. These levels are defined in Figure 2.

Figure 2. Description of security adequacy levels

Security Adequacy Level (SAL)	Suggested security mechanisms for the level	Correspondence with DOD's Hierarchical divisions (Department of Defense, 1985)	Correspondence with Strength mechanism level (Arber et al., 1999)
Low—defined as minimum protection	Password access	Division D—Minimal Protection	N/A
Basic—defined as basic security practice. It is adequate enough to protect low value data and deter unsophisticated threats	Restrictive granting of rights; enhancement of strict account policies; basic encryption	Division C—discretionary protection (Class C1, Class C2)	Basic
Medium—defined as good security practice. It is adequate enough to protect medium value data and resist sophisticated threats	Deactivation of unnecessary network services; staff training, security update plan; firewall; IPSec VPN	Division B—mandatory protection (Class B1 and Class B2).	Medium
High—defined as high security practice. It is adequate enough to protect high value data and resist high-level threats	Network and host-based Intrusion detection systems (IDS); contingency plans; vulnerability analysis tool; SSL VPN	Division B—mandatory protection (Class B3—security domains)	High
Very High—defined as a formal and very high security practice. It is adequate enough to deal with any kind of threats and protect very high value data.	Application based IDS; formal security protection	Division A—verified design (Class A1 and beyond)	N/A

Defining the security adequacy level of a business process enables one to explicitly pay attention to the security issues of a process and helps a designer to include the appropriate security mechanisms to protect the process in a network system. Figure 3 shows as an example a data flow diagram with two business processes that includes a security adequacy level for each process.

Organizational data modeling involves identifying data objects, their attributes (properties), and relationships among the data objects. The security requirements for data objects are generally ignored when developing a data model. We suggest that security requirements for data objects should be included as part of a data model. We propose to attach an appropriate security adequacy level to each data object in a data model.

Figure 4 shows an illustration of an ER model with a security adequacy level attached to each

entity type in the model. The SAL attached to an entity type specifies the level of protection needed for that entity type. The security adequacy level for data and processes should be determined in consultation with the users as well as the managers (owners) of those process and data. We now discuss the idea of a secure location model to identify network components and their security needs.

Secure Location Model

A secure location model shows not only the locations (nodes) and connections, but also the security requirements of those locations and connections. Analysts need a mechanism to include security requirements in various models along with the process and data needs of a firm. This mechanism should address the adequacy level of security of

Figure 3. A list of network security mechanisms

Network Security Mechanisms

Intrusion Detection System (IDS):
1) Network-Based IDS
2) Host-Based IDS
3) Application-Based IDS

Firewall:
1. Packet filtering
2. Proxy server
3. Stateful packet filtering

Virtual Private Network (VPN):
1. IPSec VPN
2. SSL VPN

Secure Configuration of Servers:
1. Deactivation of unnecessary network services
2. Password access protection
3. Restrictive granting of rights
4. Enforcement of strict account policies
5. Audit Logs

Network Policies and Procedures:
1. Staff training
2. Security update plan
3. Contingency plan
4. Vulnerability analysis tools

various components of a system. The security adequacy level classification discussed in Figure 2 can be used to specify security levels for various network system components.

First, process-location-security and data-location-security matrices should be developed to identify the locational usage of processes and data and to possibly revise their security adequacy levels identified previously in the process and data models. Security adequacy levels for processes and data could be influenced by their locational usage. For example, if a process or data is used from more than one location then it may require a higher level of security. Information domains should be identified next based upon the process-location-security and data-location-security matrices. An information domain is used to group a set of resources with similar characteristics and functionalities. An information domain addresses the issues of data management and data interoperability. Each location can contain one or more information domains.

Figure 4. An illustration of an ERD with security adequacy levels

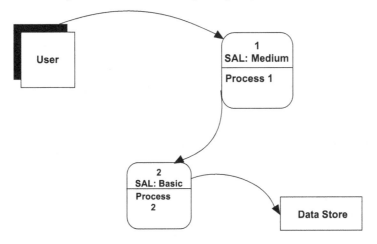

Specification of Security Adequacy Level for Processes

Note: A Security Adequacy Level of Medium for Process 1 means that Process 1 needs a Medium level of security protection.

Secure extended location connectivity diagrams should be developed after the information domains have been determined. A secure extended location connectivity diagram is an extended location connectivity diagram (Shaw & Yadav, 2001) that incorporates the identification of security adequacy levels for locations and connections. As the process and data are allocated to their appropriate locations, the corresponding process and data security adequacy levels are combined to determine the overall security levels for those locations and connections. The secure extended location diagrams should be drawn using technology independent generic symbols to represent nodes and connections in the diagram. Locations and connectivity links are labeled with security adequacy levels. Figures 8A through 8D show examples of such a diagram.

So far, we have used several types of models—process, data, and network diagrams—to identify various types of assets and resources that need to be protected. Various kinds of threats pose security risks to network assets and resources. Network security requirements should be identified from various perspectives (Yadav, 2006) while keeping in mind the various security risks for the firm. Security risks should be assessed under each view (Yadav, 2006) and prioritized based upon their expected consequences. Users and managers should be consulted in determining network security risks and requirements under each view.

The identification of security risks and their assessment allows a company to compare and evaluate consequences of various types of security risks. It also enables the company to prioritize the security risks and select, given a limited budget, the most consequential security risks for mitigation. A general process for security risk assessment can be stated as follows (Center for Medicare and Medicaid Services, 2002; Yadav, 2006):

1. Identify assets under each security view.
2. Identify sources of risk for each asset.

3. For each source of risk, we estimate its likelihood of occurrence and the consequence (impact) if the risk materializes. Using the levels of likely hood of occurrence and the levels of severity of consequence (impact), determine the risk level for each risk. Also, determine the acceptable risk level for each risk.
4. Evaluate each risk based upon the risk level and the acceptable risk level.
5. Identify security requirements and mechanisms to reduce the risk level to an acceptable level.

The above process is described in detail by CMS (Center for Medicare and Medicaid Services, 2002) and Yadav (2006).

A security risk register can be used to document the outputs of the above risk assessment process. A security risk register is a tabular representation of details about identified risks and security mechanisms for reducing those risks. Figure 5 shows a template for a security risk register.

Security views in the risk register refer to various security perspectives of a network system (Yadav, 2006). Assets are any IT or system resource that needs to be protected. Assets are identified under each security view. For each identified asset, the sources of risks are then determined. For each source of risk, the threat likelihood estimate, the consequence if the threat is realized, and the resultant risk level are computed. An acceptable level of risk is specified for each source of risk. A risk priority level is then computed based upon the resultant risk level and the acceptable risk level. Security requirements and mechanisms are then specified for reducing security threats from the sources of risks having high priority levels. Figure 6 shows a tree-view of the security risk register template shown in Figure 5. It also shows the hierarchical nature of the security risk register. For illustration, only one branch is expanded in Figure 6.

Figure 6. A security risk register template for documenting risks

A Security Risk Register Template									
Security Views	Assets	Sources of Risk	Threat Likelihood Estimate	Consequence, if the threat is realized	Resultant Risk Level	Acceptable Risk Level	Risk Priority Level	Security Requirements	Security Mechanisms

This section has discussed several ways to identify security requirements of a network system. The identified security requirements and mechanisms should be allocated and apportioned among the various components of a network system. A security mechanism is a method, tool, technique, or procedure used to enforce a security policy and to protect resources. Some examples of network security mechanisms are firewalls, intrusion detection systems, virtual private networks (VPN), and network access controls. Figure 7 shows a more complete list of network security mechanisms. For more information about network security mechanisms, please see Irvine and Levine (1999), Fisch and White (2001), Bace and Mell (2001), Rusli (2001), and Warren (2005).

The next section uses the idea of secure network architecture to represent a logical network topology and the security mechanisms apportioned among the various network components.

Secure Network Architecture

Secure network architecture can be represented using a network diagram. A network architecture diagram (NAD) and a secure network architecture diagram (SNAD) are used as a tool to model relationships among network hardware, software, processes, data, and security policies. These diagrams become the basis to simulate and evaluate network architectures. First, information enclaves and boundary controllers (Bionic Buffalo Corporation, 2000; Defense Logistics Agency, 2002) are determined under each information domain. An enclave is a set of resources that are protected at the same level as a group. An information domain may have several enclaves. Generally, an information domain is physically realized via a set of information enclaves (Bionic Buffalo Corporation, 2000). Enclaves typically contain computing resource components such as switches, servers, printers, and workstations (Defense Logistics Agency, 2002). A boundary controller protects an enclave. For example, a

Figure 7. A hierarchical (tree) view of a security risk register

A tree view of a security risk register

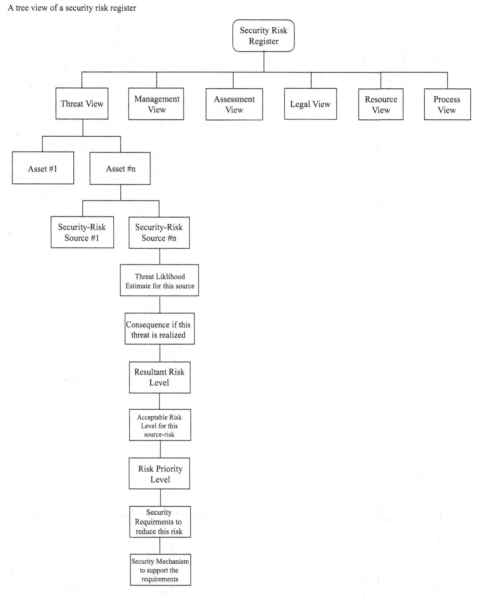

router with a firewall can act as a boundary controller. Appropriate security adequacy levels are assigned to each enclave. A network architecture diagram without security mechanisms could be created as a base network for network analysis and design. Next, the security adequacy level of each enclave is mapped to appropriate network security mechanisms to be included in the secure network architecture.

A secure network architecture diagram is then created. A secure network architecture diagram can be obviously drawn at various levels such as at the logical and physical levels. A logical level diagram uses generic symbols for nodes and links in the diagram. A physical level SNAD, on the other hand, is technology-dependent. Nodes and links in a physical level SNAD are represented by appropriate communication technology available in the market. A SNAD (logical as well as physical) should be designed using network modeling tools such as OPNET (OPNET, 2005) so that they can be simulated and evaluated for performance.

Secure Network Performance Evaluation

A network should be evaluated for various types of performance issues such as security holes, network traffic, response, and throughput. Simulation is a very powerful technique in evaluating computer networks. It is very important to use network modeling software that allows simulation of secure networks under various scenarios. A detailed discussion of network simulation and performance evaluation is beyond the scope of this article due to space and other limitations.

Network Implementation

Implementation will entail buying the required network equipment and other computing resources, and then deploying them onsite. A conversion plan to transition to the new network will have to be prepared. Users should be properly trained in the new network's security and its usage. A detailed discussion of network implementation is beyond the scope of this article.

A Comparison of Secure Network Analysis and Design Methods

In order to differentiate the SEACON method further from other methods we compare it with two existing methods, top-down network design (Oppenheimer, 2004) and secure network solutions (Whitmore, 2001). Note that we are including only those methods that address the security of networks.

While there are no standard criteria for comparing secure network design methods, the following criteria are designed to give a representative and objective view of the methods so that an organization may choose the most appropriate secure network design method for a given situation. We extend the criteria developed by Shaw and Yadav

(2001) to address the security issues in design. The security-related criteria have been developed using the notion of functional and assurance requirements of the Target of Evaluation (TOE) (Common Criteria Implementation Board, 1999a, 1999b, 1999c) and network security mechanisms. Any secure network design method should have built-in steps to guide an analyst in determining an appropriate set of network security mechanisms to be included in the overall design of a network. A method should also use a network simulation tool for analyzing and evaluating different secure network design scenarios. An extended set of comparison criteria is described below:

- **Capture of multiview security requirements:** (To what extent does the method emphasize a complete and comprehensive security requirements?)—The method should provide guidelines to identify security requirements from multiple perspectives such as legal, privacy, management, assessment, and resource (Yadav, 2006).

- **Mapping of network security mechanisms to firm's security requirements:** (To what extent does the method provide steps to relate security mechanisms to security requirements?)—The method should encourage an analyst to determine the most appropriate set of network security mechanisms to support a given set of security requirements.

- **Interplay between business and security requirements:** (To what extent does the method provide explicit steps in using security and business requirements simultaneously?)—The method should provide built-in steps for using security and business requirements together in creating network architectures.

- **Usability:** (To what extent is the method usable?)—The method should be easy for an organization to apply (Shaw & Yadav, 2001).

- **Integration:** (To what extent is the network integrated with the IS architecture?)—The method should integrate network architecture with the information system(s) in an organization.

- **Documentation:** (What level of documentation does the method provide?)—The method should provide extensive documentation including user requirements, security requirements, and network architecture.

- **Complexity:** (How easy is the method to learn and to apply?)—Ideally, the method should be relatively easy to learn and to apply.

- **Allocation guidelines:** (To what extent does the method help allocate data, processes, and security mechanisms to nodes?)—The method should provide rules and guidelines for determining which processes or data and security mechanisms to assign to each node.

- **Principles:** (What principles does the method emphasize?)—The method should be based on sound principles that have been proven effective instead of relying on intuitive ideas that have a low likelihood of success (Shaw & Yadav, 2001).

- **Outcomes:** (What are the major end products of the methodology and are the products of a high caliber?)—The end products of the method should be relevant to organizational goals and business requirements and should be of high quality.

- **Simulation:** (To what extent does the method emphasize simulation?)—The method should use network simulation tools to evaluate alternative secure network designs.

Table 1 summarizes the results of applying the criteria to each of the existing methods and to the SEACON method. The table shows that each design method has its own strength. However, the SEACON method provides the advantage of a multiview perspective of security, built-in steps

for seamless use of security and business requirements in network models, firm level integration of the network, a set of guidelines for allocating business processes and data across network nodes, and emphasis on simulation.

AN ILLUSTRATION OF THE SEACON METHOD

Consider a simple example to illustrate the applicability of the SEACON method. Although the example is not very complex, it does help illustrate the usefulness of the SEACON method. The example problem is described below. It is adapted from Shaw and Yadav (2001). The example problem has been modified to incorporate network security needs.

"SHIPIT is a fictitious firm that provides order processing services for mail order companies. The products are stored in a SHIPIT warehouse, and orders are shipped as they are received. The SHIPIT organization consists of three locations:

- The warehouse in Kansas City, Missouri,
- The office building in Dallas, Texas, and
- The call center in Albuquerque, New Mexico.

Currently, each facility has computers, but they are not integrated, and thus the only mechanism for sharing information is to print reports and physically send them to the other locations. Managers at SHIPIT believe that a computer network allowing them to share information securely over the Internet/intranet would be beneficial, and they decided to develop such a secure network using the SEACON method. The primary business driver for the company in its network design is a desire to reduce business operating costs and expedite access to various data and reports. A secure network may be a little bit more costly, but it will allow the company to run its operation with minimal or no security breaches and avoid costly

Table 1. A comparison of secure network design methods

Methods / Criteria	SEACON	Top-Down Network Design (21)	Designing Secure Solutions (28)
Multiview Security Requirements	Yes	No	No
Mapping between Network Security Mechanisms and Security Requirements	High	Medium	High
Interplay between security and business requirements	A seamless use of security and business requirements	No joint use of security and business requirements	No joint use of security and business requirements
Usability	High	High	Medium
Integration	High	Low	Low
Documentation	High	High	Low
Complexity	High	Medium	High
Allocation Guidelines	Good	None	None
Principles	Systems approach; Completeness; Consistency	Technical accuracy; Top-down development	Systems approach; Common criteria
Outcomes	Implementation	Implementation	Network model
Quality	High	High	Medium
Simulation	A secure network architecture that can be used for Simulation model and evaluation	No formal simulation	No formal simulation

security fixes down the road. As a general rule, SHIPIT wants to have every computer connected to the SHIPIT network properly administered and secured.

The DEACON method, the forerunner of SEACON method, was applied to the above example (Shaw & Yadav, 2001). In this article, we emphasize the discussion of SEACON's security-related steps. Under the SEACON method, the secure network design steps would be similar to the following:

- **Business Problem Definition:** Based upon the brief security description, we infer that SHIPIT should develop a network that provides error-free, reliable, and secure storage; sharing; and transmission of data among the facilities at SHIPIT. Appropriate security mechanisms should be built at various levels, those of application, operating system, server, and network levels to safeguard the storage, access, and flow of information on the network. More specifically:

o Network hardware and software assets such as Web servers, database servers, routers, switches, databases, and so forth, should be protected.

o Access to data stored at various locations such as the warehouse, the office building, and the call center should be allowed to only authorized personnel.

o Users should be identified and grouped in various categories and their security responsibilities should be delineated.

o User account administration, user password policy, and privilege review policy should be specified.

o Responsibility for network administration and security should be assigned to a trained and technically competent staff.

o Accounts should be promptly deleted if remained unused for 3 months.

o Accounts belonging to terminated employees should be disposed off immediately.

o Personal equipment should not be connected to the SHIPIT network.

• **Requirement Specification:** We document SHIPIT's security and business needs using process, data, and network models as discussed. We document the final set of security requirements and mechanisms in the form of a security risk register created after the secure location model was developed. The process and data models are shown in Figures 8 and 9, respectively. The security risk register in Table 4 shows security requirements under each security view. Various security views have enabled the SHIPIT firm think about security requirements not only for protecting resources and dealing with various threats but also for legal requirements and continuous security assessment.

Figure 8A. Context level DFD-SHIPIT

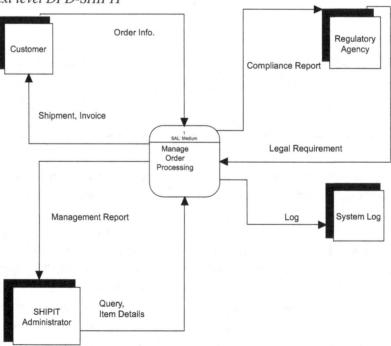

The Context Level DFD for SHIPIT: Manage Order Processing

Figure 8B. Level 0 DFD for SHIPIT

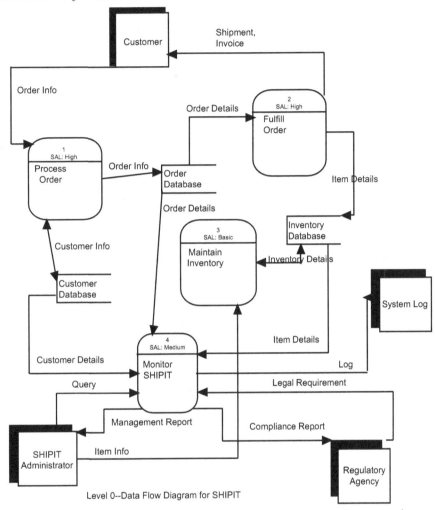

Level 0--Data Flow Diagram for SHIPIT

Secure Location Model

Figure 10 shows an initial overall location model for SHIPIT. It shows that the three locations, office, warehouse, and call center, are connected to one another. Each location shows, in parenthesis, the number of people who may use SHIPIT network. In some situations, it may be worthwhile to create an initial location model for each location. Next, we need to determine the information domains. Tables 2 and 3 show process-location-security and data-location-security matrices, respectively. These tables reveal that the call center creates customer and order data and the warehouse cre-

ates inventory data. The office uses the customer, order, and inventory data. However, the call center does more processing with the customers and orders than any of the other locations. Similarly, the warehouse does more processing with the inventory data. This leads us to propose that customer and order data should reside at the call center and the inventory data should reside at the warehouse. Even though the SHIPIT study case is not very explicit about information on Web sites and e-mails, we assume that it maintains Web site and e-mail services. We propose three information domains, Call Center, Warehouse, and Corporate Office, to segregate and group each set

Table 2. Process-location-security matrix

	Office	Warehouse	call center	security adequacy level
Process Order			**X**	**High**
Fulfill Order		**X**		**High**
Maintain Inventory		**X**	**X**	**Basic**
Monitor SHIPIT	**X**			**Medium**
Print Invoice	**X**			**Medium**

Table 3. Data-location-security matrix

	Office	Warehouse	call center	security adequacy level
Customer	**RUD**	**R**	**CRU**	**Medium**
Order	**R**	**RU**	**CRUD**	**Basic**
Inventory	**RU**	**CRUD**	**R**	**Low**

C=Create; R=Read; U=Update; D=Delete

Figure 9. Entity relationship diagram for SHIPIT

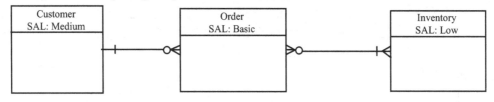

Figure 10. An overall SHIPIT location model (top level)

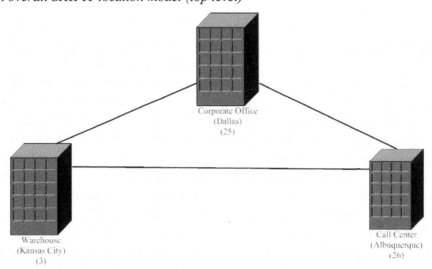

An Initial Overall SHIPIT Location Model (Top Level).

Table 4. Risk register showing risks, requirements, and mechanisms for SHIPIT-under various views

Views	Assets	Sources of Risk	Threat Likelihood Estimate	Consequence, if the threat is realized	Resultant Risk Level	Acceptable Risk Level	Risk Priority Level	Security Requirements	Security Mechanisms
Threat	Physical location (Dallas, Albuquerque, and Kansas City)	Fire	Low	Critical	High	Low	2	1. Protect against fire 2. Backup Data 3. Store backup data remotely	1. Backup 2. Equipment Security
		Earthquake	Very Low	Damaging	Low	Low	0		
	Inventory Database Server, Customer & Order Database Server	Wrong Configuration	Low	Damaging	Medium	Nil	2	1. Monitor resource integrity 2. Check Resource integrity 3. Adjust resource integrity	1. Audit trails and logs 2. Resource testing 3. Resource maintenance 4. Data back-up 5. Resource monitoring 6. Operational procedures
		Hacker	Medium	Damaging	High	Nil	3	1. Protect against intrusion 2. Protect against denial of service 3. Protect against malicious code	1. Firewall 2. Antivirus software 3. VPN
	General Purpose Server	Wrong Configuration	Medium	Damaging	High	Nil	3	1. Monitor resource integrity 2. Check Resource integrity 3. Adjust resource integrity	1. Audit trails and logs 2. Resource testing 3. Resource maintenance 4. Resource monitoring 5. Operational procedures
		Hacker	High	Damaging	High	Nil	3	1. Protect against intrusion 2. Protect against denial of service 3. Protect against malicious code	1. Firewall 2. Antivirus software 3. VPN
	Web Server	Wrong Configuration	Medium	Damaging	High	Nil	3	1. Monitor resource integrity 2. Check Resource integrity 3. Adjust resource integrity	1. Audit trails and logs 2. Resource testing 3. Resource maintenance 4. Resource monitoring 5. Operational procedures
		Hacker	High	Damaging	High	Nil	3	1. Protect against intrusion 2. Protect against denial of service 3. Protect against malicious code	1. Firewall 2. Antivirus software 3. VPN
	Mail Server	Wrong Configuration	Medium	Damaging	High	Nil	3	1. Monitor resource integrity 2. Check Resource integrity 3. Adjust resource integrity	1. Audit trails and logs 2. Resource testing 3. Resource maintenance 4. Resource monitoring 5. Operational procedures
		Hacker	High	Damaging	High	Nil	3	1. Protect against intrusion 2. Protect against denial of service 3. Protect against malicious code	1. Firewall 2. Antivirus software 3. VPN
	Operation	Technical Failure	Medium	Minor	Low	Low	0		
		Power failure	Low	Minor	Low	Low	0		
		Operational Staff Error	High	Significant	High	Nil	3	1. Verify and confirm input data and commands 2. Save data periodically	1. Staff training 2. Error proof interface
Resource	SHIPIT Internet Services	Critical Network Device Failure	Low	Significant	Medium	Low	1	1. Check resource availability 2. Monitor resource availability 3. Maintain redundancy in system	1. Power supplies security 2. Resource testing 3. Resource maintenance 4. Resource monitoring 5. Equipment redundancy
		Denial of Service Attack from the Internet	Very High	Significant	High	Low	2	1. Protect against Denial of Service 2. Protect against intrusion 3. Protect against malicious code	1. Management of outside users' access 2. Resource monitoring 3. Intrusion detection 4. Audit trails and logs 5. Internet Connection policy
	SHIPIT Data (Customer, Order, Inventory)	Hackers from the Internet	Low	Serious	High	Nil	3	1. Monitor resource integrity 2. Check Resource integrity 3. Adjust resource integrity 4. Monitor resource confidentiality 5. Check resource confidentiality 6. Adjust resource confidentiality	1. Formal standards for establishing user access 2. User ID management 3. Periodic evaluation of access rights 4. Resource monitoring 5. Audit trails and logs 6. Intrusion detection 7. Security scanning Tools
		Insider Attack	Low	Significant	Medium	Nil	2	1. Monitor resource integrity 2. Check Resource integrity 3. Adjust resource integrity 4. Monitor resource confidentiality 5. Check resource confidentiality 6. Adjust resource confidentiality	1. Formal standards for establishing user access 2. User ID management 3. Periodic evaluation of access rights 4. Resource monitoring 5. Audit trails and logs 6. Intrusion detection 7. Security Awareness and Training 8. User ID management
	Technical expertise	Loss of Key Personnel	Medium	Significant	Medium	Low	1	1. Protect from loss of key personnel	1. Succession Planning
Legal	Compliance to the Privacy Act of 1974	Violation of National Privacy Principles	Medium	Damaging	High	Nil	3	1. Establish rules for handling personal data 2. Identify Personal Identifiable Information (PII) 3. Establish proper access control for PII	1. Access policy 2. Transparency and control of access privileges 3. Audit history reporting 4. Centralized authentication and authorization 5. Audit log
	Compliance to the CAN-SPAM Act 2003	Violation of Spam Code of Practice	High	Minor	Medium	Low	1	1. Analyze legal risks for on-line environment 2. Comply with the Spam Act of 2003	1. Spam filtering 2. Spam reporting 3. Spam reduction techniques

continued on following page

Table 4. continued

Views	Assets	Sources of Risk	Threat Likelihood Estimate	Consequence, if the threat is realized	Resultant Risk Level	Acceptable Risk Level	Risk Priority Level	Security Requirements
Management	Security Policy	Inadequate Policy	Low	Serious	High	Nil	3	1. Identify faulty policy 2. Take corrective action 3. Establish security policy and procedues 4. Review security policy and procedures 5. Monitor security
	Accountability Guidelines	Vague Accountability for Individuals	Medium	Damaging	High	Nil	3	1. Review accountability policy 2. Refine accountability-assignment
		Lack of Accountability Standards	Low	Significant	Medium	Nil	2	1. Review accountability policy 2. Review accountability standards 3. Establish accountability standards
Process	Processes (Process Order, Fulfill Order, Maintain Inventory, Monitor SHIPIT)	Poorly defined Process Steps	Low	Damaging	Medium	Nil	2	1. Evaluate process 2. Rectify weak points/steps of the process 3. Secure each steps of the process 4. Train users in the secure process
	Process Control	Lack of Staff Training	Medium	Damaging	High	Nil	3	1. Train users in the secure process 2. Review secure process
		Lack of Monitoring	High	Minor	Medium	Low	1	1. Review process 2. Establish process ownership 3. Separate duties of actors involved in the process 4. Train users in the secure process 5. Review process policy
	Process Interface	Lack of Interface Design Standards	Low	Significant	Medium	Low	1	1. Review process policy 2. Review process design standards 3. Evaluate process
Assessment	Assessment Criteria	Inadequate Criteria	Medium	Significant	Medium	Low	1	1. Evaluate assessment criteria 2. Define assessment criteria 3. Define measures for each criterion 4. Collect data on measures 5. Evaluate the measures' effectiveness
		Vague Criteria	Medium	Significant	Medium	Low	1	1. Evaluate assessment criteria 2. Define assessment criteria 3. Define measures for each criterion 4. Collect data on measures 5. Evaluate the measures' effectiveness
	Assessment Method	No Assessment Method	Low	Significant	Medium	Nil	2	1. Define assessment method 2. Train users in assessment
		Inadequate Assessment Training	Low	Significant	Medium	Low	1	1. Train users in assessment 2. Evaluate assessment policy
	Assessment Standards	Inadequate Standards	Low	Significant	Medium	Low	1	1. Evaluate assessment policy 2. Define assessment standards 3. Train users in assessment

of geographically separated information resources and assets. Tables 2 and 3 also show the security adequacy levels for processes and data. This information makes it easier to determine the security adequacy levels for the location connectivity diagrams. The process-location-security matrix reveals that there are two processes concentrated in the call center. One of the processes, Process Order, requires online interaction with customers. The order processing will require a faster throughput. This suggests that there is a need to have a faster and larger capacity communication requirement for the link between the call center and the rest of the network.

A secure extended location connectivity diagram for the SHIPIT case is shown in Figures 11A, 11B, 11C, and 11D. There are two levels of the secure extended location connectivity diagrams. The first level diagram in Figure 8A shows the overall connection among the three locations, office, warehouse, and call center. Each connection is labeled with security, volume and response time requirements. The second level diagrams in Figures 11B, 11C, and 11D show the network

Figure 11A. SHIPIT secure extended location connectivity diagram (conceptual)

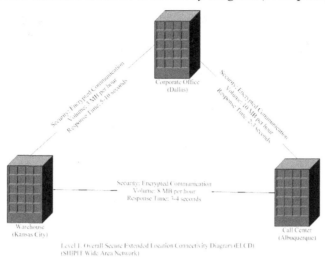

within each location. Each PC and other nodes are labeled with security adequacy level. Connections between servers and client PCs are labeled with security, volume, and response time requirements. Connections between servers are considered local and hence are considered quite fast.

- SHIPIT Secure Network Architecture: There are three enclaves, one under each information domain. Because each information domain has only one enclave, these enclaves are called by the same name as that of their information domain names. We propose to use a specialized router with a firewall as a boundary controller to protect each enclave. The appropriate security mechanisms from the security risk register should be incorporated into the secure network architecture diagram (SNAD). Figure 12 shows a logical SNAD for SHIPIT. The logical SNAD has been drawn using the SmartDraw software. The initial nodes in the diagram were derived from the secure extended location connectivity diagrams as shown in Figures 11A-11D.

Figure 12 shows a site-to-site virtual private network (VPN) design to provide a secure network environment for SHIPIT branches. A VPN design is more cost effective than designing a private network using privately leased lines. The concept of enclaves leads us to create a subnet for each enclave. SHIPIT's logical SNAD can be modeled as a hierarchical secure network model consisting of several subnets. The design of hierarchical networks and subnets are better handled and managed by network design and simulation software such as OPNET (OPNET, 2005). Due to space limitation, we do not address the network modeling of SHIPIT using network simulation software.

- Secure Network Performance Evaluation: The logical secure network architecture diagram for SHIPIT can be modeled and simulated using network design and simulation software such as OPNET (2005). OPNET provides tools and techniques to model secure computer networks. Please see OPNET (2005) for more details.

Figure 11B. SHIPIT secure extended location connectivity diagram (conceptual)—corporate office

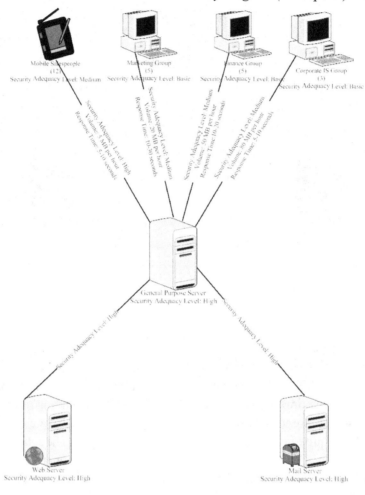

We do not discuss network performance and evaluation here due to space limitations. Discussion of network simulation and performance evaluation is quite involving and will be a subject of another research article.

CONCLUSION AND LIMITATIONS

We have proposed and discussed a new approach to designing secure computer networks for firms. The approach not only emphasizes the importance of using organizational goals and requirements in designing a secure network but also provides built-in mechanisms to capture security needs and use them seamlessly throughout the steps of analyzing and designing secure network architecture. We have proposed and used extended versions of DFD and ERD to not only capture business process and data, but also their security requirements in the same diagrams. Firms can use the SEACON method to design and implement secure computer networks that are integrated with the business requirements of that firm. An integrated

Figure 11C. SHIPIT secure extended location connectivity diagram (conceptual)—warehouse

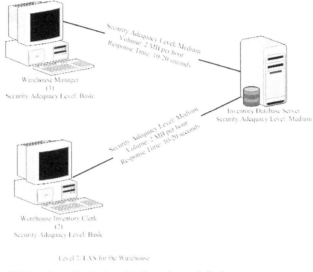

Figure 11D. SHIPIT secure extended location connectivity diagram (conceptual)—call center

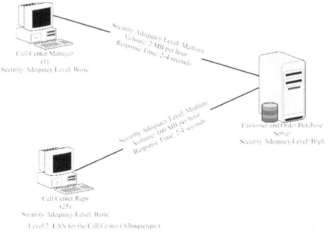

approach with built-in steps for incorporating security measures right from analysis is superior to pure technical methods because it facilitates seamless support for using business processes, security needs, and the overall IS architecture for a firm.

One of the limitations of the SEACON method is the lack of guidelines for transforming a secure network architecture into a network simulation model that can be easily tested and evaluated using network simulation software. Such guidelines will obviously have to take into account the idiosyncrasies of the target simulation software.

Figure 12. A logical secure network architecture diagram for SHIPIT

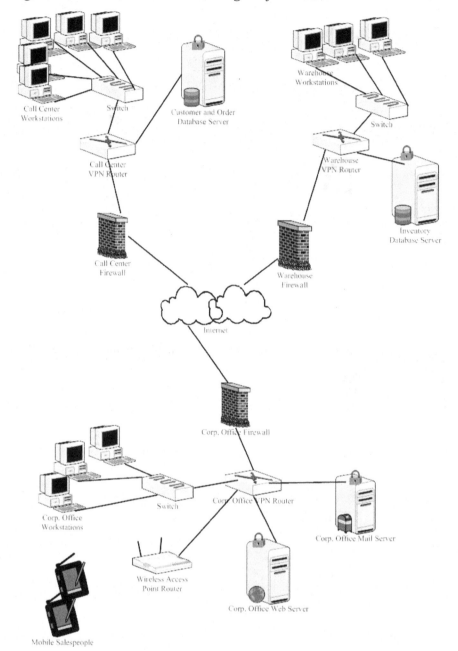

SHIPIT Secure Network Architecture Diagram

REFERENCES

Arber T., Cooley, D., Hirsch, S., Mahan, M., & Osterritter, J. (1999). *Network security framework: Robustness strategy.* Retrieved November 30, 2007, from http://csrc.nist.gov/nissc/1999/Proceeding/papers/p30.pdf

ASIS. (2003). General security risk assessment guideline. An ASIS International Guideline.

Bace, R., & Mell, P. (2001). *Intrusion detection systems.* NIST Special Publication on Intrusion Detection System. National Institute of Standards and Technology.

Bionic Buffalo Corporation. (2000). *Concept for a secure network computer.* Retrieved November 30, 2007, from http://www.tatanka.com/doc/technote/tn0110.htm

Centers for Medicare & Medicaid Services. (CMS). (2002). *CMS information security risk assessment (RA) methodology* (version #1.1). Baltimore, MD: Department of Health & Human Services.

Cisco Systems. (2001). *SAFE: A security blue print for enterprise networks.* A white paper. Retrieved November 30, 2007, from http://www.cisco.com/warp/public/cc/so/cuso/epso/sqfr/safe_wp.pdf

Common Criteria Implementation Board. (1999a). *Common criteria for information technology security evaluation, part 1: Introduction and general model* (version 2.1). Retrieved November 30, 2007, from http://csrc.nist.gov/cc

Common Criteria Implementation Board. (1999b). *Common criteria for information technology security evaluation, part 2: Security functional requirements* (version 2.1). Retrieved November 30, 2007, from http://csrc.nist.gov/cc

Common Criteria Implementation Board. (1999c). *Common criteria for information technology security evaluation, part 3: Security assurance requirements* (version 2.1). Retrieved November 30, 2007, from http://csrc.nist.gov/cc/

Defense Logistics Agency. (2002). *Enclave boundary defense.* DLIA 8500.12. Retrieved November 30, 2007, from http://www.dlaps.hq.dla.mil/dlai/i8500.12.htm

Department of Defense Standard. (1985). *Department of defense trusted computer system evaluation criteria.* DoD 5200.28-STD.

Duchessi, P., & Chengalur-Smith, I. (1998). Client/server benefits, problems, best practices. *Communications of the ACM, 41*(5), 87-94.

Fisch, E. A., & White, G. B. (2001). *Secure computers and networks: Analysis, design, and implementation.* CRC Press. Retrieved November 30, 2007, from www.crcpress.com

GAO. (1999, November). *Information security risk assessment—Practices of leading vs. accounting and information management division.* United States General Accounting Office, GAO/AIMD-00-33.

Ghosh, S. (2001). *Principles of secure network systems design.* Springer-Verlag.

Gordon, L. A., Loeb, M. P., Lucyshyn, W., & Richardson, R. (2005). *Tenth annual CSI/FBI computer crime and security survey.* Retrieved November 30, 2007, from www.GoCSI.com

Innella, P. (2001). *Designing secure networks based on the software process model.* A white paper. Retrieved November 30, 2007, from http://www.securityfocus.com/infocus/1191

Irvine, C., & Levin, T. (1999). *A note on mapping user-oriented security policies to complex mechanisms and services* (Tech. Rep.). Retrieved November 30, 2007, from http://cisr.nps.navy.mil/downloads/nps_cs_99_008.pdf

Kizza, J. M. (2005). *Computer network security.* New York: Springer-Verlag.

McMillan, R. (2005). *Computer attacks down, survey says*. Retrieved November 30, 2007, from http://www.networkworld.com/news/2005/072505-security.html

NSW. (2003). *Information security guideline for New South Wales (NSW) government, part 2: Examples of threats and vulnerabilities*. The Office of Information and Communications Technology, Department of Commerce, New South Wales. Retrieved November 30, 2007, from http://www.oict.nsw.gov.au/content/2.3.17-Security-Pt2.asp

NSW. (2003). *Information security guideline for New South Wales (NSW) government, part 3: Information security baseline controls*. The Office of Information and Communications Technology, Department of Commerce, New South Wales. Retrieved November 30, 2007, from http://www.oict.nsw.gov.au/content/2.3.17-Security-Pt2.asp

OPNET Documentation. (2005). Retrieved November 30, 2007, from www.OPNET.com

Oppenheimer, P. (2004). *Top-down network design* (2nd ed.). Indianapolis, IN: Cisco Press.

Rusli, R. (2001). *Secure system architecture and design*. A white paper. SANS GIAC Security Essentials—Practical Assignment, GSEC Web site. Retrieved November 30, 2007, from http://www.giac.org/certified_professionals/practicals/gsec/1422.php

Shaw, N., & Yadav, S. B. (2001). DEACON: An integrated approach to the analysis and design of enterprise architecture-based computer networks. *Communications of the Association for Information Systems, 7*.

Southwick, P. (2003). *Secure network design*. A white paper. Retrieved November 30, 2007, from the Hill Associates Web site: http://www.hill.com/archive/pub/papers/2003/10/paper.pdf#search='secure%20network%20design'

Survey says: Government regulations help secure networks. (2005). Sarbanes-Oxley Compliance Journal. Retrieved November 30, 2007, from http://www.s-ox.com/news/news.cfm?articleID=338

Vaidyanathan, G., & Devaraj, S. (2003). A five framework for analyzing online risks in e-businesses. *Communications of the ACM, 46*(12), 354-361.

Verdon, D., & McGraw, G. (2004). Risk analysis in software design. *IEEE Security & Privacy, 2*(4), 79-84.

Warren, P. (2005). *Ten steps to secure networking*. TechWorld. Retrieved November 30, 2007, from http://www.techworld.com/security/features/index.cfm?FeatureID=1862

Whitman, M. E. (2003). Enemy at the gate: Threats to information security. *Communications of the ACM, 46*(8), 91-95.

Whitman, M. E., & Mattord, H. J. (2005). *Principles of information security* (2nd ed.). Canada: Thomson Course Technology.

Whitmore, J.J. (2001). A method for designing secure solutions. *IBM Systems Journal, 40*(3), 747-768.

Yadav, S. B. (2006). *A six view perspective of system security—issues, risks, requirements, and mechanisms* (Tech. Rep. #ISQSYadav2006-1). Lubbock, TX: Rawls College of Business, Texas Tech University.

This work was previously published in International Journal of Information Security and Privacy, Vol. 2, Issue 1, edited by J.N.D. Gupta, S.K. Sharma, and J. Hsu, pp. 1-25, copyright 2008 by IGI Publishing (an imprint of IGI Global).

Chapter XVII
Formal Methods for Specifying and Analyzing Complex Software Systems

Xudong He
Florida International University, USA

Huiqun Yu
East China University of Science and Technology, China

Yi Deng
Florida International University, USA

ABSTRACT

Software has been a major enabling technology for advancing modern society, and is now an indispensable part of daily life. Because of the increased complexity of these software systems, and their critical societal role, more effective software development and analysis technologies are needed. How to develop and ensure the dependability of these complex software systems is a grand challenge. It is well known that a highly dependable complex software system cannot be developed without a rigorous development process and a precise specification and design documentation. Formal methods are one of the most promising technologies for precisely specifying, modeling, and analyzing complex software systems. Although past research experience and practice in computer science have convincingly shown that it is not possible to formally verify program behavior and properties at the program source code level due to its extreme huge size and complexity, recently advances in applying formal methods during software specification and design, especially at software architecture level, have demonstrated significant benefits of using formal methods. In this chapter, we will review several well-known formal methods for software system specification and analysis. We will present recent advances of using these formal methods for specifying, modeling, and analyzing software architectural design.

INTRODUCTION

It is wildly agreed that the main obstacle to "help computers help us more" and relegate to these helpful partners even more complex and sensitive tasks is not inadequate speed and unsatisfactory raw computing power in the existing machines, but our limited ability to design and implement complex systems with sufficiently high degree of confidence in their correctness under all circumstances (Clarke, Grumberg, & Peled, 1999). This problem of design validation—ensuring the correctness of the design at the earliest stage possible—is the major challenge in any responsible system development process, and the activities intended for its solution occupy an ever increasing portion of the development cycle cost and time budgets.

Two major approaches to analyze the system quality are *testing* and *verification*. Traditional and widely used quality assurance techniques based on software testing are inadequate to ensure the reliability of complex systems. In addition to the inherent limitation of testing from being able to guarantee system properties, many of today's software systems are designed to adapt in a wide range of environments and evolve over time. Because of this, the range of possible testing scenarios at code level becomes extremely large and potentially uncontrollable.

Formal methods (Harel, 1987; Hoare, 1985; Manna & Pnueli, 1992; Milner, 1989; Murata, 1989) for software specification and *verification* have been viewed as a promising way to address the problems associated with testing. These methods are precise and rigorous and can prevent and detect system defects introduced at the early stages of development, which are often more costly to fix and have more severe consequences. Despite tremendous advances (Clarke & Wing, 1996), however, widely spread application of *formal methods* in practical system development still remains to be seen (Craigen, Gerhart, & Ralston, 1995). A major cause for the problem is that results on *formal methods* are to large extent fragmented.

Formal techniques are viewed as difficult and expensive to use because their application is ad hoc, and they are too fine grained to deal with the complexity in practical-sized development. Thus it is necessary to precisely define, measure, and analyze software dependability at a level higher than source code. Recent research (Knight, 2002) has shown that it is especially important to explore technologies how to handle dependability attributes at the *software architecture* level for the following reasons:

- A *software architecture* description presents the highest-level design abstraction of a system (Shaw & Garlan, 1996). As a result, it is relative simple compared to a detailed system design. Thus it is more likely to develop an effective methodology to study dependability attributes.

- As the highest-level design abstraction, a *software architecture* description precedes and logically and structurally influences other system development products. Thus an error in a *software architecture* has a much larger impact than an error introduced at a later development stage. Prevention and detection of errors at software architectural level are thus extremely important. Hence, it is necessary to study and measure dependability attributes before the actual software systems are developed and deployed.

Many studies, especially those done at the Software Engineering Institute at Carnegie Mellon University (Kazman, Klein, & Clements, 2000), have shown that a *software architecture* reveals, influences, or even dictates many system dependability features such as reliability, performance, security, and faulty-tolerance. Therefore, the dependability attributes measured at *software architecture* level can serve as the basis to predict and validate the dependability attributes of the developed and deployed systems.

In this chapter, we will review several well-known *formal methods* for complex software system specification and analysis. We will illustrate these methods and their applications in the *software architecture model* (*SAM*) (He & Deng, 2002; Wang, He, & Deng, 1999), which is a general *software architecture* model for developing and analyzing *software architecture* specifications.

BACKGROUND

Visualizing the Structures of Software Architectures

Specification is the process of describing a system and its desired properties. Formal specification uses a language that is usually composed of three primary components: (1) a *syntax* that defines the specific notation with which the specification is represented; (2) a *semantics* that helps to define a "universe of objects" (Wing, 1990) that will be used to describe the system; and (3) a set of *relations* that define the rules that indicate which objects properly satisfy the specification.

In *SAM*, a *software architecture* is visualized by a hierarchical set of boxes with ports connected by directed arcs. These boxes are called *compositions*. Each composition may contain other compositions. The bottom-level compositions are either *components* or *connectors*. Various constraints can be specified. This hierarchical model supports compositionality in both *software architecture* design and analysis, and thus facilitates scalability. Figure 1 shows a graphical view of an *SAM software architecture*, in which *connectors* are not emphasized and are only represented by thick arrows. Each *component* or *connector* is defined using a *Petri net*. Thus the internal logical structure of a *component* or *connector* is also visualized through the *Petri net* structure.

Textually, an *SAM software architecture* is defined by a set of compositions $C = \{C_1, C_2, ..., C_k\}$ (each composition corresponds to a design level or the concept of sub-architecture) and a hierarchical mapping h relating compositions. Each composition $C_i = \{Cm_i, Cn_i, Cs_i\}$ consists of a set Cm_i of *components*, a set Cn_i of *connectors*, and a set Cs_i of composition constraints. An element $C_{ij} = (S_{ij}, B_{ij})$, (either a *component* or a *connector*) in a composition C_i has a *property specification* S_{ij} (a *temporal logic* formula) and a *behavior model* B_{ij} (a *Petri net*). Each composition constraint in Cs_i is also defined by a *temporal logic* formula. The interface of a *behavior model* B_{ij} consists of a

Figure 1. An SAM architecture model

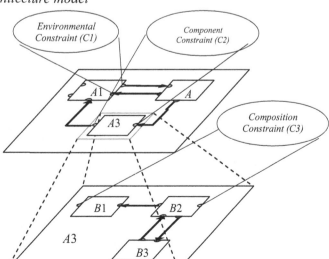

set of places (called ports) that is the intersection among relevant *components* and *connectors*. Each *property specification* S_{ij} only uses the ports as its atomic propositions/predicates that are true in a given marking if they contain appropriate tokens. A composition constraint is defined as a *property specification*; however it often contains ports belonging to multiple *components* and / or *connectors*. A *component* C_{ij} can be refined into a lower-level composition C_l, which is defined by $h(C_{ij}) = C_l$.

Modeling the Behaviors of Software Architectures

In *SAM*, the behavior of a *component* or a *connector* is explicitly defined using a *Petri net*. The behavior of an overall *software architecture* is implicitly derived by composing all the bottom-level *behavior models* of *components* and *connectors*. *SAM* provides both the modeling power and flexibility through the choice of different *Petri net* models. We have used several *Petri net* models including time *Petri nets* (Wang, He, & Deng, 1999), condition event nets, and predicate transition nets (He & Deng, 2000, 2002) in our previous work. The selection of a particular *Petri net* model is based on the application under consideration. A simple *Petri net* model such as condition event nets is adequate when we only need to deal with simple control flows and data-independent constraints; while a more powerful *Petri net* model such as predicate transition nets is needed to handle both control and data. To study performance related constraints, a more specialized *Petri net* model such as stochastic *Petri nets* is more appropriate and convenient. In the following sections, we give a brief definition of predicate transition nets (*PrT* nets) using the conventions in He (1996). Readers not interested in the technical details may skip this section, and just look at the examples.

The Syntax and Static Semantics of PrT Nets

A *PrT* net is a tuple (*N, Spec, ins*) where

1. $N = (P, T, F)$ is the net structure, in which
   i. P and T are non-empty finite sets satisfying $P \cap T = \varnothing$ (P and T are the sets of places and transitions of N respectively),
   ii. $F \subseteq (P \times T) \cup (T \times P)$ is a flow relation (the arcs of N);

2. $Spec = (S, OP, Eq)$ is the underlying specification, and consists of a signature $\mathbf{S} = (S, OP)$ and a set Eq of $\mathbf{S}$-equations. Signature $\mathbf{S} = (S, OP)$ includes a set of sorts S and a family $OP = (OP_{s_1, \ldots, s_n, s})$ of sorted operations for $s_1, \ldots, s_n, s \in S$. For each $s \in S$, we use CON_S to denote $OP_{,s}$ (the 0-ary operation of sort s), that is, the set of constant symbols of sort s. The $\mathbf{S}$-equations in Eq define the meanings and properties of operations in OP. We often simply use familiar operations and their properties without explicitly listing the relevant equations. *Spec* is a meta-language to define the tokens, labels, and constraints of a *PrT* net. Tokens of a *PrT* net are ground terms of the signature S, written $MCON_S$. The set of labels is denoted using $Label_S(X)$ (X is the set of sorted variables disjoint with OP). Each label can be a multiple set expression of the form $\{k_1 x_1, \ldots, k_n x_n\}$. Constraints of a *PrT* net are a subset of first order logic formulas (where the domains of quantifiers are finite and any free variable in a constraint appears in the label of some connecting arc of the transition), and thus are essentially propositional logic formulas. The subset of first order logical formulas contains the S-terms of sort *bool* over X, denoted as $Term_{OP, bool}(X)$.

3. $ins = (\varphi, L, R, M_0)$ is a net inscription that associates a net element in N with its denotation in *Spec* :

i. $\varphi: P \rightarrow \wp(S)$ is the data definition of N and associates each place p in P with a subset of sorts in S.

ii. $L: F \rightarrow Label_S(X)$ is a sort-respecting labeling of *PrT* net. We use the following abbreviation in the following definitions:

$$\overline{L}(x,y) = \begin{cases} L(x,y) & \text{iff } (x,y) \in F \\ \varnothing & \text{otherwise} \end{cases}$$

iii. $R: T \rightarrow Term_{OP,bool}(X)$ is a well-defined constraining mapping, which associates each transition t in T with a first order logic formula defined in the underlying algebraic specification. Furthermore, the constraint of a transition defines the meaning of the transition.

vi. $M_0: P \rightarrow MCON_S$ is a sort-respecting initial marking. The initial marking assigns a multi-set of tokens to each place p in P.

Dynamic Semantics of PrT Nets

1. Markings of a *PrT* net N are mappings M: $P \rightarrow MCON_S$;

2. An occurrence mode of N is a substitution $\alpha = \{x_1 \leftarrow c_1, ..., x_n \leftarrow c_n\}$, which instantiates typed label variables. We use $e{:}\alpha$ to denote the result of instantiating an expression e with α, in which e can be either a label expression or a constraint;

3. Given a marking M, a transition $t \in T$, and an occurrence mode α, t is α_enabled at M iff the following predicate is true: $\forall p: p \in P.(\overline{L}(p,t){:}\alpha) \subseteq M(p)) \wedge R(t){:}\alpha$;

4. If t is α_enabled at M, t may fire in occurrence mode α. The firing of t with α returns the marking M' defined by $M'(p) = M(p) - \overline{L}(p,t){:}\alpha \cup (t,p){:}\alpha$ for $p \in P$. We use $M[t/\alpha{>}M'$ to denote the firing of t with occurrence α under marking M. As in traditional *Petri nets*,

two enabled transitions may fire at the same time as long as they are not in conflict;

5. For a marking M, the set $[M{>}$ of markings reachable from M is the smallest set of markings such that $M \in [M{>}$ and if $M' \in [M{>}$ and $M'[t/\alpha{>}M''$ then $M'' \in [M{>}$, for some $t \in T$ and occurrence mode α (note: concurrent transition firings do not produce additional new reachable markings);

6. An execution sequence $M_0 T_0 M_1 T_1...$ of N is either finite when the last marking is terminal (no more enabled transition in the last marking) or infinite, in which each T_i is an execution step consisting of a set of non-conflict firing transitions;

7. The behavior of N, denoted by *Comp(N)*, is the set of all execution sequences starting from the initial marking.

The Dining Philosophers problem is a classic multi-process synchronization problem introduced by Dijkstra. The problem consists of k philosophers sitting at a round table who do nothing but think and eat. Between each philosopher, there is a single chopstick. In order to eat, a philosopher must have both chopsticks. A problem can arise if each philosopher grabs the chopstick on the right, then waits for the stick on the left. In this case, a deadlock has occurred. The challenge in the Dining Philosophers problem is to design a

Figure 2. A PrT Net model of the Dining Philosophers problem

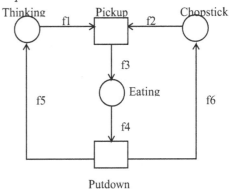

protocol so that the philosophers do not deadlock (i.e., the entire set of philosophers does not stop and wait indefinitely), and so that no philosopher starves (i.e., every philosopher eventually gets his/her hands on a pair of chopsticks). The following is an example of the *PrT* net model of the Dining Philosophers problem.

There are three places (*Thinking*, *Chopstick* and *Eating*) and two transitions (*Pickup* and *Putdown*) in the *PrT* net. In the underlying specification *Spec* = (*S*, *OP*, *Eq*), *S* includes elementary sorts such as Integer and Boolean, and also sorts PHIL and CHOP derived from Integer. *S* also includes structured sorts such as set and tuple obtained from the Cartesian product of the elementary sorts; *OP* includes standard arithmetic and relational operations on Integer, logical connectives on Boolean, set operations, and selection operation on tuples; and *Eq* includes known properties of these operators.

The net inscription (φ, *L*, *R*, M_0) is as follows:

* Sorts of predicates:
  $\varphi(Thinking)$ = $\wp$(PHIL), $\varphi(Eating)$ = $\wp$(PHIL×CHOP×CHOP),

$\varphi(Chopstick)$ = $\wp$(CHOP),
where $\wp$ denotes power set.

* Arc definitions:
  $L(f1) = \{ph\}$, $L(f2) = \{ch1, ch2\}$, $L(f3) = \{<ph, ch1, ch2>\}$,
  $L(f4) = \{<ph, ch1, ch2>\}$, $L(f5) = \{ph\}$, $L(f6) = \{ch1, ch2\}$.

* Constraints of transitions:
  $R(Pickup) = (ph = ch1) \wedge (ch2 = ph \oplus 1)$,
  $R(Putdown)$ = true.

* The initial marking m_0 is defined as follows:
  $M_0(Thinking) = \{1, 2, ..., k\}$, $M_0(Eating) = \{ \}$, $M_0(Chopstick) = \{1, 2, ..., k\}$.

This specification allows concurrent executions such as multiple non-conflicting (non-neighboring) philosophers picking up chopsticks simultaneously, and some philosophers picking up chopsticks while others putting down chopsticks. The constraints associated with transitions Pickup and Putdown also ensure that a philosopher can only use two designated chopsticks defined by the implicit adjacent relationships. Table 1 gives the details of a possible run of five dining philosophers *PrT* net.

Table 1. A possible run of five Dining Philosophers problem

Markings m_i			Transitions n_i	
Thinking	Eating	Chopstick	Fired Transition	Token(s) consumed
{1,2,3,4,5}	{ }	{1,2,3,4,5}	Pickup	ph=1, ch1=1, ch2=2
{2,3,4,5}	{<1,1,2>}	{3,4,5}	Putdown	<ph,ch1,ch2>=<1,1,2>
{1,2,3,4,5}	{ }	{1,2,3,4,5}	Pickup	ph=2, ch1=2, ch2=3
{1,3,4,5}	{<2,2,3>}	{1,4,5}	Pickup	ph=4, ch1=4, ch2=5
{1, 3, 5}	{< 2 , 2 , 3 >, <4,4,5>}	{1}	Putdown	<ph,ch1,ch2>=<2,2,3>
{1, 2, 3, 5}	{<4, 4, 5>}	{1,2,3}	Putdown	<ph,ch1,ch2>=<4,4,5>
{1,2,3,4,5}	{ }	{1,2,3,4,5}	Pickup	ph=5, ch1=5, ch2=1
{1,2,3,4}	{<5,5,1>}	{2,3,4}	Pickup	ph=3, ch1=3, ch2=4
{1,2,4}	{< 5 , 5 , 1 >, <3,3,4>}	{2}	Putdown	<ph,ch1,ch2>=<3,3,4>
{1,2,3,4}	{<5,5,1>}	{2,3,4}	Putdown	<ph,ch1,ch2>=<5,5,1>
{1,2,3,4,5}	{ }	{1,2,3,4,5}	...	...

Specifying SAM Architecture Properties

In *SAM, software architecture* properties are specified using a *temporal logic.* Depending on the given Petri net models, different *temporal logics* are used. In this section, we provide the essential concepts of a generic first order linear time *temporal logic* to specify the properties of *components* and *connectors.* We follow the approach in Lamport (1994) to define vocabulary and models of our *temporal logic* in terms of *PrT* nets without giving a specific *temporal logic.*

Values, State Variables, and States

The set of values is the multi-set of tokens $MCON_S$ defined by the *Spec* of a given *PrT* net *N.* Multi-sets can be viewed as partial functions. For example, multi-set $\{3a, 2b\}$ can be represented as $\{a \mapsto 3, b \mapsto 2\}$.

The set of state variables is the set P of places of N, which change their meanings during the executions of N. The arity of a place p is determined by its sort $\varphi\ (p)$ in the net inscription.

The set of states **St** is the set of all reachable markings $[M_0>$ of N. A marking is a mapping from the set of state variables into the set of values. We use $M[|x|]$ to denote the value of x under state (marking) M.

Since state variables take partial functions as values, they are flexible function symbols. We can access a particular component value of a state variable. However there is a problem associated with partial functions, that is, many values are undefined. This problem can easily be solved by extending state variables into total functions in the following way: for any n-ary state variable p, any tuple $c \in MCON_S^{\ n}$ and any state M, if $p(c)$ is undefined under M, then let $M[|\ p(c)\ |] = 0$. This extension is consistent with the semantics of *PrT* nets, that is, there is no token c in place p under marking M. Furthermore, we can consider the meaning $[|p(c)|]$ of the function application $p(c)$

as a mapping from states to **Nat** using a postfix notation for function application $M[|p(c)\ |]$.

Rigid Variables, Rigid Function, and Predicate Symbols

Rigid variables are individual variables that do not change their meanings during the executions of N. All rigid variables occurring in our *temporal logic* formulas are bound (quantified), and they are the only variables that can be quantified. Rigid variables are variables appearing in the label expressions and constraints of N. Rigid function and predicate symbols do not change their meanings during the executions of N. The set of rigid function and predicate symbols is defined in the *Spec* of N.

State Functions, Predicates, and Transitions

A *state function* is an expression built from values, state variables, rigid function, and predicate symbols. For example $[|p(c) + 1|]$ is a state function where c and 1 are values, p is a state variable, $+$ is a rigid function symbol. Since the meanings of rigid symbols are not affected by any state, thus for any given state M, $M[|p(c) + 1|] = M[|p(c)\ |] + 1$.

A *predicate* is a boolean-valued state function. A predicate p is said to be satisfied by a state M iff $M[|p|]$ is true.

A *transition* is a particular kind of predicates that contain primed state variables, for example, $[|p'(c) = p(c) + 1|]$. A transition relates two states (an old state and a new state), where the unprimed state variables refer to the old state and the primed state variables refer to the new state. Therefore, the meaning of a transition is a relation between states. The term transition used here is a *temporal logic* entity. Although it reflects the nature of a transition in a *PrT* net N, it is not a transition in N. For example, given a pair of states M and M': $M[|p'(c) = p(c) + 1|]M'$ is defined by $M'[|p'(c)\ |] =$

$M[|p(c)|] + 1$. Given a transition t, a pair of states M and M' is called a "transition step" iff $M[|t|]M'$ equals true. We can easily generalize any predicate p without primed state variables into a relation between states by replacing all unprimed state variables with their primed versions such that $M[|p'|]M'$ equals $M'[|p|]$ for any states M and M'.

Temporal Formulas

Temporal formulas are built from elementary formulas (predicates and transitions) using logical connectives $\neg$ and $\wedge$ (and derived logical connectives $\vee$, $\Rightarrow$, and $\Leftrightarrow$), universal quantifier $\forall$ and derived existential quantifier $\exists$, and temporal operators always , sometimes $\Diamond$, and until U.

The semantics of *temporal logic* is defined on behaviors (infinite sequences of states). The behaviors are obtained from the execution sequences of *PrT* nets where the last marking of a finite execution sequence is repeated infinitely many times at the end of the execution sequence. For example, for an execution sequence $M_0,...,M_n$, the following behavior $\sigma = <<M_0,...,M_n,M_n,...>>$ is obtained. We denote the set of all possible behaviors obtained from a given *PrT* net as $\mathbf{St}^\infty$.

Let u and v be two arbitrary temporal formulas, p be an n-ary predicate, t be a transition, x, $x_1,...,x_n$ be rigid variables, $\sigma = <<M_0, M_1, ... >>$ be a behavior, and $\sigma^k = <<M_k, M_{k+1}, ... >>$ be a k step shifted behavior sequence; we define the semantics of temporal formulas recursively as follows:

1. $\sigma[|p(x_1,...,x_n)|] \equiv M_0[|p(x_1,...,x_n)|]$
2. $\sigma[|t|] \equiv M_0[|t|]M_1$
3. $\sigma[|\neg u|] \equiv \neg \sigma[|u|]$
4. $\sigma[|u \wedge v|] \equiv \sigma[|u|] \wedge \sigma[|v|]$
5. $\sigma[|\forall x. u|] \equiv \forall x.\sigma[|u|]$

6. $\sigma[|u|] \equiv \forall n \in \mathbf{Nat}. \sigma^n[|u|]$
7. $\sigma[|uUv|] \equiv \exists k.\sigma^k[|v|] \wedge \forall 0 \leq n \leq k.\sigma^n[|u|]$

A temporal formula u is said to be *satisfiable*, denoted as $\sigma |= u$, iff there is an execution σ such that $\sigma[|u|]$ is true, i.e. $\sigma |= u \Leftrightarrow \exists \sigma \in \mathbf{St}^\infty. \sigma[|u|]$. u is *valid* with regard to N, denoted as $N |= u$, iff it is satisfied by all possible behaviors $\mathbf{St}^\infty$ from N: $N |= u \Leftrightarrow \forall \sigma \in \mathbf{St}^\infty. \sigma[|u|]$.

Defining System Properties in Temporal Logic

Specifying architecture properties in *SAM* becomes defining *PrT* net properties using *temporal logic*. Canonical forms for a variety of system properties such as safety, guarantee, obligation, response, persistence, and reactivity are given in Manna and Pnueli (1992). For example, the following *temporal logic* formulas specify a safety property and a liveness property of the *PrT* net in Figure 2, respectively:

- Mutual exclusion:
  $\forall ph \in \{1,...,k\} \neg(< ph, \_, \_ > \in Eating \wedge < ph \oplus 1, \_, \_ > \in Eating)$
  which defines that no adjacent philosophers can eat at the same time.
- Starvation freedom:
  $\forall ph \in \{1, ..., k\}\Diamond(< ph, \_, \_ > \in Eating)$,
  which states that every philosopher will eventually get a chance to eat.

FORMAL METHODS FOR DESIGNING SOFTWARE ARCHITECTURES

There are two distinct levels of *software architecture* specification development in *SAM*: element level and composition level. The element level specification deals with the specification of a single *component* or *connector*, and the composition level specification concerns how to combine (horizontal) specifications at the same abstraction level together and how to relate (vertical) specifications at different abstraction levels.

Developing Element Level Specifications

In *SAM*, each element (either a *component* or a *connector*) is specified by a tuple $<S, B>$. *S* is a *property specification*, written in *temporal logic*, that specifies the required properties of the element, and *B* is a *behavior model*, defined by a *PrT* net, that defines the behavior of the element. *S* and *B* can be viewed as the specification and the implementation respectively as in many other *software architecture* models such as Wright (Allen & Garlan, 1997). Therefore to develop the specification of an element is essentially to write *S* and *B*.

Although many existing techniques for writing *temporal logic* specifications (Lamport, 1994; Manna & Pnueli, 1992) and for developing *Petri nets* (He & Yang, 1992; Jensen, 1992; Reisig, 1992) may be directly used here. There are several unique features about $<S, B>$. First, *S* and *B* are related and constrain each other. Thus we have to develop either *S* or *B* with respect to a possibly existing *B* or *S*. Depending on our understanding of a given system; we can either develop *S* or *B* first. Second, the predicate symbols used in *S* are exterior (either input or out) ports of *B*. Third, *S* should in general be weaker than *B*, that is, *B* may satisfy more properties than *S*. Thus the view of implementation as implication is valid here. With these unique features in mind, we offer the following heuristics for developing *S* and *B*:

Heuristic 1: How to Write S

To define an element constraint, we can either directly formulate the given user requirements or carry out a cause effect analysis by viewing input ports as causes and output ports as effects. Canonical forms (Manna & Pnueli, 1992) for a variety of properties such as Safety, Guarantee, Obligation, Response, Persistence, and Reactivity are used as guidelines to define property specifications.

A simple example of applying Heuristic 1 is as follows. Let us consider a simple automated library system that supports typical transaction types such as checkout and return a book. A transaction is initiated with a user request that contains user identification, a book title, and a transaction type (checkout/return). The transaction is processed by updating the user record and the book record, and is finished by sending the user a message—either successful or a failure reason. One desirable property of an automated library system is that each request must be proposed. This property is a type of response property (Manna & Pnueli, 1992), and thus can be defined as $\forall(req).$ $(\Box(\text{Request}(req) \Rightarrow \Diamond\text{Response}(msg)))$, where *req* and *msg* stand for a request and message (Success or Failure) respectively, and Request and Response are predicate symbols, and must correspond to an input port and an output port respectively.

Heuristic 2: How to Develop B

We follow the general procedure proposed in He and Yang (1992) to develop B.

Step 1: Use all the input and output ports as places of B.

Step 2: Identify a list of events directly from the given user requirements or through Use Case analysis (Booch, Rumbaugh, & Jacobson, 1999).

Step 3: Represent each event with a simple PrT net.

Step 4: Merge all the PrT nets together through shared places to obtain B.

Step 5: Apply the transformation techniques (He & Lee, 1991) to make B more structured and / or meaningful.

Again, we use this simple library system as an example. We only provide a partial *behavior model* without the complete net inscription to illustrate the application of Heuristic 2. A more complete example of a *PrT* net specification of a library

Figure 3. (a) A PrT model of checkout; (b) A PrT model of return; (c) A connected PrT model; (d) A PrT model of checkout

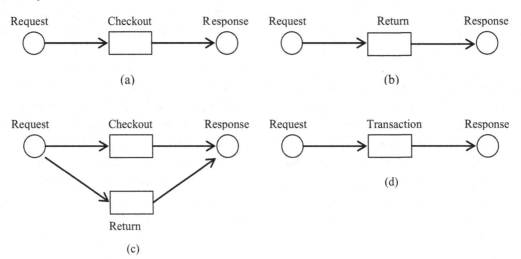

system can be found in He and Yang (1992). Since we developed a *property specification* first in this case and we identified an input port Request and an output port Response, we use them as places in the *behavior model B* according to Step 1. We can easily identify two distinct types of events: checkout and return. According to Step 3, we come up with the following two *PrT* nets Figures 3a and b, each of which models an event type. Figure 3c is obtained by merging shared places according Step 4, and Figure 3d is obtained by restructuring Figure 3c through combining Checkout and Return into a generic transaction type.

Developing Composition Level Specifications

SAM supports both top-down and bottom-up system development approaches. The top-down approach is used to develop a *software architecture* specification by decomposing a system specification into specifications of *components* and *connectors* and by refining a higher level *component* into a set of related sub-*components* and *connectors* at a lower level. The bottom-up approach is used to develop a *software architecture*

specification by composing existing specifications of *components* and *connectors* and by abstracting a set of related *components* and *connectors* into a higher level *component*. Thus the top-down approach can be viewed as the inverse process of the bottom-up approach. Often both the top-down approach and the bottom-up approach have to be used together to develop a *software architecture* specification.

Heuristic 3: How to Refine an Element Specification <S, B>

Step 1: Refining B:
A behavior model B may be refined in several ways, for example, structure driven refinement, in which several sub-components and their connectors are identified, or functionality driven refinement, in which several functional units can be identified. Although, we do not exactly know what refinement approaches are effective in general. One thing is for sure, that is, the input and output ports of the element must be maintained at a lower level. Petri net specific heuristics (He & Lee, 1991; He & Yang, 1992) may be

Figure 4. A refined PrT model of transactions

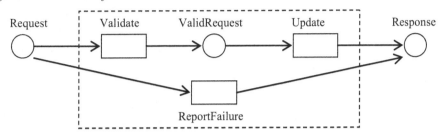

used to maintain the validity of resulting lower level B'. If only behavior-preserving transformations are used to obtain B' from B, we can assure the correctness of <S, B'> based on the correctness of <S, B>; otherwise new analysis is needed to ensure the satisfiability of S (He, 1998).

Step 2: Refining S:

Refining S into S' in general indicates the change of requirements (a special case is when S is logically equivalent to S'), and thus results in the change of B. Once S' is known, the new B' can be developed using the approach for developing element level specification. Not any S' can be taken as a refinement of S. We require that S' maintain S, which can be elegantly expressed as S' ⇒ S (Abadi & Lamport, 1991). Simple heuristics such as strengthening S always result in a valid refinement S'.

As an example, Figure 4 shows a possible refinement of transaction into two possible scenarios in the dotted box, one is for valid request and the other for invalid request. A corresponding refinement of the *property specification* is

$\forall(req).(\Box(\text{Request}(req) \land req \in \text{Valid} \Rightarrow \Diamond\text{Response}(\boldsymbol{S}))) \land$

$\forall(req).(\Box(\text{Request}(req) \land req \notin \text{Valid} \Rightarrow \Diamond\text{Response}(\boldsymbol{F})))$

where **S** and **F** stand for success and failure respectively. This refinement implies the original *property specification* and is thus a correct refinement according to Heuristic 3.

Heuristic 4: How to Compose Two Element Specifications <S_1, B_1> and <S_2, B_2>

In SAM, only a pair of related component and connector can be composed meaningfully.

Step 1: Compose B_1 and B_2 by merging identical ports.

Step 2: Compose S_1 and S_2 by conjoining $S_1 \land S_2$.

The soundness of viewing specification composition as logical conjunction has been shown by several researchers (Abadi & Lamport, 1993; Zave & Jackson, 1993).

If we view the two transaction types, Checkout and Return, in the preceding library example as two separate *components*, then Figure 3c illustrates the application of Heuristic 4.

Specify Element Instances

An element specification <S, B> obtained earlier is generic when the initial marking in B is ignored. In *PrT* net, instances sharing the same net structure are distinguished through token identifications.

Thus to obtain concrete elements, we only need to provide specific initial marking and generalize transition constraints to differentiate tokens with unique identifications. In general, there is no need to change the *property specification S*. For example, let B_1, B_2, and B_3 be three *PrT* nets with the same net structure and net inscription except the initial markings; then $<S, B_1>$, $<S, B_2>$, and $<S, B_3>$ are three element specifications. The above view shows the expressive power of *PrT* nets and first order *temporal logic* over that of low-level *Petri nets* and propositional *temporal logic*.

FORMAL SOFTWARE ARCHITECTURE ANALYSIS

Formal Analysis Techniques

A *SAM* architecture description is well-defined if the ports of a *component* are preserved (contained) in the set of exterior ports of its refinement and the proposition symbols used in a *property specification* are ports of the relevant *behavior model*(s). The correctness of a *SAM* architecture description is defined by the following criteria:

1. **Element (*Component/Connector*) Correctness:** The *property specification* S_{ij} holds in the corresponding *behavior model* B_{ij}, that is, $B_{ij} \models S_{ij}$. Note we use B_{ij} here to denote the set of behaviors or execution sequences defined by B_{ij}.
2. **Composition Correctness:** The conjunction of all constraints in Cs_i of C_i is implied by the conjunction of all the *property specifications* S_{ij} of C_{ij}, i.e. $\land S_{ij} \models \land Cs_i$. An alternative weaker but acceptable criterion is that the conjunction of all constraints in Cs_i holds in the integrated *behavior model* B_i of composition C_i; i.e. $B_i \models \land Cs_i$.
3. **Refinement Correctness:** The *property specification* S_{ij} of a *component* C_{ij} must be implied by the composition constraints

Cs_l of its refinement C_l with $C_l = h(C_{ij})$, that is, $\land Cs_l \models S_{ij}$. An alternative weaker but acceptable criterion is that S_{ij} holds in the integrated lower level *behavior model* B_l of C_l, that is, $B_l \models S_{ij}$.

The refinement correctness is equivalent to the composition correctness when the *property specification* S_{ij} is inherited without change as the composition constraint Cs_l of its refinement $C_l = h(C_{ij})$. This correctness criteria are the *verification* requirements of a *SAM* architecture description.

To ensure the correctness of a *software architecture* specification in *SAM*, we have to show that all the constraints are satisfied by the corresponding *behavior model*s. The *verification* of all three correctness criteria given can be done by demonstrating that a *property specification S* holds in a *behavior model B* and, that is, $B \models S$. The structure of *SAM* architecture specifications and the underlying *formal methods* of *SAM* nicely support an incremental formal analysis methodology such that the *verification* of above correctness criteria can be done hierarchically (vertically) and compositionally (horizontally).

Two well-established approaches to *verification* are *model checking* and theorem proving.

*   *Model checking* is a technique that relies on building a finite model of a system and checking that a desired property holds in that model. Roughly speaking, the check is performed as an exhaustive state space search that is guaranteed to terminate since the model is finite. The technical challenge in *model checking* is in devising algorithms and data structures that allow us to handle large search spaces. *Model checking* has been used primarily in hardware and protocol *verification* (Clarke & Kurshan, 1996); the current trend is to apply this technique to analyzing specifications of software systems.

- *Theorem proving* is a technique by which both the system and its desired properties are expressed as formulas in some mathematical logic. This logic is given by a *formal system*, which defines a set of axioms and a set of inference rules. Theorem proving is the process of finding a proof of a property from the axioms of the system. Steps in the proof appeal to the axioms and rules, and possibly derived definitions and intermediate lemmas. Although proofs can be constructed by hand, here we focus only on machine-assisted theorem proving. Theorem provers are increasingly being used today in the mechanical *verification* of safety-critical properties of hardware and software designs.

Element Level Analysis

For each $<S_{ij}, B_{ij}>$ in composition C_i, we need to show that B_{ij} satisfies S_{ij}, that is, $B_{ij} \models S_{ij}$. Both *model checking* and theorem proving techniques are applicable to element level analysis. In the following, we briefly introduce *model checking* technique by *reachability tree* (Murata, 1989), and theorem proving technique by *temporal logic* (He, 1995, 2001).

Model Checking

A *reachability tree* is an unfolding of a *PrT* net, which explicitly enumerates all possible markings

or states that the *behavior model* B_{ij} generates. The nodes of a *reachability tree* are reachable markings and directed edges represent feasible transitions (Murata, 1989). The main advantage of *reachability tree* technique is that the tree can be automatically generated. Once the tree is generated, different system properties can be analyzed. The main problem is space explosion when a *PrT* net has too many reachable states or even infinite reachable states. One possible way to deal with this problem is to truncate the tree whenever a marking is covered by a new marking and this results in a variant of *reachability tree*s called coverability trees. In this case, information loss is unavoidable. Thus this technique may not work in some cases. The following heuristic provides some guidelines to use the *reachability tree* analysis technique.

The basic idea of *model checking* technique for element level analysis is: (1) generating a *reachability tree* from B_{ij}; and (2) evaluating S_{ij} using the generated reachability or coverability tree. It should be noted that when a formula contains an always operator □, the formula needs to be evaluated in all nodes of the tree before a conclusion can be made.

As an example, we use the simple library system given in Figure 4 with the assumption of one valid token *req1* and one invalid token *req2* in place Request. When transition Update receives a valid request, it updates the user and book records, and generates a response *S* denoting success. When transition ReportFailure receives

Figure 5. The reachability tree of Figure 4

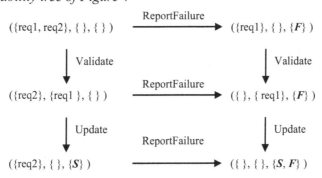

an invalid request, it produces a failure message ***F***. The resulting *reachability tree* of Step (1) is shown in Figure 5.

Based on Step (2), it is easy to see that the following *property specification*

$$\forall(req).(\square\,(\text{Request}(req) \wedge req \in \text{Valid} \Rightarrow \lozenge\text{Response}(\boldsymbol{S})))$$

is satisfied in the *reachability tree* by all three possible paths: Validate—Update, ReportFailure—Validate—Update, and Validate—ReportFailure—Update. Similarly, we can evaluate the following *property specification*: $\forall(req).(\square\,(\text{Request}(req) \wedge req \notin \text{Valid} \Rightarrow \lozenge\text{Response}(\boldsymbol{F})))$.

Theorem Proving

The basic idea is to axiomatize B_{ij} (He & Ding, 1992; He & Lee, 1990) and then use the obtained axiom system to prove S_{ij}, that is, Axiom(B_{ij}) $\vdash$ S_{ij}. The axiom system consists of general system independent axioms and inference rules and system dependent axioms and inference rules (Manna & Pnueli, 1983). Each transition in B_{ij} generates a system dependent *temporal logic* rule that captures the causal relationships between the input places and output places of the transition. The canonical form of system dependent inference rules has the form: *fired*(t/M) $\Rightarrow$ *enabled*(t/M), where t is a transition, M is a given marking. *Fired* and *Enabled* are two predicates representing the post-condition and precondition of t under M respectively. The advantage of this technique is that a syntactic approach rather than a semantic approach is used in *verification*. Since no explicit representation of states is needed, there is no space explosion problem as in the *reachability tree* technique. The main problems are that the technique is often difficult to automate and its application requires substantial knowledge of first order *temporal logic* and general knowledge of theorem proof.

To demonstrate the application of this heuristic, we axiomatize the net structure in Figure 4, and

the resulting system dependent inference rules after Step 1 are:

1. $\neg\quad M[\,|\,\mathrm{V\,a\,l\,i\,d\,R\,e\,q\,u\,e\,s\,t}(x)\,|\,]\quad \wedge$ $M'[|\text{ValidRequest}(x)|] \Rightarrow M[|\text{Request}(x)|] \wedge$ $M[|R(\text{Validate})|]$

2. $\neg M[|\text{Response}(\boldsymbol{S})|] \wedge M'[|\text{Response}(\boldsymbol{S})|] \Rightarrow$ $M[|\text{ValidRequest}(x)|] \wedge M[|R(\text{Update})|]$

3. $\neg M[|\text{Response}(\boldsymbol{F})|] \wedge M'[|\text{Response}(\boldsymbol{F})|] \Rightarrow$ $M[|\text{Request}(x)|] \wedge M[|R(\text{ReportFailure})|]$

In these inference rules, M and M' stand for a given marking and its successor marking, respectively. $R(t)$ is the constraint associated with transition t. To prove *property specification*

$$\forall(req).(\square\,(\text{Request}(req) \wedge req \in \text{Valid} \Rightarrow \lozenge\text{Response}(\boldsymbol{S})))$$

We instantiate $\lozenge$ to a marking M' and apply rule (2) to obtain $M[|\text{ValidRequest}(x)|]$, and we apply rule (1) to obtain $M[|\text{Request}(x)|]$. With some simple logical manipulations, we can easily deduce the required property.

Composition Analysis

We need to show that the connected *behavior model* B_i (again a *PrT* net) of composition C_i obtained from all the individual *behavior models* B_{ij} ($j = 1,...,k$) of *components* and *connectors* satisfies all the constraints $\wedge\, c$ in Cs_i, that is, B_i $\models \underset{c \in Cs_i}{\wedge} c$. Due to the *SAM* framework, the analysis techniques at element level can be directly applied here. This global approach works in general, but may not be efficient.

An ideal approach is to carry out the composition level analysis compositionally. In this approach, we first analyze *components* and *connectors* individually, that is, $B_{ij} \models S_{ij}$ for all *components* and *connectors* in a composition C_i, and then synthesize the properties, that is, $\wedge\, S_{ij} \vdash \underset{c \in Cs_i}{\wedge} c$. Despite some existing results on compositional *verification* techniques in *temporal logic* (Abadi & Lamport, 1993) and *Petri nets* (Juan, Tsai, & Murata, 1998), their general use and application to *SAM* are not ready yet.

The following is a modest yet effective incremental analysis approach.

Step 1: Identify partial order relationships among the *components* and *connectors* based on their causal relationships.

Step 2: Compose and analyze the *components* and *connectors* in a partial order incrementally, starting from the least element (most independent).

Step 3: Compose and analyze mutually dependent *components* and *connectors* together.

Step 4: Once we have shown that the initial condition or marking used to prove every individual element can be ensured by the composed *behavior model*, then we can conclude that all the *property specifications* hold simultaneously.

To illustrate the ideas of this approach, let us view the refined *PrT* model of transactions in Figure 4 as a composition, which consists of three trivial *components* Request, ValidRequest, and Response, and three trivial *connectors* Validate, Update, and ReportFailure. Based on the *PrT* net structure, we can identify the following incremental analysis order:

1. (Request, Validate, ValidateRequest);
2. (ValidateRequest, Update, Response);
3. (Request, Validate, ValidateRequest, Update, Response);
4. (Request, ReportFailure, Response).

where #4 is independent of the first three analyses.

To further improve the effectiveness of this approach, we are working on some Petri net reduction techniques such that the *behavior models* used in incremental analysis are simplified versions of the original *behavior models*.

Refinement Analysis

For each *component* $C_{ij} = <S_{ij}, B_{ij}>$ with $h(C_{ij}) = C_l$, we need to show that either the connected *behavior model* B_l of composition C_l satisfies S_{ij}, that is, $B_l \models S_{ij}$ or alternatively $\land Cs_l \vdash S_{ij}$. Three techniques discussed in element analysis can be used to show $B_l \models S_{ij}$. Formal temporal deduction technique (He & Ding, 1992, He, 1995) can be used to prove $\land Cs_l \vdash S_{ij}$.

As an example, if we view Figure 4 as a refinement of Figure 3d. We can easily prove the following to assure the correctness of the refinement:

$\forall(req).(\Box(\text{Request}(req) \land req \in \text{Valid} \Rightarrow \Diamond\text{Response}(S))) \land \forall(req).(\Box(\text{Request}(req) \land req \notin \text{Valid} \Rightarrow \Diamond\text{Response}(F))) \vdash \forall(req). (\Box(\text{Request}(req) \Rightarrow \Diamond\text{Response}(msg)))$.

Studying Dependability Attributes Using SAM

We have studied a variety of functional properties and several non-functional dependability attributes at *software architecture* level using *SAM* (He & Deng, 2002; Wang, He, & Deng, 1999). We have applied *SAM* to specify and analyze schedulability (Xu, He, & Deng, 2002), performance including end-to-end latency (Shi & He, 2003a; Wang & Deng, 1999; Yu, He, Gao, & Deng, 2002), security (Deng, Wang, Beznosov, & Tsai, 2003; He & Deng, 2002), fault-tolerance (Shi & He, 2002), reliability (Shi & He, 2003a, 2003b), and many other functional behavior properties such as deadlock and response (He & Deng, 2002; He, Ding, & Deng, 2002; He, Yu, Shi, Ding, & Deng, 2004; Shi & He, 2002).

Since several Petri net models and *temporal logics* as well as a variety of formal analysis techniques were used to specify and verify these system architectures and dependability attributes. Here we just briefly mentioned our approach without providing technical details.

- End-to-End Latency

  In Wang et al. (1999), time *Petri nets* (Berthomieu & Diaz, 1991) and real-time computational tree logic (*CTL*) (Emerson, Mok, Sistla, & Srinivasian, 1992) were used to specify the *software architecture* of a control and command system. End-to-end latency was then verified by generating a *reachability tree* from the time Petri net model and evaluating timing properties specified in real-time *CTL* formulas. We also used stochastic *Petri nets* to study latency (Shi & He, 2003a).

- Schedulability

  In Yu et al (2002), predicate transition nets (*PrT* nets) (Murata, 1989) and first-order linear-time *temporal logic* (*FOLTTL*) (Manna & Pnueli, 1992) were used to specify the *software architecture* of a simplified multi-media system. Timing requirements were dealt with by adding a time stamp attribute in tokens and by adding lower and upper bounds in transition constraints in predicate transition nets. Timing properties were specified in first-order *temporal logic* formulas by an additional clock variable. *Verification* of schedulability was again done using the theorem prover *STeP*.

- Security

  In He and Deng (2002), *PrT* nets and *FOLTTL* were used to specify the *software architecture* of an access authorization subsystem. Several system *component*s were explicitly modeled to handle security check process. Security policies were defined as part of transition constraints within these security-checking *component*s. Security related properties were specified using *FOLTTL*. *Verification* of security properties was done using *reachability tree* technique at the *component* level and using theorem proving at the composition level.

- Fault-Tolerance

In Shi and He (2002), *PrT* nets and *FOLTTL* were used to specify the *software architecture* a communication protocol. To handle possible communication faults such as loss of information, additional system timer *component*s were introduced to detect such losses. Fault-related properties were specified using *FOLTTL* and were verified using the symbolic model checker *SMV* (McMillan, 1993).

- Reliability

  In Shi and He (2003a, 2003b), *PrT* nets were used to model a *software architecture*. *PrT* nets were then unfolded into stochastic reward nets (SRNs). Probabilistic real-time Computation Tree Logic (*PCTL*) (Hansson & Johnson, 1994) was used to specify system reliability. The probability of system failure was then calculated using tool SPNP (Trivedi, 1999) in Shi and He (2003a) and tool SMART (Ciardo, Jones, Marmorstein, Miner, & Siminiceanu, 2002) in Shi and He (2003b).

RELATED WORK

Many *formal methods* have been developed and applied to specifying and verifying complex software systems. For example, Z (Spivey, 1992) was used to specify *software architecture* (Abowd, Allen, & Garlan, 1995), CSP (Hoare, 1985) was used as the foundation of Wright (Allen & Garlan, 1997), and CHAM (Inverardi, & Wolf, 1995) (an operational formalism) was proposed to specify *software architecture*s. Rapide (Luckham, Kenney, Augustin et al., 1995) used a multiple language approach in specifying *software architecture*s, while some language has a well-defined formal foundation (for example the specification language uses a combination of algebraic and pattern constraints), others offer constructs similar to those in a typical high-level programming language.

Two complementary *formal methods*, *Petri nets* and *temporal logic*, are used in *SAM* to define *behavior model*s and *property specification*s respectively. The selection of these *formal methods* is based on the following reasons. Well-known model-oriented *formal methods* include *Petri nets* and finite state machines. Finite state machines are simple, but have difficulty to deal with concurrent systems especially distributed systems. *Petri nets* are well suited for modeling concurrent and distributed systems, which characterize the majority of embedded systems being used by NASA and other government agencies. However, *Petri nets* are often misunderstood and even prejudiced in the U.S. Many researchers' knowledge of *Petri nets* is limited to the 1st generation low-level *Petri nets* used primarily for modeling control flows. *Petri nets* have evolved tremendously in the past 20 years, from the 2nd generation high-level *Petri nets* in 1980s (Jensen & Rozenberg, 1991) and the 3rd generation hierarchical and modular *Petri nets* in early 1990s (He, 1996; He & Lee, 1991; Jensen, 1992) to the 4th generation object-oriented *Petri nets* in late 1990s (Agha, De Cindio, & Rozenberg, 2001). More importantly, *Petri nets* have been extended in many different ways to study system performance, reliability, and schedulability (Haas, 2002; Marsan, Balbo, Conte, Donatelli, & Franceschinis, 1994; Wang, 1998), which are the central attributes of complex dependable systems. There are vast existing research results on *Petri nets* (over 10,000 publications). Despite many different types of *temporal logic*, for example, propositional vs. first-order, linear time vs. branch time, timed vs. un-timed, probabilistic vs. non-probabilistic, it is widely accepted that *temporal logic* in general is an excellent property-oriented formal method for specifying behavioral properties of concurrent systems. We are familiar with and have extensive experience in using Manna and Pnueli's (1992, 1995) linear-time first order *temporal logic*; Lamport's (1994) linear-time first order *temporal logic* (*Temporal Logic* of Actions); and Clarke and Emerson's

(1981) branch time propositional logic *CTL,* and its extension *CTL** (Clarke, Emerson, & Sistla, 1986); and various timed versions of the above *temporal logic*s (Abadi & Lamport, 1994; Alur & Henzinger, 1992; Emerson et al., 1992). One major problem of using a dual-formalism is how to integrate two *formal methods* in a consistent and meaningful way, our own research results (He, 1992; He & Ding, 1992; He & Lee, 1990) and other's work (Mandrioli, Morzenti, Pezze, Pietro, & Silva, 1996) have provided a satisfactory solution to integrate *Petri nets* and *temporal logic* in *SAM.*

Almost all ADLs support the specification and analysis of major system functional properties such as safety and liveness properties (Medvidovic & Taylor, 2000). Several ADLs also provide capabilities to represent some dependability attributes. MetaH (Binns, Engelhart, Jackson, & Vestal, 1996) supported the description of non-functional properties such as real-time schedulability, reliability, and security in *components* but not in *connectors*. Unicon (Shaw, Deline, Klein et al., 1995) supported the definition of real-time schedulability in both *components* and *connectors*. Rapide (Luckham et al., 1995) supported the modeling of time constraints in architectural configurations. The analysis of non-functional properties in these ADLs was not performed at the architecture specification level instead of during the simulation and implementation. As pointed out in Stavridou and Riemenschneider (1998), "ADLs need to be extended with appropriate linguistic support for expressing dependability constraints. They also need to be furnished with an appropriate semantics, to enable formal *verification* of architectural properties."

DISCUSSION AND CONCLUSION

Commercial pressure to produce higher quality software is always increasing. *Formal methods* have already demonstrated success in specifying commercial and safety-critical software, and in verifying protocol standards and hardware designs. In this chapter, we have provided a well-defined integration of two well-known *formal methods* predicate transition nets and first order linear-time *temporal logic* as the foundation for writing *software architecture* specifications in *SAM*. This dual *formal methods* approach supports both behavioral modeling and property analysis of *software architecture*s. Unlike many other architecture description language research efforts that primarily focus on the representation issues of *software architecture*s, we have further presented a unified framework with a set of heuristics to develop and analyze *software architecture* specifications in *SAM*. The heuristics are supported by well-developed existing techniques and methods with potential software tool assistance. We have demonstrated the applications of several of the heuristics with regard to the development and analysis in a non-trivial example. Our contributions are not limited to *software architecture* research, but also shed some light on how mature *formal methods* can be effectively used in real-world software development. While it is true that every formal method has its limits and weaknesses, it is important to rely on its strengths while avoiding and minimizing its weaknesses in practical applications. This philosophy has been used both in designing our dual *formal methods* foundation of *SAM* as well as our framework consisting of a variety of development and analysis techniques.

From our own experience in teaching and using formal methods, students can learn system modeling using high-level *Petri nets* and specification using first order *temporal logic* in a one semester course. The first author has taught these materials in several software engineering related courses in the past 15 years, and has found that the majority students can master the methods without major problems. Therefore, we are quite convinced that the *SAM* approach is practical and effective. Furthermore, we have applied *SAM* to

model and analyze the *software architecture*s of several systems, including a control and command system (Wang et al., 1999), a flexible manufacturing system (Wang & Deng, 1999), popular architectural *connector*s (He & Deng, 2000), the alternating bit communication protocol, and a resource access decision system (He & Deng, 2002). More recently, we are using *SAM* to model and analyze a middleware architecture for delivering a variety of multimedia applications based on various internet communication protocols. We have developed methods to translate Petri net models into state transition systems based on several popular model checkers including *SMV* (McMillan, 1993), *STeP* (Bjorner et al., 1995), and *SPIN* (Holzmann, 2003) for property analysis. These translation algorithms are linear to the size of given Petri net models and translations can be automated. The complexity of analysis is largely dependent on given properties. In our own experience, architecture level properties are relative simple and can be effectively checked using these model checkers.

We are carrying out more case studies to explore the effectiveness of combining different development and analysis techniques and to determine the practical limitations of each individual technique. To support this whole *SAM* framework, we are adding software *component*s to our existing *SAM* environment, which consists of a graphical editor for building behavioral models, a textual editor for defining *property specification*s, a simulator to execute behavioral models, and a translator to covert a *behavior model* in *Petri nets* into a Promela program in model checker *SPIN* for property analysis.

ACKNOWLEDGMENT

This research was supported in part by the National Science Foundation of the USA under grant HRD-0317692, and by the National Aeronautics and Space Administration of the USA under grant NAG2-1440. Huiqun Yu's work was also partially supported by the NSF of China under grant No. 60473055.

REFERENCES

Abadi, M., & Lamport, L. (1991). The existence of refinement mappings. *Theoretical Computer Science, 82*, 253-284.

Abadi, M., & Lamport, L. (1993). Composing specification. *ACM Trans. on Programming Languages and Systems, 15*, 73-130.

Abadi, M., & Lamport, L. (1994). An old-fashioned recipe for real time. *ACM Transactions on Programming Languages and Systems, 16*(5), 1543-1571.

Abowd, G., Allen, R., & Garlan, D. (1995). Formalizing style to understand descriptions of software architecture. *ACM Transaction on Software Engineering and Methodology, 4*(4), 319-364.

Agha, G., De Cindio, F., & Rozenberg, G. (Eds.) (2001).Concurrent object-oriented programming and Petri nets – Advances in Petri nets. *Lecture Notes in Computer Science, 2001*. Berlin: Springer Verlag.

Allen, R., & Garlan, D. (1997). A formal basis for architectural connection. *ACM Transaction on Software Engineering and Methodology, 6*(3), 213-249.

Alur, R., & Henzinger, T. (1992). Logics and models of real time: a survey. *Lecture Notes in Computer Science, 600*, 74-106.

Berthomieu, B., & Diaz, M. (1991). Modeling and verification of time dependent systems using time Petri nets. *IEEE Trans. Software Engineering, 17*(3), 259-273.

Binns, P., Engelhart, M., Jackson, M., & Vestal, S. (1996). Domain-specific software architectures for guidance, navigation, and control. *International Journal of Software Engineering and Knowledge Engineering, 6*(2), 201-228.

Bjorner, N. et al. (1995, November). *Step: The Stanford temporal prover – User's manual.* Technical Report STAN-CS-TR-95-1562, Department of Computer Science, Stanford University.

Booch, G., Rumbaugh, J., & Jacobson, I. (1999). *The unified modeling language – User guide.* Reading, MA: Addison Wesley.

Ciardo, G., Jones, R., Marmorstein, R., Miner, A., & Siminiceanu, R. (2002). SMART: stochastics model-checking analyzer for reliability and timing. In the *Proc. of Int'l Conf. on Dependable Systems and Networks,* Bethesda, MD, June. Los Alamitos, CA: IEEE Computer Society Press.

Clarke, E., & Emerson, E. (1981). Characterizing properties of parallel programs as fixpoints. *Lecture Notes in Computer Science, 85*.

Clarke, E., Emerson, E., & Sistla, A. (1986). Automatic verification of finite-state concurrent systems using temporal logic specifications. *ACM Trans. on Programming Languages and Systems, 8*(2), 244-263.

Clarke, E., Grumberg, O., & Peled, D. (1999). *Model checking.* Cambridge, MA: MIT Press.

Clarke, E., & Kurshan, R. (1996). Computer-aided verification. *IEEE Spectrum, 33*(6), 61-67.

Clarke, E., & Wing, J. (1996). Formal methods: state of the art and future. *ACM Computing Surveys, 28*(4), 626-643.

Craigen, D., Gerhart, S., & Ralston, T. (1995). Formal methods reality check: Industrial usage. *IEEE Trans. On Software Engineering, 21*(2), 90-98.

Deng, Y., Wang, J., Beznosov, K., & Tsai, J. P. (2003). An approach for modeling and analysis of security system architectures. *IEEE Transactions on Knowledge and Data Engineering, 15*(5), 1099-119.

Emerson, E., Mok, A., Sistla, A., & Srinivasian, J. (1992). Quantitative temporal reasoning. *Real-Time Systems, 4*, 331-352.

Haas, P. (2002). *Stochastic Petri nets: Modeling, stability, simulation.* Berlin, Germany: Springer-Verlag.

Hansson, H., & Johnson, B. (1994). A logic for reasoning about time and reliability. *Formal Aspects of Computing, 6*(4), 512-535.

Harel, D. (1987). Statecharts: A visual formalism for complex systems. *Science of Computer Programming, 8*, 231-274.

He, X. (1992). Temporal predicate transition nets – A new formalism for specifying and verifying concurrent systems. *International Journal of Computer Mathematics, 45*(1/2), 171-184.

He, X. (1995). A method for analyzing properties of hierarchical predicate transition nets. In the *Proc. of the 19th Annual International Computer Software and Applications Conference,* Dallas, Texas, August (pp. 50-55). Los Alamitos, CA: IEEE Computer Society Press.

He, X. (1996). A formal definition of hierarchical predicate transition nets. *Lecture Notes in Computer Science, 1091*, 212-229.

He, X. (1998). Transformations on hierarchical predicate transition nets: Abstractions and refinements. In the *Proc. of the 22nd International Computer Software and Application Conference,* Vienna, Austria, August (pp.164-169). Los Alamitos, CA: IEEE Computer Society Press.

He, X. (2001). PZ nets – A formal method integrating Petri nets with Z. *Information and Software Technology, 43*, 1-18.

He, X., & Deng, Y. (2000). Specifying software architectural connectors in SAM. *International Journal of Software Engineering and Knowledge Engineering, 10*, 411-432.

He, X., & Deng, Y. (2002). A framework for developing and analyzing software architecture specifications in SAM. *The Computer Journal, 45*(1), 111-128.

He, X., & Ding, Y. (1992). A temporal logic approach for analyzing safety properties of predicate transition nets. In V. Leewun (Ed.), *Information processing'92* (pp.127-133). Amsterdam: North Holland.

He, X., Ding, J., & Deng, Y. (2002). Analyzing SAM architectural specifications using model checking. In the *Proc. of SEKE2002,* Italy, June (pp.271-274). Skokie, IL: Knowledge Systems Institute.

He, X., & Lee, J. A. N. (1990). Integrating predicate transition nets and first order temporal logic in the specification of concurrent systems. *Formal Aspects of Computing, 2*(3), 226-246.

He, X., & Lee, J. A. N. (1991). A methodology for constructing predicate transition net specifications. *Software – Practice & Experience, 21*, 845-875.

He, X., & Yang, C. (1992). Structured analysis using hierarchical predicate transition nets. In the *Proc. of the 16th Int'l Computer Software and Applications Conf.,* Chicago, IL, September (pp.212-217). Los Alamitos, CA: IEEE Computer Society Press.

He, X., Yu, H., Shi, T., Ding, J., & Deng, Y. (2004). Formally analyzing software architectural specifications using SAM. *Journal of Systems and Software, 71*(1-2), 11-29.

Hoare, C. A. R. (1985). *Communicating sequential processes.* London, UK: Prentice-Hall.

Holzmann, G. (2003). *The SPIN model checker: Primer and reference manual.* Boston, MA: Addison Wesley.

Inverardi, P., & Wolf, A. (1995). Formal specification and analysis of software architectures using the chemical abstract machine model. *IEEE Transaction on Software Engineering, 21*(4), 373-386.

Jensen, K. (1992). *Coloured Petri nets.* Berlin: Springer-Verlag.

Jensen, K., & Rozenberg, G. (Eds.) (1991). *High-level Petri nets – Theory and applications.* Berlin, Germany: Springer Verlag.

Juan, E., Tsai, J. P., & Murata, T. (1998). Compositional verification of concurrent systems using Petri-net-based condensation rules. *ACM Transactions on Programming Languages and Systems, 20*(5), 917-979

Kazman, R., Klein, M., & Clements, P. (2000). *ATAM: A method for architectural evaluation.* Software Engineering Institute Technical Report CMU/SEI-2000-TR-004, Carnegie-Mellon University.

Knight, J. (2002). Dependability of embedded systems. In the *Proc. of ICSE'02,* Orlando, FL, May (pp.685-686). New York: ACM Press.

Lamport, L. (1994). The temporal logic of actions. *ACM Transactions on Programming Languages and Systems, 16*(3), 872-923.

Luckham, D., Kenney, J., & Augustin, L. et al. (1995). Specification and analysis of system architecture using Rapide. *IEEE Transaction on Software Engineering, 21*(4), 336-355.

Mandrioli, D., Morzenti, A., Pezze, M., Pietro, P. S., & Silva, S. (1996). A Petri net and logic approach to the specification and verification of real time systems. In *Formal methods for real time computing.* Hoboken, NJ: John Wiley & Sons.

Manna, Z., & Pnueli, A. (1983). How to cook a temporal proof system for your pet language. In the *Proc. Of the 10th ACM Symp. On Principle of Programming Languages,* Austin, TX, January (pp.141-154). New York: ACM Press.

Manna, Z., & Pnueli, A. (1992). *The temporal logic of reactive and concurrent systems – Specification.* Berlin: Springer-Verlag.

Manna, Z., & Pnueli, A. (1995). *The temporal verification of reactive systems – Safety.* Berlin: Springer-Verlag.

Marsan, M., Balbo, G., Conte, G., Donatelli, S., & Franceschinis, G. (1994). *Modeling with generalized stochastic Petri nets.* Hoboken, NJ: John Wiley and Sons.

McMillan, K. (1993). *Symbolic model checking.* Boston: Kluwer Academic Publishers.

Medvidovic, N., & Taylor, R. (2000). A classification and comparison framework for software architecture description languages. *IEEE Transaction on Software Engineering, 26*(1), 70-93.

Milner, R. (1989). *Communication and concurrency.* London, UK: Prentice-Hall.

Murata, T. (1989). Petri nets, properties, analysis and applications. *Proc. of IEEE, 77*(4), 541-580.

Reisig, W. (1992). *A primer in Petri net design.* Berlin: Springer-Verlag.

Shaw, M., Deline, R., & Klein, D. et al. (1995). Abstractions for software architecture and tools to support them. *IEEE Trans. on Software Eng., 21*(4), 314-335.

Shaw, M., & Garlan, D. (1996). *Software architecture.* Upper Saddle River, NJ: Prentice-Hall.

Shi, T., & He, X. (2002). Modeling and analyzing the software architecture of a communication protocol using SAM. In J. Bosch et al. (Eds.), *Proc. of the 3rd Working IEEE/IFIP Conference on Software Architecture,* Montreal, Canada, August (pp. 63-78). Boston, MA: Kluwer Academic Publishers.

Shi, T., & He, X. (2003a). Dependability analysis using SAM. In the *Proc. of the ICSE Workshop on*

Software Architectures for Dependable Systems, Portland, Oregon, May (pp. 37-42).

Shi, T., & He, X. (2003b). A methodology for dependability and performability analysis in SAM. In the *Proc. of the International Conference on Dependable Systems and Networks,* San Francisco, CA, June (pp. 679-688). Los Alamitos, CA: IEEE Computer Society Press.

Spivey, J. (1992). *Z reference manual.* London, UK: Prentice-Hall.

Stavridou, V., & Riemenschneider, R. (1998). Provably dependable software architectures. In the *Proc. of 3rd International Software Architecture Workshop,* Orlando, FL, November (pp. 133-136).

Trivedi, K. (1999). *SPNP User's Manual, version 6.0.* Department of ECE, Duke University.

Wang, J. (1998). *Timed Petri nets, theory and application.* Boston, MA: Kluwer Academic Publisher.

Wang, J., & Deng, Y. (1999). Incremental modeling and verification of flexible manufacturing systems. *Journal of Intelligent Manufacturing, 10*(6), 485-502.

Wang, J., He, X., & Deng, Y. (1999). Introducing software architecture specification and analysis in SAM through an example. *Information and Software Technology, 41,* 451-467.

Wing, J. (1990). A specifier's introduction to formal methods. *IEEE Computer, 23*(9), 8-24.

Xu, D., He, X., & Deng, Y. (2002). Compositional schedulability analysis of real-time systems using time Petri nets. *IEEE Trans. On Software Engineering, 28*(10), 984-996.

Yu, H., He, X., Gao, S., & Deng, Y. (2002). Modeling and analyzing SMIL documents in SAM. In the *Proc. of Fourth IEEE International Symposium on Multimedia Software Engineering,* Newport Beach, CA, December (pp. 132-139). Los Alamitos, CA: IEEE Computer Society Publishing.

Zave, P., & Jackson, M. (1993). Conjunction as composition. *ACM Transaction on Software Engineering and Methodology, 2*(4), 379-411.

This work was previously published in Advances in Machine Learning Applications in Software Engineering, edited by D. Zhang; J. Tsai, pp. 319-345, copyright 2007 by IGI Publishing (an imprint of IGI Global).

Compilation of References

Abdallah, S., & Lesser, V. (2005). Modeling task allocation using a decision theoretic model. In *Proceedings of the Fourth international Joint Conference on Autonomous Agents and Multiagent Systems* (The Netherlands, July 25 - 29, 2005). AAMAS '05. ACM, New York, NY, (pp. 719-726).

Abrial, J. R. (1974). Data semantics. In J. W. Klimbie & K. L. Koffemen (Eds.), *Data base management* (pp. 1–59). Amsterdam: North-Holland.

Aizamil, Z. (2005). Towards an effective software engineering course project, *ICSE'05*, St. Louis, Missouri, USA, 631–632.

Albayrak, O. (2003). Proposals to contribute computer engineers education (in Turkish), *Proceedings of the first. Elektrik Elektronik Bilgisayar Mühendislikleri Eğitimi Sempozyumu ve Sergisi (pp. 220-221)*, Ankara, Turkey.

Albayrak, O. (2007). Experiences of teaching systems analysis and design to undergraduate software engineers, *A ISSIGSAND* 2007, (pp. 109–115), Sopot, Poland.

Albayrak, O. (2007). Software engineering education: Experience and applications of requirements determination and analysis phases (in Turkish) *Proceedings of the third National Software Engineering Symposium, UYMS 2007*, (pp. 15–18), Ankara, Turkey.

Ambler, S. W. (2005). *The Elements of UML 2.0 Style*. Cambridge: Cambridge University Press.

Ambler, S. W. (last updated 2006). *Introduction to class normalization*. Retrieved 2008, from http://www.agiledata.org

Archer, C. B. (1985). A realistic approach to teaching systems analysis at the small or medium-sized college, *ACM SIGCSE Bulletin, Proceedings of the sixteenth SIGCSE technical symposium on Computer science education SIGCSE '85*, 17,1, 105–108.

Ariadne Training (2001). *UML Applied – Object Oriented Analysis and Design using the UML*. Ariadne Training Limited.

Ashforth, B. E., & Mael, F. (1989). Social identity Theory and the Organization. *Academy of Management Review, 14*(1), 20-39.

Avison, D. E., Wood-Harper, A. T., Vidgen, R. T., & Wood, J. R. G. (1998). A further exploration into information systems development: The evolution of multiview2. *Information Technology & People, 11*(2), 124-139.

Bagert, D. J. (1998). The challenge of curriculum modeling for an emerging discipline: software engineering, *Frontiers in Education Conference, FIE '98. 28th Annual, 2*, 910–915.

Bagert, D. J., Hilburn, T. B., Hislop, G. W., & Mengel, S. A. (1998). Guidelines for software education: meeting the needs of the 21st Century, *Frontiers in Education Conference, 1998. FIE '98. 28th Annual, 2*, 909.

Barki, H., & Hartwick, J. (1989). Rethinking the concept of user involvement. *MIS Quarterly 13*(1), 53-64.

Baskerville, R., & Pries-Heje, J. (2001). Racing the e-bomb: How the internet is redefining information systems development methodology. In N. L. Russo, B. Fitzgerald & J. I. DeGross (Eds.), *Realigning research and practice in information systems development: The social and organizational perspective. Ifip wg8.2 conference, boise, idaho, usa, 27-29 july 2001* (pp. 49-68). Boston: Kluwer Academic Publishers.

Baskerville, R., & Pries-Heje, J. (2004). Short cycle time systems development. *Information Systems Journal, 14*(3), 237-264.

Batini, C., Ceri, S., & Navathe, S. B. (1992). *Conceptual database design: An entity-relationship approach*: The Benjamin/Cummings Publishing Company.

Bergamaschi, S., & Sartori, C. (1998). *Chrono: A conceptual design framework for temporal entities.* Paper presented at the 17th International Conference on Conceptual Modeling, Singapore.

Bertino, E., Bettini, C., Ferrari, E., & Samarati, P. (1998). An access control model supporting periodicity constraints and temporal reasoning. *ACM Transactions on Database Systems, 23*(3), 231-285.

Bettini, C., Jajodia, S., & Wang, S. X. (2000). *Time granularities in databases, data mining, and temporal reasoning*: Springer-Verlag.

Bhattacharya, C. B., Rao, H., & Glynn, M. A. (1995). Understanding the Bond of Identification: An Investigation of its Correlates Among Art Museum Members. *Journal of Marketing, 59*(4), 46-57.

Boehm, B. (2006). A view of 20th and 21st Century Software Engineering, *ICSE'06*, Shanghai, China, (pp. 12–29).

Booch G., Rumbaugh J., & Jacobson I. (1999). *UML user guide*. Addison Wesley.

Booch, G., Rumbaugh, J., & Jacobson, I. (2004). *The UML Reference Manual*. 2nd Edition. Boston: Addison-Wesley.

Bostrom, R. P., & Heinen, J. S. (1977). Mis problems and failures: A socio-technical perspective, part 1: The causes. *MIS Quarterly, 1*(3), 17-32.

Brinkkemper, S. (1996). Method engineering: Engineering of information systems development methods and tools. *Information and Software Technology, 38*(4), 275-280.

Burkhardt, J. M., & Détienne, F., (2007). An empirical study of software reuse by experts in object-oriented design. *arXiv:cs/0702005v1*.

Burrell, G., & Morgan, G. (1979). *Sociological Paradigms and Organisational Analysis: Elements of the Sociology of Corporate Life*. Heinemann.

Burton, P. J., & Bruhn, R. E. (2004). Using UML to Facilitate the Teaching of Object-Oriented Systems Analysis & Design. *Journal of Computing Sciences in Colleges, 19*.

Calvanese, D., Lenzerini, M., & Nardi, D. (1998). Description logics for conceptual data modeling. In J. Chomicki & G. Saake (Eds.), *Logics for databases and information systems* (pp. 229-263). Kluwer.

Carroll, J. M. (2002). *Human-computer Interaction in the New Millennium*. ACM Press, Addison-Wesley.

Cavaye, A. L. M. (1995). User participation in system development revisited. *Information and Management 28*(5), 311-323.

Chaki, S., Clarke E. M., Groce, A., Jha, S., & Veith, H. (2004). Modular Verification of Software Components in C. *IEEE Transactions on Software Engineering, 30*(6), 388-402.

Chang, A., Bordia, P., & Duck, J. (2003). Punctuated equilibrium and Linear Progression: Toward a New Understanding of Group development. *Academy of Management Journal, 46*(1), 106-117.

Chen, P. P. (1976). *ACM Transactions on Database Systems, 1,* 9-36.

Chen, P. P. (1976). The entity-relationship model - toward a unified view of data. *ACM Transactions on Database Systems, 1*(1), 9-36.

Chomicki, J. (1995). Efficient checking of temporal integrity constraints using bounded history encoding. *ACM Transactions on Database Systems, 20*(2), 149-186.

Chomicki, J., & Revesz, P. (1997). Constraint-based interoperability of spatiotemporal databases. *Proc. of the 5th Intl. Symposium on Large Spatial Databases, LNCS 1262,* 142-162. Springer-Verlag.

Chomicki, J., Lobo, J., & Naqvi, S. A. (2003). Conflict resolution using logic programming. *IEEE Transactions on Knowledge and Data Engineering, 15*(1), 244-249.

Ciancarini, P. (2005). On the Education of Future Software Engineers, *ICSE'05*, St. Louis, Missouri, USA, (pp. 649–650).

Cifuentes, C., & Hughes, J. (1994). SE curriculum design: methodologies, formal methods, and life cycle models, *Proceedings of II. Formal methods Software Education Conference,* (pp. 344–346).

Clark, N. (2005). Evaluating student teams developing unique industry projects, *Australian Computing Education Conference*, Newcastle, Australia, *42*, 21–30.

Coad, P., & Yourdon, E. (1990). *Object-oriented analysis*. Englewood Cliffs: Yourdon Press.

Cockburn, A. (2000). Selecting a project's methodology. *IEEE Software, 17*(4), 64-71.

Computing Curricula 2001. Computer Science. Final Report. (2001) The Joint Task Force on Computing Curricula, IEEE Computer Society, Association for Computing Machinery. Retrieved April 23, 2006 from http://acm.org/education/curric_vols/cc2001.pdf

Currim, F. (2004). *Spatio-temporal set-based constraints in conceptual modeling: A theoretical framework and evaluation.* Unpublished Doctoral Dissertation, University of Arizona, Tucson.

Currim, F., & Ram, S. (2006). *Understanding the concept of "completeness" in frameworks for modeling cardinality constraints.* Paper presented at the 16th Workshop on Information Technologies and Systems, Milwaukee, WI.

Currim, F., & Ram, S. (2008). Conceptually modeling windows and bounds for space and time in database constraints. *Communications of the ACM, 51*(11), 125-129.

Cusumano, M. A., & Yoffie, D. B. (1999). Software development on internet time. *IEEE Computer, 32*(10), 60-69.

Dawson, R. (2000). Twenty Dirty Tricks to Train Software Engineers, *Proc. 22nd Int'l Conf. Software Eng. (ICSE 00)*, IEEE CS Press, (pp. 209–218).

Dawson, R., & Newsham R. (1997). Introducing Software Engineers to the Real World, *IEEE Software, 14*(6), 37–43.

Decree of the Minister of National Education and Sport from April 18th 2002 on designation of teaching standards for respective studies and levels of education [in Polish - Rozporządzenie Ministra Edukacji Narodowej i Sportu z dnia 18 kwietnia 2002 r. w sprawie określenia standardów nauczania dla poszczególnych kierunków studiów i poziomów kształcenia]. (2002). *Dziennik Ustaw*, 116, 1004.

Decree of the Minister of National Education and Sport from June 13th 2003 changing decree on designation of teaching standards for respective studies and levels of education [in Polish - Rozporządzenie Ministra Edukacji Narodowej i Sportu z dnia 13 czerwca 2003 r. zmieniające rozporządzenie w sprawie określenia standardów nauczania dla poszczególnych kierunków studiów i poziomów kształcenia]. (2003). *Dziennik Ustaw*, 144, 1401.

Decree of the Minister of Science and Higher Education from July 12th 2007 on designation of teaching standards for respective studies and levels of education, as well as a procedure of creating and conditions which should be satisfy in order to run cross-field and macro-field studies [in Polish - Rozporządzenie Ministra Edukacji i Szkolnictwa Wyższego z dnia 12 lipca 2007 r. w sprawie określenia standardów kształcenia dla poszczególnych kierunków studiów i poziomów kształcenia, a także trybu tworzenia i warunków, jakie musi spełniać uczelnia, by prowadzić studia międzykierunkowe oraz makrokierunki]. (2007). *Dziennik Ustaw, 164*, 1166.

Deflem, M. (1991). Ritual, Anti-Structure, and Religion: A Discussion of Victor Turner's Processual Symbolic Analysis. *Journal for the Scientific Study of Religion, 30*(1), 1-25.

DeGrace, P., & Stahl, L. H. (1990). *Wicked Problems, Righteous Solutions: A Catalogue of Modern Software*

Engineering Paradigms. Englewood Cliffs, NJ: Prentice Hall, Inc.

DeLooze, L. L. (2005). *Minimal UML Diagrams for a Data-Driven Web Site*. SIGITE.

DeMarco, T. (1978). *Structured analysis and system specification*. Englewood Cliffs: Prentice Hall.

Desouza, K. C., Awazu, Y., & Tiwana, A., (2006). Four dynamics for bringing use back into software reuse. *Communications of the ACM, 49*(1), 96-100.

Dey, D., Barron, T. M., & Storey, V. C. (1995). A conceptual model for the logical design of temporal databases. *Decision Support Systems, 15*(4), 305-321.

Dick, M. (2005). Student interviews as a tool for assessment and learning in a systems analysis and design course, *ACM SIGCSE Bulletin, Proceedings of the 10th annual SIGCSE conference on Innovation and technology in computer science education ITiCSE '05, 37*(3), 24–28.

Dobing, B., & Parsons, J. (2006). How UML is Used. *Communications of ACM, 49.*

Doherty, N. F., & King, M. (2005). From technical to socio-technical change: tackling the human and organizational aspects of systems development projects. *European Journal of Information Systems 14*(1), 1.

Dwyer, S., Richard, O., & Shepherd, C. D. (1998). An Exploratory Study of Gender and Age Matching in the Salesperson-Prospective Customer Dyad: Testing Similarity-Performance Predictions. *The Journal of Personal Selling & Sales Management, 18*(4), 55.

Dyczkowski, M., & Skwarnik, M. (2004). National Academic Institutions Curricula Review [in Polish - Prezentacja programów kształcenia w uczelniach krajowych]. In A. Nowicki (Ed.), *Doskonalenie kształcenia informatycznego na kierunku Informatyka i Ekonometria na wydziale Zarządzania i Informatyki Akademii Ekonomicznej we Wrocławiu. Część 1. Identyfikacja kształcenia w obszarze informatyki* (pp. 46-66). Wrocław: Akademia Ekonomiczna we Wrocławiu.

Dyczkowski, M., & Wójtowicz, R. (2003). The concept of computer laboratory courses for non information systems students, example of business informatics [in Polish - Koncepcja prowadzenia zajęć laboratoryjnych dla studentów kierunków nieinformatycznych na przykładzie przedmiotu informatyka ekonomiczna]. In A. Nowicki, W. Olejniczak (Eds.). *Dydaktyka informatyki ekonomicznej – kształcenie dla społeczeństwa informacyjnego* (pp. 133-138). Wrocław: Akademia Ekonomiczna we Wrocławiu.

Dymek, D., & Kotulski, L. (2006). Evaluation of Risk Attributes Driven by Periodically Changing System Functionality. *Transaction on Engineering, Computing and Technology*, vol.16 November 2006, ISSN 1305-5313, (pp. 315-320).

Dymek, D., & Kotulski, L. (2007). On the load balancing of Business Intelligence Reporting Systems. *Proceedings of the AIS SIGSAND European Symposium on Systems Analysis and Design*, University of Gdansk, (pp. 121-125).

Dymek, D., & Kotulski, L. (2007). On the hierarchical composition of the risk management evaluation in computer information systems. *Proceedings of the Second International Conference DepCoS - RELCOMEX*, Szklarska Poreba, 14-16 June, 2007, ISBN-0-7695-2850-3, IEEE Computer Society (pp. 35- 42).

Dymek, D., & Kotulski, L. (2008). Estimation of System Workload Time Characteristic using UML Timing Diagrams. *Proceedings of the Third International Conference DepCoS – RELCOMEX 2008*, IEEE Computer Society No. P3178, (pp. 9-14).

Ehrig, H., Engels, G., Kreowski, H.-J., & Rozenberg, G. (1999a). *Handbook of Graph Grammars and Computing By Graph Transformation: Volume II, Application, Languages and Tools*. World Scientific Publishing Co., NJ.

Ehrig, H., Kreowski, H.-J., Montanari, U. & Rozenberg, G. (1999b). *Handbook of Graph Grammars and Computing By Graph Transformation: Volume III, Concurrency, Parallelism , and Distribution*, World Scientific Publishing Co., NJ.

Eldredge, N., & Gould, S. J. (1972). Punctuated Equilibria: An Alternative to Phyletic Gradualism. In T. J. M.

Schopf (Ed.), *Models in Paleobiology* (pp. 82-115). San Francisco, CA: Freeman.

Ellis, H. J. C., Mead, N. R., Moreno, A. M., & Seidman, S. B. (2003). Industry/University software engineering collaborations for the successful reeducation of non-software professionals. *Software Engineering Education and Training, Proceedings. 16th Conference,* (pp. 44–51).

Elmasri, R., & Navathe, S. B. (1994). *Fundamentals of database systems* (Second ed.): Benjamin Cummings Publishing Co., Redwood City, CA.

Elmasri, R., & Navathe, S. B. (2006). *Fundamentals of database systems* (Fifth ed.): Addison Wesley.

Elmasri, R., & Wuu, G. T. J. (1990). *A temporal model and query language for er databases.* Paper presented at the Sixth International Conference on Data Engineering, Los Angeles, California, USA.

Elmasri, R., Ihab El-Assal, & Kouramajian, V. (1990, October 8-10). *Semantics of temporal data in an extended er model.* Paper presented at the Ninth International Conference on Entity-Relationship Approach, Lausanne, Switzerland.

Elmasri, R., Wuu, G. T. J., & Kouramajian, V. (1993). A temporal model and query language for eer databases. In A. U. Tansel, J. Clifford, S. K. Gadia, A. Segev & R. T. Snodgrass (Eds.), *Temporal databases: Theory, design, and implementation* (pp. 212-229): Benjamin/Cummings.

Embley, D. W., Kurtz, B. D., & Woodfield, S. N. (1992). *Object-oriented systems analysis: A model-driven approach.* Englewood Cliffs, N J: Prentice-Hall.

Engels, G., & Groenewegen, L. (2000). Object-Oriented modeling: A road map. In A. Finkelstein (Eds) *Future of Software Engineering 2000.* ACM, (pp.105-116).

Engels, G., Küster, J. M., Heckel, R., & Groenewegen, L. (2001). A methodology for specifying and analyzing consistency of object-oriented behavioral models. *The 8th European Software Engineering Conference held jointly with ESEC/FSE-9.* ACM, New York, (pp.186-195).

Enterprise Architect Home Page, *http://www.sparxsystems.com/*

Erwig, M., Güting, R. H., Schneider, M., & Vazirgiannis, M. (1998). Abstract and discrete modeling of spatio-temporal data types. *In Proceedings of ACM International Symposium on Geographic Information Systems,* (pp. 131-136).

Essinck, L. J. B. (1988). A conceptual framework for information systems development methodologies. In H.-J. Bullinger, E. N. Protonotarios, D. Bouwhuis & F. Reim (Eds.), *Information technology for organisational systems* (pp. 354-362). Amsterdam: North-Holland.

Fellers, J. W. (1996). Teaching teamwork: exploring the use of cooperative learning teams in information systems education, *ACM SIGMIS Database, 27*(2), 44–60.

Ferg, S. (1991, 23-25 October, 1991). *Cardinality constraints in entity-relationship modeling.* Paper presented at the 10th International Conference on Entity-Relationship Approach, San Mateo, alifornia, USA.

Finkelstein, C. (1990). *An introduction to information engineering: From strategic planning to information systems.*

Fitzgerald, B., Russo, N. L., & O'Kane, T. (2003). Software development method tailoring at motorola. *Communications of the ACM, 46*(4), 65-70.

Fitzgerald, B., Russo, N. L., & Stolterman, E. (2002). *Information systems development: Methods in action.* London: McGraw-Hill.

Fitzgerald, G. (1991). Validating new information systems techniques: A retrospective analysis. In H.-E. Nissen, H. K. Klein & R. Hirschheim (Eds.), *Information systems research: Contemporary approaches and emergent traditions* (pp. 657-672): Elsevier Science Publishers B.V. (North-Holland).

Flint, S., Gardner, H., & Boughton, C. (2004). Executable/Translatable UML in Computing Education. In R. Lister & A. Young (Eds.), *Conferences in Research and Practice in Information Technology, 30.*

Flower, M., Beck, K., Brant, J., Opdyke, W., & Roberts, D. (1999). *Refactoring: Improving the Design of Existing Code.* Addison-Wesley.

Forrester, J. W. (1958). Industrial Dynamics: A Major Breakthrough for Decision Makers. *Harvard Business Review, 38*(4), 37-66.

Forrester, J. W. (1961). *Industrial Dynamics.* Pegasus Communications, Waltham, MA.

Frakes, W., & Terry, C. (1996). Software Reuse: Metrics and Models. *ACM Computing Surveys, 28*(2), 415-435.

Gamma, E., Helm, R., Johnson, R., & Vlissides, J. (1995). *Design Patterns: Elements of Resuable Object- Oriented Software.* Addison-Wesley.

Gamma, E., Helm, R., Johnson, R., & Vlissides, J. (1995). *Design Patterns: Elements of Resuable Object- Oriented Software.* Addison-Wesley.

Gane, C., & Sarson, T. (1979). *Structured systems analysis: Tools and techniques.* Englewood Cliffs: Prentice-Hall.

García, F., Bertoa, M. F., Calero, C., Vallecillo, A., Ruíz, F., Piattini, M., & Genero, M. (2006), "Towards a consistent terminology for software measurement ", *Information and Software Technology, 48*(8), 631-644.

Gasson, S. (1999). A social action model of situated information systems design. *DATA BASE (ACM SIGMIS), 30*(2), 82-97.

Gersick, C. J. G. (1988). Time and Transition in Work Teams: Toward a New Model of Group development. *Academy of Management Journal, 31*(1), 9-41.

Gersick, C. J. G. (1989). Marking Time: Predictable Transitions in Task Groups. *Academy of Management Journal, 32*(2), 274-309.

Gertz, M., & Lipeck, U. W. (1995, September 17-18). *Temporal" integrity constraints in temporal databases.* Paper presented at the International Workshop on Temporal Databases, Zürich, Switzerland.

Ghezzi, C., & Mandrioli, D. (2005). The challenges of software engineering education, *Software Engineering, 2005. ICSE 2005. Proceedings. 27th International Conference,* (pp. 637–638).

Gibbs, W. W. (1994, September). Software's chronic crisis. *Scientific American,* 72-81.

Glaser, B. G., & Strauss, A. L. (1967). *The discovery of grounded theory: Strategies for qualitative research.* New York: Aldine de Gruyter.

Glass, R. L. (1995). *Software creativity.* Englewood Cliffs, NJ: Prentice Hall.

Glass, R. L. (1998). Is there really a software crisis? *IEEE Software, 15*(1), 104-105.

Gnatz, M., Marschall, F., Popp, G., Rausch, A., & Schwerin, W. (2003). The living software development process. *Software Quality Professional, 5*(3), 4-16.

Golden, D. G. (1982). Development of a systems analysis and design course, *ACM SIGCE Bulletin, Proceedings of the thirteenth SIGCSE technical symposium on Computer science education SIGCSE '82, 14*(1), 110–113.

Gorgone, J. T., Davis, G. B., Valacich, J. S., Topi, H., Feinstein, D. L., & Longenecker, H. E. Jr. (2002). *IS 2002. Model curriculum and guidelines for undergraduate degree programs in information systems.* Association for Computing Machinery (ACM), Association for Information Systems (AIS), Association of Information Technology Professionals (AITP). Retrieved April 23, 2006 from http://www.acm.org/education/is2002.pdf

Gorgone, J. T., Gray, P., Feinstein, D. L., Kasper, G. M., Luftman, J. N., Stohr, E. A., Valacich, J. S., & Wigand, R. T. (1999). *MSIS 2000. Model Curriculum and Guidelines for Graduate Degree Programs in Information Systems.* Association for Computing Machinery (ACM), Association for Information Systems (AIS). Retrieved April 23, 2006 from http://cis.bentley.edu/isa/pages/documents/msis2000jan00.pdf

Goroff, I. (1982). A systems analysis and design course sequence, *ACM SIGCE Bulletin, Proceedings of the thirteenth SIGCSE technical symposium on Computer science education SIGCSE '82, 14*(1), 123–127.

Gregersen, H., & Jensen, C. S. (1998). *Conceptual modeling of time-varying information* (No. TR-35): TimeCenter.

Gregersen, H., & Jensen, C. S. (1999). Temporal entity-relationship models - a survey. *IEEE Transactions on Knowledge and Data Engineering, 11*(3), 464-497.

Güting, R. H., Böhlen, M. H., Erwig, M., Jensen, C. S., Lorentzos, N. A., Schneider, M., & Vazirgiannis, M. (2000). A foundation for representing and querying moving objects. *ACM Transactions on Database Systems, 25*(1), 1-42.

Hammer, M., & McLeod, D. (1981). Database description with sdm: A semantic database model. *ACM Transactions on Database Systems, 6*(3), 351-386.

Hanna, H., & Mouaddib, A. (2002). Task selection problem under uncertainty as decision-making. In *Proceedings of the First international Joint Conference on Autonomous Agents and Multiagent Systems: Part 3* (Bologna, Italy, July 15 - 19, 2002). AAMAS '02. ACM, New York, NY, (pp. 1303-1308).

Hardgrave, B. C., Davis, F. D., & Riemenschneider, C. K. (2003). Investigating Determinants of Software Developers' Intentions to Follow Methodologies. *Journal of Management Information Systems, 20*(1), 123-151.

Hartwick, J., & Barki, H. (2001). Communication as a dimension of user participation. *IEEE Transactions on Professional Communication 44*(1), 21-36.

Hawthorne, M. J., & Perry D. E. (2005). Software Engineering Education in the Era of Outsourcing, Distributed Development, and Open Source Software: Challenges and Opportunities, *ICSE'05*, St. Louis, Missouri, USA, (pp. 643–644).

Hazzan, O., & Tomayko J. (2005). Teaching Human Aspects of Software Engineering, *ICSE'05*, St. Louis, Missouri, USA, 647–648.

Henninger, S. (1999). An Evolutionary Approach to Constructing Effective Software Reuse Repositories.

ACM Transactions on Software Engineering and Methodology, 6(2), 111-140.

Herbst, H. (1997). *Business rule-oriented conceptual modeling.* Heidelberg: Physica-Verlag.

Hidding, G. (1996). Method engineering: Experiences in practice. In S. Brinkkemper, K. Lyytinen & R. Welke (Eds.), *Method engineering: Principles of method construction and tool support.*London: Chapman & Hall.

Hilburn, T. B. W., & Watts S. (2002). The Impending Changes in Software Education. *IEEE Software, 19*(5), 22–25.

Hirschheim, R. A., Klein, H.-K., & Lyytinen, K. (1995). *Information Systems Development and Data Modeling: Conceptual and Philosophical Foundations.* Cambridge University Press.

Hirschheim, R., & Klein, H. K. (1989). Four paradigms of information systems development *Communications of the ACM 32*(10).

Hogg, M. A., & Terry, D. J. (2000). Social identity and Self-Categorization Processes in Organizational Contexts. *Academy of Management Review, 25*(1), 121-140.

Huang, B., & Claramunt, C. (2005). Spatiotemporal Data Model and Query Language for Tracking Land Use Change. *Transportation Research Record: Journal of the Transportation Research Board, 1902*, 107-113.

Hull, R., & King, R. (1987). Semantic database modeling survey, applications, and research issues. *ACM Computing Surveys*, 210-260.

Hunter, M. G. (1994). Excellent Systems Analyst: Key Audience Perceptions. *Computer Personnel*, (pp. 15–31).

Hwang, M. I., & Thorn, R. G. (1999). The effect of user engagement on system success: A meta-analytical integration of research findings. *Information and Management 35*(4), 229-236.

IBM Rational Unified Process, Retrieved November 05, 2008, from http://www-01.ibm.com/software/awdtools/rup/

IEEE (2004). *SWEBOK, Guide to the Software Engineering Body of Knowledge.* Los Alamitos, California.

Iivari, J., Hirschheim, R., & Klein, K. (2001). Dynamic framework for classifying information systems development: Methodologies and approaches. *Journal of Management Information Systems 17*(3), 179-218.

Introna, L. D., & Whitley, E. A. (1997). Against methodism: Exploring the limits of method. *Information Technology & People, 10*(1), 31-45.

Jackson, M. (2000). The origins of jsp and jsd: A personal recollection. *IEEE Annals of Software Engineering, 22*(2), 61-63.

Jacob, R. J. K. (1986). *ACM Transactions on Graphics, 5,* 283-317.

Jacobson, I., Christerson, M., Jonsson, P., & Overgaard, G. (1992). *Object-Oriented Software Engineering: A Use-Case Driven Approach.* Boston: Addison-Wesley.

Jayaratna, N. (1994). *Understanding and evaluating methodologies, nimsad: A systemic framework.* London: McGraw-Hill.

Jensen, C. S., Dyreson, C. E., Böhlen, M. H., Clifford, J., Elmasri, R., Gadia, S. K., et al. (1998). The consensus glossary of temporal database concepts - february 1998 version. In C. S. Jensen, J. Clifford, R. Elmasri, S. K. Gadia, P. J. Hayes & S. Jajodia (Eds.), *Temporal databases: Research and practice* (pp. 367-405): Springer.

Jonasson, I. (2000). *Developing the information systems of tomorrow - competencies and methodologies.* Unpublished M.Sc. Dissertation, University of Skövde, Sweden.

Kaminski, A., Polak, P., & Wieczorkowski, J. (2005). Process approach in MIS implementation – business process modeling tools [in Polish - Podejście procesowe we wdrażaniu SIZ – narzędzia modelowania procesów biznesowych]. In E. Niedzielska, H. Dudycz & M. Dyczkowski (Eds.), Nowoczesne technologie informacyjne w zarządzaniu, *Prace Naukowe Akademii Ekonomicznej we Wrocławiu, 1081,* 278-287.

Khalifa, M., & Verner, J. M. (2000). Drivers for Software development Method Usage. *IEEE Transactions on Engineering Management, 47*(3), 360-369.

Khatri, V., Ram, S., & Snodgrass, R. T. (2004). Augmenting a conceptual model with geo-spatio-temporal annotations. *IEEE Transactions on Knowledge and Data Engineering, forthcoming.*

Kirk, D., Roper, M., & Wood, M., (2006). Identifying and addressing problems in object-oriented framework reuse. *Empirical Software Engineering, 12*(3), 243-274.

Kirsch, L. J., Sambamurthy, V., Ko, D.-G., & Purvis, R. L. (2002). Controlling Information Systems Development Projects: The View from the Client. *Management Science, 48*(4), 484-498.

Knoke, D., & Yang, S. (2008). *Social Network Analysis* (2nd ed.) Sage Publications.

Kobylinski, A. (2004). The comparison of business informatics curriculum at the Warsaw School of Economics with model IS 2002 curriculum [in Polish - Porównanie programu nauczania informatyki gospodarczej w Szkole Głównej Handlowej w Warszawie z modelowym curriculum IS 2002]. In J. Goliński, D. Jelonek, A. Nowicki (eds.), Informatyka ekonomiczna. Przegląd naukowo-dydaktyczny, *Prace Naukowe Akademii Ekonomicznej we Wrocławiu, 1027,* 270-279.

Kontio, M. (2005). *Architectural Manifesto: Designing Software Architectures.* Part 5. Introducing the 4+1 View Model. http://www-128.ibm.com/developerworks/wireless/library/wi-arch11.

Korth, H., Silberschatz, A., & Sudarshan, S. (2005). *Database Systems Concepts.* McGraw Hill, New York.

Kotulski, L.(2006). Nested Software Structure Maintained by aedNLC graph grammar. *Proceedings of the 24th IASTED International Multi-Conference Software Engineering,* (pp. 335-339).

Kotulski, L., & Dymek, D. (2007). On the Evaluation of the Refactoring in UML Environment, *Information Systems Architecture and Technology - Information Technology and WEB Engineering: Models, Concepts and*

Challenging, Wydawnictwo Politechniki Wrocławskiej, ISBN 978-83-7493-345-2, (pp.185-193).

Kotulski, L., & Dymek, D.(2008). On the modeling timing behavior of the system with UML(VR). In M. Bubak, et al. (Eds), *ICCS 2008, part I, LNCS 5101,* (pp. 386-395).

Kotulski, L. (2000). *Model wspomagania generacji oprogramowania w środowisku rozproszonym za pomocą gramatyk grafowych.* Wydawnictwo Uniwersytetu Jagiellońskiego, Kraków, ISBN 83-233-1391-1.

Koubarakis, M. (1995, September 17-18). *Databases and temporal constraints: Semantics and complexity.* Paper presented at the International Workshop on Temporal Databases, Zürich, Switzerland.

Kraemer, K. L., & Dutton, W. H. (1991). Survey research in the study of management information systems. In K. L. Kraemer (Ed.), *The information systems research challenge: Survey research methods. Volume 3* (pp. 3-58). Boston, Massachusetts: Harvard Business School.

Kruchten, P. (1995). Architectural Blueprints – the "4+1" View Model of Software Architecture. *IEEE Software, 12.*

Kuhn, T. S. (1996). *The structure of scientific revolutions* (3rd ed.). Chicago: University of Chicago Press.

Kumar, K., & Bjørn-Andersen, N. (1990). A cross-cultural comparison of is designer values. *Communications of the ACM, 33*(5), 528-538.

Kumar, K., & Welke, R. J. (1992). Methodology engineering: A proposal for situation-specific methodology construction. In W. W. Cotterman & J. A. Senn (Eds.), *Challenges and strategies for research in systems development* (pp. 257-269): John Wiley & Sons.

Kuźniarz L., Reggio, G., Sourrooille, J., & Huzar, Z. (2002). Workshop on "Consistency in UML-based Software Development", Retrieved November 05, 2008, from http://www.ipd.bth.se/uml2002/RR-2002-06.pdf

Lai, V. S., Kuilboer, J.-P., & Guynes, J. L. (1994). Temporal databases: Model design and commercialization prospects. *DATA BASE, 25*(3), 6-18.

Lang, M. (2002, April 29-30). *The use of web-based international surveys in information systems research.* Paper presented at the European Conference on Research Methodology for Business and Management Studies (ECRM 2002), Reading, England.

Langran, G., & Chrisman, N. R. (1988). A framework for temporal geographic information systems. *Cartographica, 25*(3), 1-14.

Larmour, R. (1997). A survey into the relevance and adequacy of training in systems analysis and design. *ACM SIGCSE Bulletin, 29*(2) , 54–64.

Laverie, D. A., & Arnett, D. B. (2000). Factors Affecting Fan Attendance: The Influence of Identity Salience and Satisfaction. *Journal of Leisure Research, 32*(2), 225.

Lenzerini, M., & Santucci, G. (1983). *Cardinality constraints in the entity-relationship model.* Paper presented at the 3rd International Conference on Entity-Relationship Approach, Anaheim, California.

Liddle, S. W., Embley, D. W., & Woodfield, S. N. (1993). Cardinality constraints in semantic data models. *Data and Knowledge Engineering, 11*(3), 235-270.

Lin, L. T., & Shao, B. M. (2000). The relationship between user participation and system success: A simultaneous contingency approach. *Information and Management 37*(6), 283-295.

Lindemann, C., Lohmann, M., & Thümmler, A. (2004). Adaptive call admission control for QoS/revenue optimization in CDMA cellular networks. *Wireless Network.* 10, 4 (Jul. 2004), (pp. 457-472).

Liu, C. (2005). Enriching Software Engineering Courses with Service-Learning Projects and the Open-Source Approach, *ICSE'05*, St. Louis, Missouri, (pp. 613–614).

Locke, K. (2001). *Grounded theory in management research.* London: Sage.

Loucopoulos, P., McBrien, P., Persson, U., Schmaker, F., & Vasey, P. (1990, November). *Tempora-integrating database technology rule based systems and temporal reasoning for effective software.* Paper presented at the ESPRIT Conference, Brussels, Belgium.

Maciaszek, L. (2005). *Requirements Analysis and Systems Design*s. Addison Wesley.

Malouin, J.-L., & Landry, M. (1983). The mirage of universal methods in systems design. *Journal of Applied Systems Analysis, 10*, 47-62.

Marcinkowski, B., & Wrycza, S. (2005). Interaction Occurrences and Combined Fragments in System Dynamics Modelling with UML 2 Sequence Diagram art. In G. Nilsson, R. Gustas, W. Wojtkowski, G. Wojtkowski, S. Wrycza, & J. Zupancic (Eds.), *ISD 2005 Proceedings of the Fourteenth International Conference on Information Systems Development,* Karlstad University Studies, s (pp. 59-68), Karlstad.

Markus, M. L., & Robey, D. (1988). Information Technology and Organizational Change: Causal Structure in Theory and Research. *Management Science, 34*(5), 583-598.

Martin, J. (1990). *Information engineering, Book II: Planning and analysis*: Pearson Education.

Martin, J., & Odell, J. J. (1992). *Object- oriented Analysis And Design.* Prentice Hall.

Martin, R. C. (2003). *Agile Software Development.* Pearson Education.

Matthies, L. (1977). *The new playscript procedure.* Stamford: Office Publications Inc.

Mattia, A.M., & Weistroffer, H.R. (2008). Information systems development: A categorical analyis of user participation approaches. *Proceedings of the 41ˢᵗ Hawaii International Conference on System Sciences.*

McAllister, A. (1998). Complete rules for n-ary relationship cardinality constraints. *Data and Knowledge Engineering, 27*(3), 255-288.

McBreen, P. (2002). *Software craftsmanship: The new imperative.*Boston: Addison Wesley.

McConnell, S. (2004). *Code Complete* (2nd ed.). Redmond, WA: Microsoft Press.

McFadden, F. R., Hoffer, J. A., & Prescott, M. B. (2002). *Modern database management* (Sixth ed.): Prentice Hall.

McLeod, R. (1996). Comparing undergraduate courses in systems analysis and design. *Communication of the ACM, 39*–5, (pp. 113–121).

McMenamin, S. M., & Palmer, J. F. (1984). *Essential systems analysis.* New York: Yourdon Press.

Mellarkod, V., Appan, R., Jones, D. R., & Sherif, K. (2007). A multi-level analysis of factors affecting software developers' intention to reuse software assets: An empirical investigation. *Information & Management, 2007, 44*(7), 613-625.

Mens, T., & Tourwé, T. (2004). A Survey of Software Refactoring. *IEEE Transactions on Software Engineering, 30*(2), 126-139.

Miles, M. B., & Huberman, A. M. (1994). *Qualitative data analysis: An expanded sourcebook* (2nd ed.). Thousand Oaks, CA: Sage.

Mili, H., Mili, F., & Mili, A. (1995). Reusing Software: Issues and Research Directions. *IEEE Transactions on Software Engineering, 21*(6), 528–562.

Misic, M. M., & Russo, N. L. (1999). An assessment of systems analysis and design courses. *The Journal of Systems and Software, 45*, 197–202.

Mohagheghi, P., & Conradi, R., (2007). Quality, productivity and economic benefits of software reuse: a review of industrial studies. *Empirical Software Engineering,* May 2007, (pp. 471-516).

Mohay, G., Morarji, H., & Thomas, R. (1994). Undergraduate, graduate and professional education in software engineering in the '90s: a case study, *Software Education Conference Proceedings,* (pp. 22–25, 103–110).

Morgan, G. W., & Lear, F. A. (1994). The role of a software engineering project within an undergraduate applied computing degree, *Software Education Conference Proceedings,* (pp. 230–236).

Morgenstern, M. (1984). *Constraint equations: Declarative expression of constraints with automatic enforcement.* Paper presented at the 10th Conference on Very Large Databases, Singapore.

Morrogh, P. (2000). Is software education narrow-minded?—A position paper, *Software Engineering, 2000. Proceedings of the 2000 International Conference,* (pp. 545–546).

Muller, R. J. (2000). Databases –UML In database modeling. *MIKOM 2000* (in Polish).

Murugesan, S., & Deshpande, Y. (1999, May 16-22). *Preface to icse'99 workshop on web engineering.* Paper presented at the 21st International Conference on Software Engineering (ICSE), Los Angeles, California, USA.

Murugesan, S., Deshpande, Y., Hansen, S., & Ginige, A. (1999, May 16-17). *Web engineering: A new discipline for development of web-based systems.* Paper presented at the 1st ICSE Workshop on Web Engineering, Los Angeles, California, USA.

Myers, B., Hudson, S. E., & Pausch, R. (2000). *ACM Transactions on Computer-Human Interaction, 7,* 3-28.

N. Derrett, W. K. a. P. L. (1985). Some aspects of operations in an object-oriented database. *IEEE Database Engineering Bulletin, 8*(4), 66-74.

Naur, P., & Randell, B. (Eds.). (1969). *Software engineering: Report on a conference sponsored by the nato science committee, garmisch, germany, 7-11 october 1968.* Brussels: Scientific Affairs Division, NATO.

Nielsen, J. (1993). *Usability Engineering,* Academic Press.

Object Management Group (2006). UML Diagram Interchange v.1.0 OMG document number: formal/2006-04-04, Retrieved November 05, 2008, from http://www.omg.org/technology/documents/formal/diagram.htm

Object Management Group (2007). UML Infrastructure Specification v.2.1.2, OMG document number: formal/2007-11-04, Retrieved November 05, 2008, from http://www.omg.org/spec/UML/2.1.2/

Object Management Group (2007). UML Superstructure Specification v.2.1.2, OMG document number: formal/2007-11-02, Retrieved November 05, 2008, from http://www.omg.org/spec/UML/2.1.2/

Oinas-Kukkonen, H., Alatalo, T., Kaasila, J., Kivelä, H., & Sivunen, S. (2001). Requirements for web engineering methodologies. In M. Rossi & K. Siau (Eds.), *Information modeling in the new millennium* (pp. 360-382). Hershey, PA: Idea Group Publishing.

Olfman, L. and Bostrom, R.P. (1992). Innovative teaching materials and methods for systems analysis and design, *ACM SIGMIS Database,* 23,2, 7–12.

Olsen, D. R. (1986). *ACM Transactions on Information Systems, 5,* 318-344.

Olson, M. H., & Ives, B. (1981). User involvement in system design: An empirical test of alternative approaches. *Information and Management 4*(4), 183-195.

OMG (2005). Object Management Group. *Unified Modeling Language 2.0 Superstructure Specification.* http://www.omg.org/cgi-bin/doc?formal/05-07-04.

OMG (2006). Object Management Group. *The UML 2.1 Superstructure Convenience Document. http://www.omg.org/cgi-bin/doc?ptc/2006-04-02.*

OMG. (2004). Unified modeling language (uml), v2.0.

OMG. (2006). Object constraint language specification, v 2.0.

Omland, H. O. (1999). Educating systems analyst emphasizing the human factor, *ACM SIGCSE Bulletin, Proceedings of the 4th annual SIGCSE/SIGCUE ITiCSE conference on Innovation and technology in computer science education ITiCSE '99, 31*(3), 44–47.

Orlikowski, W. J., & Gash, D. C. (1994). Technological frames: Making sense of information technology in organizations. *ACM Transactions on Information Systems, 12*(2), 669-702.

Osborne, M. (1992). APPGEN: a tool for teaching systems analysis and design, *ACM SIGCSE Bulletin, Proceedings of the twenty-third SIGCSE technical symposium on Computer science education SIGCSE '92, 24*(1), 259–263.

Otso, K. J. (1995). A Systematic Process for Reusable Software Component Selection. *Technical Report, University of Maryland.*

Oudshoorn, M.J. and Maciunas, K.J. (1994). Experience with a project-based approach to teaching software engineering, *Software Education Conference, 1994. Proceedings.* (pp. 220–225).

Parent, C., Spaccapietra, S., & Zimanyi, E. (1999). *Spatio-temporal conceptual models: Data structures + space + time.* Paper presented at the 7th ACM Symposium on Advances in Geographic Information Systems, Kansas City, USA, 1999.

Parnas, D. (1999). Software Engineering Programs Are Not Computer Science Programs, *IEEE Software, 16*(6), 19–30.

Peckham, J., & Maryanski, F. (1988). Semantic data models. *ACM Computing Surveys, 20*(3), 153-189.

Peuquet, D., & Duan, N. (1995). An Event-Based Spatio-temporal Data Model (ESTDM) for Temporal Analysis of Geographical Data. *Int. Journal of Geographical Information Systems, 9*(1), 7-24.

Polak, P., & Polak, D. (2006). The changes in curriculum of business informatics computer laboratories in economic universities [in Polish - Zmiany w programie laboratorium z informatyki gospodarczej na uczelniach ekonomicznych]. In A. Szewczyk (Ed.), *Dydaktyka informatyki i informatyka w dydaktyce* (pp. 188-191). Szczecin: Uniwersytet Szczeciński.

Powell, T. A., Jones, D. L., & Cutts, D. C. (1998). *Web site engineering: Beyond web page design.* Upper Saddle River: Prentice Hall.

Price, R. J., Tryfona, N., & Jensen, C. S. (2000). Extended SpatioTemporal UML: Motivations, Requirements and Constructs. *Journal of Database Management, 11*(4), 14-27.

Publication, F. I. P. S. (1993). *Integration definition for function modeling (idef1x)* (No. Technical Report 184): National Institute of Standards and Technology, Gaithersburg, MD 20899.

Pullan, W. and Oliver, D. (1994). Development of an undergraduate software engineering degree, *Software Education Conference, 1994. Proceedings,* (pp. 111–117).

Rahim, M. S. M., Shariff, A. R. M., Mansor, S., Mahmud, A. R., & Alias, M. A. (2006). Volumetric spatiotemporal data model. *In Innovations in 3D Geo Information Systems, Lecture Notes in Geoinformation and Cartography,* (pp. 547-556).

Ram, S., & Khatri, V. (2005). A comprehensive framework for modeling set-based business rules during conceptual database design. *Information Systems, 30*(2), 89-118.

Ratbe, D., King, W. R., & Kim, Y.-G. (1999). The fit between project characteristics and application development methodologies: A contingency approach. *Journal of Computer Information Systems, 40*(2), 26-33.

Renolen, A. (1996). History graphs: Conceptual modeling of spatio-temporal data. *In Proceedings of GIS Frontiers in Business and Science*, International Cartographic Association, 2, Brno.

Rickman, D. M. (2000). *A Process for Combining Object Oriented and Structured Analysis and Design.* 3rd Annual Systems Engineering & Supportability Conference. Retrieved February 14, 2007 from http://www.dtic.mil/ndia/systems/ Rickman2.pdf

Rob, M. A. (2004). Issues of structured vs. object-oriented methodology of systems analysis and design. *Issues in Information Systems, 5*, 275-280.

Rob, P., & Coronel, C. (2001). *Database systems: Design, implementation, and management* (Fifth ed.): Course Technology.

Robey, D., & Markus, M. L. (1984). Rituals in Information Systems Design. *MIS Quarterly, 8*(1), 5-15.

Rochfeld, A. (1986, November 17-19). *Merise, an information system design and development methodology, tutorial.* Paper presented at the Fifth International Conference on Entity-Relationship Approach, Dijon, France.

Ross, R. G. (1997). *The business rule book: Classifying, defining and modeling rules, version 4.0* (Second ed.): Business Rule Solutions, Incorporated.

Rowley, T. J., & Moldoveanu, M. (2003). When Will Stakeholder Groups Act? An Interest- and Identity-based Model of Stakeholder Group Mobilization. *Academy of Management Review, 28*(2), 204-219.

Rozenberg, D., & Scott, K. (2001). *Applying Use Case Driven Object Modeling with UML: An Annotated e-Commerce Example*. Addison Wesley.

Rozenberg, G. (1997). Handbook *of Graph Grammars and Computing By Graph Trans-formation: Volume I, Foundations*. Ed. World Scientific Publishing Co., NJ.

Rumbaugh, J. (1995). What is a method? *Journal of Object Oriented Programming, 8*(6), 10-16;26.

Rumbaugh, J., Blaha, M., Premerlani, W., Eddy, F., & Lorensen, W. (1991). *Object-oriented modeling and design*. Englewood Cliffs, NJ: Prentice-Hall.

Rundensteiner, E. A., Bic, L., Gilbert, J. P., & Yin, M.-L. (1991, April 8-12). *A semantic integrity framework: Set restrictions for semantic groupings*. Paper presented at the Seventh International Conference on Data Engineering, Kobe, Japan.

Russo, N. L., & Graham, B. R. (1999). A first step in developing a web application design methodology: Understanding the environment. In A. T. Wood-Harper, N. Jayaratna & J. R. G. Wood (Eds.), *Methodologies for developing and managing emerging technology based information systems: 6th international bcs information systems methodologies conference* (pp. 24-33). London: Springer.

Sabau, A. (2007a). The 3SST Model: A three step spatio-temporal conceptual model. *In Proceedings of the 2nd AIS SIGSAND European Symposium on System Analysis and Design*, Gdansk.

Sabau, A. (2007b). The 3SST Relational Model. *Studia Universitatis "Babeş-Bolyai", Informatica, LII*(1), 77-88.

Sahraoui, S. (1998). Is information systems education value neutral? *Journal of Computer Information Systems, 38*(3), 105-109.

Schneider, J.-G.; Johnston, L., & Joyce, P. (2005). Curriculum development in educating undergraduate software engineers—Are students being prepared for the profession?, *Software Engineering Conference, 2005. Proceedings*. Australian, (pp. 314–323).

Schön, D. A. (1983). *The reflective practitioner: How professionals think in action*.London: Temple Smith.

Shalloway, A., & Trott, J. R. (2002). *Object oriented design – Design Patterns*. HELION (in Polish).

Shaw, M., & Garlan, D. (1996). *Software architecture: Perspectives on an emerging discipline*:Prentice Hall.

Shepard, A., & Kerschberg, L. (1984). *Prism: A knowledge-based system for semantic integrity specification and enforcement in database systems*. Paper presented at the ACM SIGMOD Conference, Boston.

Shneiderman, B. (1998). *Designing the User Interface*. Addison Wesley Longman.

Shneiderman, B. (1998). *Designing the User Interface: Strategies for Effective Human-Computer-Interaction* (3rd ed.) Addison Wesley Longman.

Shneiderman, B. (2002). *Leonardo's Laptop: Human Needs and the New Computing Technologies*. MIT Press.

Silberschatz, A., Korth, H., & Sudarshan, S. (1997). *Database system concepts* (Third Edition ed.): McGraw Hill.

Sistla, A. P., Wolfson, O., Chamberlain, S., & Dao, S. (1997). Modeling and querying moving objects. *Proceedings of the 13th IEEE International Conference on Data Engineering*, Birmingham, (pp. 422-432).

Slocombe, T. E., & Bluedorn, A. C. (1999). Organizational Behavior Implications of the Congruence Between Preferred Polychronicity and Experienced Work-unit Polychronicity. *Journal of Organizational Behavior, 20*, 75-99.

Śmiałek, M. (2005). *Understanding UML 2.0 Methods of object oriented modeling*, HELION (in Polish).

Smith, J. M., & Smith, D. C. P. (1977). *ACM Transactions on Database Systems, 2*, 105-133.

Snodgrass, R. T. (1999). Developing time-oriented database applications in sql. *Morgan Kaufmann Series in Data Management Systems*.

Snook, C. & Butler, M.(2006). UML-B: Formal modeling and design aided by UML. *ACM Transaction on Software Engineering Methodology, 15*(1), 92-122.

Song, X. (1997). Systematic integration of design methods. *IEEE Software, 14*(2), 107-117.

Spence, J. W., & Grout, J. C. (1978). Systems analysis and design in a computer science curriculum, *ACM SIGCSE Bulletin, 10*(4), 24–27.

Spinellis, D. (2007). Cracking Software Reuse. *IEEE Software, 24*(1), 12-13.

Stolterman, E., & Russo, N. (1997). *The paradox of information systems methods: Public and private rationality.* Paper presented at the 5th British Computer Society Conference on Information Systems Methodologies, Lancaster, England.

Storey, V. C. (1993). Understanding semantic relationships. *The VLDB Journal — The International Journal on Very Large Data Bases, 2*(4), 455-488.

Storey, V. C., Yang, H., & Goldstein, R. C. (1996). Semantic integrity constraints in knowledge-based database design systems. *Data and Knowledge Engineering, 20*(1), 1-37.

Strauss, A. L. (1970). Discovering new theory from previous theory. In T. Shibutani (Ed.), *Human nature and collective theory* (pp. 46-53). Englewood Cliffs, NJ: Prentice Hall.

Strauss, A., & Corbin, J. (1998). *Basics of qualitative research: Techniques and procedures for developing grounded theory* (2nd ed.). Thousand Oaks, CA: Sage.

Su, S. Y. W. (1983). A semantic association model for corporate and scientific statistical databases. *Journal of Information Sciences, 29*, 151-199.

Suchman, L. A. (1987). *Plans and situated actions: The problem of human-machine communication.*Cambridge: Cambridge University Press.

Szekely, P. A. (1996). In F. Bodart, & J. Vanderdonckt (Eds.), *Design, Specification and Verification of Interactive Systems: Proceedings of the Third International Eurographics Workshop.* Namur, Belgium.

Tajfel, H. (1981). *Human Groups and Social Categories: Studies in Social Psychology.* Cambridge, England: Cambridge University Press.

Tauzovich, B. (1991). *Towards temporal extensions to the entity-relationship model.* Paper presented at the 10th International Conference on Entity-Relationship Approach, San Mateo, California.

Taylor, P. R. (2004). Vernacularism in software design practice: Does craftmanship have a place in software engineering? *Australasian Journal of Information Systems, 11*(12), 14-25.

Ter Hofstedt, A. H. M., & Verhoef, T. F. (1997). On the feasibility of situational method engineering. *Information Systems, 22*(6-7), 401-422.

Thalheim, B. (1996, December 1-10, 1996). *An overview on semantical constraints for database models.* Paper presented at the 6th International Conference on Intellectual Systems and Computer Science, Moscow, Russia.

Thalheim, B. (2000). *Entity-relationship modeling: Foundations of database technology*: Springer-Verlag.

The Ministry of Finance GIFI. *Counteracting money laundering.*

Theodoulidis, C. I., Loucopoulos, P., & Wangler, B. (1991). A conceptual modelling formalism for temporal database applications. *Information Systems, 16*(4), 401-416.

Thomas, R., Semeczko, G., Morarji, H., & Mohay, G. (1994). Core software engineering subjects: a case study ('86–'94), *Software Education Conference Proceedings,* (pp. 24–31).

Tomer, A., Goldin, L., Kuflik, T., Kimchi, E., & Schach, S. R. (2004). Evaluating Software Reuse Alternatives: A Model and Its Application to an Industrial Case Study. *IEEE Transactions on Software Engineering, 30*(9), 601-612.

Trice, H. M., & Beyer, J. M. (1984). Studying Organizational Cultures Through Rites and Ceremonials. *Academy of Management Review, 9*(4), 653-669.

Truex, D., & Avison, D. (2003, August 4-6). *Method engineering: Reflections on the past and ways forward.* Paper presented at the 9th Americas Conference on Information Systems (AMCIS), Tampa, Florida, USA.

Trujillo, J. (2006). A Report on the First International Workshop on Best Practices of UML. *SIGMOD Record, 35.*

Tryfona, N., & Jensen, C. S. (1999). Conceptual data modeling for spatiotemporal applications. *GeoInformatica, 3*(3), 245-268.

Tryfona, N., & Jensen, C. S. (2000). Using abstractions for spatio-temporal conceptual modeling. *Proceedings of the 2000 ACM Symposium on Applied Computing,* Italy, (pp. 313-322).

Tuckman, B. W., & Jensen, M. A. C. (1977). Stages in Small Group development Revisited. *Group & Organization Studies, 2*(4), 419-427.

Turner, V. W. (1974). *Dramas, Fields, and Metaphors: Symbolic Action in Human Society.* London, England: Cornell University Press.

Turner, V. W. (1995). *The Ritual Process: Structure and Anti-Structure* (Reprint ed.). Chicago: Aldine Transaction.

Turner, V. W., & Turner, E. (1978). *Image and Pilgrimage in Christian Culture.* New York: Columbia University Press.

Underwood, R., Bond, E., & Baer, R. (2001). Building Service Brands via Social identity: Lessons from the Sports Marketplace. *Journal of Marketing Theory and Practice, 9*(1), 1.

Urban, S. D., & Lim, B. B. (1993). An intelligent framework for active support of database semantics. *International Journal of Expert Systems, 6*(1), 1-37.

Valiente, M., Genova, G., & Cerretero, J. (2005). UML 2.0 Notation for Modeling Real-Time Task Scheduling. *Journal of Object technology, 5*(4), 91-105.

Van Gennep, A. (1960). *The Rites of Passage* (M. B. Vizedom & G. L. Caffe, Trans.). London, England: University of Chicago Press

Vidgen, R., Avison, D., Wood, B., & Wood-Harper, T. (2002). *Developing web information systems: From strategy to implementation.* Oxford: Butterworth Heinemann.

Virtanen, P. (2001). Empirical Study Evaluating Component Reuse Metrics. *Proceedings of the ESCOM,* (pp. 125-136).

Vliet, H. (2005). Some Myths of Software Engineering Education, *ICSE'05,* St. Louis, Missouri, USA, (pp. 621–622).

Vliet, H. (2006). Reflections on software engineering education. *Software, IEEE, 23*(3), 55–61.

Wand, Y., & Weber, R. (2002). Research commentary: Information systems and conceptual modeling - a research agenda. *Information Systems Research, 13*(4), 363-376.

Wang, Z., Fang, Y., & Xie, X. (2005). A spatio-temporal data model based on the parcel in cadastral. *In Proceedings of Geoscience and Remote Sensing Symposium, 2.*

Ward, P. T. (1989). How to integrate object orientation with structured analysis and design. *IEEE Software, 6*(2), 74-82.

Ware, C. (2000). *Information Visualization: Perception for Design.* Morgan Kaufman.

Wasserman, S., & Faust, K. (1994). *Social Network Analysis: Methods and Applications.* Cambridge University Press.

Weisert, T. (2006). *Systems Analysis Methodology Sliding Backwards,* Chicago: Information Disciplines Inc. Retrieved January 15, 2007 from http://www.idinews.com/story.html

Wheelan, S. A. (1994). *Group Processes: A Developmental Perspective.* Needham Heights, MA: Allyn and Bacon.

Wheelan, S. A., Davidson, B., & Tilin, F. (2003). Group development Across Time: Reality or Illusion? *Small Group Research, 34*(2), 223-245.

White, M. (2000). *Leonardo: The first scientist.*London: Little, Brown & Company.

Whitley, E. A. (1998, December 13-16). *Method-ism in practice: Investigating the relationship between method and understanding in web page design.* Paper presented at the 19th International Conference on Information Systems (ICIS), Helsinki, Finland.

William, B., Frakes, W. B., & Kang, K. (2005). Software Reuse Research: Status and Future. *IEEE Transactions on Software Engineering, 31*(7), 529-536.

Wolfson, O., Xu, B., Chamberlain, S., & Jiang, L. (1998). Moving objects databases: Issues and solutions. *Proceedings of the 10th International Conference on Scientific and Statistical Database Management (SSDBM98),* (pp. 111-122).

Wollin, A. (1999). Punctuated equilibrium: Reconciling Theory of Revolutionary and Incremental Change. *Systems Research and Behavioral Science, 16*(4), 359-367.

Wolstenholme, E. F. (1990). *System Enquiry: a System Dynamics Approach.* John Wiley & Sons, New York.

Worboys, M. F. (1994). A Unified Model for Spatial and Temporal Information. *The Computer Journal, 37*(1), 27-34.

Wrifs-Brock, R., & McKean, A. (2006). *Object design – Role, responsibility and cooperation,* Helion 2006

Wroblewski, D. A. (1991). The construction of human-computer interfaces considered as a craft. In J. Karat (Ed.), *Taking software design seriously: Practical techniques for human-computer interaction design* (pp. 1-19): Academic Press.

Wrycza, S., & Marcinkowski, B. (2006). UML 2 Academic Course – Methodological Background and Survey Benchmarking. *Proceedings of ISECON 2006, 23, Dallas. AITP Foundation for Information Technology Education.*

Wrycza, S., & Marcinkowski, B. (2006). UML 2 Teaching at Postgraduate Studies – Prerequisites and Practice art. In D. Colton, & T. Janicki (Eds.), *The Proceedings of ISECON 2005, Columbus, Ohio, Volume 22, the 22ⁿᵈ Annual Conference foe Informations Systems Educa-*

tors, AITP Foundation for Information technology Education.*

Wrycza, S., Marcinkowski, B., & Wyrzykowski, K. (2005). UML *2.0 in Information Systems Modeling.* Helion 2005 (in Polish), (pp.1-448).

Wrycza, S., Marcinkowski, B., & Wyrzykowski, K. (2005a). *Systems Modeling with UML 2* (in Polish). Helion, Gliwice, (pp. 1-456).

Yamaura, T., & Onoma, A. K. (2002). University software education matched to social requests, *Cyber Worlds, Proceedings. First International Symposium,* (pp. 331–336).

Ye, Y. (2002). An Empirical User Study of an Active Reuse Repository System. *Proceedings of 7ᵗʰ International Conference on Software Reuse,* (pp. 281-292).

Ye, Y., & Fischer, G., (2002). Supporting Reuse by Delivering Task-Relevant and Personalized Information. *Proceedings of International Conference on Software Engineering,* (pp. 513-523).

Yourdon, E. (1989). *Modern structured analysis.* Englewood Cliffs: Yourdon Press.

Yuan, M. (1996). Modeling semantical, temporal, and spatial information in geographic information systems. In M. Craglia & H. Couclelis (Eds.), *Geographic Information Research: Bridging the Atlantic* (pp. 334-347). London: Taylor & Francis.

Yuan, M. (1999). Use of a three-domain representation to enhance GIS support for complex spatiotemporal queries. *Transactions in GIS, 3*(2), 137-159.

Zhou, J., & Baumann, P. (1992, October 7-9, 1992). *Evaluation of complex cardinality constraints.* Paper presented at the 11th International Conference on the Entity-Relationship Approach, Karlsruhe, Germany.

Zimányi, E., Parent, C., Spaccapietra, S., & Pirotte, A. (1997, November 26-28). *Terc+: A temporal conceptual model.* Paper presented at the International Symposium on Digital Media Information Base (DMIB '97), Nara, Japan.

About the Contributors

Akhilesh Bajaj is Chapman associate professor of MIS, at the University of Tulsa. He received a B Tech in chemical engineering from the Indian Institute of Technology, Bombay in 1989, an MBA from Cornell University in 1991, and a PhD in MIS (minor in computer science) from the University of Arizona in 1997. Dr. Bajaj's research deals with the construction and testing of tools and methodologies that facilitate the construction of large organizational systems, as well as studying the decision models of the actual consumers of these information systems. He has published articles in several academic journals such as *Management Science, IEEE Transactions on Knowledge and Data Engineering, Information Systems* and the *Journal of the Association of Information Systems*. He is on the editorial board of several journals in the MIS area. His research has been funded by the department of defense (DOD). He teaches graduate courses on basic and advanced database systems, management of information systems, and enterprise wide systems.

* * *

Ozlem Albayrak currently teaches at Bilkent University, computer technology and information systems (CTIS) Department, Turkey. Her current research interests include software engineering education, requirements engineering, software quality and empirical software engineering. She has graduate level studies on information systems at University of Maryland College Park, USA. She received her PhD from Ankara University (Financial Information Systems), MBA (Management Information Systems) and CS degrees from Bilkent University. For more than 10 years, she worked as a software engineer at all levels of software development. Contact her at Bilkent University, CTIS 06800 East Campus, Bilkent Ankara/ Turkey. ozlemal@bilkent.edu.tr. http://www.bilkent.edu.tr/~ozlemal/

Jeff Crawford is an assistant professor in the School of Accounting and Management Information Systems at The University of Tulsa. He holds a PhD in management information systems from The University of Oklahoma and an MS in telecommunications management from Oklahoma State University. Prior to his academic career, Jeff spent 7 years managing software development projects within the financial services sector and several years serving as a computer network consultant. Jeff's research interests include IT project management, small group dynamics, and IT innovation and adoption within organizations. His research has been published in the *Proceedings of the Americas Conference on Information Systems* and the *Symposium on Research in Systems Analysis & Design*, and has been presented at the *International Conference on Information Systems*, the *Annual Meeting of the Academy of Management* and the *DIGIT Workshop*.

Faiz Currim is an assistant professor in the Department of Management Sciences, Tippie College of Business, at the University of Iowa. Dr. Currim has published articles in journals like *Data and Knowledge Engineering and Communications* of the ACM. His research interests like in the area of databases and data management. This includes conceptual data modeling, database constraints, applications in healthcare, management of spatial and temporal data, XML Schema, and RFID data management.

Dariusz Dymek received the MS degree in Mathematics from Institute of Mathematic, Jagiellonian University, Kraków, 1989, the MS degree in computer science from Institute of Computer Science, Jagiellonian University, Kraków, 1991, and the PhD degree in economics from Cracow University of Economics, Krakow, 2000. He works as assistant professor at the Department of Computer Science at the Cracow University of Economics. His research interests include project management, information systems, risk management, software quality management and software development methodology.

Roy Gelbard is head of the Information System Program at the Graduate School of Business Administration, Bar-Ilan University. He received his PhD and MSc degrees in Information Systems from Tel-Aviv University. He holds also degrees in biology and philosophy. His main areas of interest are: (i) software engineering and software project management; (ii) data and knowledge modeling for data mining and decision-making.

Jason Knight was an undergraduate MIS student at the University of Tulsa as the time of this project. His research was partially funded by the Tulsa Undergraduate Research Colloquium.

Leszek Kotulski received the MS degree in Computer Science from Institute of Computer Science, Jagiellonian University, Kraków, 1979, the PhD degree in computer science from AGH University of Science and Technology, Krakow, 1984, and the DSc degree in theoretical computer science from Wroclaw University of Technology, Wrocław, 2002. He works as a professor at AGH University of Science and Technology. His research interests include graph grammars, foundation of distributed computing, agents systems and software development methodology. Prof. Kotulski is member of ACM.

Michael Lang is a lecturer in information systems at National University of Ireland, Galway. His principal research interest is methods, approaches, and techniques for business information systems analysis and design. His research has been published in a number of international journals and conferences, including *Information Systems Management, Requirements Engineering, IEEE Software, IEEE Multimedia, Information & Software Techology*, and *Communications of the AIS*. You may visit his personal Web page at: http://www.nuigalway.ie/bis/mlang/

Angela M. Mattia is an information systems doctoral candidate in the School of Business at Virginia Commonwealth University in Richmond, Virginia. Her current research interests include project management and information systems development, particularly the influence of social networks in these domains.

Przemyslaw Polak is an associate professor and the Head of the Center for Software Technology in the Department of Business Informatics (Information Systems) at the Warsaw School of Economics. He is also an independent consultant in the field of Information Systems and Information Technology. Born in

1967 in Warsaw, Poland, he graduated in 1992 and received a PhD in 2002 from the Warsaw School of Economics. He was granted scholarships from the British Council (Department of Management Science, Strathclyde University, Glasgow, UK) and the Canadian Consortium of Management Schools (Faculty of Management, University of Calgary, Canada). He received teaching mobility grants to lecture at the Fachhochschule Nordostniedersachsen, Germany and the Hasselt University, Belgium.

Sudha Ram is McClelland professor, management information systems in the Eller College of Management at the University of Arizona. Dr. Ram has published articles in such journals as *Communications of the ACM, IEEE Expert, IEEE Transactions on Knowledge and Data Engineering, Information Systems, Information Systems Research, Management Science,* and *MIS Quarterly.* Dr. Ram's research deals with issues related to Enterprise Data Management. Specifically, her research deals with Interoperability among Heterogeneous Database Systems, Semantic Modeling, BioInformatics and Spatio-Temporal Semantics, Business Rules Modeling, and Automated software tools for database design. Dr. Ram serves on editorial board for such journals as *Information Systems Research, Decision Support Systems, Information Systems Frontiers, Journal of Information Technology and Management, Journal of Database Management,* and the *Journal of Systems and Software.* She is the director of the Advanced Database Research Group based at the University of Arizona.

Andreea Sabău graduated in 2001 the Faculty of Mathematics and Computer Science, Babes-Bolyai University, Cluj-Napoca, Romania. She followed the master's degree program "Databases in Internet and Electronic Commerce" between 2001 and 2002 within the same institution. She obtained my PhD with the thesis "The Management of Spatio-Temporal Databases" in 2007, under the supervision of Prof. Dr. Leon Tambulea. Her research interests are in the areas of modeling the spatio-temporal data and designing and implementing spatio-temporal access methods. She joined the Department of Computer Science of the Faculty of Mathematics and Computer Science, Babes-Bolyai University, Cluj-Napoca, Romania in 2002 as teaching assistant, and since February 2008 she became an assistant professor within the same department. Her teaching activity includes seminars and laboratory classes for the Databases course, and the courses of transaction management and distributed databases, semistructured data and electronic commerce.

Kumar Saurabh works as a manager in Satyam Learning Center, Satyam Computer Services Ltd. Hyderabad, India. He is author of the book entitled "Unix Programming- The First Drive" published by Wiley Publications. He has over 6 years of professional experience in systems performance and capacity planning, UNIX internals, device drivers and Kernel programming, systems design and architecture, reliability and availability, operations research, simulation and modeling, system dynamics, software engineering, and network technologies. He has designed several systems stability and software consistency related methodologies to analyze and quantify hardware and software performance/capacity and availability/reliability related issues. Over the years, he has conducted several large-scale systems performance and capacity planning projects in a wide range of professional environments such as science & research, software companies and R & D products. Specific areas of expertise include UNIX systems architecture, design, setup, and maintenance, UNIX operating systems, I/O subsystem performance, performance modeling and simulation, operations research, device drivers and Kernel technologies, and all phases of the SDLC. He authored over twenty papers in international journals, proceedings of the international conferences. He is life member of ISTE. He will receive his PhD degree from Devi

Ahilya University, Indore, India shortly. He is M Tech from the same University and M Sc in computer science from Bhopal University, India.

Heinz Roland Weistroffer is an associate professor of information systems in the School of Business at Virginia Commonwealth University in Richmond, Virginia. His research has appeared in such journals as *IEEE Transactions on Software Engineering, Journal of Computer Information Systems, Expert Systems, Journal of Multi-Criteria Decision Analysis, Socio-Economic Planning Sciences*, and *Computational and Mathematical Organization Theory*. His current research interests include information systems development, decision support, and information technology for development.

Index